WHOSE JUSTICE? WHICH RATIONALITY?

Whose Justice? Which Rationality?

ALASDAIR MacINTYRE

University of Notre Dame Press
Notre Dame, Indiana

Library of Congress Cataloging-in-Publication Data

MacIntyre, Alasdair C.
　Whose justice? Which rationality?

　Includes index.
　1. Justice (Philosophy)—History.　2. Reason—
History.　3. Ethics—History.　I. Title.
B105.J87M33　1988　　　172　　　87-40354
ISBN 0-268-01942-8

Manufactured in the United States of America

FOR

Antonia Mary Pietrosanti, Jean Catherine MacIntyre,
Daniel Eneas MacIntyre and Helen Charlotte MacIntyre

Contents

Preface

In 1981 I published the first edition of *After Virtue*. In that book I concluded both that "we still, in spite of the efforts of three centuries of moral philosophy and one of sociology, lack any coherent rationally defensible statement of a liberal individualist point of view" and that "the Aristotelian tradition can be restated in a way that restores rationality and intelligibility to our own moral and social attitudes and commitments." But I also recognized that these conclusions required support from an account of what rationality is, in the light of which rival and incompatible evaluations of the arguments of *After Virtue* could be adequately accounted for. I promised a book in which I should attempt to say both what makes it rational to act in one way rather than another and what makes it rational to advance and defend one conception of practical rationality rather than another. Here it is.

In 1982 I delivered the Carlyle Lectures in the University of Oxford on "Some Transformations of Justice." In preparing the material from those lectures for publication I came to recognize that different and incompatible conceptions of justice are characteristically closely linked to different and incompatible conceptions of practical rationality. Consequently, the work of elaborating discussions of the views of justice taken by Aristotle, Gregory VII, and Hume turned out to be inseparable from that of explaining the beliefs about practical rationality presupposed by or expressed in those views of justice. What had been originally conceived of as two distinct tasks became one.

This enabled me to respond to another lacuna in *After Virtue,* one emphasized by more than one critic who misrepresented that book as a defense of "a morality of the virtues" as an alternative to "a morality of rules." Such critics failed to notice the way in which any adequate morality of the virtues was said to require as its counterpart "a morality of laws (*After Virtue,* second edition, pp. 150–152), a morality such that "knowing how to apply the law is itself possible only for someone who possesses the virtue of justice" (p. 152). A central preoccupation of this sequel to *After Virtue* is the nature of this connection between justice and laws.

Yet although this present book is a sequel to *After Virtue* in that it answers questions raised by *After Virtue,* it has been written so as to be, I hope, a work which can be read and engaged with by those who have not read *After Virtue.* In *After Virtue* I tried to address both academic philosophers and the lay reader. The danger of such attempts is that they leave both audiences dissatisfied; this is a danger which I have judged worthwhile to risk once more, if only because of a conviction that the conception of philosophy as essentially a semitechnical, quasi-scientific, autonomous enquiry to be conducted by professionalized specialists is in the end barren. There is indeed in philosophy a large and legitimate place for technicality, but only insofar as it serves the ends of a type of enquiry in which what is at stake is of crucial importance to everyone and not only to academic philosophers. The attempted professionalization of serious and systematic thinking has had a disastrous effect upon our culture.

Those readers of this present book who have also read *After Virtue* will notice that I have come to recognize more than one error in *After Virtue,* although not in any of its main contentions. I now, for example, think that my earlier criticism of Aquinas' theses on the unity of the virtues was simply mistaken and due in part to a misreading of Aquinas. But I have not referred back to *After Virtue* in the relevant passages, not so as to disguise my capacity for making mistakes, but so as to emphasize the fact that this book can be read and evaluated without any knowledge of *After Virtue.*

My debts to others are massive. I am deeply grateful to the University of Oxford for the opportunity to deliver the Carlyle Lectures, to the Warden and Fellows of Nuffield College for their hospitality on that occasion and more especially to Nevil Johnson whose care and kindness in making a variety of arrangements were notable. He and they thus enlarged a debt which I have owed to Nuffield College ever since I was a Research Fellow there. I must also record my considerable indebtedness to the National Endowment for the Humanities, which by awarding me a Fellowship in 1979–80 allowed me to prepare the ground for my treatment of the Scottish background to Hume in chapters XII–XIV, and to the Guggenheim Foundation, whose Fellowship in 1984-85 enabled me to do the fundamental work on the accounts of practical reasoning advanced by Aristotle and by Hume. But I should not have been able to use these opportunities as part of a systematic scheme of research and writing without the uninterrupted support of the Department of Philosophy and of the College of Arts and Science at Vanderbilt University. Dean V. Jacque Voegeli, Dean David L. Tuleen, and

Dr. Charles E. Scott all played a key part in making this book possible, and I thank them very much.

To the many readers and critics of *After Virtue* whose insights and comments aided the writing of this book I owe a special debt. Out of so many one nonetheless stands out: Herbert McCabe, O.P., whose pertinacious criticisms of my Carlyle Lectures have had a sustained impact on my views. I am also especially indebted for comments on drafts and for discussions of other kinds to my colleague Henry A. Teloh, to Mark D. Jordan and Ralph McInerny of the University of Notre Dame, and to my former students Donald R.C. Reed, Eric Snider, and Pamela M. Hall. My wife, Lynn Sumida Joy, supported me through this effort by exhibiting not only the virtues of justice and reasonableness but also those of charity and patience.

Yet none of this would have here resulted in a book had it not been for the hard work of preparing the final typescript by Chris Bastian and Stella Thompson. Without their conscientiousness and their intelligent care everyone else's help would have come to nothing. They therefore deserve a very special kind of thanks.

Alasdair MacIntyre

Nashville, Tennessee
April 1987

I

Rival Justices, Competing Rationalities

Begin by considering the intimidating range of questions about what justice requires and permits, to which alternative and incompatible answers are offered by contending individuals and groups within contemporary societies. Does justice permit gross inequality of income and ownership? Does justice require compensatory action to remedy inequalities which are the result of past injustice, even if those who pay the costs of such compensation had no part in that injustice? Does justice permit or require the imposition of the death penalty and, if so, for what offences? Is it just to permit legalized abortion? When is it just to go to war? The list of such questions is a long one.

Attention to the reasons which are adduced for offering different and rival answers to such questions makes it clear that underlying this wide diversity of judgments upon particular types of issue are a set of conflicting conceptions of justice, conceptions which are strikingly at odds with one another in a number of ways. Some conceptions of justice make the concept of desert central, while others deny it any relevance at all. Some conceptions appeal to inalienable human rights, others to some notion of social contract, and others again to a standard of utility. Moreover, the rival theories of justice which embody these rival conceptions also give expression to disagreements about the relationship of justice to other human goods, about the kind of equality which justice requires, about the range of transactions and persons to which considerations of justice are relevant, and about whether or not a knowledge of justice is possible without a knowledge of God's law.

So those who had hoped to discover good reasons for making this rather than that judgment on some particular type of issue — by moving from the arenas in which in everyday social life groups and individuals quarrel about what it is just to do in particular cases over to the realm of theoretical enquiry, where systematic conceptions of justice are elaborated and debated — will find that once again they have entered upon a scene of radical conflict. What this may disclose to them is not only that our society is one not of consensus, but of division and conflict, at least so far as the nature of justice is concerned, but also that to some degree that division and conflict is within themselves. For what many of us are educated into is, not a coherent way of thinking and judging, but one constructed out of an amalgam of social and cultural fragments inherited both from different traditions from which our culture was originally derived (Puritan, Catholic, Jewish) and from different stages in and aspects of the development of modernity (the French Enlightenment, the Scottish Enlightenment, nineteenth-century economic liberalism, twentieth-century political liberalism). So often enough in the disagreements which emerge within ourselves, as well as in those which are matters of conflict between ourselves and others, we are forced to confront the question: How ought we to decide among the claims of rival and incompatible accounts of justice competing for our moral, social, and political allegiance?

It would be natural enough to attempt to reply to this question by asking which systematic account of justice we would accept if the standards by which our actions were guided were the standards of rationality. To know what justice is, so it may seem, we must first learn what rationality in practice requires of us. Yet someone who tries to learn this at once encounters the fact that disputes about the nature of rationality in general and about practical rationality in particular are apparently as manifold and as intractable as disputes about justice. To be practically rational, so one contending party holds, is to act on the basis of calculations of the costs and benefits to oneself of each possible alternative course of action and its consequences. To be practically rational, affirms a rival party, is to act under those constraints which any rational person, capable of an impartiality which accords no particular privileges to one's own interests, would agree should be imposed. To be practically rational, so a third party contends, is to act in such a way as to achieve the ultimate and true good of human beings. So a third level of difference and conflict appears.

One of the most striking facts about modern political orders is that they lack institutionalized forums within which these fundamental disagreements can be systematically explored and charted, let alone there being any attempt made to resolve them. The facts of disagreement themselves frequently go unacknowledged, disguised by a rhetoric of consensus. And when on some single, if complex issue, as in the struggles over the Vietnam war or in the debates over abortion, the illusions of consensus on questions of justice and practical rationality are for the moment fractured, the expression of radical disagreement is institutionalized in such a way as to abstract that single issue from those background contexts of different and incompatible beliefs from which such disagreements arise. This serves to prevent, so far as is possible, debate extending to the fundamental principles which inform those background beliefs.

Private citizens are thus for the most part left to their own devices in these matters. Those of them who do not, very understandably, abandon any attempt to think through such issues systematically are generally able to discover only two major types of resource: those provided by the enquiries and discussions of modern academic philosophy and those provided by more or less organized communities of shared belief, such as churches or sects, religious and nonreligious, or certain kinds of political association. What do these resources in fact afford?

Modern academic philosophy turns out by and large to provide means for a more accurate and informed definition of disagreement rather than for progress toward its resolution. Professors of philosophy who concern themselves with questions of justice and of practical rationality turn out to disagree with each other as sharply, as variously, and, so it seems, as irremediably upon how such questions are to be answered as anyone else. They do indeed succeed in articulating the rival standpoints with greater clarity, greater fluency, and a wider range of arguments than do most others, but apparently little more than this. And, upon reflection, we should perhaps not be surprised.

Consider, for example, one at first sight very plausible philosophical thesis about how we ought to proceed in these matters if we are to be rational. Rationality requires, so it has been argued by a number of academic philosophers, that we first divest ourselves of allegiance to any one of the contending theories and also abstract ourselves from all those particularities of social relationship in terms of which we have been accustomed to understand our responsibilities and our interests. Only by so doing, it has been suggested, shall we arrive at a genuinely neutral, impartial, and, in this way, universal point of view, freed from the partisanship and the partiality and onesidedness that otherwise affect us. And only by so doing shall we be able to evaluate the contending accounts of justice rationally.

One problem is that those who agree about this procedure then proceed to disagree about what precise conception of justice it is which is as a result to be accounted rationally acceptable. But even before *that* problem arises, the question has to be asked whether, by adopting this procedure, key questions have not been begged. For it can be argued and it has been argued that this account of rationality is itself contentious in two related ways: its requirement of disinterestedness in fact covertly presupposes one particular partisan type of account of justice, that of liberal individualism, which it is later to be used to justify, so that its apparent neutrality is no more than an appearance, while its conception of ideal rationality as consisting in the principles which a socially disembodied being would arrive at illegitimately ignores the inescapably historically and socially context-bound character which any substantive set of principles of rationality, whether theoretical or practical, is bound to have.

Fundamental disagreements about the character of rationality are bound to be peculiarly difficult to resolve. For already in initially proceeding in one way rather than another to approach the disputed questions, those who so proceed will have had to assume that these particular procedures are the ones which it is rational to follow. A certain degree of circularity is ineliminable. And so when disagreements between contending views are sufficiently fundamental, as they are in the case of those disagreements about practical rationality in which the nature of justice is at stake, those disagreements will extend even to the answers to the question of how to proceed in order to resolve those same disagreements.

Aristotle argued in Book Gamma of the *Metaphysics* that anyone who denies that basic law of logic, the law of noncontradiction, and who is prepared to defend his or her position by entering into argumentative debate, will in fact be unable to avoid relying upon the very law which he or she purports to reject. And it may be that for other laws of logic parallel defenses can be constructed. But even if Aristotle was successful, and I believe that he was, in showing that no one who understands the laws of logic can remain rational while rejecting them, observance of the laws of logic is only a necessary and not a sufficient condition for rationality, whether theoretical or practical. It is on what has to be added to observance of the laws of logic to justify ascriptions of rationality—whether to oneself or to others, whether to modes of enquiry or to justifications of belief, or to courses of action and their justification—that disagreement arises concerning the fundamental nature of rationality and extends into disagreement over how it is rationally appropriate to proceed in the face of these disagreements. So the resources provided by modern academic philosophy enable us to redefine, but do not themselves seem to resolve the problems of those confronting the rival claims upon their allegiance that are made by protagonists of conflicting accounts of justice and of practical rationality.

The only other type of resource generally available in our society to such persons is that which is supplied by participation in the life of one of those groups whose thought and action are informed by some distinctive profession of settled conviction with regard to justice and to practical rationality. Those who resorted or resort to academic philosophy hoped or hope to acquire thereby a set of sound arguments by means of which they could assure themselves and others of the rational justification for their views. (Those who resort instead to a set of beliefs embodied in the life of a group put their trust in persons rather than in arguments. In doing so they cannot escape the charge of a certain arbitrariness in their commitments, a charge, however, which tends to carry little weight with those against whom it is directed) Why does that charge carry so little weight?

(Partly it is a matter of a general cynicism in our culture about the power or even the relevance of rational argument to matters sufficiently fundamental.) Fideism has a large, not always articulate, body of adherents, and not only among the members of those Protestant churches and movements which openly proclaim it; there are plenty of secular fideists. And partly it is because of a strong and sometimes justified suspicion by those against whom the charge is leveled that those who level it do so, not so much because they themselves are genuinely moved by rational argument, as because by appealing to argument they are able to exercise a kind of power which favors their own interests and privileges, the interests and privileges of a class which has arrogated the rhetorically effective use of argument to itself for its own purposes.)

Arguments, that is to say, have come to be understood in some circles not as expressions of rationality, but as weapons, the techniques for deploying which furnish a key part of the professional skills of lawyers, academics, economists, and journalists who thereby dominate the dialectically unfluent and inarticulate. There is thus a remarkable concordance in the way in which apparently very different types of social and cultural groups envisage each other's commitments. To the readership of the *New York Times,* or at least to that part of it which shares the presuppositions of those who write that parish magazine of affluent and self-congratulatory liberal enlightenment, the congregations of evangelical fundamentalism appear unfashionably unenlightened. But to the members of those congregations that readership appears to be just as much a community of prerational faith as they themselves are but one whose members, unlike themselves, fail to recognize themselves for what they are, and hence are in no position to level charges of irrationality at them or anyone else.

We thus inhabit a culture in which an inability to arrive at agreed rationally justifiable conclusions on the nature of justice and practical rationality coexists with appeals by contending social groups to sets of rival and conflicting convictions unsupported by rational justification. Neither the voices of academic philosophy, nor for that matter of any other academic discipline, nor those of the partisan subcultures, have been able to provide for ordinary citizens a way of uniting conviction on such matters with rational justification. Disputed questions concerning justice and practical rationality are thus treated in the public realm, not as matter for rational enquiry, but rather for the assertion and counterassertion of alternative and incompatible sets of premises.

How did this come to be the case? The answer falls into two parts, each having to do with the Enlightenment and with its subsequent history. It was a central aspiration of the Enlightenment, an aspiration the formulation of which was itself a great achievement, to provide for debate in the public realm standards and methods of rational justification by which alternative courses of action in every sphere of life could be adjudged just or unjust, rational or irrational, enlightened or unenlightened. So, it was hoped, reason would displace authority and tradition. Rational justification was to appeal to principles undeniable by any rational person and therefore independent of all those social and cultural particularities which the Enlightenment thinkers took to be the mere accidental clothing of reason in particular times and places. And that rational justification could be nothing other than what the thinkers of the Enlightenment had said that it was came to be accepted, at least by the vast majority of educated people, in post-Enlightenment cultural and social orders.

Yet both the thinkers of the Enlightenment and their successors proved unable to agree as to what precisely those principles were which would be found undeniable by all rational persons. One kind of answer was given by the authors of the *Encyclopédie,* a second by Rousseau, a third by Bentham, a fourth by Kant, a fifth by the Scottish philosophers of common sense and their French and American disciples. Nor has subsequent history diminished the extent of such disagreement. It has rather enlarged it. Consequently, the legacy of the Enlightenment has been the provision of an ideal of rational justification which it has proved impossible to attain. And hence in key part derives the inability within our culture to unite conviction and rational justification. Within that kind of academic philosophy which is the heir to the philosophies of the Enlightenment enquiry into the nature of rational justification has continued with ever-increasing refinement and undiminishing disagreement. In cultural, political, moral, and religious life post-Enlightenment conviction effectively has acquired a life of its own, independent of rational enquiry.

It is therefore worth asking whether the Enlightenment may not have contributed to our present condition in a second way, not only by what its achievements in propagating its distinctive doctrines led to, but also by what it succeeded in excluding from view. Is there some mode of understanding which could find no place in the Enlightenment's vision of the world by means of which the conceptual and theoretical resources can be provided for reuniting conviction concerning such matters as justice on the one hand and rational enquiry and justification on the other? It will be important in trying to answer this question not to trap ourselves by, perhaps inadvertently, continuing to accept the standards of the Enlightenment. We already have the best of reasons for supposing that those standards cannot be met, and we know in advance, therefore, that from the standpoint of the Enlightenment and its successors any account of an alternative mode of understanding will inescapably be treated as one more contending view, unable to vindicate itself conclusively against its Enlightenment rivals. Any attempt to provide a radically different alternative standpoint is bound to be found rationally unsatisfactory in a variety of ways from the standpoint of the Enlightenment itself. Hence it is inevitable that such an attempt should be unacceptable to and rejected by those whose allegiance is to the dominant intellectual and cultural modes of the present order. At the same time, since what will be introduced will be a set of claims concerning rational justification and its requirements, those whose nonrational convictions flout any such requirement will be equally apt to be offended.

Is there, then, such an alternative mode of understanding? Of what did the Enlightenment deprive us? What the Enlightenment made us for the most part blind to and what we now need to recover is, so I shall argue, a conception of rational enquiry as embodied in a tradition, a conception according to which the standards of rational justification themselves emerge from and are part of a history in which they are vindicated by the way in which they transcend the limitations of and provide remedies for the defects of their predecessors within the history of that same tradition. Not all traditions, of course, have embodied rational enquiry as a constitutive part of themselves; and those thinkers of the Enlightenment who dismissed tradition because they took it to be the antithesis of rational enquiry were in some instances in the right. But in so doing they obscured from themselves and others the nature of some at least of the systems of thought which they so vehemently rejected. Nor was this entirely their fault.

To those who inhabit a social and intellectual tradition in good working order the facts of tradition, which are the presupposition of their activities and enquiries, may well remain just that, unarticulated presuppositions which are never themselves the objects of attention and enquiry. Indeed generally only when traditions either fail and disintegrate or are challenged do their adherents become aware of them as traditions and begin to theorize about them. So the claim that most of the major moral and metaphysical thinkers of the ancient, medieval, and even the early modern world are only to be understood adequately when placed in the context of traditions, of which rational enquiry was a central and constitutive part, does not in any way involve the claim that these thinkers were themselves concerned with, let alone provide an adequate account of, the nature of such traditions. Those thinkers who are explicitly concerned with tradition as their subject matter are generally later thinkers, such as Edmund Burke and John Henry Newman, who already in some way or other are or have been alienated from those traditions about which they theorize. Burke theorized shoddily, Newman theorized with insight, but both did so in an awareness of a sharp antithesis between tradition and something else, an antithesis which was unavailable to the earlier inhabitants of the kind of tradition with which I am concerned.

The concept of a kind of rational inquiry which is inseparable from the intellectual and social tradition in which it is embodied will be misunderstood unless four considerations are borne in mind. The first has already been touched upon: the concept of rational justification which is at home in that form of enquiry is essentially historical. To justify is to narrate how the argument has gone so far. Those who construct theories within such a tradition of enquiry and justification often provide those theories with a structure in terms of which certain theses have the status of first principles; other claims within such a theory will be justified by derivation from these first principles. But what justifies the first principles themselves, or rather the whole structure of theory of which they are a part, is the rational superiority of that particular structure to all previous attempts within that particular tradition to formulate such theories and principles; it is not a matter of those first principles being acceptable to all rational persons whatsoever— unless we were to include in the condition of being a rational person an apprehension of and identification with the kind of history whose culmination is the construction of this particular theoretical structure, as perhaps Aristotle, for example, in some measure did.

Second, not only is the mode of rational justification within such traditions very different from that of the Enlightenment. What it is that has to be justified is also conceived very differently. What contend, according to the theories of the Enlightenment, are rival doctrines, doctrines which may as a matter of fact have been elaborated in particular times and places, but whose content and whose truth or falsity, whose possession or lack of rational justification, is quite independent of their historical origin. On this view the history of thought in general, and of philosophy in particular, is a discipline quite distinct from those enquiries concerned with what are taken to be the timeless questions of truth and rational justification. Such history concerns who said or wrote what, which arguments were as a matter of fact adduced for or against certain positions, who influenced whom, and so on.

By contrast, from the standpoint of tradition-constituted and tradition-constitutive enquiry, what a particular doctrine claims is always a matter of how precisely it was in fact advanced, of the linguistic particularities of its formulation, of what in that time and place had to be denied, if it was to be asserted, of what was at that time and place presupposed by its assertion, and so on. Doctrines, theses, and arguments all have to be understood in terms of historical context. It does not, of course, follow that the same doctrine or the same arguments may not reappear in different contexts. Nor does it follow that claims to timeless truth are not being made. It is rather that such claims are being made for doctrines whose formulation is itself time-bound and that the concept of timelessness is itself a concept with a history, one which in certain types of context is not at all the same concept that it is in others.

So rationality itself, whether theoretical or practical, is a concept with a history: indeed, since there are a diversity of traditions of enquiry, with histories, there are, so it will turn out, rationalities rather than rationality, just as it will also turn out that there are justices rather than justice. And it is at this point that a third consideration has to be borne in mind, for it is on this that the adherents of the Enlightenment will understandably fasten. You reproach us, so those adherents will say, with an inability to resolve the disagreements between rival claims concerning principles to which any rational person must assent. But you are instead going to confront us with a diversity of traditions, each with its own specific mode of rational justification. And surely the consequence must be a like inability to resolve radical disagreement.

To this the proponent of the rationality of traditions has a twofold reply: that once the diversity of traditions has been properly characterized, a better explanation of the diversity of standpoints is available than either the Enlightenment or its heirs can provide; and that acknowledgment of the diversity of traditions of enquiry, each with its own specific mode of rational justification, does not entail that the differences between rival and incompatible traditions cannot be rationally resolved. How and under what conditions they can be so resolved is something only to be understood after a prior understanding of the nature of such traditions has been achieved. From the standpoint of traditions of rational enquiry the problem of diversity is not abolished, but it is transformed in a way that renders it amenable of solution. Finally, it is crucial that the concept of tradition-constituted and tradition-constitutive rational enquiry cannot be elucidated apart from its exemplifications, something which I take to be true of all concepts, but something which it is more important not to neglect in some cases than in others. The four traditions which in this book are used to exemplify that concept are important for more than one reason. Each is part of the background history of our own culture. Each carries within itself a distinctive type of account of justice and of practical rationality. Each has entered into relationships of antagonism or of alliance and even synthesis, or of both successively, with at least one of the others. Yet at the same time they exhibit very different patterns of development.

So the Aristotelian account of justice and of practical rationality emerges from the conflicts of the ancient *polis,* but is then developed by Aquinas in a way which escapes the limitations of the *polis.* So the Augustinian version of Christianity entered in the medieval period into complex relationships of antagonism, later of synthesis, and then of continuing antagonism to Aristotelianism. So in a quite different later cultural context Augustinian Christianity, now in a Calvinist form, and Aristotelianism, now in a Renaissance version, entered into a new symbiosis in seventeenth-century Scotland, so engendering a tradition which at its climax of achievement was subverted from within by Hume. And so finally modern liberalism, born of antagonism to all tradition, has transformed itself gradually into what is now clearly recognizable even by some of its adherents as one more tradition.

That there are other bodies of tradition-constituted enquiry which not only merit attention in their own right but whose omission will leave my argument significantly incomplete is undeniable. Three in particular have to be mentioned. The derivation of Augustinian Christianity from its biblical sources is a story whose counterpart is the history of Judaism, within which the relationship of the devoted study of the Torah to philosophy engendered more than one tradition of enquiry. But of all the histories of enquiry this is the one which, perhaps more than any other, must be written by its own adherents; in particular for an Augustinian Christian, such as myself, to try to write it, in the way that I have felt able to write the history of my own tradition, would be a gross impertinence. Christians need badly to listen to Jews. The attempt to speak for them, even on behalf of that unfortunate fiction, the so-called Judeo-Christian tradition, is always deplorable.

Second, I have tried to give Hume his due in respect of his accounts of justice and of the place of reasoning in the genesis of action. Had I tried to do the same for Kant, this book would have become impossibly long. But the whole Prussian tradition in which public law and Lutheran theology were blended, a tradition which Kant, Fichte, and Hegel tried but failed to universalize, is clearly of the same order of importance as the Scottish tradition of which I *have* given an account. So that once again more needs to be done.

Third, and at least as important, Islamic thought requires treatment not only for its own sake but also because of its large contribution to the Aristotelian tradition, but this too I have had to omit. And, finally, the kind of story which I shall try to tell requires as its complement not only Jewish, Islamic, and other postbiblical narratives, but also the narratives of such sharply contrasting traditions of enquiry as those engendered in India and China. Acknowledgment of such incompleteness does nothing to correct it, but at least it clarifies the limitations of my enterprise.

That enterprise by its very nature has to take, initially at least, a narrative form. What a tradition of enquiry has to say, both to those within and to those outside it, cannot be disclosed in any other way. To be an adherent of a tradition is always to enact some further stage in the development of one's tradition; to understand another tradition is to attempt to supply, in the best terms imaginatively and conceptually available to one—and later we shall see what problems can arise over this—the kind of account which an adherent would give. And since within any well-developed tradition of enquiry the question of precisely how its history up to this point ought to be written is characteristically one of those questions to which different and conflicting answers may be given within the tradition, the narrative task itself generally involves participation in conflict. It is therefore with an emphasis upon the necessary place of conflict within traditions that I have to begin.

II

Justice and Action
in the Homeric Imagination

Heraclitus said that justice is conflict and that everything comes to pass
in accordance with conflict. John Anderson, who understood Heraclitus in the light of John Burnet's account of him in *Early Greek Philosophy,* argued that Heraclitus' insight provided the key to understanding the nature of social institutions and social orders. They are milieus
of conflict, arenas within which opposing modes of belief, understanding, and action engage in argument, debate, and, at extremes, war, as
Heraclitus also noted. But conflict is not merely divisive. By engaging
the contending parties in ongoing, shifting, but, at times, stable relationships, it becomes integrated into and integrative of those forms of
social and civil life within which, as in the universe at large, the transgression of the measures of justice brings retribution (fragments XLIV
and LXXXVII in Charles Kahn *The Art and Thought of Heraclitus,*
Cambridge, 1979, pp. 49 and 69). The history of any society is thus
in key part the history of an extended conflict or set of conflicts. And
as it is with societies, so too it is with traditions.

A tradition is an argument extended through time in which certain
fundamental agreements are defined and redefined in terms of two kinds
of conflict: those with critics and enemies external to the tradition who
reject all or at least key parts of those fundamental agreements, and
those internal, interpretative debates through which the meaning and
rationale of the fundamental agreements come to be expressed and by
whose progress a tradition is constituted. Such internal debates may
on occasion destroy what had been the basis of common fundamental
agreement, so that either a tradition divides into two or more warring
components, whose adherents are transformed into external critics of
each other's positions, or else the tradition loses all coherence and fails
to survive. It can also happen that two traditions, hitherto independent
and even antagonistic, can come to recognize certain possibilities of
fundamental agreement and reconstitute themselves as a single, more
complex debate.

⌊ To appeal to tradition is to insist that we cannot adequately identify either our own commitments or those of others in the argumentative conflicts of the present except by situating them within those histories which made them what they have now become⌋ And insofar as those present argumentative conflicts concern the nature of justice, that of practical reasoning, and their mutual relationship, the relevant histories cannot be made intelligible without a recognition of the degree to which they are an extension and a continuation of a history of conflict found in the Athenian social and cultural order during the fifth and fourth centuries B.C. This is, of course, not the only antecedent history of which they are an extension and a continuation. What happened under King Josiah at Jerusalem in the seventh century—with the redefinition of the relationship of the people of the Kingdom of Judah to a history whose central event was the giving of the divine law to Moses on Mount Sinai —is also inescapably part of the past without which our present cannot be made adequately intelligible. But even the understanding of divine law has in certain important episodes been partially but crucially determined by modes of argument and interpretation stemming from Athenian debates.

⌈We inherit from the conflicts of the social and cultural order of the Athenian *polis* a number of mutually incompatible and antagonistic traditions concerning justice and practical rationality. ⌋The two with which I shall be concerned received their classical statements from Thucydides as well as from certain of the sophists and teachers of rhetoric and from Aristotle respectively. But neither of them can safely be abstracted for expository purposes from the overall context of debate within which each defined itself in opposition to a whole set of others. And the terms of that debate were set by that body of oral and written matter which provided educated Athenians with those shared understandings without which clearly articulated disagreements and conflicts are impossible. Central to that body of oral and written matter were the *Iliad* and the *Odyssey*. From Homer, therefore, Athenians had to begin. And we who find one of the two most important of our own beginnings with respect to justice and practical rationality in the conflicts of the Athenians have therefore no alternative but to begin with Homer too. That beginning requires the discovery of some way to express to ourselves in English prose what has to be learned from a poet speaking a Homeric Greek in which, happily or unhappily, many of our own present-day thoughts about justice and practical rationality could not even be expressed.

Ever since the Homeric poems were first translated into English, the Homeric word '*dikē*' has been translated by the English word 'justice'.

But the changes which have taken place in modern English-speaking societies as to how justice is to be understood have rendered this translation more and more misleading. This is far from the only respect in which the Homeric poems have gradually become less translatable, but it is one of the most important. For the use of the word '*dikē*', both by Homer and by those whom he portrayed, presupposed that the universe had a single fundamental order, an order structuring both nature and society, so that the distinction which *we* mark by contrasting the natural and the social cannot as yet be expressed. To be *dikaios* is to conduct one's actions and affairs in accordance with this order.

It is over this order that Zeus, the father of gods and human beings, presides; and it is over particular communities within this order that kings preside, dispensing, if they are just, the justice that Zeus has entrusted to them. Of the uses of *dikē* in the *Iliad* all refer either to a judgment by a judge in a dispute or to a claim by a participant in a dispute. A particular *dikē* is straight if it accords with what *themis* requires, crooked if it departs from it. *Themis* is what is ordained, what is laid down as the ordering of things and people. A king judges straightly when he judges in accordance with the *themistes,* the ordinances given by Zeus. Kingship, divine governance, and cosmic order are inseparable notions, and the words '*dikē*' and '*themis*' are nouns derived from two of the most basic verbs in the Greek language, '*dikē*' from the root of '*deiknumi*', 'I show' or 'I indicate', '*themis*' from that of '*tithēmi*', 'I put' or 'I lay down'. *Dikē* is what is marked out; *themis* is what is laid down. And these nouns are tied to the verbs so that what we are dealing with is, not dead etymology, but a way in which the nature of cosmic order is presupposed in a great deal of everyday speech.

Both Zeus and those kings to whose rule Zeus has entrusted the *themistes* enforce *dikē* by punishing those who violate it. If therefore the subject of a king is wronged, it is to the king that he should appeal for right judgment in his favor. And so also with Zeus. Zeus protects especially those whose place in the established order is unclear or threatened: the stranger and the suppliant.

The order over which Zeus and human kings reign is one structured in terms of hierarchically ordered social rules. To know what is required of you is to know what your place is within that structure and to do what your role requires. To deprive another of what is due to someone occupying his role or to usurp the role of another is not only to violate *dikē*; it is to infringe upon the *timē*, the honor of the other. And if I am dishonored, as Achilles was by Agamemnon, then I am required to seek redress.

To do what my role requires, to do it well, deploying the skills necessary to discharge what someone in that role owes to others, is to be *agathos*. '*Agathos*' comes to be translatable by 'good', and '*aretē*', the corresponding noun, by 'excellence' or 'virtue'; but since originally to be *agathos* is to be good at doing what one's role requires, and since the primary all-important role is that of the warrior-king, it is unsurprising that '*aretē*' originally names the excellence of such a king. One who does what it is proper for a king to do, preserving his *timē* as a king, may nonetheless act in a way not well designed to preserve *dikē*. Agamemnon in dishonoring Achilles did not cease to be *agathos* (*Iliad* I, 275).

'*Aretē*' comes, of course, to be used of qualities other than those of warrior-kings, but in the Homeric poems it still names only qualities which enable an individual to do what his or her role requires. Yet these are qualities praised not only because they enable an individual to do what his or her role requires, but also because they enable one both to act in accordance with what his or her role requires and to preserve or restore the order that is *dikē*. So in the *Iliad* Nestor is *eu phroneōn* (I, 253) in speaking with the purpose of ending the quarrel of Agamemnon and Achilles, and in the *Odyssey* Telemachus is said by Eurycleia to have acted with *saophrosunē* (XXIII, 30) in not revealing his father's plans prematurely; the same quality was ascribed to him much earlier (IV, 158) when he was at the court of Menelaus. In both cases what was ascribed to him was knowing how to act *both* effectively in his role *and* in a way which sustains rather than violates the overall order of things. And Nestor's counsel to others is designed to produce the same restraint that Telemachus exerts in respect of himself.

Thinking well (*eu phronein*) or soundly (*saophronein*) is a matter of reminding oneself or another of what *aretē* and *dikē* require. But most often in the Homeric poems it is only *aretē* that is in question. What is it to consider the claims of *aretē* in deciding how to act? In the *Iliad* (XI, 400 et seq.) there is a point at which Odysseus is left alone upon the battlefield. He conducts a dialogue with himself, or rather with his *thumos*: ". . . what is to happen to me? If I flee frightened of their numbers, that will be a great evil; but if I am taken alone, that is more terrible. . . . But why does my *thumos* say these things to me? For I know that the bad [*kakoi*] leave the battle, but that he who is excellent [*aristeuesi*] in fighting must stand his ground boldly . . ." (XX, 404–410). Odysseus reminds himself, or rather his *thumos*, of what he knows: whoever is *agathos* as a warrior, rather than *kakos*, stands fast; and it would be natural enough for us to say of him that he gives himself a reason for acting as he does. But this could be misleading if it suggested that Homer was ascribing to Odysseus a process of reasoning. Odysseus makes no inferences. What he does is to call to mind what he knows in order to counteract the effect upon his *thumos* of a disturbing passion, fear. What he says to himself stands to the action that he then performs, not as a premise to a conclusion, but as a statement of what is required to a performance of that requirement.

What does the word '*thumos*' mean in such a context? To translate it by 'soul' or 'spirit', as Liddell and Scott suggested at least for some examples of its use, or by '*mens*' or '*animus*', as Henricus Stephanus did, is acceptable if we divest these words of many of their familiar associations. Someone's *thumos* is what carries him forward: it is his self as a kind of energy; and it is no accident that it comes to be used not only of the seat of someone's anger but of the anger itself. Passions such as fear or anger or sexual longing swell the *thumos* and lead to action, often of a destructive kind. Such passions are inflicted upon us; in experiencing them we may have *atē,* blind infatuation, visited upon us. The gods may for their own purposes or to punish us be the authors of such inflictions and visitation, and the gods may equally caution us against yielding to them, as Athena does Achilles when he has an impulse to slay Agamemnon.

This conception of the relationship of the passions to the *thumos* precludes us from understanding the passions as affording reasons, let alone good reasons, for someone to act in a particular way. The passions are on this view causes which by swelling the *thumos* divert someone from doing what he would otherwise do, what it would be appropriate for him to do. When Odysseus invokes what he knows to be the right way to behave in order to inhibit the effects of fear, he is not weighing two alternative reasons for action. It is rather that he calls upon his *aretē* to give him strength of purpose to overcome the passion.

Thus not only do the precepts which embody the injunctions of *aretē* and *dikē* not stand to the actions which they enjoin as reasons, but the passions are not to be thought of as providing an alternative set of reasons for action. Of course, when later on the Homeric poems are read by those who inhabit quite different types of culture, it is easy to misread them in this and a variety of related ways. So later readers project back on to the Homeric poems those forms of deliberation which are the prologue to action, those modes of decision-making, those patterns of practical reasoning which they themselves employ. Consider in this light the lines in Book I of the *Iliad* (189–192) in which Homer describes Achilles' response to Agamemnon's dismissive speech in which Agamemnon asserts his claim to Achilles' prize, the slave woman Briseis, "so that you may know how much mightier than you I am. . . ." Achilles is poised for a moment between on the one hand drawing his sword in order to kill Agamemnon or on the other curbing his *thumos*. George Chapman, who published his translation in 1598, wrote:

> Thetis' son at this stood vext. His heart
> Bristled his bosome and two waies drew his discursive part—
> If, from his thigh his sharpe sword drawne, he should make
>   room about
> Atrides' person slaughtring him, or sit his anger out
> And curb his spirit. While these thoughts striv'd in
>   his blood and mind . . .

Alexander Pope in his *Iliad* of 1715 by contrast translated:

> *Achilles* heard, with Grief and Rage opprest,
> His Heart swell'd high, and labour'd in his Breast.
> Distracting Thoughts by turns his Bosom rul'd,
> Now fir'd by Wrath, and now by Reason cool'd:
> That promps his Hand to draw the deadly Sword,
> Force thro' the *Greeks,* to pierce their haughty Lord;
> This whispers soft his Vengeance to controul,
> And calm the rising Tempest of his Soul.

And in Robert Fitzgerald's version, published in 1974, the same passage became:

> A pain like grief weighed on the son of Peleus,
> and in his shaggy chest this way and that
> the passion of his heart ran: should he draw
> long sword from hip, stand off the rest, and kill
> in single combat the great son of Atreus,
> or hold his rage in check and give it time?

Chapman had been educated at Cambridge and there would have had to read the *Nicomachean Ethics* in the high age of Renaissance Aristotelianism. So he ascribes to Achilles a "discursive part" and rival "thoughts" in his "mind." According to Pope, Achilles is torn in eighteenth-century fashion between reason and passion. And Fitzgerald portrays Achilles in the psychological style of the present age as subject to alternating impulses of passion. Each translator uses an idiom familiar in his own time, the presupposition of whose use is some contemporary well-articulated account of the determinants of action and of the corresponding psychology imputed to the agent. Homer's Greek, however, says nothing of discursive part or of reason vying with passion or indeed of any "passion of his heart" in a modern sense. Homer speaks of heart (*ētor*) and, a few lines later, of midriff (*phrēn*) as physical organs. All psychology in Homer is physiology.)When we use this physiological vocabulary to express what for us now are distinctively psychological notions, we cannot but speak figuratively, at least most of the time. But Homer did not in using these particular words speak figuratively. There is, therefore, a crucial sense in which, although we can with the appropriate aids of philological and historical scholarship understand the Homeric poems, they cannot be translated even by a word-for-word rendering. For if these words are understood as words of contemporary English without gloss or paraphrase—and it makes no difference whether it is the contemporaries of 1598, those of 1715, or those of 1974 who are in question, or whether the language of translation is English, French, or German—they will often not mean what Homer's words mean; and if those words *are* understood in their genuine Homeric sense, it is only by means of adequate gloss and paraphrase and not simply through those words.

This is not only a matter of the transition from physiology to psychology; and it is not something that could be remedied by better translation. (Who could do better than Chapman, Pope, and Fitzgerald?) To understand someone as poised between alternative courses of action in any adequately determinate way requires understanding their situation in a way that cannot be neutral between radically different modes of conceiving the relations between what human beings do and the prologues to and/or determinants of their actions. Each translator cannot but, if he is to be intelligible to his intended audience, blend Homer's idiom with that of his own age, and the better the translator the more subtly it will be, transmuting Homer's quite alien preconceptions into more familiar ones. This is why each particular cultural milieu needs its own translations of Homer, and it is why the path to understanding Homer is through understanding the specific limitations of each translation as well as its achievements.

I have argued, then, that in the Homeric poems the prologues to action ought not to be represented, except where a clear justification can be provided, in terms of later conceptions, and that when they are so represented, this is a consequence of misunderstanding generated by a necessary infirmity of the translator's act. But it may be suggested not only that I have at the very least exaggerated the difference between Homer and ourselves, but also that I can easily be shown to have done so by, for example, reading on from line 192 to lines 205–218. For here Athena urges restraint upon Achilles on behalf of Hera as well as herself by telling him that if he restrains himself, he will receive gifts worth three times that of which he is being deprived. And Achilles answers that it is necessary to heed the words of two goddesses, "however angered in one's thumos; for so it is better [*ameinon*]. Whomever obeys the gods, they especially listen to." Achilles here speaks in two different ways about doing what Athena bids. He is reminded by Athena, just as Odysseus reminded himself, that it is the part of the *agathos* (*ameinon* is simply the comparative of *agathon*) not to allow one's passion-swollen *thumos* to dictate one's actions. But he also reasons from a means-end generalization, just as we do: doing what the gods command now secures their favor later on. And in so doing he certainly makes an inference as to what he should do, just as we do.

Moreover, the making of inferences which appeal to causal generalizations in this way is, of course, commonplace in the Homeric poems: Eurylochus points out the consequences of sailing at night (*Odyssey* XII, 286–290); Odysseus, those of slaying the sheep of Helios (XIV, 320–323); and Eumaeus, Telemachus, Eurycleia, and indeed, implicitly or explicitly, almost every character in Homer does and must reason similarly. It is the ability so to reason that constitutes a large part of the resourcefulness which is Odysseus' distinctive characteristic and merits the stock epithet applied to him, '*polumētis*' ('of many devices'). And when causal generalizations are invoked in the Homeric poems, the interest in them is always the practical interest of some agent trying to act effectively. There are no would-be theorists in the *Iliad* or the *Odyssey*. Yet even means-end reasoning in the Homeric poems has, compared with later times and places, a restricted function.

What differentiates means-ends reasoning in the Homeric poems from later reason-giving is that it does not, except in a secondary way, answer the agent's question "What am I to do?" The agent already has envisaged the action that he or she is to perform; what he or she reasons to is *either* a reminder that he must curb his *thumos* if he is to perform it or else must suffer baneful consequences (for example, not have the gods hear his prayers) *or* a conclusion that he or she must perform such and such other actions if he or she is to do what is required (as, for example, Odysseus reasons that he must have the bow if he is to kill the suitors, and Penelope that she must unravel her weaving if she is to fend the suitors off). If they are to do what they envisage as required of them, they must first do certain other things. So in a secondary way they derive conclusions about what to do next, but they are able to do so only because they already know independently of their reasoning what action it is that they are required to perform.

This makes the reasoning of agents represented in the Homeric poems significantly different in its function from that of the reasoning of agents as represented by later theorists of practical reasoning, whether in fifth- and fourth-century Athens or in other successor societies. For such theorists have characteristically offered us accounts of practical reasoning in which one or more of the following three types of reasoning are represented. In some ancient and medieval accounts the agent reasons from premises about what the good for agents of his or her kind is, conjoined with premises about his or her situation, to conclusions which are actions; in some modern accounts the agent reasons from premises about what he or she wants, conjoined with premises about how what he or she wants is to be obtained, to conclusions which are decisions or intentions to act in a particular way; and in some early modern accounts the agent, motivated to satisfy some desire, selects according to some rational criterion an action as a means to the satisfaction of that desire. In all three types of case the question confronting the agent, to which his or her practical reasoning provides an answer, arises because the agent does not know what to do. It is only after the question "What am I to do?" has been answered by means of some such piece of practical reasoning that the rational agent knows what action or actions are required of him or her now or in the foreseen future. And this makes all these later types of reasoning agent very different from Homer's characters.

There are, of course, ways of redescribing episodes in the Homeric poems so that they will seem to fit one of these patterns. That is what Chapman, Pope, and Fitzgerald do. But to do so always involves some degree of anachronistic misconception. And generally the temptation to misconception is most dangerous when it is embodied in the use of expressions that can apparently be applied correctly and insightfully to the actions and characters of the Homeric poems, and that do also find application to contemporary transactions, but are able to perform both functions only in virtue of shifts in meaning and in criteria of application. Consider "self-interest." Agents in the Homeric poems can certainly be said always to act in their own interests as they understand them, but the interest of an individual is always his or her interest *qua* wife or *qua* host or *qua* some other role. And since what is required of one in one's role is to give what is due to those others occupying roles that stand in determinate relation to one's own, king to kinsman or subject, swineherd to master or fellow servant, wife to husband and other kin, host to stranger and so on, there is not the same contrast between what is to one's own interest and what is to the interest of others as that which is conveyed by modern uses of 'self-interest' and cognate terms.

In our modern uses of such expressions we often presuppose some account of human nature in which actions are the expression of or are caused by desires and according to which chains of practical reasoning always terminate in some "I want" or some "It pleases me." From this point of view every reason for action is a reason for some particular individual, and it is therefore a mistake to suppose that there could be good reasons for someone to do something independently of his or her motivation. And we envisage the desires which provide such motivation as capable of being organized either so that they serve the purposes of socially cooperative achievement or in a way that produces instead a mutually frustrating competitiveness. In this context a contrast between the altruistic individual who gives weight to the desires of others and the egoistic individual who does not, and between the cooperative qualities of the one and the competitive qualities of the other, is completely at home. But to use these same contrasts in elucidating Homeric attitudes and actions, as some scholars have done, is to risk grave distortion. Why?

We are apt to suppose under the influence of this type of modern view that desires are psychologically basic items, largely, even if not entirely, invariant in their function between cultures. This is a mistake. The role and function of desires in the self-understanding of human beings vary from culture to culture with the way in which their projects and aspirations, expressions of need and claims upon others, are organized and articulated in the public social world. Where someone moves toward a goal deliberately and intentionally, it is not necessarily or always the case that this is or is taken to be because that person is moved by a desire or even, in some wider sense, by a passion. Whether it is so or not will depend in important part on the way in which in the relevant culture the relationships between the inner world of purposes, felt needs, pains, pleasures, emotions, desires, and the like and the public social world of actions, claims, excuses, pleas, duties, and obligations are organized. The inner world may mirror, be responsive to, be compensating for, or be reactive against the constitutive elements of the public social world. Even the possession of some concept of a unified inner self is not culturally necessary, and one culture that functioned very well without it was that portrayed in the Homeric poems.

Hugh Lloyd-Jones (*The Justice of Zeus,* 1971) has suggested that if the arguments of Hermann Frankel to the conclusion "that Homer had no coherent articulated view of the self" were sound, this "would rule out the possibility that the *Iliad* is a poem in which justice . . . plays any significant part" (pp. 8–9). And he pours scorn on Bruno Snell's thesis (*Die Entdeckung des Geistes,* 1964) that the Homeric characters

were incapable of genuine decision-making because of the lack of coherence in the Homeric psychology. Lloyd-Jones is, of course, right in
holding Snell's conclusion to be false; but some of Snell's premises are
true, and Frankel's thesis is also true, but does not have the drastic consequence which Lloyd-Jones ascribes to it.

To be able to make decisions and to move from action to action in
the specific way that Homer's characters do requires a recognition by
those characters of just the three types of constituent of their social
world which I have already identified: the requirements of *dikē* and
aretē, the incursions and distractions provided by *thumos,* and the
truth and practical relevance of certain causal generalizations. But it
requires no more than this; it does not require that Homer's characters
understand their own decision-making in terms of a coherent psychology of the self. That they lack such a psychology places severe constraints upon the type of decision-making in which they can engage
and upon the type of reasoning that can bear upon it. Moreover, it
would be as difficult for us to develop an entirely consistent account
of what constitutes, in anything like our sense of those words, volun-
tariness and responsibility in the Homeric poems as it would be to construct an entirely consistent theology from what Homer says about the
gods. But even to attempt either of these exercises would already be
an essay in misunderstanding. Responsibility in Homer is a socially
defined and socially established concept. You are responsible for everything for which your role requires that you be held answerable. To
want to add to this some conditions derived from some account of psy-
chic causality is neither possible nor necessary.

So Hermann Frankel was right, but Lloyd-Jones is also right in his
essential contention. And it is crucial for the defense of the view which
I have taken of the way in which action and decision-making are conceived in the Homeric poems that both should be. But what is peculiarly important is that the connection between the forms of decision-
making and the order of *dikē,* which Lloyd-Jones emphasizes, is clearly
perceived. Central to every culture is a shared schema of greater or
lesser complexity by means of which each agent is able to render the
actions of others intelligible so that he or she knows how to respond
to them. This schema is not necessarily ever explicitly articulated by
agents themselves, and even when it is so articulated, they may make
mistakes and misunderstand what it is that they do in understanding
others. But an external observer, particularly one coming from an alien
culture, cannot hope to understand action and transaction except in
terms of such an interpretative schema. So it is with us as observers

of the archaic society represented in the Homeric poems, and what the construction of an accurate Homeric schema reveals is that it is the conjunction of the constraints of *dikē* and *aretē* with the incursions and diversions of *thumos* which in large part both define and provide a classification of types of action in such a way that a particular action can be identified and responded to by others. Decision-making has to be what it is in key part because justice is what it is. The characterization of action and of the prologues to action make ineliminable reference to the cosmic order of *dikē*. The cosmic order can be transgressed, but the consequences of transgression are themselves signs of that same order.

The Homeric poems are not philosophical treatises. The conceptual schema which they embody is revealed to us only in its range of concrete applications. The connection between different parts of it are not rigorously articulated. Nonetheless, the coherence of the Homeric *Weltanschauung* enables us to identify two features of the Homeric conceptions of *dikē* and of the reasoning of agents which are transmitted to their post-Homeric successors. The first is a matter of the way in which each of these conceptions is embedded in and draws part of its distinctive character from the larger conceptual scheme in which it is at home. It is not just that the conception of *dikē* and that of practical reasoning are interrelated; neither can be understood adequately apart from quite a number of other concepts. So also to understand the subsequent history of these Homeric concepts and their successors will likewise be inseparable from understanding, in some measure at least, the larger history of these successive, changing conceptual schemes in terms of which they come to be articulated.

Second, whatever else 'justice' names, it names a virtue; and whatever else good practical reasoning may require, it requires certain virtues in those who exhibit it. This subsequent history will then inescapably be a history of the relationship of practical reasoning and of justice to the virtues and more generally to conceptions of human good. That at the Homeric stage the elucidation both of *dikē* and of the nature of reflection upon prospective action should have required discussion also of *aretē* and of *agathos* will turn out to have been required not only for its own sake but as a necessary preliminary to the later history, a history which, while it both puts in question and transforms what is inherited from Homer, also preserves to a remarkable degree features of the Homeric standpoint. Indeed, the point has been reached at which it is important to think in terms not so much of *the* Homeric standpoint as of Homeric standpoints.

The Homeric poems themselves were, of course, composed over a long period of time, and for certain purposes it would be crucial to contrast not only the standpoint of the *Iliad* with that of the *Odyssey* but also the different stages which can be distinguished within each poem with each other. For the moment, however, I can put the problems which these contrasts present on one side. It is sufficient for my immediate purposes to remark upon the way in which certain dominant Homeric themes and concepts furnished a background to the thought and action of fifth- and fourth-century Athenians, and more especially upon the way in which fifth- and fourth-century embodiments of, responses to, and reactions against those Homeric themes and concepts provided both essential parts and aspects of the materials for and the contexts of practical reasoning and deliberation.

To understand these themes and concepts as Homeric, even when in successive transformations they have been developed and elaborated in a manner that is quite alien to their Homeric origin, is essential to understanding them at all. Athenian thought and Athenian practice were, among other things, dialogues with Homeric voices. And what even the non- and anti-Homeric voices in those dialogues said is genuinely intelligible only when interpreted in terms of their relationship to the Homeric voices. But this is only one of the ways in which Athenian arguments and conflicts begin from Homer.

All practical reasoning arises from someone's asking the question "What am I to do?" The asking of that question itself has point only when some reason has presented itself to the agent, or has been presented to him or her, for doing something other than that which he or she would in the normal way of things have next or at least quite soon proceeded to do. Good reasons for action, when they are effective in action-guiding, are causes, and a cause is always something that makes a difference to an outcome. In the case of human action most of the time in most circumstances the processes and procedures on which good (or bad) reasons for action impinge causally are those of the normal day with its schedule of routine activities and cessation from activity. This conception of the normal day, and of the normal month, the normal year, and so on, is of the first importance to understanding action and reasoning about action in any culture. The structure of normality provides the most basic framework for understanding action. Acting in accordance with those structures does not require the giving or the having of reasons for so acting, except in certain exceptional types of circumstance in which those structures have been put in question. Meals are eaten at certain prescribed times in certain prescribed company without anyone having to give reasons either to themselves or to others for so doing; likewise, work of the type assigned to those of each particular role and status is assigned to certain scheduled periods; rituals both occupy parts of the routinized day and reinforce the habits of structured activity; and both serious play and casual pursuits have their own structure and their own place in the larger structures.

So acting upon certain specific reasons is usually exceptional and in normal circumstances is intelligible only in terms of and against the background of the structures of normality. It is departing from what those structures prescribe which requires the having and the giving of reasons. And an adequately good reason for action is therefore in the first instance a reason good enough for doing something other than that which normality prescribes. Of course, when a reason is judged to outweigh the requirements of the customary structure, there is in the background the possibility of a not-yet-formulated judgment of some kind as to how good the reasons are for doing what the customary structure prescribes. And so reasoning which justifies particular requirements of that structure may emerge from the reasoning which puts it in question. But only in this secondary way do agents find reasons for doing what is normally prescribed. Indeed, one of the functions of the structures of normality is that by making it unnecessary for almost everybody almost all the time to provide justifications for what they are doing or are about to do, they relieve us of what would otherwise be an intolerable burden. But this does not mean that the structures of normality may not themselves be understood, independently of and prior to any reasoning, as worthy of respect; and when they are so understood, it is commonly because the structures of normal life are taken to be a local expression of the order of the cosmos.

So classical Greeks, like Greeks of the archaic period, for the most part understood the forms and structures of their communities as exemplifying the order of *dikē;* and what gave literary expression to that understanding above all else was the recitation and the hearing and the reading of the Homeric poems. In fifth- and fourth-century Athens those poems had an important place in the structures of normality; not only were they taught systematically to Athenian boys, but their recitation at the festival of the Panathenaia underlined the identity of the Athena who stays Achilles' hand at the beginning of the *Iliad* and brings about peace and reconciliation at the end of the *Odyssey* with the Athena whose cult is the core of Athenian religion and whose statue shows whose temple the Parthenon is. And Athena, the favored daughter of Zeus, acted in Zeus' name when, in Aeschylus' version of the story, she established the specific justice of the Athenian *polis* in the original institution of jury trials. The "equally voted *dikē*" (*Eumenides* 795) which acquitted Orestes exhibited "the light-bearing testimony of Zeus" (797). So the institutionalization of justice at Athens is in a very clear sense taken to be the local expression of the justice of Zeus. And in so understanding themselves and the structure of their everyday life Athenians necessarily understood themselves at least partly in Homeric terms: only partly, not only because more than poetry informed that understanding, but also because Homer's poetic successors had made their own additional contributions, as the reference to Aeschylus reminds us.

Moreover, it is not only that Homer's successors elaborate new ways of understanding the Homeric scheme; it is important now to recall the point that I put on one side a little earlier, that the Homeric poems themselves in the various chronological layers represented therein give expression to an ongoing history of conceptual change. There are already in the *Iliad* tensions between what *aretē* requires and what *dikē* requires. Later post-Homeric development moves toward rendering the relationship between these two problematic in a way which finally generates the problems of practical reasoning which Socrates, Plato, and Aristotle successively confronted. We therefore have to understand the Homeric inheritance in Athenian social life and culture as functioning in two distinct ways. It both is partially constitutive of the everyday ordering of the usually to-be-taken-for-granted structures of that life and culture, and it provides some, perhaps most, of the concepts and modes of understanding which in becoming problematic put key aspects of that ordering and those structures in question. What then was it that rendered originally Homeric concepts and modes of understanding problematic?

Consider first the way in which individual concepts take on a life of their own, so that in their development their relationships to other concepts change. '*Aretē*' is post-Homeric uses is sometimes narrowed in its application, sometimes widened. So that sometimes—in inscriptions on grave stones, for example—it means much the same as '*andreia*': courage, manliness. And in such inscriptions it is often coupled with '*sōphrosunē*' where that word means "prudent caution." In this pairing *aretē* is the virtue of assertion, of knowing how and when to dare; *sōphrosunē*, the virtue of restraint, of knowing when to pause or draw back. But *aretē* and *aretai* come to be used of the whole range of human virtues, and radical disagreement over what virtue consists in cannot but be expressed as disagreement over what *aretē* is and concomitantly over what is good and what is best.

Good (*agathos*), as I pointed out earlier, is used first of all of those who are good at doing what is required of each person inhabiting his or her own particular role by excelling at the types of task so required. If I do what it is good for me to do, I will be approved of by those who want to see human beings do what is required of them, and they will generally be those who uphold the order of *dikē*. So that to call someone *agathos,* in its original use, is not just to express approval; it is generally to express the kind of approval that is characteristic of those who are themselves good and just. One has to say "generally" because on occasion someone may for reasons deriving from some particular context disapprove of someone's behavior, as Nestor does of Agamemnon's toward Achilles, and yet have to admit that they have not acted in a way that violates what is required of an *agathos. Dikē, sōphrosunē,* and *aretē* are generally, not universally, concordant in the Homeric poems. But this lack of universal concordance is not the only or even the most important source of subsequent post-Homeric disagreement.

Homer himself perceived very clearly that the notion of achievement which *aretē* embodies has two distinct, albeit closely related, dimensions. To achieve is to excel, but to achieve is also to win. What is the relationship between achievement understood as excellence and achievement understood as victory? The context in which that relationship has to be understood is that of the agōn. The *agōn* is a formal rule-governed contest, and the rules are designed to allow each contestant a fair opportunity to exhibit his excellence in activity of some particular kind. Under the conditions of a fair rule-governed contest the contender who excels will also be the contender who wins and receives the prizes and above all the kudos, the glory of winning because one is excellent. In the light of this account one aspect of the relationship between excellence and victory is crucial: the standards by which excellence is to be judged and the standards by which it is determined who has won on a particular occasion are distinct. Under maximally fair conditions the more excellent contender will generally be the winner, and on this understanding of the concepts of excellence and of victory this is a conceptual truth. If under such conditions I habitually lose, my claim to be the more excellent *must* be false. But even under such conditions the less excellent may occasionally defeat the more excellent, because, for example, of luck (the sun blinded the more excellent contender at a crucial moment) or a rare moment of error on the part of the more excellent contender. So that by "more excellent" we do not *mean* "victorious"; "more excellent, but defeated" is not a contradiction, as Hector recognized when, having affirmed his own pre-eminence as a warrior, he nonetheless foresees his own defeat (*Iliad* VI, 440–465).

What is the relationship of this contrast between excellence and winning to the central topics of our enquiry? Two points are immediately obvious. First, in giving even the most elementary account of that contrast it was impossible to say how excellence is evaluated within the context of an *agōn* without making use of the concept of a certain kind of justice, that of fairness in the conditions of competition, a fairness that involves an equality of tasks and standards in evaluating rival competitors. And it is also obvious enough that a certain kind of injustice, unfairness in the same respects, will not only impede the making of true evaluative judgments, but may also furnish a means whereby on occasion the less excellent can defeat the more excellent. Second, both kinds of achievement, that of excellence and that of victory, will require effective practical reasoning; and it will be important to learn whether and, if so, how the kind of practical reasoning necessary for the achievement of excellence differs from that necessary for the achievement of victory. To go beyond what is thus obvious requires an exploration of the way in which changing uses of *agathos* and *aretē* among fifth- and fourth-century Greeks are informed by aspects of this conceptual contrast, so that disagreements about both justice and practical reasoning can also be understood as informed by continuing conflicts over the relationship of excellence to winning. The formal *agōn* retained its central place throughout fifth- and fourth-century Greek history, institutionalized in the Olympic and Pythian games, in the contests between tragic and comic poets at Athens and elsewhere, in political debates, in trials in the law courts, and later still in philosophical disputation. But outside those institutions the concept of the *agōn* also found application. Certain events in Greek history were remembered as having provided agonistic occasions in which victory had been a sign of Greek excellence: most notably, the defeats of the Persians by the Athenians at Marathon and Salamis. But historical events also exhibited the difference between being excellent and being victorious, most notably in the Spartan sacrifice at Thermopylae.

How then are excellence, understood as the Greeks understood it, and winning, also understood as the Greeks understood it, related? How far and in what ways does caring about the one involve caring about the other? How far and in what ways does caring about the one exclude caring about the other? One difficulty in answering these questions is this: if we go to particular episodes in Greek, or rather in Athenian, history for our answers, we shall have the advantage of staying close to the evidence and will lessen the dangers of ignoring its constraints; but just because the interest of such particular episodes for our inquiry lies in the extent to which they exemplify and exhibit the part played by an overall conceptual scheme in constituting social life, no set of particular studies will by itself yield answers. I shall therefore proceed as follows. In the next chapter I will construct an account of a conceptual contrast in terms of which, so I shall argue, post-Homeric Greeks developed their Homeric inheritance. This account should be read initially as an as yet untested hypothesis; its value lies only in the extent to which it can subsequently be put to work to provide a cogent interpretation of the relationships between a variety of contending practical and theoretical Athenian positions. Obviously, in constructing it I have had in mind the conflicts and debates for which it is designed to provide an interpretation. But it can only function in the way that I hope that it will by itself being constructed at a level of conceptual abstraction which distances it for the moment from the detail of Athenian realities.

III

The Division of the
Post-Homeric Inheritance

To what standards did post-Homeric Greeks, and more especially Athenians, appeal in making judgments about human excellence? It was part of their Homeric inheritance to believe that excellence is to be judged in terms of the standards established within and for some specific form of systematic activity. To be good is to be good at some activity or in the performance of some role situated within such an activity. There are at least seven types of systematic activity in which in the Homeric and post-Homeric worlds such standards of excellence are elaborated and applied. They are: warfare and combat; seamanship; athletic and gymnastic activity; epic, lyric, and dramatic poetry; farming both arable and the management of animals; rhetoric; and the making and sustaining of the communities of kinship and the household and later of the city-state. To this list architecture, sculpture, and painting were to be added, as were the intellectual enquiries of mathematics, philosophy, and theology.

Such types of activity are often interrelated. Qualities of body, mind, and character acquired in one may play a useful or essential part in achieving success in another. Moreover, all of them require the same kind of disciplined apprenticeship in which, because initially we lack important qualities of mind, body, and character necessary both for excellent performance and for informed and accurate judgment about excellence in performance, we have to put ourselves into the hands of those competent to transform us into the kind of people who will be able both to perform well and to judge well. What is it that we have to learn from them?

We have to acquire both in performance and in judgment the ability to make two different kinds of distinction, that between what merely seems good to us here now and what really is good relative to us here now, and that between what is good relative to us here now and what is good or best unqualifiedly. The first distinction is of course one that can only be applied retrospectively. It is a distinction involved in someone's identification at some later stage of his or her own earlier mistakes, either in performance or in judgment. It is a distinction which will inform later judgments upon one's earlier mistakes in a rational, well-grounded way only if one is able to explain what it was about one in an earlier state that led one into error.

The second kind of distinction is that between what is a good — perhaps the best possible — performance for someone at his or her present stage of educational development relative to his or her particular talents and capacities and what would be the best kind of performance which can now be envisaged by those best qualified to judge, the distinction, for example, between excellent apprentice work and a supremely excellent masterpiece. But it is important to note that the kind of judgments which we make invoking this second type of distinction are themselves subject to later judgments invoking the first kind of distinction. What seemed to us at one stage a perfect performance may later be recognized either as imperfect or as less perfect than some later achievement. That is to say, in all these areas there is not only progress in achievement but also progress in our conception and recognition of what the highest perfection is.

The concept of the best, of the perfected, provides each of these forms of activity with the good toward which those who participate in it move. What directs them toward that goal is both the history of successive attempts to transcend the limitations of the best achievement in that particular area so far and the acknowledgment of certain achievements as permanently defining aspects of the perfection toward which that particular form of activity is directed. Those achievements are assigned a canonical status within the practice of each type of activity. Learning what they have to teach is central to apprenticeship in each particular form of activity.

What can never be done is to reduce what has had to be learned in order to excel at such a type of activity to the application of rules. There will of course at any particular stage in the historical development of such a form of activity be a stock of maxims which are used to characterize what is taken at that stage to be the best practice so far. But knowing how to apply these maxims is itself a capacity which cannot be specified by further rules, and the greatest achievements in each area at each stage always exhibit a freedom to violate the present established maxims, so that achievement proceeds both by rule-keeping and by rule-breaking. And there are never any rules to prescribe when it is the one rather than the other that we must do if we are to pursue excellence.

Excellence and winning, it is scarcely necessary to repeat, are not the same. But it is in fact to winning, and only to excellence on the occasions when it does in fact produce victory, that a certain kind of reward is attached, a reward by which, ostensibly at least, excellence is to be honored. Rewards of this kind—let us call them external rewards —are such goods as those of riches, power, status, and prestige, goods which can be and are objects of desire by human beings prior to and independently of any desire for excellence. In societies and cultures, such as that represented in the Homeric poems, in which the pursuit of these latter goods and that of excellence are to some large degree linked together within the dominant social institutions, any incompatibilities between the human qualities required for the pursuit of such goods and the qualities required for the pursuit of excellence are apt to remain latent and unacknowledged. But when social change transforms institutions, so that the systematic pursuit of excellence in some area or areas becomes incompatible with the pursuit of the goods of riches, power, status, and prestige, the differences between the two types of pursuit and between the goods which are their objects become all too clear.

What qualities of body, mind, and character are generally required to achieve such goods as those of riches, power, status, and prestige? They are those which, in the circumstances in which a given person finds him or herself, enable that person both to identify which means will be effective in securing such goods and to be effective in utilizing those means to secure them. Let us call these qualities of body, mind, and character the qualities of effectiveness, and the goods which provide these qualities with their goal and their justification the goods of effectiveness.

It is at once clear that some of the qualities characteristically and generally necessary to achieve excellence and some of the qualities characteristically and generally necessary to achieve the goods of effectiveness are the same: steadfastness of purpose, for example. But it is equally clear that these two sets of qualities also differ in striking ways, so that what is accounted a virtue in the perspective afforded by the goods of effectiveness will often be very different from what is accounted a virtue from the standpoint of the goods of excellence. Consider in this respect what each characteristically makes of justice, temperateness, courage, and friendship.

In relation to both the goods of excellence and the goods of effectiveness a disposition to obey certain rules of justice will be accounted a virtue, but the justification of the rules, the content of the rules, and the nature of the binding force that the rules have for those who accept their authority is different in the two cases, and these differences are rooted in the fundamental contrast between excellence on the one hand and effectiveness on the other, both defined in terms of performance in the *agōn.* One who excels is one who wins under conditions of fairness, as we noted earlier. Moreover, someone who is genuinely excellent has to impose the constraints of fairness upon him or herself, if only because to know how to judge oneself or others excellent, which is part of excellence, involves fairness in judging. The same standards have to be applied to performances under the same standard conditions, appropriate allowances have to be made where someone performs under conditions either more difficult or easier than the standard conditions, and the beginner and the advanced performer must be judged in appropriately different ways. These constraints are expressed in formulas used to define justice: each person and each performance has to be accorded what is due to him or her and to it in respect of merit, like cases being judged on equal terms, unlike with the right degree of proportionality.

The content of justice is thus defined in terms of merit and desert. To be wronged is to be the recipient of undeserved harm inflicted intentionally by someone else; to be unlucky by contrast is to be the recipient of harm from nature, by accident. To redress wrong is to restore the order in which the appropriate goods, whatever they are, are distributed according to desert. But at this point a problem arises. If excellence is always the specific excellence of some particular form of activity, then desert in respect of excellence is presumably also correspondingly specific, and there will be a multiplicity of standards of desert, each independent of the others. So the question will arise: How are the goods of honor and those of the external rewards of excellence to be apportioned among different kinds of achievement? How is the desert of the good soldier to be compared to that of the good farmer or the good poet? Failure to provide some standard in terms of which relative achievement and relative desert can be appraised would leave the members of a community without the possibility of any overall shared standard of just apportionment and just recognition. It would deprive them of any standard which could be what any legitimate claimant to the names '*dikē*' and '*dikaiosunē*' has to be, an expression of some unitary order informing and structuring human life. But how could such a standard be provided?

The only form of community which could provide itself with such a standard would be one whose members structured their common life in terms of a form of activity whose specific goal was to integrate within itself, so far as possible, all those other forms of activity practiced by its members and so to create and sustain as its specific goal that form of life within which to the greatest possible degree the goods of each practice could be enjoyed as well as those goods which are the external rewards of excellence. The name given by Greeks to this form of activity was 'politics', and the *polis* was the institution whose concern was, not with this or that particular good, but with human good as such, and not with desert or achievement in respect of particular practices, but with desert and achievement as such. The constitution of each particular *polis* could therefore be understood as the expression of a set of principles about how goods are to be ordered into a way of life. *The* good for human beings would be the form of life that was best for them; to enjoy what is best is to flourish, to be *eudaimōn;* and what both the constitution and the life of a particular polity express is a judgment as to what way of life is best and what human flourishing consists in.

The ordering of goods within a *polis* was not only a matter of ranking goods hierarchically, by understanding some goods to be valued only for their own sake, others as both for their own sake and for the sake of some further good, and others yet again as only to be valued as means to some further good. It was also a matter of identifying the place of each good within the patterns of the normal day and month and year, so that there would be in some cities at least a time of the year when tragic poetry received its due and a time when comedy did so, and also of identifying both which section of the citizens it was whose peculiar good each particular good was, as the good of excellence in military combat was peculiarly the good of the young, and which section of the citizens it was to whose care the achievement of each particular good peculiarly belonged, as the goods of farming to the farmers and the goods of healing to the guild of physicians, the Asclepiadae.

To what rational principles can appeal be made in such an overall ordering of goods, so that that ordering may be rationally justifiable? It is, of course, this question which must be answered by any theory of practical reasoning that aspires to show what it is for the citizen of the *polis qua* citizen — the citizen who acts in accordance with the ordering of goods established in his particular *polis* — to act rationally. And it is evident that only in the light of such a theory could the justice of any particular *polis,* understood in this way, be justified. For the justice of a *polis* on this view, both in its apportionment of goods and in its correction of wrongdoing, is expressed in the actions of its citizens as they in different ways and with different degrees both of devotion and of success pursue the goods of excellence and reason as to what to do in order to achieve such goods.

Yet at once it needs to be remarked that this was only one way in which the justice of the *polis* and the practical rationality of its citizens came to be understood. From another contrasting and antagonistic perspective the justice of the *polis*, both as a quality of individual citizens and as an ordering of the city, was understood as directed not toward the goods of excellence but toward those of effectiveness. To understand this alternative conception of justice adequately, it is necessary as a preliminary to emphasize the complexity of the relationships between the goods of excellence and those of effectiveness.

It would be a large misconception to suppose that allegiance to goods of the one kind necessarily excluded allegiance to the goods of the other. For on the one hand those forms of activity within which alone it is possible to achieve the goods of excellence can only be sustained by being provided with institutionalized settings. And the maintenance of the relevant institutional and organizational forms always requires the acquisition and retention of some degree of power and some degree of wealth. Thus the goods of excellence cannot be systematically cultivated unless some at least of the goods of effectiveness are also pursued. On the other hand it is difficult in most social contexts to pursue the goods of effectiveness without cultivating at least to some degree the goods of excellence, and this for at least two reasons. The achievement of power, wealth, and fame often enough requires as a means the achievement of some kind of genuine excellence. And, moreover, since the goods of effectiveness are those goods which enable their possessor to have or to be, within the limits of contingent possibility, what he or she wants, whenever what someone whose fundamental allegiance is to the goods of effectiveness just happens to want, for whatever reason, to be genuinely excellent in some way, goods of effectiveness will be put to the service of goods of excellence.

It is, however, always possible for a particular individual or social group systematically to subordinate goods of the one kind to goods of the other, and the fundamental conflicts of standpoint in much Greek and especially Athenian life were provided by those who did so. In the actual social orders of city-states not only was recognition accorded to both sets of goods, but it was often enough accorded in a way that left it indeterminate where the fundamental allegiance of those who inhabited that social order lay. So it was, as I have already suggested, with the order portrayed in the Homeric poems; so it was for the most

part in Periclean Athens. Only when certain kinds of practical and theoretical issues—those in which different fundamental allegiances in respect of goods require systematically different and incompatible answers
to centrally important practical questions—claimed the attention of a
particular social group did they either discover for themselves where
it was that their own allegiance had already been given or else for the
first time clearly give their allegiance to one set of goods rather than
the other.

What made this indeterminateness possible was the fact that one and
the same institutionalized set of rules and procedures in the administration of justice may over a wide range of cases be equally compatible
with the pursuit of either set of goods, while an ambiguous political
rhetoric may for long periods leave it quite unclear, to those who utter
it as much as to their hearers, that there are any decisive choices between types of good which need to be made. Nonetheless, there are
some continually recurring issues which make it difficult to avoid the
making of such choices, and these in time reveal the radical character
of the difference between a justice defined in terms of the goods of excellence, that is, a justice of desert, and a justice defined in terms of
the goods of effectiveness. What is distinctive about the latter kind of
justice?

Under the normal conditions of life in human societies each person
can only hope to be effective in trying to obtain what he or she wants,
whatever it is, if he or she enters into certain kinds of cooperation with
others and if this cooperation enables both him or her and those others
generally to have rationally well-founded expectations of each other.
Thus a rule-governed mode of social life will be required, and it will
be important, if obedience to the rules is to be a means to the goods
of effectiveness, that disobedience to the rules should carry certain penalties. A well-designed penalty is one which attaches to disobedience
to the rules a cost assessed in terms of the goods of effectiveness such
that for most people most of the time it will outweigh any benefit that
is likely to accrue from disobedience.

What the rules of justice will have to prescribe is reciprocity, and
what is to be accounted as reciprocity, what is to be exchanged for what,
will depend on what each party brings to that bargaining situation of
which the rules of justice are the outcome. When I speak of a bargaining situation in this regard, I am not suggesting that there was once
in fact an historical episode in which the rules of the justice of cooperative effectiveness were arrived at through negotiation. It is rather the
case that in any given stage of a particular social order's history the

interactions of various groups and individuals will have provided each
with varying degrees of influence upon how the rules of justice are to
be construed and applied. Thus, where the justice of cooperative effectiveness prevails, it will always be *as if* justice was the outcome of a
contract, an episode of explicit negotiation. And the various groups
and individuals will behave accordingly. Those who are least vulnerable
to having the pursuit of their own ends frustrated by others will be in
a position to demand most and to give least in terms of the rules governing the distribution of power and other resources; those who are
most vulnerable will be in a position to demand least. But the rules
will have to be at least minimally acceptable to almost all for them to
function as rules of justice for any extended period of time, and this
will characteristically involve that some of the same constraints are imposed on those who are relatively rich and powerful as well as on those
who are relatively weak and powerless.

The contrast between the two conceptions of justice in respect of
both content and justification scarcely needs to be spelled out further.
Justice as what is due to excellence in the one case, justice as what is
required by the reciprocity of effective cooperation in the other, will,
as I have already emphasized, often enough require the same or similar
rules. But there will clearly be large areas in which not only the standards but also the verdicts of each kind of justice will differ over particular cases and will do so precisely because of the different types of
justification which each has to invoke. Corresponding to these differences is a difference in the kind of binding force that each set of rules
possesses for those who acknowledge them. Someone who breaks the
rules of the justice of excellence primarily harms him or herself, whether
or not others are harmed. The harm to oneself is that of depriving oneself in some specific way of an opportunity to achieve the goods at
which one is aiming. That a breach of the rules of justice is indeed
such a harm will not always be clear even to those whose allegiance
is genuinely to some good of excellence, and therefore such justice will
have to be enforced, especially upon those who are in the initial stages
of apprenticeship in the pursuit of some excellence. The discipline of
punishment within such a scheme is, however, only justifiable because
and insofar as the punishment educates those upon whom it is inflicted;
it has to be the kind of punishment which they are able to learn to
recognize as being to their own benefit. So one mark of some particular local conception of justice being an example of justice defined in
terms of the goods of excellence is that its protagonists will have to
maintain, if they are consistent, that it is always better for his or her

own sake for someone who commits an injustice to be punished than to escape unpunished. And this is markedly not the case with a justice defined in terms of the goods of cooperative effectiveness.

The rules of justice thus defined are such that to break them primarily hurts others and not oneself. To commit injustice may sometimes and perhaps in certain types of circumstance will almost always be to one's own disadvantage, but only because one will by so doing tend both to antagonize others and to make it less likely that the rules of justice will be observed on those many occasions when it is in one's own interest that they should be obeyed. One will thus lessen one's chances of securing needed cooperation from others. But these harms to oneself will be a consequence, not of one's acts of injustice by themselves, but of such acts accompanied by a recognition on the part of others that one has been guilty of them. Hence someone who is able to commit an injustice in such a way that others remain ignorant that he or she has done so benefits him or herself and incurs no harm. Thus, one is a rational agent bound by the rules of justice only to the extent to which one cannot commit injustice with impunity.

In respect of the goods of excellence those who administer and enforce justice will themselves be required to be just; for if they did not have a regard for justice, it could only be because they had failed to understand how the rules of justice function in relation to the goods to which they had given their allegiance and so they would be incompetent in evaluating merit and desert. Indeed, the administration of the rules of justice will be involved in the relationships of master to apprentice within any of the forms of activity in which excellence is the goal, since just punishment in the context of the justice of desert has a primarily educational function. By contrast, the most important function of punishment in a justice defined in terms of the goods of effectiveness is deterrence, and what is required of those who administer the rules of justice is that they are effective in deterring injustice. For this they need both to be skilled in applying the relevant stock of true generalizations about what types of cause have deterrent effects and to have a strong interest in maintaining and in themselves observing the rules of justice, an interest which may be secured by the institutionalized provision of benefits outweighing those to be achieved by the maladministration of justice. But it can be true of them, as it cannot be true of those who are well qualified to administer the justice of desert, that were they not to have such an interest, they would not be just. Unsurprisingly, therefore, the question "Who should rule?" has a very different answer in respect of the goods of effectiveness from that which it has in respect of those of excellence. For the adherents of each have to conceive of the point and purpose of politics and the *polis* in a very different way. Those who subordinate the goods of excellence to those of effectiveness will, if they are consistent, understand politics as that arena in which each citizen seeks to achieve as far as possible what he or she wants within the constraints imposed by the various forms of political order, and the answer to the question "Who should rule?" will be "Whoever has both the skills and the interest to maintain or to promote each type of order." Which type of order someone promotes will of course depend upon his or her own interests. Politics as a theoretical study will from this point of view be primarily concerned with how far rival interests can be promoted and yet also reconciled and contained within a single order. By contrast, for those whose fundamental allegiance lies with the goods of excellence politics as a theoretical study will primarily be concerned with how a regard for justice relevantly conceived can be promoted so as to increase a shared understanding of and allegiance to the goods of the *polis* and only secondarily with conflicts of interest, especially insofar as they may be destructive of movement toward such a shared understanding and allegiance.

The two rival conceptions of justice differ in one other important way. For justice defined in terms of the goods of excellence, justice as a virtue of individuals is definable independently of and antecedently to the establishment of enforceable rules of justice. Justice is a disposition to give to each person, including oneself, what that person deserves and to treat no one in a way incompatible with their deserts. The rules of justice, when they are in good order in terms of this conception of justice, are those rules best designed to secure this outcome if they are observed by everyone, including both the just and the unjust. So someone may obey the rules of justice and yet be an unjust person who obeys the rules only from, for example, fear of punishment. But for the justice that is designed to serve the goods of effectiveness a perfectly just person is no more and no less than someone who always obeys the rules of justice; until there exists an enforceable set of rules defining what is required of the relationships of each person to every other in the pursuit of their particular goals, the concept of justice lacks any content. When such rules have given it content, the virtue of justice is nothing other than the disposition to obey those rules. So the virtue of justice is, on this latter view, secondary to and definable only in terms of the rules of justice.

Yet although the relationship of the virtue of justice to the rules of justice differs in the two conceptions, it is true for both not only that justice as a virtue is one of a whole range of virtues, but also that the upholding of justice both in the social order and as a virtue in individuals requires the exercise of a range of virtues other than justice. Examples of such justice-sustaining virtues are temperateness, courage, and friendship. And each of these is differently conceived from each of the two alternative standpoints.

The differences between the way in which temperateness is to be accounted a virtue in respect of the goods of excellence and the way in which it is to be so accounted in respect of the goods of effectiveness precisely parallel the differences that arise over justice. What temperateness prescribes in respect of the goods of excellence is a directed disciplining and transformation of the desires, aversions, and dispositions of the self so that someone incapable of excellence in performance or judgment becomes, so far as possible, someone capable of both. Thus temperateness is a virtue which transforms both what I judge to be a good and what I am moved by as a good. By contrast, in respect of the goods of effectiveness temperateness is a virtue only because and insofar as it enables me to achieve more efficiently goods antecedently recognized as such and desired. Temperateness is the virtue which overcomes frustration by oneself in one's pursuit of one's own satisfaction, just as justice is the virtue which overcomes frustration by others.

In the case of courage the differences are of another kind. From both points of view the ability to endure and the ability to confront a variety of harms and dangers are to be valued. But both the range of relevant harms and dangers and what one may be required to sacrifice in confronting them and why differ significantly. It is a common characteristic of both standpoints that the relevant range of harms and dangers will be understood to vary with the specific good or goods aimed at. Just as the harms and dangers which have to be faced and overcome in order to be excellent as a poet are not at all the same as those which have to be faced and overcome in order to be excellent as a soldier, so the harms and dangers which confront someone trying to increase his or her wealth are characteristically different from those which confront someone trying to increase his or her political power. Moreover, the self-endangering character of courage makes it important in another way. How much each of us cares for or is concerned about any person, group, institution, practice, or good is measured — cannot but be measured — by the degree to which we would be prepared to take risks and face harm and danger on their behalf. And the claim that some person or group or institution or practice is the bearer of some very great good, in a way or to a degree that I myself am not, always at the very least raises the question of whether, if a condition of that bearer of good being preserved and defended is that I should be prepared to die, I do not owe it to that person or group or institution or practice to be so prepared to die.

With some of the goods of excellence it is only too obvious that from time to time one must put one's life at stake. One cannot excel in the practice of war without being so prepared, and one cannot excel as one engaged in founding or sustaining some settled form of human community without providing for its defense, a defense which requires that for the sake of the good of that community some persons have to be willing to risk their lives. But this is also required in some circumstances in respect of the goods of effectiveness. Consider, for instance, the way in which prestige can function as such a good.

Homeric heroes and some of their later Greek heirs characteristically valued above all that form of prestige which consists in being honored and famous both in one's lifetime and after one's death. Someone who treated honor as so great a good would have had to be willing to risk death and to die bravely, for honor of that kind was accorded only to those who were so willing. And in the reciprocity which governs relationships defined in terms of the goods of cooperative effectiveness certain privileges may be accorded only to those who are prepared to die bravely in battle. So Homer shows us Sarpedon urging Glaucus to join him at the point of danger in battle, by reminding him that both honor and princely possessions are accorded them by the Lycians, just because they are expected to risk their lives in this way. Courage in this particular kind of social order is therefore to be accounted a very important virtue as much by those who value the goods of effectiveness as by those who value the goods of excellence.

Wanting to be regarded well by others and wanting the pleasure of liking and being liked by others can come to have a central place among the goods of effectiveness. Insofar as they do occupy such a place, an additional motive, over and above that afforded by the benefits of reciprocity, is provided for obedience to the rules of justice. And indeed the kind of cooperativeness which is originally valued only as a means to the goods of effectiveness may itself engender the kind of relationships in which a larger and deeper sociability is at home. So the very process of trying to obtain what one values may change what it is that one values. But of course the sociability thus valued will itself be valued for the pleasure and the utility which it affords to those who partake of it. And so from the standpoint of the goods of cooperative effectiveness friendship is a virtue precisely insofar as it is a source of pleasure and utility.

From the standpoint of the goods of excellence, however, friendship is a matter of more than pleasure and utility, although it may involve both of these. It is a type of relationship of mutual regard which arises from a shared allegiance to one and the same good or to one and the same set of goods. Characteristically the affections and the affective enjoyment of relationship supervene upon this regard, and characteristically friends are useful to one another. But what matters most in this kind of relationship is that each cares for the other primarily because of the relationship of each to the good.

In the Homeric poems the distinction between these two kinds of friendship had not yet been formulated and could not have yet been formulated. Within the archaic conceptual scheme of the Homeric poems friendship is either a kin relationship or a relationship resting on past vows which have laid upon two or more men the same obligations as those which arise from kinship. To be a friend, therefore, is to owe and to recognize that one owes to some other in virtue of an established social relationship. And as with friendship, so it is also with the other virtues and most notably with justice. In the Homeric poems the distinction between types of good and types of virtue has not yet emerged. But in the post-Homeric world of Athenian fifth-century social life, although Homeric ways of imagining and understanding oneself retained great power, nonetheless the social and political transformations of the Athenian order made it impossible to avoid raising questions for which Homer could furnish no answer, precisely because those questions resulted from the dissolution of the Homeric vision into disparate and incompatible elements. So where Homer imaginatively integrated what were potentially conflicting conceptions of goodness, of justice, and of other virtues into a largely coherent vision of social order, fifth- and fourth-century Athenians made those potential conflicts actual in the course of debating with themselves and with others large issues of practice and of theory. And the thesis which I am now able to advance is that when those conflicts became explicit, the underlying issues involved in them are best understood in terms of a systematic and radical disagreement over whether it is the goods of excellence or those of cooperative effectiveness which are to define the goals of the *polis* and with them the mode of life to which Athenians are to give their fundamental allegiance.

Only, of course, upon certain exceptional and rare occasions did it occur that any clear and unqualified statement of either standpoint was either defended or challenged, and it was even rarer for such an occasion to produce a confrontation between those who championed an unquestioning deference to the goods of cooperative effectiveness and those committed to a defense of excellence even in circumstances in which the consequence of such an allegiance was plainly to incur undeserved defeat and humiliation. Often enough it was instead in the course of conflicts in which two or more adherents of one and the same standpoint disagreed radically among themselves as to how to act in a particular situation that the shared presuppositions of their standpoint were explicitly articulated. So it was, for example, in the debate in the Athenian assembly over the Mytilenean revolt, when both the main speakers for the two opposing points of view, Cleon and Diodotus, took it for granted that the only fundamental question at issue was how Athenian power might be rendered more effective in the future. When Diodotus did urge that the Mytilenean democrats did not *deserve* to be put to death, it was as part of an argument designed to show that treatment of this kind would lose Athens useful friends in other cities, and it was the utility and only the utility of that friendship to which he appealed. So Cleon and Diodotus agreed in presupposing a fundamental allegiance to the goods of effectiveness.

When that allegiance was challenged, as I shall argue that it was, for example, by Sophocles, both in the *Oedipus Tyrannus* and in the *Philoctetes,* and by Socrates, it was naturally enough issues concerning the nature of justice which became central. But when fundamental controversy about justice thus becomes explicit, the problem of how to reason practically and theoretically about justice becomes inescapable. When it does so, another and more surprising level of disagreement between the standpoint of the goods of excellence and that of the goods of cooperative effectiveness comes to light. For it emerges that what is accounted *a good reason for action* is very different for those for whom the context of practical reasoning is provided by a form of activity specified by one or more of the goods of excellence from what is so accounted by those for whom the context of practical reasoning is provided by an understanding of social life as an arena in which each individual and each group of individuals seek to maximize the satisfaction of his or her own wants and needs. These are two practical rationalities, not one, and so at a later stage the question must arise of whether it is possible to have good reasons for giving one form of practical rationality precedence over the other. Wherein do these two kinds of practical reasoning differ?

The reasons for action which I and others take to be good reasons for action—and the ascription of which by others to me and by me to others will form the basis for those judgments upon each other's conduct which will be crucial to the flourishing or failing of our co-operation—will in the case of the goods of excellence be such that each of us will have had to learn what they are and how to judge concerning them as part of their education into that specific form of activity which aims at those particular goods. Such reasons will thus have force for us only insofar as we care about and understand the goods specific to that form of activity. So the first premises of our practical reasoning, premises in the formulation of which we shall gradually improve as we come to understand better the good or goods which we are pursuing, will concern those goods; they will be the starting point, the *archē,* of our reasoning. Moreover, in order to reason well we shall have had to learn how systematically to accord merit where it is due, that is, we shall have had, in the context of that particular specific form of activity, to acquire the virtue of justice, conceived in terms of desert.

Justice, conceived in terms both of fairness in respect of the conditions of the *agōn* and of desert in respect of the outcome of the *agōn,* was originally, it will be recalled, a concept which found its application only within the context of particular forms of activity. In order that justice so conceived should play the part assigned to *dikē* and to *dikaiosunē* in the Homeric and post-Homeric orders, it was necessary that its scope should be that of the whole life of the community of a *polis.* And it achieved that scope because and insofar as the systematic conduct of the life of the *polis* constituted a higher-order, integrative form of activity, whose *telos* was the achievement of a structured communal life within which the goods of the other forms of activity were ordered, so that the peculiar *telos* of the *polis* was not this or that good, but *the good and the best* as such. And just as justice and the other virtues can therefore be understood as dispositions whose exercise is necessary to secure not merely the goods of this or that form of activity, but also the overall good of the *polis,* the good and the best, so also practical reasoning becomes ordered to the overall good of the *polis,* to the good and the best.

Such practical reasoning will take place in two stages. In the first the reasoner will deliberate in the light of his own situation and circumstances as to what proximate good must be pursued if the ultimate *telos* of the good and the best is to be achieved. In the second the reasoner will move from a premise or premises about the proximate good conjoined with a premise or premises about the way in which his circumstances provide an occasion for realizing it to a conclusion which will be an action. Those premises will be good reasons for action for anyone whose *telos* is the good and the best, for anyone, that is, who not only acts *qua* citizen of a *polis* but also understands the activities of the *polis* and his own actions in terms of the achievement of the goods of excellence. Whether a particular person happens to be moved to action by them will depend not only on such an understanding but also on whether that particular reasoner has progressed sufficiently far in his education into the intellectual and moral virtues to judge correctly as to their truth and relevance. So the soundness of a particular practical argument, framed in terms of the goods of excellence, is independent of its force for any particular person.

By contrast, where the goods of cooperative effectiveness are concerned, no consideration counts as a reason except in respect of its actually motivating some person. And there are no standards by which a reason can be judged a good or a bad reason independently of its being a reason which provides some particular agent with a motive for action. Those psychological states in virtue of which I am moved to action, whatever they are—desires, needs, aspirations, drives—constitute the *archē* of my action. My practical reasoning begins not from some good, let alone some good of which it may be that I cannot as yet have an adequate conception, but from myself understood as directed toward something by way of need or desire, whose obtaining or achievement will satisfy me. Hence cooperation with others demands recognition of their reasons for action as *good reasons for them,* not as *good reasons as such,* and such cooperation requires the creation of a framework for bargaining, within which each may offer to the other considerations designed simultaneously both to appeal to the other in virtue of what he or she wants or is aiming at and to promote one's own goals. In the case of the goods of excellence the good which gives point and purpose to the cooperation of individuals on a given occasion is a good independently of and antecedently to the cooperation of those particular individuals; it is for the sake of that good that they come together. In the case of the goods of effectiveness any common good at which cooperation aims is derived from and compounded out of the objects of desire and aspiration which the rival participants brought with them to the bargaining process. The type of allegiance which those participants give to the rules of justice and what rules of justice they acknowledge will, as I said earlier, depend upon what rules had to be mutually observed to bring into being and to sustain that bargaining process in such a way that each participant can enjoy the maximum benefit from it.

So the two rival standpoints which I have delineated involve, at least in their extreme versions, radically incompatible conceptions not only of goods and of justice and other virtues but also of politics and of practical rationality. It is in the moral and political history of fifth- and fourth-century Athens that these incompatibilities are given their classical expression both in practice and in theoretical enquiry.

IV

Athens Put to the Question

What is to be learned from Athenian political history about the development of conceptions of justice and of practical reasoning is perhaps best understood in terms of the relationships between four different and incompatible Athenian ways of understanding the role of Athens in the later fifth century, each of them playing an important part in shaping later discussions of the problems of justice and of practical reasoning. The chief, but far from the only author of the first of these, was Pericles; his collaborating coauthors were all those of his fellow citizens, at the time the vast majority, for whom Pericles succeeded in articulating in both his speeches and his policies an image of themselves which they were only too eager to acknowledge and to make their own. The other three modes of understanding all involved reaction against or at least critical reflection upon the Periclean interpretation of Athens. They are to be found in the works of Sophocles, of Thucydides, and of Plato, all of them members of the Athenian ruling elite, the first two, like Pericles himself, holding office as general (*stratēgos*) at key times before or during the Peloponnesian War. And since it is the Periclean understanding that evokes responses from the other three, it is with Pericles that we ought to begin. But to begin with Pericles is, it turns out, to return to our true starting point, Homer.

For the understanding of themselves with which Pericles furnished the Athenians was in surprising measure Homeric. Modern scholars often and rightly draw our attention to the extent to which Pericles, at least as portrayed by Thucydides, exemplified attitudes characteristic of and specific to the later fifth century (see, for example, Lowell Edmunds *Chance and Intelligence in Thucydides,* Cambridge, Mass., 1975). But what is remarkable is the degree to which those contemporary elements in Pericles' utterances were integrated into a largely Homeric vision. It may, of course, be thought implausible to ascribe Homeric attitudes to Pericles, since as a leader of the democratic party he was often opposed by those aristocratic conservatives for whom appeal to Homeric models and precedents was so central. But here again what is remarkable in Pericles' utterances and policies is the way in which Homeric thoughts and attitudes have been given a new democratic content while retaining their distinctively Homeric character. Pericles may have offered a distinctively fifth-century and Athenian version of the Homeric ethos, but it was still the Homeric ethos.

So the individual member of the Athenian demos would generally no doubt have found it impossible to understand himself as an Homeric hero, but what Pericles offered him instead was an account of Athens itself as hero-figure and of his citizenship as providing him with a share in that *aretē* which once belonged only to kings. Consider in this respect first of all the virtues which Pericles ascribed to Athens. They are, it seems, much the same virtues that his Athenian followers ascribed to Pericles.

Isocrates was to say of Pericles that he surpassed all other citizens in being *sōphrōn, dikaios,* and *sophos*. '*Sōphrosunē*' had been used in a variety of ways in post-Homeric Greece. As the name of an aristocratic virtue it had been used to characterize a man who could have aggrandized himself beyond due limit but preferred deliberately to curb himself, so that he might enjoy *hēsuchia*, that peacefulness of spirit in which the victor deservedly rests after the *agōn*. It came also to be the virtue more generally associated with knowing who one is and what one's place in the world is, so that restraint may be exercised in not exceeding the limits set by that place. But that cannot be what Isocrates meant in speaking of Pericles. Here it had become the virtue, not of setting constraints upon one's goals, but of moving with due and deliberate caution in one's choice of means. And although Pericles did not use the word '*sōphrosunē*', he praised the Athenians in the Funeral Oration because they did not act until they had instructed themselves in debate, being of all men the most given to reflection before they acted. In so doing they were also able to learn. So Pericles also says of himself and his fellow Athenians that they are lovers of wisdom. (Thucydides II, 40, 3, and II, 40, 1; throughout my use of Thucydides depends on my acceptance of the arguments of Donald Kagan in 'The Speeches of Thucydides and the Mytilene Debate' *Yale Classical Studies* 24, 1979.) And the justice which Isocrates ascribed to Pericles, Pericles himself had ascribed to the Athenians generally for their practice of treating free citizens equally before the law, their respectful fear in face of the law and especially of those laws which are for the advantage of those to whom injustice had been done. To this last point we shall have to return later.

It is right to emphasize that in this period not only '*sōphrōn*' but also such other virtue words as '*dikaios*' and '*sophos*' no longer mean quite the same as did their Homeric predecessors, and the conception of law in the Athenian democracy was not the same as that of Homeric *themis*. To be *sophos* had always involved knowing how to appeal to *gnōmē,* but when Pericles appeals to *gnōmē,* he is appealing no longer to traditional received wisdom but instead to that intelligent learning from experience to which some of the sophists and Euripides had also appealed. So generally the virtue words as used by and about Pericles have been democratized in a way that enables Pericles to claim for the ordinary Athenian citizen virtues which the older Greek aristocrats had tried to reserve for themselves. In what way, then, can these appeals nonetheless form part of an authentically Homeric vision?

They do so first by the way in which Pericles reproduces both in his praise of the Athenians in the Funeral Oration and in his exhortations to them there and in other speeches the central Homeric injunction of father to son. "Always to be the best and preeminent above others" was both the injunction of Hippolochus to Glaucus and that of Peleus to Achilles (*Iliad* VI, 208, and XI, 784). It is also what Pericles tells the Athenians that they are and must continue to be.

Second, just as in Homer, to be supremely excellent and to win are treated as so closely linked that no possibility of incompatibility between the pursuit of the prizes of virtue and the pursuit of virtue itself appear to exist. It is by his *aretē* that at Athens someone is judged fit for public office, says Pericles (Thucydides II, 37, 1); and it is part of the *aretē* of the Athenians that they acquire friends by accomplishing things on their behalf. But this cultivation of *aretē* at home and abroad is not just in the interest of being virtuous: it also serves the pursuit of wealth and power and has led to hitherto unsurpassed achievement in their acquisition.

Third, wealth and power are not pursued solely for their own sake. They are pursued also for the sake of honor and glory, and in prizing the honor and glory of Athens Athenians behave in respect of their citizenship and their city just as Homeric heroes did. So Pericles in the Funeral Oration could tell the Athenians to remember that in old age what they would look back upon with satisfaction was not profit but honor (II, 44, 4), and in his speech designed to curb Athenian dissatisfaction with the war, after the plague and the second Spartan invasion of Attica, he could remind them that those who, like themselves, wanted to accomplish something would be moved by the thought that they would be remembered for ever as the greatest of Greek cities (II, 64, 3–4).

Fourth, and finally, just as the Homeric hero treated what he perceived as the attempt to impose limits upon his achievement by others as a challenge that must be repelled, so is it also with Athens, on Pericles' view: ". . . if it was necessary either for us to yield immediately to our neighbours' dictates or to preserve our superiority by accepting dangers, then he who flees the danger is more to be blamed than he who accepts it" (II, 59, 1). The dictates to which Pericles referred were those of the Spartans and their allies, and it is instructive to remember the resemblance between Pericles' words and the remarks of the Athenian envoys to the assembly of the Spartans and their allies, which took place just before the outbreak of war. The Athenians had learned to speak with a Periclean voice.

The Periclean image of Athens was then in these various ways Homeric. It was, of course, Homer transposed and put to new uses, but it was still Homer. And most notably just as in the Homeric poetic vision of the heroic social order, although the goodness of excellence and the goodness of victory are distinguished, there is no suggestion that the pursuit of the two is incompatible or that it might be necessary to choose between them, so in the Periclean rhetorical vision of the Athenian social order the same holds. Pericles praises the Athenians for their pursuit of a variety of goods; there is no place in his vision of Athens for even the slighest suggestion that achievement in respect of one kind of good might be destructive in respect of another. The Periclean vision is epic; it is not tragic.

Yet the implementation of specifically Periclean policies, even if by successors who lacked Pericles' own restraint, pointed toward the inadequacy of the Periclean view. Pericles had praised the autonomy of Athens and of its citizens. But the complaint against Athens was most generally that in transforming the Delian League into an empire Athens had denied to other cities the autonomy which she claimed for herself. The Athenians in retort made three claims: it had long been established that the more powerful prevail over the weaker and no one, prior to the Athenians, had allowed a plea of justice to prevail over advantage; nonetheless, the Athenians had accepted equality with the other cities in their empire in lawsuits, even under conditions to their own disadvantage; and those cities, instead of exhibiting gratitude, resented their inequality, both when a legal decision went against them and when Athens had simply imposed its imperial will (I, 77, 1–4).

This response was irrelevant to what was the crucial point for the Spartan allies: whatever the Athenian subject cities had or enjoyed was no more than Athens allowed them to have or enjoy. Underlying all the Athenian claims was Pericles' boast that the Athenians do good to their friends, rather than receive good from them, and in fact whatever good may have been in fact rendered to the subject cities was conferred upon them whether they wanted it or not. But was there any good? And what was it?

The Delian League had at first existed for the sake of what all its members had recognized as a genuinely common good, naval protection against the Persian empire, a protection secured for the cities joining it by the contributions made by all the members either in the form of ships or of money. The Athenians in 454 had unilaterally transferred the treasury of the League from Delos to Athens, refused by the use of force to allow cities to secede from the League, and used monies from the treasury for such self-interested projects as that of the building of the Parthenon. So in the name of the continuing good of naval protection now only dubiously needed—Athens had made peace with Persia in 449—Athens transformed the League into an empire.

The final Athenian response to the accusations of the Spartan allies concerning the imperialism of Athens was to invite the Spartans to accept arbitration, *dikē*. The Spartan reply was that the Athenians had already committed injustice (*adikein*) (I, 79) and on this ground voted for war.

What emerges from this interchange is the way in which in Athenian thinking the place of justice in the relationship of citizen to citizen within the *polis* is one thing, that of justice in the relationship of the *polis* to those outside it quite another. Within the *polis* equality in status under the laws specifies the type of participation to which every citizen is entitled. Office and its rewards are to be assigned to those who deserve them by reason of ability and achievement. Every citizen is free not only to participate in the life of the city but also to pursue his own ends, and each will be able to do so all the more successfully by reason of that participation. Those ends may be those of excellence, of wealth, or of power. There is on the Periclean view nothing in the pursuit of any one of these that needs to be destructive of the good of the city or of any other individual citizen.

To be wronged, therefore, as a citizen would involve willful and unnecessary interference with one's activities by some other person. The laws on a Periclean view are to be regarded with fearful respect because they protect against such wrongs. But in the relationship of the *polis* to those outside it no such conception of wrong would be warranted. It is not that there is no place at all for the application of rules of justice. When two approximately equal powers confront one another, and neither can have rationally warranted expectations of being able to impose their will upon the other, then necessity may compel both to agree to arbitration by some just standard, the kind of arbitration which the Athenians invited the Spartans to accept. But this is the limiting case in the application of the general rule accepted by the Athenians: the stronger may and always do impose their will upon the weaker. Notice that this rule is interpretative as well as action-guiding. It justifies our understanding of the motives of others in a particular way, whatever those others may say to the contrary; indeed, if we apply this rule, we shall recognize in what others say to the contrary a device by which they seek to impose their will upon us. And the use of this rule as both action-guiding and interpretative finds successive embodiment in the policy decisions and actions of the Athenians in relation to three city-states which refuse to conform themselves to the Athenian will.

The first of these, Samos, one of the leading members of the Delian League, was responding to an Athenian intervention. Samos was in dispute in 441 with Miletus, another subject city, over the possession of Priene. Miletus appealed to the Athenians, who sent a naval expedition to Samos, where they enforced an alteration of the constitution, took one hundred hostages whom they placed upon the island of Lemnos, and set up a garrison. With the aid of Pissuthnes, the Persian satrap of Sardis, the Samians successfully revolted, rescued the hostages, and handed over the Athenian garrison to the Persians. The Athenians put down the revolt by besieging Samos until the Samians were induced to make terms which involved not only the destruction of their defenses and the handing over of their fleet to the Athenians, but also the giving of further hostages and the paying of an indemnity for the cost of the war. The *stratēgos* who led the expedition against Samos was Pericles.

In 428 during the first phase of the Peloponnesian War Mytilene, also a subject city, revolted against Athens and looked to Sparta for help, but was forced to surrender because of grain shortages. The Athenians accepted the surrender only on terms that left the treatment of Mytilene entirely in the hands of the Athenian assembly. The assembly first voted to execute all the adult males and to sell all the women and children into slavery, a policy advocated by Cleon, Pericles' successor as chief spokesman for the Athenian democrats. But the Athenians were then persuaded by Diodotus that a milder policy was more advantageous to them.

A third city-state, that of the island of Melos, was not a subject city and was neutral in the war. But in 416 the Athenians sent a force to require the submission of the Melians. Thucydides has recorded a dia-

logue between the Melian leaders and envoys from the Athenian expedition in which the Athenians state with great clarity the principle
defining the justice of effectiveness: "that in human disputation justice
is then only agreed on when the necessity is equal; whereas they that
have odds of power exact as much as they can, and the weak yield to
such conditions as they can get" (V, 89, Hobbes' translation). Both here
and elsewhere, notably in the speech which Euphemus makes to the
Syracusans in Book VI, Thucydides represents Athenian spokesmen as
rejecting any justice of reciprocal desert as holding between peoples.
Euphemus says: "And we make no fine speeches either about how because
we alone overthrew the barbarian or because we risked dangers for the
sake of the freedom of these men [that is, the Peloponnesians] rather
than for that of all the Greeks, including our own, it is fair that we
rule" (VI, 83). And, indeed, when the Melians reply to the Athenians,
they too are represented as arguing that the Athenians should respect
principles which pay regard to the advantage of the Melians as well
as their own, precisely because it will be to their own (that is, the Athenian) greater advantage to do so. For, so the Melians point out, the
consequences of applying the principle of the right of the stronger without qualification is that you will invite others, in changed circumstances,
to appeal to the same principle in their dealings with you. That is to
say, the Melians suggested to the Athenians a more sophisticated conception of the justice of effectiveness, one which the Athenians on that
particular occasion rejected—Melos was compelled after a long siege
to surrender, and all its adult males were killed, while its women and
children were enslaved—but which over ten years later, in the closing
months of the Peloponnesian War, was to inform Athenian fears that
they too might be treated in defeat as the Melians had been.

Thus the goods of effectiveness are paramount in the relationship
of the Athenians to other city-states. And the place, the very limited
place, assigned to justice and the kind of justice envisaged are just those
which the paramountcy of the goods of cooperative effectiveness requires. But those goods were also valued in part for what they made
possible in, for example, the building of the Parthenon: excellence too
can be served by cooperative effectiveness. But the nature of the relationship between the two kinds of good can never emerge, so long as
the images of Periclean rhetoric continue to dominate. For what the
Periclean attitude obscures from view, as I remarked earlier, is any suggestion that the paramountcy of effectiveness in external relationships
might perhaps be such as to damage the pursuit of excellence at home;
and it equally obscures the possibility that individual aspiration to either

excellence or effectiveness might injure the good of the city. Central to Periclean rhetoric is the unargued and never wholly spelled out claim that all the goods which Athenians pursue can be pursued in harmony with one another and above all that the individual citizen may pursue his own good, whether that of excellence or wealth or power, in also pursuing the good of the city. Hence the Periclean conception of what Lowell Edmunds (op. cit., p. 84) has called "the primacy of the polis" is not presented as in any way incompatible with a multiplicity of views by individual citizens as to what their flourishing may consist in. It is indeed the achievements in respect of both *polis* and individual which in Pericles' words make "our city as a whole an education for Greece" and one that "needs no praise from Homer or any other poet" (Thucydides II, 41, 1 and 4). Athens is not only an epic hero; it is also its own epic poem. So Athens on this Periclean view provides for the rest of Greece what the *Iliad* and the *Odyssey* provided for the schooling of Athenian boys.

Perhaps this preempting of the Homeric image by Pericles explains in part why conservative, aristocratic politicians found it so difficult to respond successfully to Pericles and to his successors. For they above all treated the Homeric texts as canonical. But they also faced another kind of difficulty. Those who respond to periods of rapid and disruptive change by appealing for a retention of or a return to the ways of the past, to the customary, to the traditional, always have to reckon with the fact that in an established customary social order those who follow its ways do not have and do not need good reasons for so doing. The question of what constitutes *a good reason for action* is thrust upon them only when they are already confronted by alternatives, and characteristically the first uses of practical reasoning will be to justify the pursuit of some good not to be achieved by following the customary routines of the normal day, month, and year. It is only later when these routines have more largely and more radically been disrupted that the question of whether it was not in fact better to follow the older ways unreflectively can be raised, and when the conservative offers his contemporaries good reasons for returning to an earlier relatively unreflective mode of social life, his very modes of advocacy provide evidence that what he recommends is no longer possible. So in Aristophanes' comedies the conservative figures portrayed are in part comic victims because forced into the very rhetorical modes which they abhor in order to argue against those modes. And Aristophanes himself is so plainly a conservative sympathizer that this is significant evidence of the power of the Periclean imagination.

This imaginative vision of Athens was systematically communicated in, but never itself argued for, in Pericles' speeches. Indeed it could not have been argued for within the limitations of Periclean rhetoric. And the limitations of that rhetoric are not accidental but derive from the kind of *technē* which rhetoric had so far been understood to be.

Plutarch in his life of Theseus speaks of the cultivation at Athens of a *deinotēs politikē* (cleverness in politics) which includes the ability to speak effectively. And the assembly and the law courts had of course nourished a practice of debate, of the making of rival speeches, a practice which is then reflected in the great debates within tragic dramas from Aeschylus onward. What matters about such debate is that an effective speaker is one who succeeds in contriving to bring others to accept his particular conclusions upon the matter in question by starting out not from his, but from their, the audience's, premises. And since such debate is concerned to bring about joint and cooperative action, the relevant premises will embody an appeal to what the audience considers desirable. In appealing to such premises an effective speaker will have to recognize which of two different approaches it is necessary for him to adopt.

If the premises from which his audience are prepared to argue will yield the conclusion which it is the speaker's aim to induce his audience to adopt, provided only that they also accept additional premises about the means necessary to secure those ends which they already find desirable, then the speaker will need to do no more than convince his audience of the truth of what he has to say about the relevant means-ends relationship. And Pericles in his appeals to what *gnōmē* and *empeiria* have to teach (II, 62, 5, and I, 142, 5) exemplifies this kind of reasoning. But he also exemplifies a quite different kind of appeal.

On occasion an audience may initially be in a frame of mind such that from no premises about what they at first believe to be desirable could an argument be constructed whose conclusion would be that which it is the speaker's aim to reach. In such a case the speaker has the task of altering his audience's attitudes and so their judgments as to what is desirable; he has to change their desires by allaying their fears, enlarging their hopes or whatever else is necessary for his purposes. And at this, too, Pericles excelled: "Whenever indeed he saw them inopportunely confident, he would speak so as to cow them into fear, and by contrast when they were unreasonably frightened, he would again restore their confidence," reported Thucydides (II, 65, 9), after having pointed out that Pericles was able to get a hearing from the Athenians

even when saying what they did not want to hear, because of his reputation for honesty and his refusal to flatter the assembly.

Periclean rhetoric thus had to be both argumentative and manipulative. The patterns of argument give evidence of a deductive sophistica-
tion that is indebted both to the use of evidence in forensic contexts
and to the forms of inference used by sixth- and fifth-century natural
philosophers, and most notably by the Eleatics. But deductive argument only warrants a conclusion when there is adequate reason to believe its premises true, and effective practical deductive argument requires at least one premise which characterizes some action or object
or state of affairs as something which is in fact desired. Where everyone
agrees on what is desirable or advantageous in some particular situation, then the adducing of the relevant premise is unproblematic. When
in the *Iliad* alternatives present themselves, what is advantageous is unproblematic in just this way. So Deiphobus considers whether to fight
alone or alongside some other Trojan, "and to him thinking it seemed
more advantageous to go after Aeneas" (*Iliad* XIII, 458–459), for advantage is what brings victory, and victory is always desirable. And
so in the debate over Mytilene, Cleon, Pericles' successor in leadership
of the democratic party, and Diodotus are able to argue in favor of alternative courses of policy from premises shared both by the two speakers
and by their audience about what is advantageous for Athens. But when
no such shared premises are available, what resources does the orator
possess? A presupposition, albeit an unrecognized presupposition, of
Periclean rhetoric as practiced was that only nonrational forms of persuasion were available. So a thesis about where the line is to be drawn
between what can be subject to rational argument and what cannot
was already presupposed by the practices of Periclean debate. Plato was
to argue that just this presupposition must underlie any democratic
politics, but it was in its peculiarly Periclean form that such a presupposition first clearly played a part in Greek life. What was thereby excluded from rational argument and enquiry?

The answer is: that shared background of beliefs about the desirable and undesirable which provide for democratic Athenians the first
and ultimate premises of their arguments. So the issues which divide
such Athenians from those who hold systematically different views about
or conceptions of the desirable and the undesirable are not open to
rational debate or to rational enquiry. They have to be treated within
the Periclean framework as a surd, a given. Hence the issues which divide those whose fundamental allegiance is to the goods of cooperative
effectiveness and to a conception of justice derived from such an alle-

giance from those whose fundamental allegiance is to the goods of excellence and to the corresponding conception of justice were rationally undebatable within a Periclean framework, and indeed could not be spelled out explicitly before the closing stages—twenty years after the death of Pericles himself—in the life of Periclean Athens. For what I am calling the Periclean view was not and could not have been articulated in the way that a philosophical theory can and must be. The importance of rhetoric to that view was not only that rhetoric provided for Pericles and for most of his Athenian contemporaries their mode of public deliberation; the Periclean vision was itself inseparable from the rhetoric by means of which it was expressed, a work of an imagination which took form in the building and sculptures of the Parthenon as well as in words. Images are more fundamental to the Periclean standpoint than either concepts or arguments.

Vico argued that the human understanding in the course of moving from the age of gods through the age of heroes to the age of men transforms itself from a poetic mode to which the imaginative universal is central to a rational mode in which the imaginative universal is replaced by the intelligible universal. This conceptual transformation is indeed the one that was enacted in the passage from Homer to Plato. And when I call the Periclean vision of Athens Homeric, I do so in order to stress not only its Homeric content—Athens itself as Homeric hero, guided by Athena just as Achilles was—but also the fact that in its self-articulation it was still closely tied to poetry rather than to philosophy. Nonetheless, the recognition by his contemporaries that Pericles distinguished himself by his rationality and by his appeals to rationality is also very much to the point. What Pericles did in translating a Homeric view into concrete mid- and late-fifth-century terms was also to expound that view in a way that made it available for later rational criticism at a more fundamental level than was available immediately either to Pericles himself or to his political contemporaries.

Both Thucydides and Plato, although in very different ways, were to undertake this task. But the radical criticism of Periclean attitudes and beliefs was first initiated in a mode much closer to that of Periclean rhetoric itself. The Periclean orator was an actor in the public drama of Athens, and dramatic poetry had both imaginative and to some degree rational resources fully adequate to provide dramatic countertheses to rhetorical theses, even though neither tragic nor comic drama could have provided any rational resolution of the issues raised in criticism of the stances of Pericles and his successors. But it was in fact in tragic and comic drama that some of its key limitations and the need to transcend them were first identified. The most important commentator upon Pericles' successors was Aristophanes. But upon Pericles himself it was Sophocles: "the resemblances between Oedipus and Pericles, though it is true that they have often been exaggerated and over interpreted, are still striking and not to be lightly dismissed" wrote Bernard M. W. Knox in his *Oedipus at Thebes* (New Haven, 1957, p. 63). The two resemblances to the Oedipus of *Oedipus Tyrannus* which Knox emphasizes — and *Oedipus Tyrannus* is after all a play about a city suffering from a plague, presented to the Athenians at a time when their own city had recently suffered from a plague — are the way in which Pericles combined the kind of unquestioned authority characteristic of a *turannos* (and that was what Pericles' political opponents said that he was) with a large deference to public opinion and the fact that Pericles belonged to a family under a hereditary curse because of a sacrilegious murder by an ancestor. But Knox lays his greatest emphasis, not upon these resemblances between Pericles himself and Oedipus, but upon the resemblances between Oedipus and Periclean Athens.

Pericles himself had described the Athenian empire as a tyranny, and it had been Pericles who not only boasted of the wealth and the *technē* of the Athenians in their exercise of power, but who also claimed that in consequence the Athenians suffered from the envious resentment of others. So Oedipus too is represented as saying in explaining the envious resentment of Creon: "O wealth and *turannis* and *technē* succeeding *technē* in the competition of life, how much envy is stored up in you . . ." (380–383).

What Sophocles attacked in *Oedipus Tyrannus* was Periclean and Athenian *hubris,* that violence expressive of pride which Sophocles' chorus declare to be the begetter of tyrannical power. And he attacked this particular Athenian *hubris* for an impious confidence in the effectiveness of the skillful use of power, a confidence which had displaced a proper care and respect for the relationship of the city to divine law. But if *Oedipus Tyrannus* was indeed the political play which Knox takes it to be, its message was either unheard or, if heard, rejected. The trilogy of which *Oedipus Tyrannus* was a part failed to win the first prize when it was produced in 427 or 426, even though the play itself was to be regarded by Aristotle as the exemplar of tragic drama, and Pericles' successors retained all those aspects of Periclean policy which invited the accusation of *hubris.*

When Sophocles came to present his penultimate play, the *Philoctetes,* in 409, Athens was in a very different condition. The destruction of the expedition to Syracuse and the revolution of the Four Hundred had shaken the Athenian democracy, but its recovery of power from the oligarchs and a series of naval victories had provided it for a time at least with renewed possibilities of preserving itself. It was thus opportune and urgently necessary to raise again the questions of what justice within a political community is, of what justice toward those external to the community is, and the relationship of both to the expedient and the advantageous. And these are the questions raised by the *Philoctetes.*

The action of the play takes place on the barren island of Lemnos where Philoctetes was abandoned by the Greeks on their way to Troy, when in the sanctuary of the goddess Chryse he was bitten by a snake. The wound, which drove him at intervals to agonized screaming, made him apparently nothing but an unnecessary burden to the expedition. For nine years he has survived without human contact in the bleakest of conditions. His only resource is his magical bow and arrows. Philoctetes had been—indeed would be again—a great archer, and when he aided the dying Heracles, Zeus' half-mortal son, by lighting the funeral pyre that would deliver Heracles from *his* agony, Heracles had made him a gift of the bow and arrows. During the nine years that Philoctetes had been on Lemnos the Greeks had failed to take Troy. But now they have learned from a prophecy of the Trojan seer Helenus that only with the weapons of Philoctetes will they take Troy. So Odysseus, experienced and resourceful, and Achilles' son, the young and inexperienced Neoptolemus, have been sent to Lemnos.

The political content of the play is plain. The large problem that confronts the Greeks at Troy is the same large problem that confronts the Athenians in 409: How may a long-drawn-out war be brought at last to a successful conclusion? The Athenians cannot hope to avoid defeat at the hands of Sparta without the cooperation of some of those to whom in the past they have done undeserved harm; the Greeks cannot hope to defeat the Trojans without the aid of Philoctetes. But it is not only in this overall way that Sophocles relates the action of the play to the situation of Athens. If the Athenians had understood *Oedipus Tyrannus* in the way that Knox suggests that it is to be understood, they may have perceived it as in part a partisan attack on the Periclean democracy. But in the *Philoctetes* Sophocles is careful to make it clear that the play is, not about the actions of a party, but about the way in which all Athenian citizens, including himself, have to confront the issues raised by their common history. He achieves this by the way in which he alludes in the play to his own past part in Athenian public life.

To be a tragic or comic dramatist at Athens was necessarily in any case to be a public and political figure, but Sophocles had played additional roles. The play is about an exile left against his will on Lemnos. Whom had the Athenians held against their will on Lemnos? The hostages from Samos in 441. And who were the Athenian *stratēgoi* who had done this? Pericles was the chief of them, but one of his colleagues was Sophocles, elected, so it was said, because of the success of the *Antigone*. And although by 409 that was long ago, Sophocles had as recently as 413 been one of the special commissioners elected after the news of the disaster at Syracuse reached Athens. So Sophocles, even at the age of eighty-seven, speaks not against those with power, but as one of those sharing power who needs to know how it is to be used. But it is not only in placing the action of the play on Lemnos that he relates it to his own life as a public figure. At the close of the play Philoctetes is promised a cure for his wound from the Asclepiadae, the descendants and followers of Asclepius in the healing art. The cult of Asclepius had been established at Athens before the temple sanctuary on the Acropolis was ready for the god's reception; until it was ready, the house of Sophocles had been chosen as the god's house, and Sophocles therefore stood in a singular relationship to the Asclepiadae.

We ought by now to have learned from Karl Reinhardt (*Sophocles,* trans. H. and D. Harvey from the third German edition of 1947, Oxford, 1979) that the tragedy is centrally that of Neoptolemus, who is confronted by two incompatible sets of demands and who in yielding to each in turn fails to be and do what he ought. At the outset Neoptolemus is presented as one who both, like any well-brought-up young Athenian, respects the honorable and shuns the disgraceful; but also, like any well-brought-up young Athenian, he wants not only to excel but to be seen to excel by winning. To this Odysseus is able to appeal when he persuades Neoptolemus of the necessity of skillful deceit if the bow is to be obtained for the Greeks. Odysseus is what he is in the *Odyssey:* cunning, resourceful, a master of stratagems whose behavior is controlled by one overriding aim, that of securing victory for the Greeks by first securing the bow. The goods of effectiveness are recognized as overriding. But so they are too, even if in a very different way, for Philoctetes.

Philoctetes has been reduced by the extremity of his deprivation to devote himself to survival by whatever means are available. At the first moment that opportunity offers he is determined to escape from that deprivation. Revenge upon those who made him suffer is his only other goal. Philoctetes is as unheeding of the needs of the Greeks as Odysseus is of the needs of Philoctetes.

Neoptolemus has two reasons for agreeing to undertake what Odysseus orders him to do. Not only does he wish to take Troy, but he has been sent to Lemnos by the Greek generals who have legitimate authority over him. Yet at the outset he has said that he would prefer to lose, having acquitted himself finely, than to win, having been bad in so doing. So there is an initial recognition that one can be *kakos* (bad—the opposite of *agathos*) and win. But if he were to be *agathos* and *kakos* and lose, in what would he have excelled? It is perhaps because Neoptolemus has no clear answer to this—his standards are no more than the conventional Periclean standards of a young upper-class Athenian, the kind of standards which an Alcibiades would also have originally been taught to respect—that he falters throughout the play, first in one direction, then in another. And the first evidence of this is the speech with which Odysseus is able to overcome his scruples about deceiving Philoctetes, an act of persuasion which Odysseus confirms with an invocation of three gods: Hermes, the god of ruses; *Nikē,* Victory conceived as a Divine Being; and Athena Polias, Athena as the guardian of the city. Odysseus thus identifies the goods of effectiveness, the goods of victory with the cause of Athens understood theologically. And since *Philoctetes* turns out to be an essentially theological drama, this is not unimportant.

When, after first successfully deceiving Philoctetes, Neoptolemus is shocked into a change of mind (*metanoia*) by the spectacle of Philoctetes' suffering, he turns himself into an instrument of Philoctetes' purposes, just as earlier he had served those of Odysseus. Neoptolemus now recognizes that by taking the bow which *deservedly* belongs to Philoctetes—it was Heracles' reward for his virtues of courage and friendship and a recognition of his excellence as an archer—he has behaved unjustly in respect of desert. And so the justice of desert, justice conceived in terms of the goods of excellence, for the moment receives its due. That justice requires Neoptolemus to return the bow. But when he and Odysseus engage in assertion and counterassertion about their now rival and incompatible views of justice, this is all that it amounts to. Neither is able to uphold assertion by argument. Neoptolemus cannot argue, does not even seem to have the thought of arguing, that it is for the good of the Greeks as a whole that justice as desert should not be violated and that the undeserved wrongs of exiling Philoctetes on Lemnos and of attempting to steal his bow should now be redressed.

Pericles, as I noticed earlier, had said in the Funeral Oration that the Athenians had a peculiar regard for "those laws which are enacted for the advantage of those to whom injustice has been done and those unwritten laws the breach of which incurs shameful disgrace," (II, 37, 3) just that kind of disgrace which Neoptolemus sees in his own earlier behavior toward Philoctetes. So that it is not only Odysseus who is able to appeal to elements in the Periclean view; Neoptolemus is also able so to appeal. And what the dialogue between them brings out is the potential incoherence of that view, the coexistence within it of potentially incompatible ways of conceiving the relationship of Greek to Greek and of the bonds which unite Athenians. But just as it is one of the limitations of Periclean rhetoric that rival conceptions of what justice requires cannot have their claims evaluated rationally within its framework, so this is also a limitation of Sophoclean tragedy, a limitation from our point of view, that is, not from that of Sophocles.

For Sophocles offers what is in the Homeric perspective a conservative rejoinder to Pericles, a restoration of an older version of the Homeric vision. He does indeed enable us to see in the Periclean transmutation of Homer the incoherence of the Periclean image of Athens and the way in which it raises for the Athenians questions to which it cannot provide an answer. But Sophocles himself treats these same questions as ones to which there is and can be no rational answer; the only resolution can come from the appearance of a god.

Euripides had popularized the *deus ex machina* as a dramatic device. But Karl Reinhardt pointed out that in the *Philoctetes* what we are presented with is not just one more example of this by 409 all-too-conventional device. The plot requires, not an arbitrary disentangling by the intrusion of the supernatural, but the discovery of a standard for action which merely human resources have been unable to supply. That standard to which Neoptolemus has been unable to appeal throughout the play, but which he has needed so badly, turns out to be a divine standard, and not just the standard of any god. "The god—it is Heracles, the very god whose primal presence has been felt throughout the play—appears as the visible standard against which man is measured" (pp. 190–191). And Heracles comes to turn Philoctetes and Neoptolemus and even Odysseus back into the path planned for them by Zeus. It is the justice of Zeus to which Sophocles appeals to provide the standard which human beings cannot provide for themselves. And the justice of Zeus, *dikē*, is the underlying order of the universe within which alone human justice finds point, purpose, and justification

To this fundamental Homeric conception of the divinely ordained cosmic order Sophocles appeals in order to respond to questions which neither Homer nor his characters were able even to raise. But in returning us to the Homeric framework Sophocles provides a response, but

not an answer. The reconciliation of Philoctetes, Odysseus, and Neoptolemus is at the *ad hoc* bidding of Heracles: nothing is learned or
could be learned within this framework about how more generally the
rival claims of the justice of effectiveness and of the justice of desert
are to be evaluated. That those claims can only be rightly evaluated
within a theological framework is indeed part of what Sophocles says
to his fellow citizens. And perhaps what he meant them — and us — to
learn is that there is no way of addressing these claims generally, but
we always have to wait upon the voice of some divine being. Yet even
if this is what Sophocles intended, another possibility has to be inves-
tigated: Sophocles' response is inherently defective, not on account of
what he says, but because tragic drama is not the kind of genre which
can provide adequate answers to the kind of questions about justice
which the *Philoctetes* poses, and it is only when the questions about
justice and practical reasoning are posed together, as they can only be
within the genres of philosophical enquiry, that either set of questions
becomes answerable. These were to be Plato's claims, but although the
critique of dramatic poetry was essential to Plato's enterprise, it was
not most fundamentally against dramatic poetry, but rather against the
systematic cultivation of the goods of effectiveness, that Plato directed
his attack. His chosen opponents were certain of the teachers of rhetoric and certain sophists. And both for the sake of understanding Plato's
contentions, and for the sake of understanding those sophistic theses
which have their own independent importance for my larger argument,
it is necessary not to pass directly from Sophocles to Plato, but instead
first to consider further one crucial aspect of the background against
which Plato conducted his dispute with the sophists, the conduct of
the Athenians in the Peloponnesian War and their subsequent defeat.

Plato, not only in the early dialogues but in such maturer works as
the *Meno* and the *Republic,* portrayed conversations between Socrates
and a variety of interlocutors which are not only represented as occur-
ring in the period when the Peloponnesian War is in progress, but which
on occasion stand in some direct relationship to events during that war.
So the systematic criticism of the claims of the teachers of rhetoric is
made against Gorgias of Leontini in the dialogue named after him.
What part had Gorgias played in Athenian history? It was he who came
to Athens in 427 as a member of an embassy from Leontini in order
to persuade the Athenians to intervene in Sicily, a request to which the
Athenians acceded. That first expedition to Sicily was the precursor
of the expedition of 415 whose disastrous defeat fatally weakened Athenian power. So in a very important way Gorgias' rhetorical skill was

among the causes of the defeat of Athens. Who were the generals who initially commanded that first expedition? Chariades, who was killed early on in a naval battle, and Laches. Who were the generals who initially commanded the second expedition? Lamachus, who was killed early, and Nicias. So in a very important way Laches and Nicias contributed to Athens' defeat. And who in the *Laches* are the interlocutors of Socrates, represented by Plato as defective in their understanding not only of the *aretē* of courage but of the relation of that *aretē* to *aretē* as such, and therefore as defective in *aretē*? Laches and Nicias.

As in the *Gorgias* Plato is offering his explanation of what brought about the ruin of the Athenians. In both cases the theses which he is challenging are ones advanced by Thucydides. I do not mean of course that he had Thucydides' history explicitly in mind, although he may well have had. I do mean that he was responding to a view of Athenian history during the Peloponnesian War to which Thucydides gave lucid and detailed expression. And this is true not only in dialogues such as the *Gorgias* and the *Laches* but equally later on in the *Republic*. The defeat of Athens in 404 had been accompanied by the overthrow of the democracy and the rule of the pro-Spartan extremists among the oligarchical party, who came to be known as the Thirty Tyrants. The center of resistance to the Thirty Tyrants was the Peiraeus, and it is here that the conversation represented in the *Republic* takes place, a conversation in which Socrates' central arguments entail that it is of the nature of democracy that it prepares the way for tyranny. Of the characters present during the conversation, Cephalus, the rich old man, had been a friend of Pericles; his sons Lysias and Polemarchus were, as democrats, marked down for execution by the Thirty Tyrants, and Polemarchus was in fact killed, while Lysias became a leader in the restoration of democracy; Plato's elder brothers Glaucon and Adeimantus, who had already served in the army at Megara, were the nephews of Critias, the author of a poem in praise of the Spartan constitution, and himself the most influential and the most extreme of the Thirty Tyrants; and Socrates, who had been allowed to remain at Athens by the Thirty, had refused to obey their illegal order to arrest Leon of Salamis, thus risking execution, but had nonetheless been executed in 399 on the basis of accusations by leaders of the restored democracy. The *Republic* is thus in part a dialogue among those who are to meet unjust deaths at the hands of the protagonists of both oligarchy and democracy; it is to be read as a dialogue about why oligarchy and democracy are by their nature unjust forms of polity. But how does any of *this* relate to Thucydidean themes in the way in which the *Gorgias* and the *Laches* palpably do? To answer this question it is necessary to identify Thucydides' own standpoint in relation to the events about which he wrote his history.

Three features of that standpoint are crucial. First, Thucydides separates *aretē* and intelligence, a separation apparent in the contrasting careers of Nicias and Alcibiades. Thucydides' verdict upon Nicias, after he has recounted how he surrendered to the Syracusans and was executed by them, was that he was of all the Greeks the one who least deserved such a misfortune "because the conduct of his entire life had been regulated by *aretē*" (Thucydides VII, 86, 5). Nicias had thought the project of the second Sicilian expedition ill-judged, but he had lacked the intelligence to sway the assembly, in the way Pericles had been able to do. Alcibiades had the intelligent skill to persuade audiences difficult to persuade, just as Pericles did, and Thucydides portrays him exercising this skill in persuading the soldiers at Samos not to return to Athens to overthrow the Four Hundred in 411 (VIII, 86, 5–6). But Alcibiades lacked the Periclean *aretai* which would have enabled him both to exercise cautious restraint, a respect for limits, and to recognize how his individual achievement related to that of the city. The flaw of the leaders who succeeded Pericles, said Thucydides, was that they pursued their own profit rather than that of the city. Pericles himself had combined a practical intelligence, which he could use in rhetorical manipulation as well as in devising policy, with *aretai* of the appropriate kinds. But these are presented in Thucydides' portrait as distinct and independent traits, and it is no more than a contingent fact about Pericles that he possessed both.

Second, in the social world, as Thucydides represents it, there is and can be only that justice which the strong find it in their own interest to uphold. And this is true within city-states as well as of the relationships between them. When those with the power to do so think it in their interest to overthrow the existing form of government within their own *polis,* they take to civil war. When members of the same political faction have the power and the desire to outbid rival leaders, they take to factional strife. It is unsurprising that Hobbes should have concluded from his reading of Thucydides that either justice has to be imposed by power or there will be no justice. But it does not follow that Thucydides himself was a premature Hobbesian. Plutarch (*Nicias* 29) tells us that after the Athenian defeat at Syracuse some of the enslaved Athenians were able to gain their freedom by reciting passages from Euripides' plays. In some of those plays, notably the *Trojan Women* and the *Hecuba,* the vision of justice is remarkably similar to that of Thucydides. And Peter Green has remarked upon how the closing words of the chorus in the former play would be a fitting epitaph to Thucydides' narrative of the closing episodes of the Athenian disaster at Syracuse. But the harsh necessity of which Euripides speaks in that chorus is the necessity of the cosmic order. Writing of the *Trojan Women,* Hugh Lloyd-Jones has said: ". . . the Greeks go too far in their revenge . . . we know from the start that they will presently meet with disaster, as they do according to the epic tradition. The justification of Zeus is from the beginning harsh . . ." (*The Justice of Zeus,* p. 153). And Thucydides too can be read as presenting us with a vision of cosmic order in which those who allow themselves to pursue their own aggrandizement without due regard for limits meet the same kind of fate that they inflicted upon others. If so, the nature of things appears not in any divine intervention, as with Sophocles—Thucydides is always contemptuous of appeals for divine intervention—but in the order of events themselves; and such a theology was in its own way as much part of the Homeric inheritance as the beliefs of Sophocles were. It reflects an insight possessed by the Homer of the *Iliad,* although not by his characters, that nobody both wins and remains a winner. In the long run we are all going to be defeated, and the prospect of ignominious death or slavery awaits everyone and not just those who are now defeated. Thucydides has of course translated this part of the Homeric *Weltanschauung* into entirely secular terms. What this translation offers us is a conception of justice as entirely at the service of effectiveness, a justice to which desert is irrelevant except when those who happen to have the power at a given time choose to make it relevant. There is no appeal beyond the realities of power.

Third, Thucydides was centrally concerned with the place of rhetoric in the social and political world. He took Pericles to have been supreme in rhetorical achievement, and the rhetoric with which he was concerned was the manipulative rhetoric employed so successfully by Pericles and so unsuccessfully by Nicias. Marc Cogan (*The Human Thing,* Chicago, 1981, especially chapter 6) has argued compellingly that when Thucydides asserted that from his history the reader would be able to learn not only what events did happen but also what kind of event will happen in accordance with human reality (*kata to anthrōpinon*) (Thucydides I, 22, 4), what he was identifying as the underlying human reality was the connection between rhetorical deliberation and political action. It is this connection, so Cogan suggests, through which on Thucydides' view the relationship between individual actions and the projects of the *polis* as a whole have to be understood. If that is so, then it is in those public deliberations in which individuals urge, either upon their own fellow citizens or upon the citizens of some other city, the adoption of one policy rather than another that the form of practical reasoning, as Thucydides understood it, is exhibited. By the devices of rhetoric, understood as both Pericles and Thucydides understood it—rhetoric, that is to say, in accordance with the teaching of Gorgias—individuals bring it about that one kind of action rather than another is performed. Since such rhetoric must, as I argued in discussing Pericles himself, exclude from its scope any rational evaluation of ends or of rival conceptions of justice, it follows that the fundamental connection which a skilled rhetorician has to establish between himself and his audience has to be nonrational. He cannot offer his audience any rationally defensible account of the ends which, on his view, he and they ought, if they are rational, to pursue; he has instead to appeal to ends which he and they do in fact already share and to hopes and fears defined in terms of those ends. As a member of a community held together by sympathetic feeling and by coincidence of interest, the rhetorician appeals to other members of that same community. Within this context, of course, the rhetorician will reason about means, arguing either that, given that such and such is his and the audience's shared end, they should adopt such and such means (as Alcibiades argued in urging approval of the Sicilian expedition) or that, given that such and such are the limited means which that the audience possess, they should pursue their shared end only in such and such a limited way (as the Athenians were forced to argue after their great losses in Sicily). Thucydides' own concern with human affairs is of course one which leads him to stress the differences between what speakers and audience alike intended to bring about by the implementation of their deliberative decisions and what actually occurred. Here chance (*tuchē*) and especially ill-fortune (*dustuchia*) enter human affairs. But what he also shows us is how a particular understanding of the role of deliberation in human affairs can provide a partial causal explanation of human actions and their outcomes.

In so doing Thucydides provided a paradigmatic version of the account of human social order and relationships which has to be presupposed by any rational exposition and defense of what is involved in allegiance to the goods of cooperative effectiveness and to the corresponding conception of justice. Later defenders of that allegiance have appealed to other, later historians, and modern defenders of the same allegiance often appeal to what they take to be the findings of the social sciences. But it is doubtful whether any later historian or any modern social scientist has any matter of substance to add in this respect to what we can learn from Thucydides. Thus Thucydides' account of human social order and relationships has to be challenged by anyone engaged in challenging the claims to allegiance of the goods of cooperative effectiveness. Hence it is unsurprising that Plato's extended argument in the *Republic* can so easily be read as a rejoinder to Thucydides.

V

Plato and Rational Enquiry

I have ascribed to Thucydides three theses: *aretē* is one thing and practical intelligence quite another and their conjunction is merely coincidental; there is only as much justice and the kind of justice to be had in the social world as the strong and powerful allow there to be; and rhetorical deliberation as practiced by those who had learned from Gorgias and his pupils is the best way for human beings to answer questions about what to do. It is the overriding purpose of Plato's mature political philosophy to deny all three of these theses and to do so by means of a theory which lays bare both the connections between them and the connections between the theses with which he wishes to replace them. What links the Thucydidean theses is a single presupposition: the goods of effectiveness are bound to prevail over those of excellence and the goods of excellence will be prized only insofar as those who prize the goods of effectiveness permit them to be. This presupposition Plato denies by providing for the first time a well-articulated theory as to what human excellence in fact consists in and why it is rational in the light of that theory always to subordinate the goods of effectiveness to those of excellence.

Plato's denial of the first Thucydidean thesis, that *aretē* is one thing and practical intelligence quite another, rests upon arguments designed to show that without *aretē* you cannot be either theoretically or practically rational and that without rationality you cannot have *aretē*. So Thucydides' conception of Nicias as someone genuinely possessing *aretē* was simply a mistake, a mistake identified in the *Laches,* when Nicias is shown to be in a state of confusion not only about the virtue of courage but also about the nature of virtue in general. And a key part of Plato's view is that not to understand what virtue is precludes one from being virtuous.

Of course not only Nicias fails by Plato's standard. Plato also argued that Pericles and such predecessors in building the Athenian empire as Themistocles, Miltiades, and Cimon were lacking in virtue; more specifically, they were defective in *sōphrosunē* and *dikaiosunē*, (*Gorgias* 503c, 515–517, and 519a). What then is the justice, the *dikaiosunē*, which they lacked? Plato's rejection of the Thucydidean view that justice is nothing but what the strong make it incorporates a large measure of agreement with Thucydides about what actually happens. What people generally take to be justice is indeed what the strong make it. And justice, rightly understood, requires a type of *polis* which it is extremely improbable that anyone will be able to construct. So that on Plato's view justice is absent from the social and political world in an even more thoroughgoing way than Thucydides recognizes. Nonetheless, the Thucydidean point of view concerning the place of justice in the world embodies, from a Platonic standpoint, an illusion.

First, those who lack justice will not only fail in excellence by the standard of genuine virtue, but they will also fail in respect of effectiveness, a failure which they themselves will be unable to understand correctly. Unjust policies, whether timocratic or plutocratic oligarchies, democracies or tyrannies, come to ruin because of their injustice and because of the injustice of their rulers. In this lies the cause of the kind of failure which Thucydides had ascribed to *tuchē*. So justice and virtue are causally efficacious in the social and political world in a way quite incompatible with Thucydides' view.

Plato's third denial concerns both the nature of Periclean rhetoric and the alternative to it. Because the rhetoric of Gorgias is a mode of nonrational manipulation, its use makes citizens worse. The rhetorician has to appeal to his audience; he has to gain their approval for what he wants. So he will flatter them and play upon their hopes and fears in a way that strengthens their irrationality. What is the alternative? It is the rhetoric used by that orator who is himself a good man and whose rhetoric is a genuine *technē* (*Gorgias* 506d), unlike the mere *empeiria* (*Gorgias* 500e) of the Periclean rhetorician. When Plato contrasts *technē* and *empeiria*, by that very contrast he challenges the assimilation of these not only by Pericles himself (Thucydides I, 162, 5–9) but more generally by speakers reported by Thucydides (Lowell Edmunds, *Chance and Intelligence in Thucydides*, pp. 26–27). Where Plato and Pericles differ is in their conception of *technē*. On the Periclean view a *technē* is a skill or body of skills based on means-end generalizations which are derived from *empeiria*. On Plato's view no one is master of a *technē* who does not understand how and in what way the end which that specific *technē* serves is a good, and that understanding requires a knowledge of goods and good in general. How is such knowledge to be acquired?

Plato in answering this question had both to rely upon what he had learned from Socrates and also to transcend the limitations of Socratic method. From Socrates he inherited both a negative use of deductive argument as deployed in his method of refutation (*elenchos*) and a standard of truth. Like Socrates he believed that the first step toward truth had to be the use of *elenchos* to exhibit the unreliability of our preexisting beliefs. For by involving his interlocutors in inconsistency concerning the nature of courage, or piety, or justice, or whatever, Socrates showed them not only that not everything that they believed on that subject could be true, but also that they had no resources for deciding which parts of what they believed were false and which, if any, true. Socrates thus avoided the requirement imposed upon the Periclean rhetorician of being only able to argue from premises to which the audience had already given their assent, a requirement which reappears in the later history of both rhetoric and of philosophy in a variety of forms, the latest of which is the appeal to shared intuitions, so basic to some recent types of philosophy.

Yet if we cannot begin in a nonquestion-begging way from what we already believe, how can we begin at all? The Socratic answer is: by starting out from anyone's thesis, our own or anyone else's indifferently, provided that it is rich enough in content and formulated in such a way as to invite serious attempts at refutation. Every attempt at refutation from any point of view should be carried through as far and as systematically as the participants in the enquiry are able. That thesis which most successfully withstands all attempts to refute it—characteristically, of course, such a thesis will have had to be modified and reformulated in the course of its encounters with a variety of objections—is that which claims our rational allegiance. It is true of a true thesis that it is one which is able to withstand any objection whatsoever—and to call a thesis true is to be committed to holding that it will never be refuted. Hence "is true," if truly predicated, is true for all times and places: "is true" is a timeless predicate. So Socrates says to Callicles in claiming that reason is on his side (*Gorgias* 509a–b): "If you or someone yet more forceful are not able to break through [the chains of argument which hold fast my position], then it will be impossible for anyone to speak rightly on such a subject matter other than in the way that I am speaking now . . . just as on this occasion, I have never encountered anyone who was able to assert an alternative position and not fall into absurdity. Therefore I assume that things are as I have said. . . ." Yet notice that Socrates is able to conjoin these assertions with a quite unironic avowal that "I do not know what is the case as to these matters" (509a5, a clause inserted between the first two sections quoted above). He does not claim to *know,* presumably because he takes it that a claim to knowledge asserts or implies that the thesis in question lies beyond any possibility of refutation, and no thesis established by the methods of Socratic dialectic, understood as it is understood in the *Gorgias,* can ever be placed beyond *any* possibility of refutation (see on this Gregory Vlastos 'Introduction: The Paradox of Socrates' in *The Philosophy of Socrates,* ed. Gregory Vlastos, Notre Dame, 1980, pp. 1–21, esp. pp. 10–11). If, therefore, Plato had advanced no further than the Socrates of the *Gorgias* did (and I take it, in spite of the amount of scholarly disagreement on the issue, that the *Gorgias* is one of the last dialogues in which Plato is giving us an accurate historical representation of the views of Socrates), he too would have had to place genuine knowledge, as against rationally warranted belief, as beyond the scope of dialectic. What has happened then to enable Plato in the *Republic* to make knowledge a state of the soul which can be arrived at through the practice of dialectic?

The *Republic* unfolds dramatically. In its dramatic structure there are four successive episodes. Three of the four take their form from the *agōn.* The first of these occupies Book I. Where Thucydides had portrayed agonistic encounters between rival rhetoricians, Plato portrays an encounter between Socrates and the successive protagonists of the Periclean standpoint: Cephalus, the friend of Pericles; Polemarchus, who reiterates the standpoint of Odysseus in the *Philoctetes* that justice consists in doing good to one's friends and harm to one's enemies; and finally Thrasymachus, a sophist and professional teacher of rhetoric from Chalcedon. The only surviving work by him is the opening of a speech written for delivery in the Athenian assembly (by someone else — not being a citizen, Thrasymachus could not have addressed the assembly himself) that is Periclean or Thucydidean in the way that it contrasts practical competence on the one hand and chance on the other. And Lowell Edmunds (op. cit., pp. 14–15) has pointed out how closely what Plato says about Thrasymachus's rhetorical skill in the *Phaedrus* resembles what Thucydides says of Pericles' own rhetorical talents.

Thus Book I defines that to which Plato is primarily opposed. The focus of the exchanges between Socrates and Thrasymachus is the conception of *technē.* For Thrasymachus, as for Pericles, a *technē* is a skill or set of skills equally available to serve the interests of anyone intelligent and experienced enough to employ it. For the Platonic Socrates, as I noted earlier, a *technē* is a skill or set of skills directed in its exercise to the service of a good, a good of which the agent has to have genuine knowledge and understanding. But in Book I what Socrates has to deploy against Thrasymachus' rhetorical aggression is no more than what the dialectic of the *elenchos* provides, and for two distinct reasons that version of dialectic cannot provide what Socrates needs in his encounter with Thrasymachus. The first is that there are no true meeting points, no shared standards to be appealed to, for the two contending parties. Each in his conversational practice exemplifies his own conception of his own *technē* and is correspondingly unresponsive to what is said by the other. The second is that the dialectic of the *elenchos* is inherently incapable of supplying what the Platonic Socrates now needs to supply, namely, a rationally grounded conception of goods and of the good which can claim the status of knowledge. Unsurprisingly, Book I ends inconclusively, and indeed to exhibit this outcome was evidently Plato's purpose in writing the book.

A first difference between Book I and the dramatic episode of Books II–V (up to 473b) is the difference in character between Thrasymachus on the one hand and Glaucon and Adeimantus on the other in their responses to Socrates. In the *Gorgias* Plato had made it clear that successful engagement in dialectic requires certain initial virtues of character, virtues which enable one to follow those procedures of questioning and refutation truthfully, candidly, and carefully. Glaucon and Adeimantus satisfy these requirements as Thrasymachus did not. Books II–IV tell the story of the refutation by Socrates of the account of justice which they outline and defend in the first part of Book II, an account which not only seems to have been the one presupposed by Thrasymachus, but one which provides a rational justification for the view of justice taken by Thucydides, according to which the strong would do without justice altogether if they could; only the limitations in their strength compel them to compromise with others and to agree upon a set of rules which provides each person wtih the best chance of securing whatever it is that he or she wants in a way that is compatible with adequate protection against being victimized by others bent on satisfying their own wants. The justice at first defended by Glaucon and Adeimantus is the justice of effectiveness.

Against this Socrates deploys the twin notions of a *polis* and a *psuchē* which are in good order. The *polis* which is in good order is one in which each citizen is able to perfect him or herself in that form of activity for which his or her soul is peculiarly fitted. The *psuchē* which is in good order is one which is able to perfect itself in its activity, because reason provides it with knowledge of its goods, and the love

which motivates it is for the objects of reason—reason itself according
to Plato has the power to move to action—rather than those of passion
or appetite. The underlying concept of goodness has as its focus a conception of perfected excellence in a type of activity specific to a particular type of person. A virtue is a quality of character necessary for
the achievement of such a good. And justice is the key virtue because
both in the *psuchē* and the *polis* only justice can provide the order
which enables the other virtues to do their work. What is disorder in
the *psuchē?*

It is the pursuit of the satisfaction of the appetites and the emotions
for the sake of that satisfaction, rather than only as disciplined by the
virtues of temperateness, courage, and justice, so that the appetites and
emotions are appropriately transformed. In characterizing this pursuit
as incompatible with the achievement of that good which is the perfection of human agents *qua* agents Plato not only provides an outline
of the first systematic theoretical vindication of the goods of excellence
over against the goods of effectiveness, but he also defines the most
fundamental difference between Socrates and himself on the one hand
and the whole sophistic movement on the other.

The sophistic movement has had two very different reputations in
the modern world. Until the early nineteenth century Plato's accounts
of the teachings of individual sophists and his verdict upon both their
argument and their influence largely predominated. The negative connotations of 'sophistry' in everyday English reflect this predominance
from the fourteenth century onward. But with the publication of George
Grote's *History of Greece,* which appeared in ten volumes from 1846
to 1856, a quite new perspective on the history of Greek thought and
politics was supplied. Grote was a disciple of the older Mill and a friend
of the younger, a utilitarian and a partisan of liberal democracy, and
a succession of utilitarians, positivists, and pragmatists have seen in
the sophists their own predecessors. In two respects at least they have
been right.

The sophists anticipated their modern apologists in denying that any
standard of right action is to be found which is independent of the wants,
satisfactions, and preferences of individual human beings. There is, of
course, room for a large number of disagreements as to how such a
standard is or ought to be constructed out of the materials afforded
by individual wants, satisfactions, and preferences, but these disagreements all require a rejection of the view that there is or could be some
standard of right action which could be at odds with what human beings generally want. A counterpart to this denial is the belief that hu-

man wants, satisfactions, and preferences provide an empirical basis for morality. Being themselves prior to and independent of any set of moral judgments or discriminations, they provide good reasons for adopting one type of standard for making such judgments and discriminations rather than another.

Utilitarians, positivists, pragmatists, and their contemporary heirs proceed from these shared starting points very differently from the way in which fifth-century sophists proceeded—and do not of course agree with each other. But there are two features of these shared starting points which are equally crucial for the encounter between Plato and the sophists and for modern controversies. The first of these points us back to Callicles' grudging, uncandid, and sullen withdrawal from the argument with Socrates in the *Gorgias* and to the almost, but not quite, complete silence of Thrasymachus through nine books of the *Republic*. Socrates has indeed in one way refuted the central theses of Callicles in the *Gorgias* and of Thrasymachus in Books II to IV of the *Republic*, but he has done so by arguing from premises and on the basis of presuppositions which not only do Callicles and Thrasymachus reject, but which neither they nor any follower of the sophistic movement could have had any good reason to accept. The premises and presuppositions of the Platonic account certainly entail the falsity of any sophistic view and vice versa. But neither account is able to supply sufficient reasons for any sophisticated adherent of the opposing view to admit that a refutation has occurred. Plato gives no evidence—except perhaps for the all too ambiguous prolonged silences of Thrasymachus —that he recognized this aspect of the arguments of Books II to IV. But it is of central importance in evaluating the dialectical method of those books, understood as an exemplification and extension of the claims of the *Gorgias* concerning truth and justification.

What those claims amounted to was the thesis that we owe our rational allegiance to that statement or set of statements, that *logos,* about a given subject matter which has best withstood refutation so far. But what if, concerning one and the same subject matter, there are two mutually incompatible sets of statements, each able to withstand refutation in its own terms, neither able to refute the other in terms that would be acceptable to the protagonists of that other? This is a question never posed by Plato, but it will be important to ask what materials for an answer, if any, are supplied in the later books of the *Republic*. And it is important in characterizing contemporary moral philosophy to recognize how the inability of Socrates and Plato on the one hand and of the sophists on the other to produce what their opponents could recognize as a refutation of their position is mirrored in the inability of the adherents of contemporary rival moral philosophies to resolve *their* disagreements.

A second feature of the disagreement between Plato and the sophists which is equally relevant to contemporary disputes concerns the appeal to wants, satisfactions, and preferences. When I briefly described the Homeric psychology of human agency in chapter II, I remarked that in different cultures the desires and emotions are organized differently and that there is therefore no single invariant human psychology. I now have to add to this that different forms of psychological organization of the personality presuppose different evaluative and moral judgments. Wants, satisfactions, and preferences never appear in human life as merely psychological, premoral items to which we can appeal as providing data that are neutral between rival moral claims. Why not?

In every culture emotions and desires are norm-governed. Learning what the norms are, learning how to respond to the emotions and desires of others, and learning what to expect from others if we exhibit certain types and degrees of emotion or desire are three parts of one and the same task. What the norms govern is a set of three-term relations: *a particular type or degree of emotional reaction or of aspiration to fulfill a desire* is justified in *such and such a range of situations* when exhibited by *such and such a type of person filling such and such a particular type of social role.* If I do not know how the relations between these are norm-governed, then I will not understand, for example, why others react as they do to what they judge to be my unjustified anger or what it is that makes their indignation at my anger justified and so acceptable to people in general in a way that my anger is not. Nor will I understand why certain aspirations to fulfill certain desires will be treated as justified if exhibited by the occupants of some social roles, but not others. And, that is to say, when desires and emotions are understood in the context of interaction and interpretation which are constituted by particular cultures, it becomes evident that they can only function as they do if characterized in terms provided by one specific set of norms of justifications. Thus, to exhibit a particular pattern of emotions and desires, to treat them as appropriate or inappropriate in one type of situation rather than another, is always to reveal a commitment to one set of justifying norms rather than another. But such a commitment is always to one distinctive evaluative and moral position rather than another. For the justifying norms which govern both emotions and desires and their interpretation either embody or presuppose a rank ordering of goods and evils. Hence at any particular stage in the historical development of any particular culture the established patterns of emotion, desire, satisfaction, and preference will only be adequately understood if they are understood as giving expression to some distinctive moral and evaluative position. Psychologies thus understood express and presuppose moralities.

From this it does not follow that such patterns of emotion, desire, satisfaction, and preference, whether in individuals or in social and cultural groups, cannot be treated instead in detachment from their evaluative background, as some kind of nonmoral, natural, precultural given. The passions thus understood then become that in terms of which norms and evaluations are justified, themselves beyond justification because part of nature. And goods may then be defined in terms of the satisfaction of desire, either that of each particular individual or that of people in general. This is how many characteristically modern moral philosophers have understood evaluation, and this is how their sophistic ancestors understood it. What members of neither group have understood, however, is that in conceptualizing and understanding the passions in one way rather than another, indeed in treating the passions as part of nature defined independently of culture rather than as an expression of culture, they were already adopting one particular evaluative standpoint, derived from their culture's understanding of nature.

Because this is the case, the issues which divided Plato from the sophists cannot be settled by appeal to empirical psychological considerations. Both the Platonic Socrates and the sophists claim that their own specific conception of justice is according to nature (*kata phusin*). But from the Platonic standpoint the nature of each kind of thing is to be specified in terms of the good toward which it moves, so that the adequate characterization of human nature and of the passions as part of that nature requires reference to that good; while, from the sophistic standpoint, the nature to which appeal is made is how things are independently of and prior to all evaluation. From the Platonic standpoint nature has to be conceptualized from the standpoint of the best that human culture affords; from the sophistic standpoint culture has to be understood as part of physical nature. In characterizing the opposing standpoints in this way, in terms of the modern antithesis of nature and culture instead of, or rather as well as, the Greek antithesis of nature and customary law, of *phusis* and *nomos,* I do of course incur the danger of being misunderstood anachronistically. But the danger needs only to be remarked to be avoided, and it is worth incurring in order to emphasize the continuity of fifth- and fourth-century debates with those conflicts which are their modern heirs. And in both cases the difficulty in resolving such disagreements rationally arises from their systematic and wide-ranging character.

Thereby the difficulty posed for the dialectical method elaborated in the *Gorgias* and practiced in Books II to IV of the *Republic* is accentuated. No matter how successfully a set of given statements—an account of justice, for example—resists refutation, it seems that it can do so only on the basis of its own particular assumptions; and, as we have already seen, on the basis of some alternative set of assumptions, some other rival incompatible set of statements may also resist refutation with equal success. To transcend this limitation of dialectical method, as it has been so far elaborated, Plato would have to provide a way of arriving at conclusions in such a way as to free them from dependence on any particular set of assumptions. And this is how he himself defines his task at the end of Book VI (511b–c) and with it a new scope for dialectic. Dialectic is to be the science of the intelligible and as such is to provide a new resource of rationality.

The new starting point for dialectic, constructed so as not to displace its older starting point in the thickets of disagreement and refutation, but so as to supplement it, is a conception of the goal of enquiry. Failure in respect of dialectic as understood in the *Gorgias* would be of two kinds: one might fail by advancing a thesis that succumbed to refutation; or one might fail by defending one's thesis in such a way so that it and one became able to escape refutation only by being self-enclosed, bound into some narrow circle of consistency from which all possible counterexamples and objections had been excluded by some initial definition. To avoid this latter risk of failure it is necessary to frame one's theses so that they are as open to refutation as adequacy of formulation will allow: that is to say, so that we may have as much opportunity as possible to discover whether or not they are false. And what we want to learn is indeed whether or not they are false and not merely whether or not they are false from such and such a point of view, or in such and such circumstances, or if exemplified in such and such a way. This conception of being false as such is central to the Platonic conception of rationality, just because it is the counterpart to the conception of truth as such.

To engage in intellectual enquiry is then not simply to advance theses and to give one's rational allegiance to those theses which so far withstand refutation; it is to understand the movement from thesis to thesis as a movement toward a kind of *logos* which will disclose how things are, not relative to some point of view, but as such. And the conception of what each kind of thing is as such not only gives a direction to the enquiry that it would otherwise lack but also provides a resource for correcting and reformulating our successive theses as we aspire to move from hypothesis to unconditional assertion. So the terminus and *telos* of enquiring into what justice is has to be an account of justice as such, of the *eidos* of all partial and one-sided exemplifications and one-sided elucidations. The theory of forms is primarily a theory of inquiry, a theory ignorance of which by those engaged in enquiry will necessarily lead them to fail, because they will not understand adequately what they are doing. In what way is this so?

A central contention of at least some sophists was that what is the case is just what appears to be the case to someone or other. 'Is' and 'is true' are always to be reinterpreted reductively as saying no more than is said by 'Seems to be to such and such persons' or 'Seems to be true to such and such persons'. All claims are made from some point of view, and any attempt to speak in a way that overcomes relativity and one-sidedness is foredoomed to failure. So too have urged some modern pragmatists and some modern Nietzscheans. One type of reply would begin by conceding immediately that it may well be the case that there is no way of exempting oneself from the partialities and one-sidedness of particular times, place, and social and cultural positions, that no thesis can be advanced but from some particular standpoint. But it then adds that if there were no more to matters than that, we should be unable to distinguish between two distinct ways in which an enquiry may proceed.

Consider two different possible outcomes of looking back upon an enquiry which has already proceeded for some time. It may be that such a retrospective examination may reveal that although a variety of theses have been advanced, defended in various formulations and reformulations, and then refuted or abandoned, to be replaced by others, still no overall direction has emerged. The movement from one dominating thesis or set of theses to another does not amount to progress. But it may instead be the case that a retrospective examination shows, not merely a movement without direction, but progress pointing toward a goal. What characteristics would the latter have to possess, the former have to lack? Four seem to be crucial.

First, the later stages of the enquiry would have to presuppose the findings of the earlier. I do not mean by this that at the later stages what had at some earlier stage been taken to be findings would always be confirmed. It is rather that some at least of the later stages would afford us a point of view from which it would be possible to identify and to characterize the findings of earlier stages in a way in which that

would not have been possible at those stages. And it would be the findings thus characterized which the later stage would have to presuppose
in moving the enquiry further on.

Second, where there has been at an earlier stage unresolved and, at
that stage, unresolvable disagreement, it must at some later stage become possible to provide an explanation both of why the disagreement
occurred and of why it was then and with those resources unresolvable. Thus the later stages provide a theory of error and falsity to account for inadequacy at earlier stages.

Third, it has to become possible to provide at later stages a successively more adequate conception of the good of the enquiry. By
"more adequate" I do not mean merely a conceptually richer and
more detailed characterization but also one which enables the enquiry
to be better directed. Thus successive retrospective examinations of the
enquiry so far would provide fuller accounts of the goal of the enquiry, and in turn successive characterizations of that goal would furnish stronger grounds for directing the enquiry in one way rather than
another.

Fourth, this gradually enriched conception of the goal is a conception of what it would be to have completed the enquiry. One and the
same conception is to provide both the enquiry with its *telos* and the
subject matter of the enquiry with its explanation. So that to arrive
at it would involve being able to provide a single, unified explanation
of the subject matter and of the course of the enquiry into that subject
matter. Let us call the conception which provides this explanation the
archē: adequately specified as it can only be at the point at which enquiry is substantially complete, it will be possible to deduce from it
every relevant truth concerning the subject matter of the enquiry; and
to explain the lower-order truths will precisely be to specify the deductive, causal, and explanatory relationships which link them to the *archē*
and which show that, given the nature of the *archē,* they would not
be other than they are. But the *archē* will also afford an understanding
of why each of the successive stages by which it was approached was
distinct from it as well as a characterization of the specific type of error
that would have been involved in mistaking each of these stages for the
completion of the enquiry. For each of these stages will have been
marked both by less and less partial insight and yet also by a continuing one-sidedness. Only from the standpoint of the completion of the
enquiry, of a finally and fully adequate conception of the *archē,* is such
one-sidedness left behind. Does it follow that to adopt this view of
what progress in rational enquiry consists in commits one to holding

that one can finally exempt oneself from the one-sidedness of a point of view? Not at all. This account of progress in rational enquiry is consistent *either* with the view that by attaining the standpoint afforded by a completely adequate conception of the *archē* one can indeed achieve final exemption from such one-sidedness and partiality *or* with the rival and incompatible view that one cannot. If the latter is the case, then although one can definitely progress toward the final completion of rational enquiry, that completion lies at a point which cannot itself be attained. Hence we would be rescued by the progress of that enquiry from the one-sidedness of any particular point of view; we would still be guided by a conception of what it would be to understand things as they are absolutely, and not just relating to some standpoint, even if such final understanding is not in fact to be attained.

Return now to Plato. The denial of the sophists that we can say what justice is, rather than what it seems to be to such and such persons (so that justice at Athens is what it seems to be to the Athenians, justice at Sparta what it seems to be to the Spartans), requires a rejection of the possibility of this kind of rational enquiry with respect to justice. For it involves a rejection of any conception of justice, understood in terms of timeless, impersonal, and nonperspectival truth, which could function as the *archē* of such an enquiry into the nature of justice. It is then the possibility of this kind of enquiry which Plato needs to vindicate. How far does the argument of the *Republic* provide just such a vindication? We can only approach the task of answering this question by first reconsidering the structure of Plato's overall argument in the *Republic*.

I remarked earlier that the *Republic* falls into four sections, three of them agonistic, with Socrates' principal adversaries being in Book I Thrasymachus, in Books II–V (up to 473b) Glaucon and Adeimantus, and in Book X Homer and the rest of the poets and tellers of tales. But from 473c onward in Book V Socrates does not carry forward the enquiry through agonistic, dialectical interchange, but rather he expounds and teaches directly, even though the conversational question-and-answer form is preserved. What the argument so expounded concludes is that only those educated through many years in mathematics and dialectic can achieve adequate understanding (*epistēmē*) of the object of the enquiry. Hence arises the central apparent paradox of the *Republic*. The kind of education of which the prologue is described in Books II and III and the completion in Book VII is necessary if and only if *epistēmē* of the forms is what Socrates claims it to be; but no one can know whether this is true or not unless they have had that kind of education. And no one participating in the conversations of the *Republic* has had such a training. Hence neither Glaucon nor Adeimantus nor any other participant has been supplied within the *Republic* with the knowledge which they need. So the third part of the *Republic* (Books V, 373c–VII) is a description of how to complete the enquiry and arrive at its *archē,* an understanding of the form of justice in the light afforded by the form of the Good, but it is not itself and could not be the completion of that enquiry. It follows that the *Republic* is by intention a radically incomplete book. It tells us what structure and content a theory which could rationally warrant its account of justice would have to possess. But it does not itself provide such a theory. It is less surprising then than it might otherwise be that when the Platonic Socrates returns to the *agōn* with his contentions against Homer and the other poets in Book X, after making the case against mimetic poetry, he says that the friends of the poets must be allowed to reply on their behalf and then turns away to another topic, that of the immortality of the soul. About the immortality of the soul Plato recounts the myth of Er. That myth violates two of the educational prohibitions proposed in Book II: it includes direct speeches (615c–616a and 617d–e), and thus is an example of the mimesis which has just been condemned, and it speaks of the underworld in precisely the kind of way that was condemned earlier (compare 387b–6 with 616a). Nothing could make it clearer that Socrates is disclaiming for himself the status of one who speaks from the standpoint of achieved *epistēmē:* he remains one who appeals to images and diagrams, and therefore who has not yet apprehended the forms.

The *Republic* is therefore to be understood as presenting, not a completed theory of forms, but rather a program for constructing such a theory. (Because I take this view of what is said about forms in the *Republic,* my argument does not require a commitment to any one out of the rival contending views on those substantive problems concerning the nature of the forms which have been debated ever since H. F. Cherniss 'The Philosophical Economy of the Theory of Ideas' *American Journal of Philology* 57, 1936: 445–456, except on one crucial issue. This is the character of the forms as standards, standards which can be invoked and applied only by those able to provide the requisite *logos.* Here my view derives from that taken by R. C. Cross 'Logos and Form in Plato' *Mind* LXIII, 252, 1954: 433–450.) The stages of this proposed construction to some degree satisfy the four conditions for an enquiry which exhibits rational progress toward a *telos,* which I stated earlier. For the disagreements of Book I become intelligible in a new

way when recharacterized in terms of what we learn about such disagreements subsequently, especially in Books VIII and IX. We are now
able to recognize Thrasymachus as having a democratic soul; Polemarchus and Cephalus, plutocratic souls. The argument of Books II to IV
had already revealed the systematic character of the differences between
Socrates and Thrasymachus in a way that Book I does not. Thus at
later stages the earlier arguments are recharacterized and to some degree corrected, in just the way that the first and second conditions require.

In Book I the good pursued in the enquiry is to show somehow or
other what is defective in various views of justice. In Books II to IV
the good has become that of providing an adequate definition of justice, understood in terms of the tripartite *polis* and the tripartite *psuchē*.
Given such a definition, what could not be resolved in Book I can be
resolved. But it turns out that the kind of definition provided is not,
by itself, rationally adequate. And by Book VII we have learned what
has to be supplied to make it adequate, the kind of progress required
by the third condition.

Further examples could be added to strengthen the argument that
the first three of the conditions which must be satisfied by any enquiry
which is making rational progress toward its completion are to some
extent at least satisfied by Plato's representation of such enquiry in the
Republic. But what about the fourth? This is the condition which concerns the function of the *archē* in directing the enquiry. And it is a condition which Plato's account of enquiry cannot satisfy just because that
epistēmē which would provide the requisite grasp of the *archē* is
necessarily unavailable to those such as Socrates, Glaucon, Adeimantus and the others who have not yet left behind the realms of images
and diagrams, who have not yet escaped from the cave. Hence what
Plato offers us is radically incomplete. And what we have to learn from
the *Republic* finally is as much a matter of the uncompleted character
of Plato's project as it is of the claims made about the nature of justice.
Only with an adequate specification of an *archē* for the understanding
of justice would the Platonic account of justice have been rationally
vindicated against the sophistic. Recognizing that such a specification
is not furnished in the *Republic* is crucial for understanding what Plato
contributed to the conflicts about justice: not a doctrine, but a dilemma,
and a dilemma which gives definitive form to subsequent debate.

The dilemma is this: *either* the life of the reasoning human being
can be shown to have its *archē* in the sense defined earlier *or* the sophistic and Thucydidean view of human reality prevails. Notice that
it is the form of Plato's argument rather than its precise content which

provides the dilemma. Plato in the *Republic* has his own particular account of the goods of excellence and of the justice of excellence, involving the tripartite structures of state and soul. But the connection between what is specific to Plato's account of justice and his account of how one must enquire if the *epistēmē* of justice is one's *telos* is never stated in any close and precise terms. And what Plato has succeeded in stating at this point are conditions which *any* successful rational defense of the goods of excellence and of a justice defined in terms of them will have to satisfy.

At this point readers aware of the variety of later philosophical debate may object by enquiring whether these are after all the only alternatives. Can there not be some other basis for rejecting the sophistic and Thucydidean view? To this the reply must be that what we are pursuing is an actual history of argument and debate and that within that history the alternatives come to be defined in this way. Later, of course, even in the ancient world new ways of thinking about justice and practical reasoning emerge, for example, Stoicism. But any later third alternative must itself presuppose that the Platonic project, as Plato adumbrates it in the *Republic,* has proved incapable of successful completion.

The dilemma with which the *Republic* finally confronts its readers is in an important way the outcome of the history of conceptions of justice and their relationship to conceptions of practical and theoretical reasoning so far. If one begins with a society informed by the Homeric imagination and tries to answer the questions raised at each stage for the members of such a society by the working out of the understanding of themselves provided by that imagination in actual historical terms, then one is led in the end inescapably to the problems posed by the *Republic*. For these problems at last give clear philosophical definition to those conflicts between the goods of excellence and the goods of effectiveness which were articulated in turn in terms of Periclean rhetoric and politics, of tragic drama and of Thucydides' history. Plato made of the sophists partners in posing these problems in a way that provided, so as it was to turn out, a permanent part of the framework for all subsequent discussion and even for contribution to that discussion where historical origins were not merely not Homeric, but quite alien to the Homeric imagination. This is why the reading and the continuous rereading of the *Republic* remains indispensable to moral and cultural education. I do not mean to suggest by saying this that themes are not going to be introduced both into the discussion of justice and into that of practical reasoning which are both of the first importance and also unknown to Plato.

This is not the only reason why it has often been the case that the importance of the dilemma posed by the *Republic,* more especially when it is read in relation to Thucydides' history (a way of reading defined for recent generations by David Grene's *Man In His Pride,* Chicago, 1950—later mistitled *Greek Political Theory*), has often been obscured from view. For the issues posed by that dilemma in relation both to justice and to practical reasoning have been transformed in a variety of ways in the course of their subsequent history. And when the issues posed by that dilemma reappear in other conceptual guises, it is all too easy to fail to recognize the kinship of the protagonists of one alternative or the other to Plato and either Thucydides or some one of Plato's sophistic adversaries. Another source of such failure is a misreading of Aristotle, or rather a whole series of misreadings of Aristotle, which have in common that they represent Aristotle's thought as though its relationship to Plato's was merely one of historical accident. Aristotle may on this view have learned this or that from Plato in the course of criticizing and rejecting certain Platonic doctrines, but his philosophy was independent of Plato's and can be appropriated by us independently of Plato's. The Aristotle whom I am going to present is by contrast one whose own fundamental enterprise was to complete, and in so doing to correct, Plato's project. The *Nicomachean Ethics* and the *Politics* are, on the view that I am taking, to be understood as sequels to the *Republic* in which the *archē,* whose adequate characteristics Plato could not provide, is specified in such a way that it can provide the ultimate *telos* of practical activity and the justification and specification of the virtues, including justice. The questions which Aristotle answers are Platonic questions.

The central importance of Aristotle's moral and political philosophy derives on this view from the claim that in essentials it solves the problem posed by the dilemma presented by a reading of the *Republic.* And the importance of other subsequent moral and political philosophies will then turn on whether they do or do not impugn, vindicate, or correct and supplement Aristotle's answers to Plato's questions. Yet, of course, such a view of the history of moral and political philosophy not only must seem eccentric in the context of a culture such as our own, defined by the Enlightenment and its heirs. It is a view of that history which would have seemed eccentric in the fourth century and indeed in many periods thereafter. In the fourth century it was important that Plato's true successors seemed to be those who continued in the Academy under the leadership of Plato's nephew, Speusippus. And in fact a conception of what is specific to Platonism which derived from Speusippus (a conception which understands the knowledge of the forms in terms of a particular kind of construal of mathematics) contributed importantly to concealing the continuity of Aristotle's thought with Plato's.

Moreover neither Plato nor Aristotle provided the focal point for fourth-century Athenian discussion of moral and political issues. If any single person did so, it was Isocrates. Isocrates, born eight years or so before Plato in 436, outlived him by ten years, dying in 338. Isocrates more than anyone else not only perpetuated the rhetoric of the Periclean and immediately post-Periclean periods but also turned that rhetoric into an educational system. Historians of philosophy tend to give Isocrates only marginal attention, and if what was important about Isocrates was to be measured by either argumentative rigor or conceptual insight, they would be right. But the importance of Isocrates lay in his offering an alternative to philosophy understood as Socrates, Plato, and Aristotle had defined it. Isocrates praised *aretē* and *dikaiosunē* and asserted that his teaching of rhetoric fostered them. But he was opposed to dialectic, and when he praised Athens for philosophical achievement, it was clearly the masters of rhetoric that he had in mind. Teaching is to be by examples of what is good and honorable. In so teaching, Isocrates directly challenged the Platonic Socrates of the *Meno,* who argued that examples cannot give us the kind of knowledge of virtue that we need, just as, in his praise of his own teacher Gorgias, Isocrates directly challenged the Platonic Socrates of the *Gorgias.* Yet if Isocrates disdained dialectical enquiry and argument of a kind that he took to be harmfully abstruse, why should we pay him any attention at all?

The answer is that if the sophistic alternative turns out to be true, then there are no objective and independent standards of justice or indeed, more fundamentally, of truth to which appeal can be made against the *de facto* standards upheld by particular groups. But if this is the case, disagreement about those *de facto* standards can only be resolved by means of nonrational persuasion; and the most effective means of nonrational persuasion is the type of rhetoric taught and practiced by Isocrates.

Isocrates looked back to the catastrophic defeat of Athens in the Peloponnesian War and understood that defeat in a way very different from either Thucydides or Plato. What had led to that war and so to that defeat was Greek disunity. What the Greeks needed was a restoration of that unity, the unity forged in the wars against the Persians. And since only under a monarchy could order and unity be enforced, he became in the end the protagonist of a united Greek attack on Persia under the leadership of some king who would be afforded hegemony over the *poleis*. But what mattered in the lasting influence of Isocrates and the system of education which he founded was not the particular policies which he advocated, but the way in which he gave canonical form to rhetoric as a means of education whose overriding aim is effectiveness in persuasion rather than truth through enquiry. He decisively broke the links between practical and theoretical discourse. And in so doing, of course, he was once again at odds with Plato, whose project requires that practical discourse be made dependent on the outcome of theoretical enquiry. Isocrates was no Callicles or Thrasymachus, but the very ways in which Isocrates differed from them, his bland, unargued assumption that virtue and justice can be understood without dialectic is far more dangerous to culture and society than the brutal questioning of Callicles and Thrasymachus. The sophists have had philosophically far more distinguished descendants than Isocrates. But it is through the influence of Isocrates in the ancient world and of his modern heirs that they have been effective as protagonists of the goods of cooperative effectiveness. The dilemma posed by the reading of the *Republic* is therefore to be understood as confronting us at two levels. At that of theory the alternatives are best defined in terms of Plato's theses and the countertheses of Thucydides and of the sophists, but at the level of political practice the alternative to Plato then and now was provided by Isocrates.

VI

Aristotle as Plato's Heir

Two dominant images of human life emerge from post-Homeric reflection. Both are images of aiming and striving. According to the one, human beings aim at excellence. Some may misconceive what excellence is, and many may fall short of attaining that at which they aim. But all, whatever their degree of achievement, are measured by a standard which they did not make but which they discover, first within various *technai* in which they engage and then within the project of achieving the good and the best. Plato makes it part of that project to replace, as far as possible, the images and narratives of the poet and the storyteller by the concepts and arguments of the philosopher. But even he, as is plain from the *Republic*, cannot describe the philosophical enterprise in a way which completely discards image and myth. The task of moving through the final stages in the Viconian journey from the imaginative universal to the conceptual universal still remains to be accomplished.

A second and rival image is that according to which human beings aim at a particular kind of power, the power of remaking the social and natural world, so far as possible, into conformity with one's own desires. The exercise of this power may be frustrated by failures in judgment springing either from inadequate intelligence or from an inability to resist the temptation of *hubris* or by failures in tenacity of purpose. Accuracy in judgment is peculiarly important when it concerns the need to form alliances with some in order to overcome the obstacles presented by the opposition of others to one's projects. It is also important in enabling one to secure the service of those whose excellence may enable one to overcome or circumvent a variety of obstacles and frustrations. This image, like its rival, is originally Homeric and, in this also like its rival, receives its final definitive elaboration as an image in the fourth century. But while that rival is presented through Plato's contrast between the ideal and the actual, the image of human life as a striving after success in doing whatever it is one wants to do is finally exemplified in the actions and achievements of Alexander of Macedon.

It is important to remember that Aristotle was both Plato's pupil and Alexander's tutor. In the latter role—also perhaps in virtue of his father's position as physician to an earlier king of Macedon and certainly in virtue of his friendship with Antipater, Alexander's viceroy in Greece—he was identified with the Macedonian ruling elite who were confronted by three quite different claims to their allegiance. Not only were Macedonian institutions and customs challenged by the form of life of the Greek *polis,* so that to be both Macedonian and Greek involved difficult choices. But both Macedonian custom and Greek politics were increasingly rejected by Alexander in his self-glorifying adoption of the style and substance of the Persian monarchy. Callisthenes, Aristotle's nephew and his collaborator in drawing up the lists of the victors in the Pythian games, for which they were both honored at Delphi, accompanied Alexander on his expedition against Persia as the historian of Alexander's deeds. Callisthenes understood his task as a Greek: he was to be the Homer who narrated the deeds of the new Achilles. Unsurprisingly he was among those in Alexander's circle antagonized by Alexander's transformation from Greek *hēgemōn* to Persian monarch. Alexander had him executed.

Aristotle could not, therefore, have evaded the question posed at the level of political practice for Antipater and Callisthenes, that of whether and how the mode of life of the Greek *polis* could be justified against its rivals. Aristotle provided the materials for a response to this question by constructing two original interrelated arguments, each of some complexity. The first is designed to show that it is the good and the best which alone supplies an *archē* for human beings when they are fully rational and which also, by supplying the *telos* for human action, provides the key concept for a framework of theoretical explanation by appeal to which the varying outcomes of human action can best be explained, insofar as they depend upon the exercise or the failure to exercise human powers and abilities, and not upon chance and accident. Rational practice and the theoretical explanation of practice are informed by the same concepts.

Since the conceptions of activity, of excellence, and of the relationship between them which Aristotle expounds and defends are precisely those embodied in those particular types of activity in which Greeks pursued specific types of physical and intellectual excellence—it is no accident that Aristotle had a role in the Pythian games as well as in the Academy and the Lyceum—what emerges is a defense of the goods of excellence and of the virtues, more particularly of justice, understood in terms of those goods. It is Plato's project which Aristotle vindicates and, so I shall suggest, completes; Alexander's which he discredits. And since Aristotle is engaged in furnishing us with an account of a type of human life within which the various specific goods are integrated. Since it is only the institutionalized forms of the *polis* which, not only on Aristotle's view but on that common to educated Greeks, provided such an integrated form of life, Aristotle's account of the good and the best cannot but be an account of the good and the best as it is embodied in a *polis*. Thus once again it is on the side of Plato and against Alexander that Aristotle contends.

His second argument, however, involves him in a partial rejection, or at least correction, of Plato. He agrees of course with Plato in passing a negative judgment upon the Athenian democracy, one no doubt reinforced by Aristotle's Macedonian sympathies. For it had been the Athenian democrats, led by the untruthful, corrupt, and golden-mouthed Demosthenes, who had opposed Philip of Macedon's ambitions (for an excellent account of the influence of his Macedonian sympathies upon Aristotle see H. Kelsen 'Aristotle and Hellenic-Macedonian Policy' *Ethics* 48, 8, 1937). And it was to be the Athenian democrats who on Alexander's death made it unsafe for Aristotle to remain at Athens. But Aristotle was nonetheless committed to defend the actuality of the *polis,* as Plato had not been. No actual *polis* on his view completely exemplified the best possible type of *polis,* but some features of that best possible type had in fact been exemplified. And the second most important fact about the best possible type of polis was that it was possible. Aristotle was no utopian. When Demetrius of Phalerum, an Athenian pupil of Aristotle's pupil Theophrastus, became the ruler of Athens from 317 to 307 as a result of the military intervention of Cassander, he introduced a form of oligarchy whose constitutional and legislative inspiration was Aristotle's *Politics*. The *Politics* could then be used as a handbook for practice in a way quite alien to the spirit of the *Republic*. Thus Aristotle's standpoint on the *polis* separated him not only from Alexander but also from Plato.

Plato and Thucydides had been in agreement and Socrates and Thrasymachus had been represented by Plato as being in agreement that justice as it is defined and characterized by the Socrates of the *Republic* is nowhere to be found in any actual *polis*. The justice of which Aristotle offers an account in Book V of the *Nicomachean Ethics* by contrast exhibits justice-as-it-ought-to-be-understood as implicit in the practice of justice-as-it-is. The justice of actual *poleis* is held to be in varying ways defective, but it is in studying the principles implicit in those varying forms that we discern how those defects are all departures from or failures to achieve a form of justice which would be the best justice of the best kind of *polis*. So Aristotle's method of political enquiry was to make a collection of constitutions—just as in his zoological studies he made collections of sea and land creatures—in order to discover what form of constitution could be treated as the paradigm in relation to which all deviations from it could be classified in terms of the various types of misunderstanding and failure which they embody.

This method of moving from a set of particulars to a universal, to the concept of the form which those particulars to different degrees exemplify, Aristotle called *epagōgē*. The standard modern translation of '*epagōgē*' by 'induction' does no harm, provided that we distinguish carefully between what Mill and other modern writers have meant by "induction" and what Aristotle meant by "*epagōgē*." *Epagōgē* involves inference but is more than inference; it is rather that scientific method through which the particular varyingly impure or distorted exemplifications of a single form can be understood in terms of that form—as particular varyingly impure examples of carbon can all be understood by chemists to exemplify the single atomic structure which makes them each an example of *carbon*—so that the concept of that structure provides within atomic and molecular theory the *archē* both for their classification and for their explanation. The mode of apprehension in which the mind grasps such an *archē* Aristotle calls *nous*.

It is not only by means of *epagōgē* that *nous* attains its comprehension of *archai*, of first conceptions and principles. When someone proposes that the *archē* of some particular science or some particular type of activity is such and such or when there is debate over a number of rival and conflicting proposals of that kind, it is by means of another kind of dialectical argument—Aristotle regards *epagōgē* also as part of dialectic—namely, that process in which a particular thesis or theory justifies itself over against its rivals through its superior ability in withstanding the most cogent objections from different points of view, that a conclusion about what the *archē* is is arrived at. And once again it is *nous* which grasps what the conclusion is. *Nous*, that is to say, is the exercise of a capacity for understanding what the conclusion is of a nondemonstrative mode of argument or enquiry. The principles which *nous* grasps are those *from* which we argue in setting out those sound deductive arguments which have the status of demonstrations. Demonstration is thus dependent on dialectic for the acquisition of the premises which provide it with a starting point. And this, as I suggested above, is equally true of theoretical enquiry and of practical reasoning,

unsurprisingly perhaps since the first principles of theoretical enquiry
into the nature of practical reasoning and of the practical reasoning
which issues in action are one and the same.

Aristotle distinguishes between *epistēmē,* scientific knowledge, which
involves universals and *phronēsis,* practical intelligence, which is concerned with particulars as well. But inability to exercise *phronēsis* can
have two different sources. We may fail to identify the characteristics
of a particular which are relevant to the actions that we should be about
to perform either for lack of experience of the relevant set of particulars or from inadequate *epistēmē,* so that we do not understand the
universal, the concept of the form which *this* particular exemplifies
(*Nicomachean Ethics* 1131a 11–25). Someone with extensive experience
of particulars, but who is by reason of his or her lack of *epistēmē* unable to appeal to argument (*logos*), may be better at judging what is
the case or what to do correctly than is someone whose *epistēmē* provides them with arguments, but who has inadequate experience of particulars (*Metaphysics* 981a 23–24). Yet if someone is judging rightly,
although only on the basis of experience, then the principles of right
action will be implicit in what he or she does. They will provide the
unarticulated major premises which in conjunction with his or her judgments as to the particular aspects of situations entail that action which
is the correct conclusion of sound practical argument.

Just because this is so we can by *epagōgē* from the judgments and
actions of such persons move toward the formulation of true *archai,*
supplementing that *epagōgē* by a dialectical enquiry in which we evaluate the best-supported opinions as to the relevant *archai* advanced so
far. And it is of course because there are a variety of rival and conflicting opinions, opinions which direct enquiry and guide action in different and incompatible ways, that it is crucial not to remain at the level
of *empeiria,* experience of particulars—the kind of experience to which
Pericles and Thucydides had appealed—or *gnōmē,* but instead to attain knowledge of the *archai, nous.*

Those *archai,* if correctly formulated, will furnish us with the first
principles for the explanation of how and why human enterprises and
activities are better or worse at achieving those goods which provide
them with their *telos,* and they will do so precisely by formulating adequately an account of those goods and their place in or relationship
to the good and the best. They will also furnish, by so doing, the kind
of account of that *telos* which human beings need in order to aim at
it in their actions, thereby providing the ultimate major premise of
such practical reasoning: "Deductive inferences about what is to be

done have as an *archē* 'Since the *telos* and the best is such and such'"
(*NE* 1144a31–33).

Nous then grasps those first principles without which both theoretical enquiry and practical activity are blind, inadequately guided, and prone to error: ". . . on the one hand in demonstrations *nous* apprehends the unchanging and primary definitions, on the other in practical reasonings it apprehends what is ultimate and contingent, the second premise. For these are the *archai* of that for the sake of which, since it is from the particulars that the universals are derived. Therefore, of these we must have perception, and this is *nous*" (*NE* 1142b1–5). It is the ultimacy, not further to be justified, of the claim that *this* particular is a *such and such,* the comprehension of the form which is embodied in *this* particular, which *nous* provides as the counterpart to its comprehension of the universal as such, the concept of the form as such. For to comprehend the form as such just is to comprehend it as embodied in particulars, including *this* particular. So although Aristotle does indeed contrast the *epistēmē* of universals with the particularity of *phronētic* concerns, the two are clearly linked. (Although I differ from Normal O. Dahl in his translation of this particular passage, his discussion of how Aristotle's views are to be interpreted in *Practical Reasoning, Aristotle, and Weakness of Will,* Minneapolis, 1984, pp. 41–48 and 277–872, is much the most illuminating in the literature, and I hope that I have learned enough from his general views, with which I am in large agreement. I am also indebted to Daniel T. Devereux 'Particular and Universal in Aristotle's Conception of Practical Knowledge' *Review of Metaphysics* 39, 1986, and most fundamentally to Henry Teloh's two papers 'Aristotle's Metaphysics Z' *Canadian Journal of Philosophy* 9, 1979, and 'The Universal in Aristotle' *Apeiron* 13, 1979, and to A. C. Lloyd *Form and Universal in Aristotle,* Liverpool, 1981).

There is thus the closest of parallels between Aristotle's revision of Plato in respect of his account of the relationship of universals and forms to particulars and in respect of his political and moral philosophy. Where Plato contrasts the form and the realm of particulars, emphasizing their disparity, Aristotle understands the form as confronted only in the particulars, albeit often imperfectly so exemplified; where Plato contrasts the ideal polity and the realm of actual *poleis,* emphasizing their disparity, Aristotle understands the type of *polis* which is the best as conforming to a standard which is already implicitly embodied and acknowledged, albeit in important ways, within the practices of actual Greek politics. And this is why the findings of political enquiry, as Aristotle understands them, can be brought to bear upon the choices between Macedonian custom, Greek political practice, and Alexander's seduction by Persian despotism.

Yet by emphasizing the contrast between Aristotle and Plato even to this extent I may be in danger of obscuring the equal or even greater importance of the unity and continuity of their enterprise. It is all too easy to relapse into the long-established and highly misleading view of Plato and Aristotle as representing fundamentally distinct and opposed philosophical alternatives, a commonplace for centuries, and still not without adherents. But the kind of scholarly interpretation of both Plato and Aristotle which had been invoked in the last century by Thomas Case and in this by Werner Jaeger to support this view of their opposition has not survived the work of G. E. L. Owen (see especially 'The Platonism of Aristotle' *Proceedings of the British Academy* 50, 1965). What now sustains this kind of conception is the revival of an essentially Neoplatonic view of Plato, in one version by John Findlay, in another by Iris Murdoch. The view which I shall be taking lies at the opposite end of the spectrum of interpretations. For, as I have already remarked, I understand Aristotle as engaged in trying to complete Plato's work, and to correct it precisely insofar as that was necessary in order to complete it. This is in part a matter of following Owen and others in recognizing both how far Aristotle's criticisms of some of Plato's earlier positions are either substantially identical with or a further development of Plato's own criticisms of those positions and how far Aristotle's original constructions are still informed by Platonic goals and make use of Platonic materials. But it is also in part a matter of going somewhat further than this, by understanding certain of Aristotle's major arguments as directed to answering either questions posed by Plato or questions to which Plato had given unsatisfactory answers.

There are, of course, specific areas in which Plato and Aristotle, on any plausible account at all, are sharply opposed — concerning the nature of mathematical truths, for example. But in ethics and politics Aristotle is not so much opposing, as redoing, the work of the *Republic*. Plato himself redid that work in his own way in the *Laws,* and it is worth observing the close parallels at some key points between the direction taken by Plato in moving from the *Republic* to the *Laws* and Aristotle's thought. Where in the *Republic* Plato used '*eidos,*' so that a knowledge of the forms involves turning away from the world of experience, in the *Laws* he uses '*eidos,*' just as Aristotle does, to mean 'species,' and experience has a crucial part in the acquisition of that ability to discriminate species rationally which is what a knowledge of *eidē* now consists in. Where in the *Republic* *'epistēmē'* is the word for the kind of knowledge which is necessary for a ruler, the words commonly used of the wise and knowledgeable ruler in the *Laws* are *phronimos* and its cognates, the same words used by Aristotle of those who are practically intelligent. And just as Aristotle is in the *Politics,* Plato in the *Laws* is concerned with such practical considerations as how too great inequities of property may disrupt the life of a *polis,* a discussion to which Aristotle explicitly refers in the *Politics.*

These are not the only continuities between Plato's later thought and Aristotle's political and ethical doctrines. Aristotle in both the *Nicomachean Ethics* (1137b 13–14) and the *Rhetoric* (1374a 25–b3) recognizes the need for a type of exercise of practical judgment which cannot be guided by rules because it concerns a situation whose relevant particulars are not captured by the best formulated rules so far available, and he also recognizes that it is of the nature of sets of rules that no matter how well formulated they may be, they cannot provide for all such eventualities. But this too had already been suggested in the *Politicus* (294a–c).

Moreover, Plato's attitudes to the course of Athenian history, originally very different from those which Aristotle was to exhibit, show the same tendencies in his later writings to approximate to Aristotle's positions. Earlier his attitude is one of large and near universal condemnation. In the *Gorgias* Pericles and Cimon, Miltiades and Themistocles, are all attacked. And the *Republic* provides just the theoretical background necessary to sustain those condemnations. But by the time that Plato came to write the *Laws* his attitude had been modified. In Book III (698a 9–701b 3) Plato ascribed to the Athenians at the time of the Persian Wars a well-ordered constitution in which the hierarchical division into four classes ensured that the relations of rulers to ruled and of both to the laws were what they ought to be. And it is clear that what he then looked back to was the Athenian constitution prior to 462 when Ephialtes deprived the Areopagus of most of its powers. In the *Constitution of Athens* it was just this same period to which Aristotle looked back with approbation: "During this period Athenians were governed well" (XXIII,2), and, in sharp contrast to the *Gorgias,* Themistocles is praised for his *dikaiosunē* (XXIII,3). (I am not of course concerned with the accuracy of either Plato's or Aristotle's beliefs about Athenian history.) I do not want to overemphasize the resemblances and continuities. It would be both an exaggeration and an oversimplification to say either that Aristotle always remained some sort of a Platonist or that Plato gradually became an Aristotelian, but either assertion would be the simplified exaggeration of a complex truth. The part of that truth which is important to my own discussion is the extent to which and the way in which Aristotle's writings on ethics and politics ought to be read as solving or resolving the problems posed by the *Republic*.

There is, however, one crucial respect in which Aristotle at first sight seems to be so radically at odds with the Plato of the *Republic* that it endangers this understanding of their relationship. For although Plato in the *Republic* initially defines justice in terms of relationships within the tripartite *polis* in Book IV, he ascribes the characteristics of a *polis* to the characteristics of the individual persons who compose it—Whence else, he asks, could the characteristics of the *polis* be derived? (435e2) And a central thesis of the *Republic* is that justice in the individual *psyche* can exist and be for the good of that *psyche,* no matter how unjustly that individual is treated by the *polis.* So Plato appears to believe that justice as a virtue, or rather as the key element in the virtue of the individual human being, is independent of and antecedent to the justice that is the ordering of the *polis.*

That this is an adequate characterization of Plato's view might well be thought to be supported by recalling Plato's own most important political experiences. Plato after all did abandon the prospect of participation in Athenian politics because of the injustice of the death of Socrates. And his experiences at the courts of Dionysius I and Dionysius II, during his visits to Syracuse, and the subsequent fate of his friend Dion would surely have reinforced a negative view of the possibility of transforming any actual *polis.*

Aristotle however represents a tradition of thought, in which he is preceded by Homer and Sophocles, according to which the human being who is separated from his social group is also deprived of the capacity for justice. So Homer, in a passage which Aristotle quotes (*Politics* 1253a6), makes Nestor say of the man who lacks a clan (*aphrētōr*) that he is also lacking in *themis (Iliad* IX, 63). Sophocles has Philoctetes declare that when deprived of friends and of a *polis,* he became "a corpse among the living" (*Philoctetes,* 1018) and it is as a consequence of this that he is unable to respond justly to Neoptolemus. Thus Aristotle is articulating at the level of theoretical enquiry a thought inherited from the poets when he argues in Book I of the *Politics* (1252b28–1253a39) that a human being separated from the *polis* is thereby deprived of some of the essential attributes of a human being. This is a passage whose importance for the interpretation of everything that Aristotle wrote about human life cannot be underrated, and it is peculiarly crucial for understanding his claims about justice, practical reasoning, and their relationship.

Aristotle uses two analogies to make his central point. A human being stands to the *polis* as a part to its whole, in a way analogous both to that in which a hand or foot stands to the body of which it is a part and to that in which a piece in a board game (we may think of chess or checkers—the Greek game referred to by Aristotle resembled the latter) stands to a game in which it is deployed. Detach a hand from its body; it then lacks both the specific function and the specific capacity of a hand: it no longer in the same sense is a hand. Abstract a piece from such deployment in a game; it too is deprived thereby of function and capacity. What is it that a human being is deprived of, if radically separated from the life of the *polis*?

Dikē is the ordering of the *polis,* declares Aristotle, but he understands this in a way that relates his claim to the Homeric use of '*dikē*'. For the *polis* is human community perfected and completed by achieving its *telos,* and the essential nature of each thing is what it is when it achieves its *telos*. So it is in the forms of the *polis* that human nature as such is expressed, and human nature is the highest kind of animal nature. The Homeric view of *dikē* as the order of the cosmos thus reappears in the Aristotelian view of *dikē* as the ordering of what is highest in nature. *Dikē* orders by the giving of just judgments, and justice (*dikaiosunē*) is the norm by which the *polis* is ordered, a norm which lacks application apart from the *polis*. So the first answer to the question of what it is that a human being separated from the *polis* is deprived is: *dikaiosunē*. But to be deprived of *dikaiosunē* involves certain other deprivations.

In the *Nicomachean Ethics* (Book VI, 1144a7–1145a11) Aristotle discusses the interdependence of practical intelligence (*phronēsis*) and the virtues of character. Because Aristotle believed that the possession of each of those virtues requires the possession of the others, he uses both the singular *aretē* and the plural *aretai* to speak of them. Virtue is required if there is to be a right choice of actions, and it is *phronēsis* which issues in right action; so there is no *phronēsis* without *aretē*. But equally there can be no *aretē* without *phronēsis*. The person whose actions are formed by both *aretē* and phronēsis has, according to the discussion in the *Politics,* developed originally, biologically given capacities, which could, however, have been developed instead so that they were put to the service of injustice. And this is how they would have been developed in a human being deprived of the law and justice which only the *polis* affords. Hence the *polis* is required for *aretē* and for *phronēsis,* as well as for *dikaiosunē.* Separated from the *polis,* what could have been a human being becomes instead a wild animal.

There is thus the sharpest of contrasts, on this Aristotelian view, between the human being disciplined and educated by the justice of the *polis* and the human being lacking such discipline and education in respect both of the virtue of justice and of the ability to engage in practical reasoning. The rules of justice cannot be understood as the expression of, nor will they serve to fulfill, the desires of those not yet educated into the justice of the *polis.* So the understanding of the rules of justice proposed by Thrasymachus and elaborated by Glaucon and Adeimantus has to be rejected, and with it not only that of later heirs of Thrasymachus, such as Hobbes, but also any account of justice or right which prescribes that the desires of every individual are equally to be taken into account in deciding what it is right to do. So all utilitarian doctrines which prescribe that *everyone* is to count for one, that everyone's desires are to be weighed equally in calculating utility and, with it, right, from Bentham to contemporary utilitarians and egalitarians, are deeply incompatible with Aristotle's standpoint. For what those deprived of the justice of the *polis* want cannot provide any measure for justice.

I suggested earlier that Plato, by contrast, on one highly plausible reading of the *Republic* does not take the justice of the individual to be dependent on that of the *polis,* but rather vice versa. But this reading ignores one of Plato's central theses, the full force of which emerges only in Books VI and VII: only an education within a community led, disciplined, and taught by philosophers will provide that knowledge of the forms, including the form of justice, without which one cannot be virtuous. The philosophical community has for the Plato of the *Republic* taken the place of the *polis* as the society within which one can become both just and practically intelligent, as in Plato's own life leadership of and participation in the community of the Academy had doubtless come to supply what he would otherwise have gained from participation in political activity. But to this it may be retorted: What about Socrates?

Socrates was after all, it may be urged, the paradigm of the just and practically intelligent human being, so far as Plato was concerned. Yet surely Socrates did not learn his justice and his practical intelligence *from* the Athenian *polis,* and he spent his life at odds with those who represented what educated Athenians took to be justice. There are two replies to this. We ought first to remember how in the *Crito* Socrates expresses his sense of gratitude for a debt which is more than can be repaid to the *polis* and to its laws for the part which they played in his education and upbringing. But even if, unlike Socrates himself, we viewed him as someone whose moral and intellectual virtues were not formed by participation in the life of the *polis,* we need not treat him as a counterexample to Aristotle's thesis in Book I of the *Politics.*

Aristotle, like most Greeks, recognized the existence of exceptional persons who themselves inhabiting communities in a state of some disorder were able to play the role of a lawgiver, providing their *polis* with a new constitution and by so doing to establish or reestablish possibilities of virtue in a *polis* which it had previously lacked. Such had been Solon at Athens and Lycurgus at Sparta. And Socrates may be regarded analogously as the founder in some sense of a philosophical community whose structure Plato institutionalized in the Academy. To recognize that the Academy or the Lyceum could to some degree at least discharge the functions which Aristotle ascribes only to the *polis* is not unimportant. For just because Aristotle's account of the nature of justice and of that of practical reasoning embeds them so thoroughly in the context of the practices of the *polis,* it would be all too easy to conclude that in societies such as our own, which not only are not organized in the form of a *polis,* but to whose culture the concept of a *polis* is quite alien, what Aristotle has to say about justice and practical reasoning must be irrelevant. But if at least those features of the *polis* which are minimally necessary for the exercise of justice and of practical rationality can be exhibited by forms of social order other than those of the *polis,* then the grounds for that change of irrelevance may fail. And I have suggested that in the account of institutionalized philosophical community which Plato offers us in the *Republic*—presumably an idealized view of the Academy—we have an example of just such a form of social order.

There is therefore no incompatibility between two of my purposes in giving an account of what Aristotle has to teach us about justice and about practical reasoning. One is to insist, for the overall interpretation of Aristotle's thought, upon the importance of his view that it is within one specific kind of social context that the intellectual and moral virtues of human beings characteristically have to be exercised and that apart from certain features of that kind of social context the concept of those virtues must for the most part lack application. The other is to claim that not only are Aristotle's arguments the outcome—the final outcome as he more or less takes them to be, the provisional outcome as I take them to be—of a sequence of thought which begins from Homer, but that they provide a framework on the basis of which and by means of which later thinkers can extend and continue Aristotle's enquiries in ways which are both unpredictably innovative and genuinely Aristotelian.

My thesis has of course been that the post-Homeric debates and conflicts within Athenian society of the fifth and fourth century generated not one subsequent tradition but two. But the non-Aristotelian, the anti-Aristotelian tradition, whose founding authors are the sophists and Thucydides, has now for the purposes of my immediate argument to be put on one side. What that argument does require is attention to two other features of Aristotle's philosophy which later turned out to be important in enabling it to generate a tradition of thought and enquiry. The first of these is a characteristic of dialectic as Aristotle understood it. I described earlier how it is by dialectical argument that we arrive at the formulation of the first principles, the *archai* of any enquiry or body of scientific thought. And it is also through the use of dialectical argument that we construct those deductive structures linking *archai* to the subordinate truths derived from them in an explanatory hierarchy.

The finished structure of a completed science is then an extended demonstrative argument, moving from those fundamental first truths which cannot but hold true of the subject matter of the particular science to their ultimate consequences in the realm of phenomena. Commentators who have not assigned sufficient importance to the fact that Aristotle's account of this kind of structure, in the *Posterior Analytics,* for example, is an account of what a science would be in its completed form, in which the final results of enquiry were presented, and *not* an account of what a science in the course of construction, a science as a form of enquiry, is, have tended to present Aristotle's own thought as though it were or claimed the status of a completed, or almost completed, system.

It is of crucial importance, however, not only that what Aristotle presents us with are accounts of sciences which are still in the process of construction, the ideal deductive and explanatory hierarchy furnishing a conception of the *telos* toward which scientific enquiry moves, but also that the dialectical procedures by means of which those tasks of construction are carried out never present us with a conclusion which is not open to further revision, elaboration, emendation, or refutation. Dialectic is essentially unfinished at any point in its development. If we do rest in a conclusion reached by dialectical argument, it is only because no experiences have led us to revise our belief that in our *epagōgai* so far, *nous* has indeed apprehended the needed universal concepts for the foundation of our *archai* and that no alternative opinion advanced has been able better to withstand objections than that at which we had already arrived. But the possibility of further dialectical development always remains open, and it is this which renders possible the work of a tradition elaborating upon, revising, emending, and even rejecting parts of Aristotle's own work, while still remaining fundamentally Aristotelian.

A second feature of Aristotle's philosophy turned out to be important in the formation of those particular Aristotelian traditions which flourished within medieval Islamic, Jewish, and Christian communities. Central to the argument which I am developing is that the *polis,* and indeed a particular conception of the *polis,* provided the framework within which Aristotle developed his accounts of justice, of practical reasoning, and of the relationship between them. But this must not be allowed to obscure the fact that Aristotle understood that movement from human potentiality to its actualization within the polis as exemplifying the metaphysical and theological character of a perfective universe. His is a universe structured in a hierarchical way—that is why the hierarchical structure of the sciences is appropriate for giving a realist account of such a universe—and each level of the hierarchy provides the matter in and through which the forms of the next higher level actualize and perfect themselves. The physical provides the material for biological formation, the biological the material for human formation. Efficient and material causes serve final and formal causes.

The question of whether or not this conception of the character of the universe has been refuted has often been equated with the question of whether or not the mechanics which late medieval physicists derived from Aristotle was refuted by Galileo and Newton. But the justification for this equation, as some later Scholastic thinkers understood, is very far from obvious. What is clear is that the Aristotelian scheme provides a link between science and the type of ultimate explanation provided by rational theology and that this kind of link, although far from absent in the science of Galileo and Newton, has disappeared in nineteenth- and twentieth-century science. But if this has rendered Aristotle's thought less credible in recent centuries, it was precisely the fact that he provided a warrant for rational theology, in connecting such a theology to the rest of the sciences, that assisted his assimilation by medieval Islamic, Jewish, and Christian thinkers.

What matters for my present argument is the claim that it is not merely the *polis* but the *kosmos* itself, the very order of things, which provides the context within which justice and practical rationality are related. What this claim amounts to can only emerge in the discussion of those later Aristotelians for whom it was so crucial. They for the most part read Aristotle's political and moral texts as part of the fabric of Aristotle's overall system of thought. The characteristic vice of their expositions at its worst was to treat those works ahistorically, seeing in Aristotle no development from one work to another, as though a completed system was there from the outset in Aristotle's mind and only had to be written down part by part. The characteristic vice of our expositions is quite the reverse. Our curricular divisions, as well as our scholarly habits of mind, lead us to treat the *Politics* as the concern for one sort of scholar, the *Posterior Analytics* as that of another, and so on. Even Aristotle's own remark, that ethics is a branch of politics, is ignored by those who discuss the *Nicomachean Ethics* in independence of the *Politics*. It will be one of the central tasks of my own account to suggest that this cannot be done without distorting our understanding of the *Nicomachean Ethics*.

Finally, it is perhaps necessary to say that it is the understanding of the *Nicomachean Ethics* with which I shall be principally concerned. Ancient and medieval traditions agree in treating the *Nicomachean Ethics* as the work in which Aristotle presents us with his most mature and best-developed opinions by contrast with the *Eudemian Ethics,* which has been almost universally understood to be an earlier work. Modern commentators have almost universally agreed with their predecessors. But recently Anthony Kenny (*The Aristotelian Ethics,* Oxford, 1978) has argued more powerfully than had been done previously that the *Eudemian Ethics* has at least as great a claim as the *Nicomachean Ethics,* and possibly a greater claim, to be regarded as the work in which Aristotle's thought takes on its mature and final form.

It is very clear that the *Eudemian Ethics* throws light upon Aristotle's views on some topics in a way and to an extent that the *Nicomachean Ethics* does not, and Kenny's argument puts every reader of Aristotle in his debt by what he says about these matters. But the difficulties in accepting Kenny's view that those books of the *Eudemian Ethics* which are not common to it and to the *Nicomachean Ethics* are later and better than the corresponding books of the *Nicomachean Ethics* are substantial. They have been set out by T. H. Irwin in a review of Kenny's book (*The Journal of Philosophy* LXXVII, 6, 1980), and I take them to provide adequate grounds for holding that Kenny's arguments should not be allowed to outweigh the testimony of tradition.

VII

Aristotle on Justice

Expositions of Aristotle on justice characteristically make little or no reference to his account of practical reasoning; and discussions of Aristotle on practical reasoning, or on the theory of action more generally, are apt to say nothing about justice. But since my central claim will be that Aristotle's thought on each of these topics is intelligible only in the light of what he says about the other, and both only in the light of what he says about the *polis,* I cannot explain why on Aristotle's view justice is a virtue and what is involved in being just without discussing the essential part which practical reasoning plays in someone's being just, or say what practical reasoning is without explaining why, on Aristotle's view, no one can be practically rational who is not just.

In a *polis* of free citizens the good citizen must have both the knowledge and the ability both to rule and to be ruled. To be good at ruling requires the same kind of excellence as is required in a good man. And we cannot be good at ruling without knowing how to be a good citizen under the rule of others. Therefore goodness in the *polis* (and we have already seen that human excellence requires the *polis*) requires the ability to exercise specific virtues *both* in the way in which one who is ruled over needs the virtues *and* in the way in which one who rules needs them. Examples of such needed virtues are *sōphrosunē* and *dikaiosunē.* So justice as one and the same virtue nonetheless imposes somewhat different requirements upon citizens in each of these different social roles (*Politics* III, 2, esp. 1277b 12–21).

The citizen *qua* citizen is required not only to obey but to respect the law. And the word '*dikaiosunē*' is used, so Aristotle says, in one of its senses, for everything which the law requires, that is, for the exercise of all the virtues by each citizen in his relationships to other citizens. This large and general requirement is to be distinguished from what is required by '*dikaiosunē*', used in a narrower sense, as the name of one particular virtue. In this sense *dikaiosunē* is of two kinds, distributive and corrective. Corrective justice has the function of restoring, so far as is possible, that just order which was partially destroyed by some unjust action or actions. Distributive justice consists in obedience to that principle of distribution which defines the order protected by corrective justice.

What principles in fact govern the distribution of goods within each particular *polis* differs, so Aristotle observes, from one type of political constitution to another. And when we ascribe justice to an action or an agent in virtue of an act or a disposition conforming to the principle of distribution constitutionally established in that person's particular *polis,* all that we are ascribing is justice relative to that principle. The justice which is ascribed absolutely—that is, without qualification —is the justice which accords with the principle of distribution which is or would be established in the best type of *polis* (*Politics* VII, 1238b 36–39). What type of *polis* is that?

It is unsurprisingly that in which the best citizens rule and in which what is rewarded is virtue. Everyone, says Aristotle, agrees that justice in distribution must be in accordance with desert of some kind; where they disagree is upon what kind of desert it should be. Different types of *polis* and different parties within a *polis* hold correspondingly different views of desert. Democracy favors equal allocations between all free citizens, and oligarchy a restriction in the distribution of certain goods, the goods of public office, to classes privileged by reason of either wealth or birth. But the type of constitution favored by Aristotle, and called by him 'aristocracy', rewards according to virtue (*NE* V, 1131a 24–29). Aristotle's description of this type of constitution depends in part unfortunately upon his belief that participation in certain types of occupation—those of artisans, merchants, and farmers—precludes the requisite exercise of the virtue necessary for participation in the active life of the best kind of *polis* (*Politics* VII, 1328b 34–1329a 2). Although members of the groups which are so occupied discharge functions necessary for sustaining the life of the *polis* and are to be parts of the *polis,* they are not to be citizens. One of the errors of democracy, on Aristotle's view, is that it is unselective in admitting members of all these classes to citizenship; the error of oligarchy is that it selects by making distinctions which are irrelevant to virtue.

Modern readers of Aristotle often understandably disapprove of these exclusions by Aristotle, just as they also disapprove of the exclusion from citizenship of women (Aristotle believed that women could not exercise the requisite control over their emotions) and of Aristotle's justification of slavery (Aristotle believed that some people by nature are incapable of ruling themselves and therefore are natural slaves). The crucial question is: What kind of mistake was involved in these exclusions and to what extent do they damage Aristotle's claims? Part of Aristotle's error may well have arisen from a kind of fallacious reasoning typical of ideologies of irrational domination. Its premises are often enough in part true and are indeed made true by the effects of irrational domination. Those reduced to the condition of slavery do to some large extent become irresponsible, lacking in initiative, anxious to avoid work, and incapable of exercising authority. Women faced with incompatible role demands and deprived of education—required as changing circumstances dictate to be as quietly compliant as Ismene or Chrysothemis *and* as resourcefully loyal to family as Antigone or Electra—will often enough exhibit strong and undisciplined emotion. Aristotle's mistake, and the mistake of others who have reasoned similarly, was not to understand how domination of a certain kind is in fact the cause of those characteristics of the dominated which are then invoked to justify unjustified domination.

It is therefore important to ask whether such assertions can be excised from Aristotle's thought without denying his central claims about the best kind of *polis*. And it seems clear that they can (although for another view see chapter 4, Susan M. Okin *Women in Western Political Thought*, Princeton, 1979). For the claim that in the best kind of *polis* the distribution of public offices and the honoring of achievement will be in accordance with excellence, that is, with virtue, is independent of any thesis about what kinds of persons are or are not capable of excellence. What Aristotle's invalid arguments direct our attention to is that in the best kind of *polis* the participation of women or of artisans would require a restructuring of their occupational and social roles of a kind inconceivable to Aristotle himself, although envisaged, in the case of women at least, by Plato. Moreover, it may well be the case that there *are* occupations which are peculiarly suited to the exercise of civic virtue—Thomas Jefferson thought that the life of a yeoman farmer was of this kind—or which, by focusing upon goals inimical to those of the best kind of *polis,* are peculiarly inimical to virtue— Dante thought that this was true of banking.

What therefore remains so far at least unscathed in Aristotle's account of the best kind of *polis* is the thesis that a political constitution which is designed to promote the exercise of virtue in political life will need to concern itself with the occupational structure of the *polis*. It is also clear that although Aristotle's account of the hierarchical ordering of the best kind of *polis* rests on certain mistakes, the best kind of *polis* will have an hierarchical order. This is because it has to school its citizens in the exercise of the virtues. The hierarchy of the best kind of *polis* is one of teaching and of learning, not of irrational domination.

Aristotle thinks of human life in the best kind of *polis* in terms of stages: childhood to puberty, puberty to twenty-four, the life of the adult in full vigor, and the life of the experienced older adult. In both the earlier stages the young person needs to receive education into both the virtues of character and those of intelligence. As a young man the citizen owes the *polis* his service as a soldier. Later he owes it his service in public office, including both administrative magistracies and service as juror in the courts and as legislator in the assembly. As he moves from role to role, both as one who is ruled and one who rules, he will need, if he is to merit honor, to learn how to exercise a whole range of virtues. But in all of them he will especially need to learn both to understand the principle of just distribution and to be moved by a disposition to abide by it. To do so he will have to come to recognize who owes which good to what persons in a variety of situations, something which in Aristotle's view requires experience and habituation, as well as right reason.

Justice thus occupies a key position among the virtues. Because of the different types of achievement in different types of situation, because of the different character of the goods which are at stake in different types of situations, it will be impossible to judge justly, and consequently impossible to act justly, unless one can also judge correctly in respect of the whole range of the virtues. The courage and skill required in military actions, the temperateness required in respect of pleasures, the liberality or munificence which deserves well of the *polis* because of the provision of resources for public use, the intellectual and aesthetic excellence which makes this dramatist or lyric poet deserve the prize rather than that, all these may at different times have to be judged rightly if a just judgment is to be made. But since on Aristotle's view it is impossible generally to judge consistently aright concerning a particular virtue without possessing the virtue, it seems to follow that someone who makes just judgments must not only be just but also temperate, courageous, generous, and the like. This is perhaps why in the key passage from the *Politics* which I cited earlier (1253a 31–37) Aristotle equates the absence of *dikaiosunē* with that of *aretē* itself.

Distributive justice then consists of the application of a principle of desert to a variety of types of situation. But concepts of desert have application only in contexts in which two conditions are satisfied. There must be some common enterprise to the achievement of whose goals those who are taken to be more deserving have contributed more than those who are taken to be less deserving; and there must be a shared view both of how such contributions are to be measured and of how rewards are to be ranked. Both these conditions are satisfied in the life of the *polis*. It is an enterprise which aims at the achievement of human good as such, and to this shared enterprise different occupations and different public offices contribute in different ways and to different degrees. Thus that achievement has to be measured by considering both how important the role or office discharged by some particular citizen is and how well he has performed in it. The structure of the *polis* also embodies agreement upon how achievement is to be measured, not only in its ranking of the goods achieved by those filling different offices and roles—general, tragic poet, farmer, orator, stonemason, or whatever—and by its ranking of honors conferred, but also negatively by its scale of punishments and deprivations.

What these socially embodied agreements which are partially constitutive of a *polis* succeed in integrating and ordering are all those goods specific to the forms of activity in which post-Homeric Greeks had come to recognize impersonal and objective standards of excellence: warfare and combat, athletic and gymnastic performance, poetry of various kinds, rhetoric, architecture, and sculpture, farming and a variety of other *technai*, and the organization and sustaining of the *polis* itself. So the goodness of a citizen is in key part constituted by his goodness *qua* horseman or *qua* soldier or *qua* dramatic poet, and the goodness of someone who is a craftsman is in key part his goodness *qua* flutemaker or bridlemaker. Activities are hierarchically ordered by the *for the sake of* relationship: excellence at flutemaking is for the sake of excellence at fluteplaying, excellence at bridlemaking for the sake of excellence at horseriding, excellence at horseriding in part for the sake of military excellence, military excellence for the sake of political excellence.

Political excellence and above all the excellence of the legislator consist in being good at ordering goods both generally and in particular types of situation. It does not follow, and it is not in Aristotle's view the case, that the only goods at which the *polis* aims are political. The *polis*, at least the best kind of *polis*, is directed toward achieving all the goods of its citizens, and for human beings the highest good to be achieved, that which in an individual life is that for the sake of which all other activity is undertaken, is *theōria*, a certain kind of contemplative understanding. The virtuous activities which enable someone to serve the *polis* well culminate and are perfected in an intellectual achievement which is internal to the activity of thinking (*Politics* VII, 1325b 14–23).

Thus there is no incompatibility between the pursuit of civic and the pursuit of individual virtue. The virtue with which the good man discharges his social roles carries him forward finally to the perfecting of his own soul in contemplative activity. And the goods internal to contemplative activity, those achieved when human intelligence apprehends that for whose sake all else in the universe exists and so completes its own activity, are such that in the light of them the excellences achieved in exercising the rest of virtue—those of the life of political virtue, in which *dikaiosunē* and *phronēsis* are central—are recognized as secondary (*NE* 1178a9). The happiness achieved in political life is purely human; the happiness of contemplative activity moves to a higher level, "divine in comparison with human life" (*NE* 1177b32).

We are now in a position to situate Aristotle's claims about justice within that Greek debate which I have characterized in terms of a rivalry between the protagonists of the goods of excellence and those of effectiveness. Aristotle says that we may in our activities aim at the fine or noble (*to kalon*) or the expedient or the pleasurable, and the good man does indeed aim at the fine, which he values for its own sake as well as for its part in constituting *eudaimonia*. But this does not mean that the good man does not on occasion aim at the expedient, just as it does not mean that he does not give a due place to pleasure in his life. The difference between the virtuous person and others lies rather in this, that what is expedient for the virtuous person, just as what gives pleasure to him, is very different from what is expedient either for the vicious person or for the person of merely undisciplined desire. What someone takes to be to his advantage depends upon what he is aiming at, and the aims of the good man are very different from those of either the vicious or the undisciplined (*akratēs*). So that even to raise from within Aristotle's framework the question of whether the goods of expediency or advantage are to be treated as overriding is to invite the rejoinder: What kind of person's expediency or advantage?

From the standpoint of a protagonist of the goods of effectiveness— a Callicles or the Athenian delegates on Melos—this rejoinder has no force. For his or her conception of effectiveness or advantage is one that has to be definable independently of and antecedently to any particular account of the virtues or excellences, such as Aristotle's, since it is that definition which is to provide the standard by which the claims of all such accounts are to be judged. Thus, at the core of this conception is a notion of the human individual as such with *whatever* desires or goods he or she may have as providing the measure of value, an individual as yet innocent of determinate beliefs about the human good or about moral rules, since it is this individual who has to decide what beliefs on these matters it is rational for him or her to adopt, given his or her desires and goals. From Aristotle's point of view this is to make the standard of right action in the *polis,* not what the good man would do, but what anyone who consulted his or her own interest, whether of virtuous or vicious character, would do; it is precisely the error of both oligarchies and democracies that they permit participation in political deliberation and decision-making to just such persons. From the point of view of the protagonists of the goods of effectiveness the *polis* is primarily always an arena of rival interests, whether this fact is acknowledged or not, and each type of *polis* can be expected to express the particular interests of the class of persons who dominate it, just as Thrasymachus argues in *Republic,* Book I. Thus the disagreement between the two sides is not only over the comparative ranking of the goods of effectiveness compared with those of excellence but even more fundamentally over the question of how and within what conceptual framework both excellence and effectiveness are to be understood.

From Aristotle's point of view the standpoint of the protagonists of the goods of effectiveness is one which precludes rationality in action. For it is the case—and here I have to look ahead to Aristotle's account of practical reasoning—that on Aristotle's view being virtuous is a prerequisite for such rationality. But even to say this without further elucidation makes it clear that for Aristotle the content of the notion of rational decision has to be very different from what it is for the protagonists of the goods of effectiveness. For them rational action can only be action based upon a rational calculation of what means will at least cost to the satisfaction of their desires achieve the ends proposed to them by their dominant desires, whatever those desires may be. Yet from an Aristotelian standpoint no such calculation can be rational. Why not?

The virtues are, on Aristotle's view, dispositions to act in specific ways for specific reasons. Education into the virtues involves the mastery, the disciplining, and the transformation of desires and feelings. This education enables one to exercise the virtues so that one not only values each of the virtues for its own sake, but understands the exercise of the virtues as also being for the sake of being *eudaimon,* of enjoying that kind of life which constitutes the good and the best life for human beings. And the knowledge which enables one to understand why this kind of life is in fact the best is only to be had as a result of having become a virtuous person. But without this knowledge rational judgment and rational action are impossible. To be uneducated in the virtues is precisely to be unable as yet to judge rightly what is good or best for oneself.

There is an important analogy between how a capacity for right judgment in respect of the good life for human beings as such is developed within the context provided by the *polis* and how capacities for more particular species of right judgment are developed in the context of all those more particular forms of activity within which standards of excellence are recognized. Just as an apprenticeship in sculpture or architecture is required in order to recognize what excellent performance in these arts consists in, just as training in athletic skills is necessary to recognize adequately what excellence in athletic performance is, so a capacity for identifying and ordering the goods of the good life, the achievement of which involves the ordering of all these other sets of goods, requires a training of character in and into those excellences, a type of training whose point emerges only in the course of the training. Learning of this kind, as of other kinds, is what the uneducated, left to themselves, do not and cannot want: "those engaged in learning are not at play; learning is accompanied by pain" (*Politics* VIII, 1239a29).

It follows that for those who have not yet been educated into the virtues the life of the virtues will necessarily seem to lack rational justification; the rational justification of the life of virtue within the community of the *polis* is available only to those who already participate more or less fully in that life. The *Nicomachean Ethics* and the *Politics* should therefore be read as directed to a particular type of audience, that composed of the mature citizens of a *polis*. They alone will have had the kind of experience which will enable them to understand the standards and values implicit in the life of any tolerably well-ordered *polis,* standards and values which when made explicit provide the principles of order for the constitution and the institutions of the best kind of *polis,* as Aristotle presents it. The immature are excluded from this audience, because not yet sufficiently experienced or disciplined in respect of their passions (*NE* 1095a2–8), while those outside the *polis* will have had the wrong sort of education. And of course there are examples of the *polis* in which fundamental mistakes either about the *telos* of human life or about the virtues as means to that *telos* result in the more or less systematic miseducation of the citizens. How then does it stand with *us* as modern readers of Aristotle? It is clear that at the very least we are required in the first instance to identify ourselves imaginatively with the standpoint of the citizen of a well-ordered *polis*. A modern would-be critic of Aristotle, who necessarily has had a political and cultural education very different from that presupposed in his readers by Aristotle, will be unable to understand, let alone criticize, Aristotle's theses unless he or she discards for the moment at least the standpoint of modernity. For even Aristotle's vocabulary cannot be correctly rendered into an idiom which presupposes the characteristic beliefs of modernity. Consider, for example, the difference between Aristotle's answer to the question of what the vice of injustice consists in and characteristically modern answers.

We have already noticed that justice, like the other virtues, is valued *both* for its own sake *and* for the sake of the *telos,* the kind of life which it is best for human beings to live, because justice, like the other virtues, enables us to avoid those vicious states of character incompatible with the living out of that kind of life. To each virtue there correspond two such vicious states of character. To act virtuously is to act in accordance with a mean, a middle state between the two extremes of vice. The two extremes in the case of *dikaiosunē* are that of acting so as to aggrandize oneself, whether one's deserts entitle one to it or not, and acting so as to suffer injustice voluntarily, that is, to undergo undeserved harm or less than one's deserved good. The former, Aristotle remarks, is a more important vice than the latter, and he sometimes writes as if simply equating injustice with that vice. Its name is *pleonexia* (1129b9), and Hobbes may have been the first writer in English to explain '*pleonexia*' as meaning "a desire of more than their share" (*Leviathan* 15). But although when someone commits injustice because of this character trait, often enough the injustice will involve trying to take more than one's share, what is due to one, the character trait itself, *pleonexia,* is no more or no less than simple acquisitiveness, acting so as to have more as such.

In his discussion of the place of money in human life in Book I of the *Politics* Aristotle identifies the mistakes made by those who exemplify one version of this trait, those who seek to acquire more and more money without limit: "The cause of this condition is zeal for life, but not for the good life" (1257b41). Such a pursuit of wealth without limit may be either for its own sake or for the sake of the limitless bodily pleasures which, it is believed by some, can be procured by limitless wealth. In either case the character trait exhibited in and developed by such activity will not be directed in accordance with that mean which guides toward the *telos* of the good life for human beings.

Just as Hobbes' translation of '*pleonexia*' is misleading rather than mistaken, and for that reason all the more dangerous, so is the recent translation by T. H. Irwin (who also cites Hobbes: *The Nicomachean*

Ethics, Indianapolis, 1985, pp. 331 and 413), who uses the English word 'greed'. But 'greed' is, as Irwin notes, the name of a type of desire, whereas '*pleonexia*' names a disposition to engage in a type of activity; and in English we treat 'greed' as the name of one motive for activities of acquisition, not as the name of the tendency to engage in such activities simply for their own sake. What such translations of '*pleonexia*' conceal from us is the extent of the difference between Aristotle's standpoint on the virtues and vices, and more especially his standpoint on justice and the dominant standpoint of peculiarly modern societies. For the adherents of that standpoint recognize that acquisitiveness is a character trait indispensable to continuous and limitless economic growth, and one of their central beliefs is that continuous and limitless economic growth is a fundamental good. That a systematically lower standard of living ought to be preferred to a systematically higher standard of living is a thought incompatible with either the economics or the politics of peculiarly modern societies. So prices and wages have come to be understood as unrelated — and indeed in a modern economy could not be related — to desert in terms of labor, and the notion of a just price or a just wage in modern terms makes no sense. But a community which was guided by Aristotelian norms would not only have to view acquisitiveness as a vice but would have to set strict limits to growth insofar as that is necessary to preserve or enhance a distribution of goods according to desert.

Justice thus imposes negative constraints, but they are constraints upon the vicious and upon the *enkratic,* the disciplined person, not upon the virtuous. The unjust person will not be able to achieve his goals without violating the canons of distribution of goods according to desert, and what gives such persons pleasure will to some significant degree be denied to them by such a distribution of goods. The *enkratic* person is the person who has learned how to control his desires, so that the doing of virtuous acts is not rendered impossible by those desires, but the desires themselves have not yet been transformed by the virtues. Thus to some degree at least *enkratic* persons act virtuously in spite of, not because of, their desires. And such persons will experience the exercise of virtues in general and of justice in particular as a matter of negative psychological constraints. But it will not be so with the virtuous, who differ from the *enkratic* in that they no longer take pleasure in what is contrary to virtue and indeed take pleasure in the exercise of the virtues themselves. Just actions are among those which the virtuous want to perform for their own sake as well as for the sake of the part they play in constituting and effecting the good life for human beings.

To say that just actions are to be pursued for their own sake is to say, not that nothing can outweigh the requirements of justice, but that the whole notion of weighing the requirements of justice against something else is from the standpoint of the virtuous a mistake. For that an action should be just is not merely one among the preferences of the virtuous person, competing as a requirement with other preferences. It is rather that being just is taken to be a condition of achieving any good at all and that being just requires caring about and valuing being just, even if it were to lead to no further good. It is in part in this aristocratic carelessness about consequences that the nobility, the fineness of the exercise of such virtues resides. It was this trait, this elegance of style which virtue possesses, which the Spartans at Thermopylae exhibited when they combed their hair before fighting to their deaths (Herodotus VII, 207; my example, not Aristotle's); and this same fineness belongs in appropriate measure to every just action performed just because it is just.

The person who violates the mean of justice, not by *pleonexia,* but by the action of taking less of some particular good than is his due, may well have done what is in fact unjust—although Aristotle notes that he may have behaved in this way because he had thereby obtained more of some other good (1136b 21–22)—but he will not have voluntarily inflicted injustice upon himself. For no one could do that since no one could knowingly inflict unqualified harm upon oneself, and to do injustice is to do unqualified harm. This indeed must be so if justice is to be valued for its own sake.

There is a crucial distinction, of course, between a just action performed because it is just, the kind of action which is performed by a genuinely just person, and a just action performed from some other motive. There are some types of action which it is always unjust to perform, actions by their nature unjust. But the motive to abstain even from actions of this type will not always be justice as a character trait; fear of punishment or obloquy may so motivate, and such fear may itself be either an expression of a virtuous respect for the laws and for the good opinion of the virtuous or an expression of some vicious character trait, such as cowardice. It is indeed because just actions can be performed by those who are not, or not yet just, that education into the virtue of justice has the structure that it does.

We become just by first performing just acts (*NE* 1103a 31–1103b 2), acts which *ex hypothesi* are not yet expressions of the character trait of justice and which we cannot ourselves as yet rationally justify. How then do we know *which* acts to perform and what can be our motivation in performing them? Plainly we have to learn from those others who already possess the moral education which we so far lack which acts are to be performed as just, and it is presumably in order to please those others that we act in accordance with their precepts. What we will learn from those precepts is that certain rules of distribution are always to be observed and that, conformably with this, certain types of action which would always violate such rules are never to be performed.

Having learned how to apply the predicates 'just' and 'unjust' in such cases, we shall have to go on to learn how their use has to be extended to characterize cases in which types of action otherwise and generally, but not universally, prescribed or prohibited as just or unjust require a judgment which takes account of circumstances which provide grounds for a judgment which would in the absence of that type of circumstance be false. And in learning when circumstances are and when they are not thus relevant, we shall be learning how to move from judgment in simpler to judgment in more complex cases. This complexity of judgment which justice requires is the kind of complexity which makes enquiry into the nature of justice less of an accurate science than is, for example, mathematics. Aristotle ranks enquiries and bodies of knowledge, both theoretical and practical, in terms of the degree of accuracy (*akribeia*) appropriate to each (1094b 11–16). Politics as a whole, the science of which enquiry into the nature of justice is a part, the study of which issues in and is expressed in good practice, good activity, is ranked with the less rather than the more accurate sciences. What then does Aristotle mean by "accuracy"?

A science is accurate insofar as "it is concerned with things which are prior in definition and simpler" (*Metaphysics* M 1078a 9–10), and elsewhere Aristotle makes it clear that it is insofar as a conception derived from the basic concepts and premises of a science (those prior in definition) has to be qualified in the light of additional independent premises that it is less simple and hence less accurate (see *NE* 1148a 10–11, *Metaphysics* Z 1030a 28–4, and the excellent elucidation of this area of Aristotle's thought in chapter 4 of J.D.G. Evans *Aristotle's Concept of Dialectic,* Cambridge, 1977, pp. 85–89). As one moves from the simpler to the more complex cases, therefore, in applying the terms 'just' and 'unjust', one needs to be more and more adept in knowing how to bring to bear the relevant additional independent premises. Knowledge of these premises is acquired only through experience. This is why the young, who as yet lack the relevant range of experience, are not yet capable of embarking upon ethical enquiry, but must rather first cultivate those habits which will enable them not only to acquire that range of experience, but also to discipline their passions, so ridding them of their other disqualification for ethical enquiry (*NE* 1094b 28–1095a8).

We can understand what is involved here better if we characterize this process of moral education, using a notion of which Aristotle himself does not make use in this connection, that of a rule. What the novice learns from his instructors is how to apply a relatively simple rule; certain types of action are characterized as just, certain as unjust, and the novice acquires the disposition to do what the rule prescribes by understanding how to identify the relevant range of acts and by habitually performing them. The novice is next able to learn what the *logos* of justice is: how to supply a rational justification for the performance of just acts and to find application for that justification to a range of cases not covered by the original formulation of the rule of justice. What the Aristotelian account requires here in the way of successful learning is precisely what the Platonic Socrates showed time and again by the use of *elenchos* that his interlocutors had hitherto failed to learn. Consider one Platonic example.

The elementary formulation of the rule of justice requires that if I am in possession of something which justly belongs to another, I should return it to that other. But what if that other has become mentally deranged and the possession in question is a knife? How is the rule of justice to be formulated so as to apply in such a case? What has to be supplied is a *logos* which will provide the *same* fundamental justification *both* for the application of the original formulation of the rule to the central cases to which it clearly did apply *and* for the treatment of this new type of case. There is no objection to understanding the outcome of this process of learning in terms of the acquisition of a more and more sophisticated ability to supply a rational justification for the application of a more and more complex rule or set of rules. But it is crucial also to understand that neither the movement from a less to a more sophisticated ability to judge how the rules of justice apply and to justify those judgments nor the corresponding movement from the use of simpler versions of the rule of justice to the use of more complex versions are themselves rule-governed forms of activity. How then are they governed?

The movement of learning consists in the development of at least two related sets of dispositions, two virtues, that of justice itself and that of *phronēsis,* of practical intelligence. *Phronēsis* is the exercise of a capacity to apply truths about what it is good for such and such a type of person or for persons as such to do generally and in certain types of situation to oneself on particular occasions. The *phronimos* is able to judge both which truths are relevant to him in his particular situation and from that judgment and from his perception of the relevant aspects of himself and his situation to act rightly. The virtue of justice, like any other moral virtue, cannot be exercised without *phronēsis* also being exercised. For truths about what is just are a subclass of truths about what is good, and the ability to embody them in action is the *phronētic* ability to embody these truths in action in the requisite way in particular cases.

That Aristotle did not consider *phronētic* activity itself to be rule-governed—even although it involves, in the case of justice at least, the application and extension of rules—is clear. For in exercising *phronēsis* we understand why this particular situation makes the exercise of some particular moral virtue or the application of some particular rule of justice in acting in some particular way the right thing to do. And there are no rules for generating this kind of practically effective understanding of particulars. Aristotle draws an analogy with geometry: "it (*phronēsis*) is at the opposite extreme to *nous*. For *nous* is concerned with definitions of which there is no (further) account, while *phronēsis* is of what is ultimate not in respect of knowledge, but of perception, not the perceptions of each of the senses, but that by which we perceive that the ultimate element in some mathematical problem is a triangle; for there too there will be a terminus" (*Nicomachean Ethics* 1142a 25–29). The analogy is with the geometer who in discovering how to construct a given type of plane figure has to identify the basic elements from which he has to begin and who has no rule to tell him which these are (I am indebted to David Wiggins' illuminating paraphrase of this passage in 'Deliberation and Practical Reason' *Proceedings of the Aristotelian Society 1975–6,* reprinted in J. Raz (ed.) *Practical Reasoning,* Oxford, 1978, p. 148). Aristotle discusses a parallel problem in arithmetic in the *Posterior Analytics* (II, 96a 33–b1) when he analyzes the concept of a triad into its elements, the concepts of number, odd and prime in two senses. So also in practical reasoning the identification of the relevant particular elements of a situation cannot be rule-governed. That there *must* in evaluative judgment and action be some such non-rule-governed form of activity is also clear for a reason which Aristotle never discusses, perhaps because he did not consider these issues in terms of the concept of a rule. Let us suppose that *phronēsis* were itself to be rule-governed, that in exercising it we not only on occasion apply rules to particular cases, but that we have and follow rules in so applying rules. Then either these second-order rules will themselves be applied by means of the exercise of some non-rule-governed capacity or some third-order set of rules will be involved in knowing how to apply the second-order rules, and so on. So we are faced with these alternatives: *either* we have to posit an infinite hierarchy of rules *or* there is a kind of activity which may involve the application of rules to instances, but which is not itself rule-governed. And since there are compelling reasons for rejecting the former, we have good reasons to accept the latter conclusion. But if this conclusion is to be used to support an Aristotelian standpoint, then it is important to be able to say what it is about this kind of non-rule-governed activity which renders it capable of rational justification.

In attempting to make phronētic judgments about particular cases I can make mistakes. My judgments can be false or true. A false judgment will be one which does not identify correctly the good or goods which are at stake in this particular situation, either because I have misunderstood the situation or because my understanding of the relevant good or goods, for example, justice, is inadequate. It follows that true judgments will be those which make or presuppose a correct account of the relevant good or goods, of their relevance to this particular situation, and of the situation itself. So to move from a lesser or a greater ability to make true judgments will require an increasingly adequate conception of the good and the best for human beings and of the range of goods, such as justice, which are constitutive parts of the good and the best. What, on Aristotle's view, makes one such conception more adequate than another?

Even to sketch in outline a compelling answer to this question is impossible without going further not only into Aristotle's view of practical reasoning but also into his view of the relationship of practical to theoretical reasoning than is practicable at this stage of the argument. But it is possible to say this: the *telos* of theoretical enquiry in ethics is to elaborate a fully adequate and rationally defensible conception of the good and the best; the more nearly such a conception is approached, the greater will be the range of political and moral phenomena — actions, judgments, dispositions, forms of political organization — which prove susceptible of explanation within the conceptual and theoretical scheme whose ultimate and basic principle is the conception of the good and the best; and the methods of argument which Aristotle uses both in elaborating and in justifying such explanations are in part demonstrative and in part those types of dialectical argument discussed in the *Topics,* including *epagōgē.*

So in extending the range of judgments concerning, for example, justice, by moving from the simpler to the more complex, the *phronimos* does not and cannot make use of any rule or criterion; but nonetheless there is a standpoint from which the adequacy of his judgments can be evaluated. Retrospectively surveyed, the judgments and actions of the *phronimos*—that is, if the *phronimos* is indeed judging and acting as a *phronimos* should—will turn out to be such as would be required by an adequate conception of the good and the best. How then is an adequate conception of the good and the best to be acquired?

In trying to answer this question we confront what has seemed to some a paradox. In order to become adequately *phronētic* in judgment and in action, it is necessary to be guided by an adequate conception of the good and the best. Yet in order to achieve an adequate conception of the good and the best, it seems necessary first to be able to perform the requisite *epagōgē* on those experiences in which we have made right phronetic judgments. We cannot judge and act rightly unless we aim at what is in fact good; we cannot aim at what is good except on the basis of experience of right judgment and action. But the appearances of paradox and circularity are deceptive. In developing both our conception of the good and the habit of right judgment and action—and neither can be adequately developed without the other—we gradually learn to correct each in the light of the other, moving dialectically between them.

Two features of this dialectical movement are especially worth remarking. It is in practice one of Aristotle's criteria for a successful correction of a false view that we are able to explain why we might expect such a view to be generated if our overall standpoint is correct. So Aristotle's dismissal of the life of money-making as the good life for human beings in Book I of the *Nicomachean Ethics* is reinforced by his account of how the life of money-making generates false beliefs about the *telos* of human life in Book I of the *Politics*.

More importantly the use which we make of *epagōgē,* in moving from particular examples of what we take to be right judgment and action to a view of what the good and the best consist in, is supplemented by that other resource of dialectic, the confronting of alternative and rival opinions, especially of those most plausibly and cogently argued, by each other, so that we may arrive at a conclusion as to which of these best survives the strongest objections which can be advanced on the basis of the others. This is the type of enquiry concerning rival and competing opinions about what the life of *eudaimonia* is which Aristotle conducts in Book I of the *Nicomachean Ethics,* so illustrating his thesis (*Topics* I, 101a 36–101b 2) that it is in the study of the first principles of each science that dialectic finds one of its principal uses.

The *phronimos* can then always look forward to the vindication of his present judgments by their according with that conception of the good and the best which dialectical enquiry establishes. But at the time at which he has to judge and act he may not yet be in a position to invoke such a conception and so may well have no standard external to his own judgment to which to appeal. Nonetheless, he will discover, as we noticed earlier, that as he develops the virtue of *phronēsis,* his judgments will increasingly be informed by a grasp of modifying and circumstantial considerations which did not inform his original simpler rule-governed judging. What will this amount to in judgments concerning justice? Justice is a matter of what is fair, that is, of *to ison,* the equal. What the equality of justice consists in is in like cases being treated alike and in proportional differences in merit being treated according to that proportion. So a distribution is just, if and only if, it preserves between two cases where the recipients are unequal in merit a proportionately unequal distribution (*NE* 1131a 10–1131b 24). The application of this kind of rule-governed proportionality in distributive justice obviously presupposes a rank-ordering of actions as meritorious or undeserving and a rank-ordering of goods to be distributed, while in corrective justice it presupposes a rank-ordering of harms and deprivations which may be imposed as more or less serious punishments.

A judge who administers the laws which express and enforce this conception of justice is of course, insofar as his decisions and judgments are governed by those laws, rule-governed in his activity; but notice that those rules, the laws, must have been the work of some legislator or legislators who in formulating those same laws had no such rules to guide them. And a judge will from time to time be confronted with cases about which the existing laws yield no clear answer or perhaps no answer at all. In those situations the judge too lacks rules and must exercise *phronēsis,* just as the legislator had originally done. The area into which the judge moves in so acting is that of what Aristotle calls *epieikeia,* that of reasonable, although not rule-governed, judgment. In the specifically legal context of Aristotle's discussion in which '*epieikeia*' is related to '*dikaiosunē*'—Aristotle says that *epieikeia* is not the same as justice, but it is not generically different either (*NE* 1137a 33–34)—'*epieikeia*' is usually translated by 'equity' (see also *Topics* VI, 1141a 16, for the same type of use of '*epieikeia*') And since "equity" is used in English law to name something very like that type of exercise of legal judgment to which Aristotle is referring, it is understandable that English scholars should have so translated it. Nonetheless, that

"*epieikeia*" does not mean "equity" is quite clear not only from its range
of uses by other authors but also by Aristotle's use of it and its cognates
in other contexts (e.g., *Politics* 1308b 27 and 1452b 34 or *Nicomachean
Ethics* 1107b 11), where the most generally apt translation is "reasonable." Why does that matter?

Aristotle remarks that sometimes we use "*epieikēs*" as though it were
a synonym for "good" (*NE* 1137a 35–1137b 1) and insists that "*epieikeia*"
is aptly used as the name for a kind of justice which corrects that justice which would consist in the application of already laid down rules
(1137b 11–24). But in Book VI Aristotle also makes it clear that he takes
it that the whole area of life with which *phronēsis* is concerned can
be characterized as that in which *epieikeia* is required (1143a 19–24 and
28–32). Thus, what the judge does in the case where he cannot simply
follow and apply a rule provided by a legislator, but has to go beyond
that rule in some way, exemplifies what more generally any *phronimos*
must from time to time do, not only in order to be just but in order
to exemplify any of the virtues adequately. What is said about *epieikeia*
in purely legal contexts holds of practical life and reasoning in general.
Thus Aristotle's discussion of the reasoning involved in being just exemplifies his view of rational agency in general. And this is true of some
other features of his discussion of justice.

Since the possession of any virtue requires an ability to distinguish
between what is good *haplōs* from what is good only relative to some
particular situation or some particular set of persons, so, as I noticed
earlier, being just requires an ability to distinguish what is just *haplōs*
from what is just relative to the provisions of a particular constitution.
Any adequate grasp of this distinction will require a more general understanding of the distinction between the natural and the conventional
elements in justice. There is indeed natural justice (*NE* 1134b 18–1135a 5),
that which is invariant from city to city, and the standard of natural
justice is the justice of the best kind of *polis*. But in every city, including
the best, some elements of justice must be such as are assigned by local
convention, for example, the precise ransom to be given for a prisoner
or the way in which the successful discharge of a particular public office
is to be honored. Note that to say that certain penalties or rewards are
assigned to desert by convention does not entail that it is only a matter
of conventional rather than natural justice that the citizens of a particular city should obey their own conventions. Aristotle says too little
about the distinction between natural and conventional justice for us
to be other than cautious in drawing inferences from what he does say.
But it would be consistent with what he asserts to hold that natural

justice would generally require the citizens of a constitutional *polis* to abide by their own conventions. And Aristotle certainly believed that citizens were bound by their regard for justice to respect the terms agreed upon in commercial treaties or treaties of military alliance between their own *polis* and some other.

Aristotle also says that although there is natural justice, everything in justice is susceptible of variation (1134b29–30), whether natural or conventional: that is, as a matter of fact, human beings differ in their formulation of the rules of justice, so that there is no formulation of any such rule which is universally held—except among the gods. But here he is presumably not challenging his own view that there is natural justice, particularly since earlier in Book II he had asserted bluntly that certain types of action and passion are blamed as bad in themselves (the adjective used is *phaulos*). The passions thus unconditionally condemned are *Schadenfreude,* shamelessness and envy; the types of action similarly condemned are adultery, theft, and murder (1107a8–14). These are the kind of actions that will have been prohibited in his code of laws by any virtuous legislator; judgments based upon them, whether of judges or of ordinary citizens, will be applications of those rules which generally at least can be made without *epieikeia.* But it is what the younger citizen learns from those rules about what justice and other virtues consist in, about the classes of action which are prohibited or enjoined as such, which provides the material both for that exercise of judgment which when fully trained becomes *phronēsis* and for that process of *epagōgē* which issues in the formulation of adequate concepts of the particular virtues and of virtue and goodness in general, so that the theoretical understanding can come to provide an *archē* from which practical reasoning may draw its most fundamental premises. But before we turn to consider Aristotle's account of the reasoning which makes use of such premises, we need to notice some other features of Aristotle's account of justice.

Justice in the fullest and proper sense governs only the relationships of free and equal citizens within a *polis.* It is not just that the *polis* and its institutions are necessary in order to bring into being just persons and a just order; it is also that the scope of justice in the fullest and proper sense is the individual *polis.* Certain other relationships and transactions can indeed be called "just" or "unjust" by analogy: the relationships of husband and wife within the household, of father to children, and of master to slaves. And here once again what Aristotle says is deformed by his beliefs about women and about the nature of slaves. Yet even Aristotle recognizes that justice will be violated in a household if a husband simply imposes his will in areas where his wife should have her say; then he governs in a way contrary to desert (*NE* VIII, 1160b36).

Aristotle's understanding of the ideal household mirrors his understanding of the best kind of *polis* not only in respect of the kind of justice involved—one in which desert or merit is the principle—but also in respect of the kind of friendship involved. And it is important to recognize that on Aristotle's view the norms of justice govern the relationships of those who in one way or another are also and more fundamentally bound to each other by ties of friendship. For justice by itself is insufficient as a bond (*NE*, 1155a27). Both justice properly so-called and friendship of the highest kind are founded on a shared allegiance to and embodiment of the virtues in general and the good for the sake of which the virtues are pursued. In exercising the virtues and pursuing the good and the best we need our friends to aid us when we are mature, just as we needed teachers when we were immature. The kind of mutual dependence involved is different from that of the young, who are too much moved by feeling in their friendships; what friendship of the highest kind requires includes feelings but also a fixed disposition toward that virtue and that good which is the virtue and good of the friend as well as of oneself.

Aristotle's discussion of friendship refocuses our attention upon one central and crucial feature of his account of the virtues in general and of justice in particular, a feature to which I drew attention at the outset. Justice, both as a virtue of the individual and as an ordering of social life, is only to be achieved within the concrete institutionalized forms of some particular *polis*. The norms of justice have no existence apart from the actualities of each particular *polis*. But it does not follow that there is nothing more to the norms of justice than what they are taken to be in each particular *polis* at some particular time. Just because the *polis* is defined functionally as that form of human association whose peculiar *telos* is the realization of good as such, a form of association therefore inclusive of all forms of association whose *telos* is the realization of this or that particular good, the citizens of each *polis* have the rational resources to judge their own city as succeeding or failing in doing and being what a *polis* at its best does and is.

So there is no standard external to the *polis* by which a *polis* can be rationally evaluated in respect of justice or any other good. To apprehend what a *polis* is, what the good is which is its function to achieve, and to what extent one's own *polis* has successfully achieved that good, all require membership in a *polis*. Without such membership, as we saw earlier, one is bound to lack essential elements of the education into the virtues and of the experience of the life of the virtues which is necessary for such apprehension. But more than this, one is bound also to lack the capacity to reason practically.

That one cannot be just, on Aristotle's view, without the capacity to reason practically, that *dikaiosunē* requires *phronēsis,* has, I hope, been made abundantly clear by the preceding argument. But since practical reasoning, as Aristotle understands it, involves the capacity to bring the relevant premises concerning goods and virtues to bear on particular situations and since this capacity is inseparable from, is indeed a part of, the virtues, including justice, it is also the case that one cannot be practically rational without being just. And for reasons which are in essentials the same as those which entailed the conclusion that one cannot be just apart from membership in some particular *polis,* one cannot be practically rational apart from membership in some particular *polis.* That one's rationality should be not merely supported by but partly constituted by one's membership in and integration into a social institution of some one particular type is a contention very much at odds with characteristically modern views of rationality. It is therefore crucial to ask what kind of justification Aristotle offers for his view and how he elaborates it in detail. To these questions I now turn.

VIII

Aristotle on Practical Rationality

Whom does Aristotle address in those works in which he speaks about practical reasoning? By and large they are works upon which he was engaged while teaching at Athens in the Lyceum after 338, although the relevant passages in *De Anima* Book III probably belong to an earlier period. We must therefore presume their primary audience to be the students of the Lyceum, students whom Aristotle treats as aware of Plato's having put in question the beliefs of the ordinary educated Athenian about the *polis*. And those ordinary educated Athenians more generally, from the ranks of whom many of Aristotle's students must have been drawn, were his secondary audience. What Aristotle offers that audience is threefold. First, he furnishes an account of what it is for an educated agent to act rationally, from that agent's own point of view. And to do so he has to identify the kinds of reason which must move a rational agent to action and the standards to which they must conform in order for them to be adequately good reasons. This account, therefore, is of practical as well as theoretical import and contributes to the practical task of ethics, as Aristotle conceives it (*NE* 1103b 27–29).

Second, Aristotle's account of practical reasoning provides a way of classifying and understanding defects and failures in practical rationality, so that it becomes clear how it would be appropriate for a rational person to respond to the actions of the less than rational. More particularly, Aristotle enables his fourth-century Greek audience to understand how different types of political constitution facilitate or constrain the activities of the rational agent, so that the relationship between being a good citizen of this or that particular *polis* with this or that particular type of constitution and being a rational human being can be grasped.

Aristotle's account of practical reasoning also has a third function, one arising primarily out of his more purely scientific enquiries. As any adequate account of practical reasoning must, his is intended to supply a causal explanation of the genesis both of rational action and of less than rational action. This explanatory project finds its place within Aristotle's purely theoretical enquiries about the genesis of human and animal behavior; hence the importance of texts from Book III of the *De Anima* (700b 36–701b 1) in supplementing what Aristotle says in Books I, II, and VI of the *Nicomachean Ethics,* in Books I and II of the *Eudemian Ethics,* and in Book I of the *Politics.* Yet it is important nonetheless to recognize the practical and political relevance of these enquiries about causality. For only if and insofar as good reasons are the causes of actions, and only if and insofar as those good reasons are causally efficacious just because and to the extent that they are good reasons, are there any rational agents. Any account of practical rationality which fails as a causal account fails altogether. How then and by what must someone be moved to action if he is to be accounted practically rational, as Aristotle understands practical rationality?

Such a person must first of all be moved by a belief about what good it is best for him here and now to achieve. But for it to be rational to be moved by that belief, that belief itself must be rationally well-grounded; it must be supported by adequately good reasons. What different kinds of reasons will these have to include? On Aristotle's view the individual will have to reason from some initial conception of what is good for him, being the type of person that he is, generally circumstanced as he is, to the best supported view which he can discover of what is good as such for human beings as such; and then he will have to reason from that account of what is good and best as such to a conclusion about what it is best for him to achieve here and now in his particular situation. It is this double movement of thought which Aristotle describes in the *Metaphysics:* ". . . in practical matters the procedure is to move from the goods for each person to how what are goods generally can be the goods for each . . ." (2, 1029b 5–7). And in Book V of the *Nicomachean Ethics* he warns against supposing that the individual need go no further than identifying what is good as such, when, having just distinguished goods which are so only for certain individuals in certain circumstances from what are unqualifiedly goods, he says of the latter: "Human beings pray for and pursue these, but they ought not to do so; they should pray that what is unqualifiedly good may be their good, but it is their goods that they should choose" (1129b 4–6).

The individual's belief, then, that *this* is the specific good to be achieved by him in this particular situation will be rational only if no less than five related abilities have been exercised. First, that individual must have been able to characterize the particular situation in which he finds himself, so that the features of that situation relevant to immediate action have become salient. Second, he must have been able to reason, by the use of *epagōgē* and of other dialectical modes of reasoning, from knowledge of what are goods for him to a more or less adequate concept of the good as such. Third, in order so to reason he must also be able to understand his goods *qua* participant in a variety of types of activity appropriate to someone of his age, at his stage of educational development, engaged in his particular occupation, and so on. And fourth, he must have been able to reason from his understanding of the good in general, the unqualifiedly good, to a conclusion about which out of the specific goods which it is immediately possible for him to achieve he should in fact set himself to achieve as what is immediately best for him.

Each of these abilities will have had to be developed through training in highly specific contexts. But there is a fifth ability, the ability to deploy the four others in conjunction, which will also have had to be systematically trained. This is the ability exhibited in the exercise of the virtue of *phronēsis,* and while it is his own actions as such with which the *phronimos* is concerned, one cannot learn to pursue one's own overall good except in the context of the household and the *polis,* for "someone presumably does not have a good of his own without participation in the management of a household and without a polity" (*NE* 1142a 9–10). So it is within the household and the *polis* — and especially in the *polis* — that one will have had to learn how to exercise this fifth ability and to exhibit the dispositions which are evidence of possessing it.

Yet although the exercise of all these abilities in the formation of a true and justified belief about what is one's own immediate good is a necessary condition for the genesis of rational action, it is only a necessary condition. If someone's desires are not desires to do what reason discloses it is best for that person to do, or if that person's dispositions to act are not systematically organized and directed to serve such desires for the ends proposed by reason, then that person will be open to being moved by considerations which distract his attention from or otherwise make him ignore what he knows to be best, and so what he does will not be what it is best or even good for him to do. So Aristotle distinguishes in his earlier writings on these topics two species of appetite (*orexis*), that which is rational wish (*boulēsis:* for an account of *boulēsis* see *NE* 1113a 15–1113b 2) and that which is not. All *orexis* has as its object something taken to be good, but *orexis* may be distracted from what is really good by a desire (*epithumia*) for what would be immediately and momentarily satisfying (*De Anima* 433a 23–30 and 433b 7–10; *NE* 1111b 12–13).

Aristotle distinguishes a number of different sources of error in action. One is immaturity. The young, as I noticed earlier, may reason badly from lack of experience and, even if they reason well, may still be misled by untutored passions, but so also may those who, although no longer youthful, have never developed maturity of intelligence and character (*NE* 1093a 2–10). A second source of error is lack of education, both in the development of the appropriate habits and in intellectual training (*NE* 1095b 4–6 and 1179b 23–29; *Politics* Book VIII). Those without the requisite education will characteristically err in three ways. Their habits and dispositions to act will not direct their activity to its true *telos,* and their passions will distract them. "For someone who lives according to passion would not listen to an argument designed to redirect him, nor would he understand it" (*NE* 1179b 26–27). Thus they will also and thirdly make intellectual mistakes and exhibit intellectual limitations in reasoning about what to do.

The immaturity of the young is of course one and the same in every *polis* and indeed in every social order. The adequacy of the education provided for them will vary from *polis* to *polis*. How adequate it is in any particular *polis* will depend upon the degree to which those who rule have well founded true beliefs about the good and the best and exhibit the virtue of *phronēsis* in acting upon them. In a city where false beliefs are inculcated by the basic laws, as at Sparta, the citizens as a whole will be led astray and will fail in respect of *aretē* and of their good, *eudaimonia* (*Politics* 1333b 11–31). But even in a city in which this is not the case, one mark of educational failure will be a tendency on the part of individual citizens to identify as *the* good and *the* best some good which is merely an external by-product of those activities in which excellence is achieved—money or honor, for example (*Politics* 1257b 40–1258a 14; *NE* 1095b 22–31). Such errors are evidence of an individual having failed to understand the way in which goods are rank-ordered, a failure which involves a defective conception of the overall character of the best life for human beings as structured in the best kind of *polis*.

There is, however, another kind of failure which is neither a matter of false beliefs about the good, resulting from an inadequate or distorted education, nor a matter of simple immaturity. Consider the case of an individual who has learned enough to know what the good is, in the sense that if this question and cognate questions as to why the good is what it is are posed to him, either by himself or by others, he gives correct answers, understanding and meaning what he says. It follows that his intellectual instruction must have been sufficient to inform him adequately and that his passions and habits have been at least orderly enough to permit him this degree of intellectual instruction. Nonetheless, from time to time, instead of doing what the good and his good requires, this individual yields to passion-generated impulses and does what is contrary to his good and to the good. Such an individual is not vicious (*NE* 1146b 22–24). The vicious person deliberately and on principle sets himself to do what is contrary to his good and to the good, because he has made false judgments about what the good and his good consist in. This type of individual fails in another way; his passions are not yet under his rational control, because in one way or another his knowledge of what is good is not brought to bear on them (*NE* 1146b 31–1147a 24). He is incontinent, *akratic*. The kind of person who does not suffer from *akrasia,* but who successfully controls the passions which would otherwise result in occasions of *akratic* breakdown, the *enkratic* continent person, is not the same as the virtuous person, just as the *akratic* is not to be identified with the vicious. The *enkratic* person knows what it is good and rational to do and does it, but his passions have not yet been fully transformed, so that his pleasures and pains are those of the wholly virtuous. So the *enkratic* person does what the rational and virtuous person does, but his motivations are not the same as those of the fully virtuous. It is in spite of his passions, at least to some degree, that he does what he does in judging and acting rightly, although his character is sufficiently formed to issue in *prohairesis,* rational desire (*NE* 1111b 14–15).

In the transition from immaturity to rationality the conditions of the *akratic* and of the *enkratic* represent moments of incomplete development. But development toward what? I have up to this point summarized what Aristotle has to say about various types of failure and inadequacy in respect of practical rationality, but it will only, of course, be in the light afforded by an account of what it is to be successfully and adequately practically rational that the nature and significance of failure and inadequacy can emerge. Even so, one crucial point emerges from the discussion so far. The remedy for each kind of failure and inadequacy in respect of practical rationality, which Aristotle catalogues, is on his view the acquisition or exercise of one or more of the virtues. One cannot be practically rational without being virtuous, any more than one can be virtuous without being practically rational. And what holds of the virtues generally holds more specifically of justice. The person who habitually yields to *pleonektic* impulses, or who does not yield to them only when inhibited by fear or by a desire to please, will be distracted thereby from that directedness toward the good and his good which rationality requires; the person who does not require what is due to him will also be paying or have paid inadequate attention to what his good is and so will also fail in respect of rationality. Justice is a precondition of practical rationality. But what then *is* practical rationality?

On Aristotle's account its exercise on particular occasions involves two stages. What immediately precedes and generates action is that form of deductive reasoning which commentators have called "the practical syllogism," although Aristotle himself never uses that expression. Such a syllogism consists of two premises or sets of premises, a first initiating premise (often somewhat misleadingly referred to as the major premise) in asserting which the agent declares what good is at stake in his acting or not acting as he should, and a secondary premise (correspondingly referred to as the minor premise) in asserting which the agent declares what the situation is in which, given that this good is at stake, action is required. The conclusion drawn from these premises is the required action (*DA* 434a 16–21, *De Motu Animalium* 701a 7–25, *NE* 1146b 35–1147a 7 and 1147a 25–31).

Every practical syllogism is a performance by a particular person on a particular occasion. It is tied down to that particular occasion both by the here and now reference of the referring expressions in the secondary premise and by the fact that it is the particular person who utters the syllogism whose good is specified by the initial premise and by whom the action which is the conclusion is to be done. Hence the soundness of a practical syllogism depends upon who utters it and on what occasion, and in this respect a practical syllogism differs radically from Aristotle's theoretical syllogisms in which there is no place for singular referring expressions—it is this which makes the idiom of major and minor premises somewhat inappropriate to the practical syllogism.

Before, however, the premises of a practical syllogism can be affirmed by a practically rational agent, the particular syllogism has to be constructed. The first stage in the exercise of practical rationality, preceding the utterance of the practical syllogism, is that in the course of which the syllogism is constructed, the stage to which Aristotle gives the names '*boulē*' and '*euboulia*' (*NE* 1112a 18–1113b 14). An agent who is defective in his rationality may well have engaged in no previous activity of rational construction. Yet such an individual will also be moved by what can be represented as a conjunction of premises, the first expressive of his desire, the second referring to the particularities of his situation. So Aristotle gives an example of a syllogism in which the agent is moved by *epithumia,* in this case presumably thirst-inspired *epithumia:*

"Drinking is what I should do; this is drink" (*DMA* 701a 32) — and the utterer immediately drinks. But this is not the practical syllogism of rationality, for whether or not *epithumia* of this kind is to be yielded to has not been considered, and we should remember that in the *De Anima* the biddings of *epithumia*, which always responds immediately to a present stimulus, are contrasted with and represented as being in conflict with the rational biddings of *nous* (*DA* 433b5-10: Aristotle here uses *nous* where later on he would instead have spoken of *phronēsis*).

What then distinguishes nonrational animals in the generation of behavior from human beings, insofar as they are successfully rational animals, is that the desires and dispositions of such human beings are ordered to what they have truly judged to be their good, rather than by *epithumia* ungoverned by such judgment. That such and such is the good of this particular individual or of this type of individual or of this set of individuals is true or false independently of whether or not he or they or anyone else happen in fact to desire that good. What the major premise of a practical syllogism affirms is an individual's judgment as to what his good is; what such a premise affirms, when the individual is fully rational, is a well-founded and true judgment. That premise, whether true or false, will only be effective in generating action if the individual's desires and dispositions are ordered accordingly. But the premise itself says nothing about desire; in all Aristotle's examples what is affirmed is that something is "good for" or "needed" or the like. The minimal predicate is the bare gerundive "should be done by me." Hence it is misleading, for example, to translate the Greek "*poteon moi*" as "I want to drink" instead of as "Drinking should be done by me." What gives practical force to a practical syllogism for the agent who utters it is not itself mentioned in the syllogism.

The rational agent then is set the task of constructing a major premise which states truly what good it is which is his particular good here and now. How is such a premise to be constructed? The good specified in it will provide his action with its immediate *telos* and, as his immediate first premise, will be the immediate *archē* of his about-to-be-performed action. But the good specified in it will only be his genuine good if it not merely is consistent with but is derivable from *the archē*, the set of ultimate first principles and concepts, which specifies the good and the best for human beings as such. The completion of this derivation is the central task of deliberation.

There is an initial problem here to which Gilbert Ryle first drew our attention (*The Concept of Mind*, London, 1949, p. 67). If all rational action is to be preceded by deliberation, while deliberation is itself a form of rational activity, as it surely must be on Aristotle's view of it, we seem to be committed to a vicious infinite regress. For any particular piece of deliberation would, in order to be rational, have to be preceded by some further piece of deliberation, and so proceed *ad infinitum*. But Aristotle can be understood in such a way as not to be open to this charge, and indeed it is on other grounds more reasonable so to understand him. What makes deliberation itself rational is its conforming to certain standards. If on some particular occasion either questions of whether these standards are in fact being conformed to or questions about what the standards themselves are arise, it is necessary for rationality that we should be able to pursue those questions by deliberating about how to deliberate. But it is not a necessary condition of rational deliberation that we *always,* on every occasion of action, should so further deliberate.

Indeed, what matters about rational action is primarily, not that we have deliberated immediately before embarking upon any particular action through the enunciation of some practical syllogism, but that we should act as someone would have done who had so deliberated *and* that we should be able to answer truly the question "Why did you so act?" by citing the relevant practical syllogism and the relevant piece of deliberation, even if these had not actually been rehearsed by us on this particular occasion. But of course in order for this to be the case, it will also have to be the case that often enough we have deliberated explicitly and so performed the tasks necessary for constructing a practical syllogism.

The chain of derivations which is constructed in deliberation is also a chain of "for the sake of" relationships. The good which we are immediately to achieve is to be achieved either for the sake of itself or also or only for the sake of some other good. If it is for its own sake that an immediate particular good is to be achieved, then it is always also as a constitutive part of that life of the good and the best which is the *telos* for human beings. So that only the supreme good is valued *only* for itself.

Thus at each stage of the deliberative process an individual bent upon rational action enquires: If such and such is the good which constitutes the *telos,* what means must I employ to achieve that good? So if *the* good is to be achieved only in and through adequate participation in the life of the *polis* and I am eighteen years old, then the means will be that of performing my military service. I then must ask: If the good to be achieved is the performance of military service, what means, given my circumstances, shall I need to employ or acquire? And the answer, given those circumstances, may be: I need to acquire and fit out a horse to serve in the cavalry. Then in turn I shall ask: What means do I need to adopt, to fit out my horse? And the answer may be: I must make or acquire a bridle. So the goods of bridle-making serve the goods of horsemanship, and the goods of horsemanship serve, among others, those of military service. It is this feature of deliberation which Aristotle characterizes by saying that we deliberate about what conduce to ends, *peri tōn pros ta telē,* and not about ends (*NE* 1112b 11–12).

More than one commentator has pointed out that what conduces to an end either may be what is more commonly in English called a means—that is, some activity distinct from an end-state, which is causally efficacious in producing that end-state, as the building of a wall may be a means to enjoying shelter from the wind—or it may be a means instead in the sense of a constitutive part of an end which is some whole including and requiring that part, as the making of the opening moves in a game of chess is a means to the end of playing a game of chess.

The deliberative task of rational construction is then one which issues in an hierarchical ordering of means to their ends, in which the ultimate end is specified in a formulation which provides the first principle or principles from which are deduced statements of those subordinate ends which are means to the ultimate end. What is an ordered hierarchy of "for the sake of" relations leading to the *archē* is also a deductive hierarchy descending from the *archē.* It is only of course by invoking additional premises, independently supported, that deliberation can arrive at an end product in which the particular types of circumstance of *this* particular agent can be understood to make it the case that for him to pursue the good and the best involves the here-and-now pursuit of this highly specific good. And, as I explained in the previous chapter, one of the marks of *phronēsis* is that someone is able to identify just which circumstances are relevant and therefore which premises must be utilized in the deliberative construction.

Deliberation then first moves to a beginning, an *archē,* with a view to the construction of an argument which concludes with an end product to which Aristotle gives the name *prohairesis.* It is important to examine in turn the character of that *archē,* the types of argument which link *archē* to *prohairesis* and the nature of *prohairesis.* How then is the *archē* to be understood? Aristotle says that we do not deliberate about ends, but it is of course his view that we reason nondeliberatively about ends and about that first end which is the *archē.* Only insofar as such reasoning has furnished some rationally supported conception of the *archē* can we embark upon the tasks of deliberation with rational confidence. Hence the conception of a single, albeit perhaps complex, supreme good is central to Aristotle's account of practical rationality. Yet it is just this conception which most, if not all, recent moral philosophers find quite implausible. Those, for example, who identify a good with any object of desire—or perhaps with any object that would be desired, were the person who desires provided with adequate factual information—cannot but recognize, if they are realistic, and generally do recognize the variety, heterogeneity, and incommensurability of such objects. Aristotle does of course in the very first sentences of the *Nicomachean Ethics* identify the good with that toward which everything is directed, acknowledging at the same time a variety of goods and therefore of aims. But that variety, as Aristotle conceived it, is susceptible of a kind of ordering of which characteristically modern conceptions of goods are incapable. So it has sometimes been claimed, and cogently from the standpoint of modernity, that there can be no uniquely rational way of ordering goods within a scheme of life, but rather that there are numerous alternative modes of ordering, in the choice between which there are no sufficient good reasons to guide us. And one way to understand Aristotle's point of view is to consider why he would have had to reject this kind of modern account.

On this account the individual human being confronts an alternative set of ways of life from a standpoint external to them all. Such an individual has as yet *ex hypothesi* no commitments, and the multifarious and conflicting desires which individuals develop provide in themselves no grounds for choosing which of such desires to develop and be guided by and which to inhibit and frustrate. From Aristotle's point of view such an individual has been deprived of the possibility of rational evaluation and rational choice. And it is precisely because it is the *ergon*, the peculiar task of human beings to evaluate, to choose, and to act *qua* rational beings that human beings cannot be understood in detachment from their necessary social context, that setting within which alone rationality can be exercised.

That necessary context, that setting, is provided by the *polis*, understood as the form of social order whose shared mode of life already expresses the collective answer or answers of its citizens to the question "What is the best mode of life for human beings?" From within and only from within a given *polis*, already provided with an ordering of goods, goods to be achieved by excellence within specific and systematic forms of activity, integrated into an overall rank-order by the political activity of those particular citizens, does it make sense to ask: "In the light of the evaluations and the resources of dialectical reasoning which we now possess can we construct a better account of the supreme good than any hitherto suggested?" Which is to say, it is a condition of asking and answering questions about the *archē* of practical rationality that one is already a participant within a form of community which presupposes that there is a supreme, albeit perhaps complex, human good.

It may be illuminating to consider an analogy with modern natural science. From a standpoint outside that of any established scientific community, on the basis of data uncharacterized in terms of any established theory, there are and can be no sufficiently good reasons to suppose in respect of any particular subject matter or area of enquiry, let alone in respect of nature as such, that there is one true fundamental explanatory theory. Only for the inhabitants of such a community, who already possess some established theory or theories and who have so far characterized the data in terms of it or them, can the question be put: In the light of the norms of evaluation which we now possess, which of the presently competing overall theories is the best, or can we conceive of a better? That there is a true theory to be found is a presupposition of the ongoing activity of the scientific community; that there is a supreme good for human beings is a presupposition of the ongoing activity of the *polis*.

It is unsurprising then that in Book I of the *Nicomachean Ethics* Aristotle argues as to which, if any, of the presently competing accounts of the supreme good ought to prevail or whether a better account than any of them can be constructed, but he offers no argument at any point to the conclusion that there *is* such a good. (It has sometimes been alleged that *NE* 1094a 18–22 is such an argument, and it has also been charged that it is a fallacious argument, and indeed were it such an argument, it would be fallacious; but it is in fact only a conditional assertion whose first clause says that "*If* there is some *telos* of actions which we wish for its own sake and for the sake of which we wish whatever else we wish . . ." and which nowhere says, let alone argues, that there is such a *telos*.)

What the *archē* is is of course established by the theoretical enquiries of dialectic — including *epagōgē* from the experience of exercising phronetic judgment — and not by deliberation. In deliberation the agent argues from the *archē* as to what means must be adopted to move toward it. Nor of course is it by deliberation that the matters of circumstance which must be taken into account in the course of deliberation are established. That is the work of perception, which furnishes deliberation with further premises to use in the construction of that deductive argument whose first premise of all begins "Since the *telos* and the best is such and such . . ." (*NE* 1144a 31–33). But of course that complete argument does not have to be constructed on every occasion or even perhaps on many occasions; it will characteristically be only parts of that larger argument, parts concerned with particular subordinate goals to the achievement of which means have to be devised, which will be invoked in everyday deliberation. Nor is it the case, as I noticed earlier, that every action has to be immediately preceded by deliberation if it is to be rational. One may act rationally on the basis of perhaps long previous deliberation.

The account of Aristotle's view of rational action which I have given thus assigns the following parts to deliberation and to the practical syllogism. Deliberation is that process of argument which provides the practical syllogism with its premises. The sound practical syllogism is the immediate precedent and determinant of rational action. In so understanding Aristotle I am of course agreeing with John M. Cooper (*Reason and Human Good in Aristotle,* Cambridge, Massachusetts, 1975; Cooper should, of course, be absolved from any responsibility for my view of Aristotle in general), and in this respect I am disagreeing even with those of his recent critics from whom I have in other ways learned most, such as Norman O. Dahl (*Practical Reason, Aristotle and Weakness of Will,* Minneapolis, 1984).

Cooper, however, in one way weakens his case unnecessarily. He follows W.F.R. Hardie (*Aristotle's Ethical Theory,* Oxford, 1968) in pointing out that the rational devising of means for given ends, which deliberation consists in, requires nonsyllogistic reasoning. But by suggesting that deliberative reasoning is exclusively nonsyllogistic, he and Hardie encounter the objection that Aristotle asserts that deliberation can fail by employing an unsound syllogism (*NE* 1142b 21–26) and also holds that some means-ends reasoning can be cast in syllogistic form (*Posterior Analytics* 94b 8–12). These difficulties have been most cogently urged in favor of an alternative interpretation of Aristotle by Fred D. Miller ("Aristotle on Rationality in Action" *Review of Metaphysics* XXXVII, 3, 1984). But there is no need to deny and, on more general grounds concerning means-ends reasoning, as well as in the light of these passages, there is every reason to assert that deliberation must involve *some* syllogistic reasoning, but it is not and could not be exclusively syllogistic. Deliberation, by its very nature, will have to employ a variety of types of reasoning in its constructive tasks; so analogously, the construction of scientific theories involves the use of a variety of types of reasoning, including deductive reasoning.

What deliberation issues in, except in the case of the *akratic* person, is *prohairesis,* a word usually translated in the key passages in Aristotle by 'choice' and, more recently by T.H. Irwin, by 'decision'. But these translations, as translations of Aristotle's semitechnical use of *'prohairesis'*, are misleading for two reasons. First, the English words 'choice' and 'decision' have as much application to the selection of actions by the *akratic* as they do to that by the virtuous and the vicious, while *prohairesis* is restricted by Aristotle to the latter (*NE* 1111b 14–15 and 1139a 33–35). And second, when Aristotle explicitly tells us what he means by *'prohairesis'*, he says that it may be called either "*orektikos nous*" or "*orexis dianoētikē,*" that is, either desiring thought or desire informed by thought. And whatever we mean by "choice" or "decision" in English, we do not mean that.

What matters is that *prohairesis* can only issue from the deliberations of those whose formed character is the result of the systematic disciplining and transformation of their initial desires, by the virtues if they have conceived correctly of their good or by the vices if they have misconceived their good. What *prohairesis* unites is desire whose object is the agent's true good, as that agent rightly or wrongly understands it, and the thought of the concrete form that the achievement of that good must take, supplied by deliberation. Without that desire the deliberation could not issue in effective *practical* rationality. What then forms the desire rightly? "Virtue makes the *prohairesis* right" (*NE* 1144a 20) and "Virtue makes the project right" (1144a 7–8), while *phronēsis* cooperates in identifying the means leading to the goods to which virtue has directed our desires (1144a 8–9).

There is no practical rationality then without the virtues of character. The vicious argue unsoundly from false premises about the good, while the *akratic* ignores the sound arguments available to him. Only the virtuous are able to argue soundly to those conclusions which are their actions, and this is so in consequence of two distinct parts that the virtues play and have played in their lives. In their initial training it was the acquisition of virtuous habits which enabled the virtuous to perform those actions in reflection upon which they first formulated, even if initially in skeletal form, those principles of action which define human excellence, the various virtues and indeed the good and the best itself. Moreover, in so doing they became able to engage in theoretical enquiry about practice, as well as in practical enquiries, deliberations (Aristotle calls deliberation a type of enquiry, *zetesis, NE* 1112b 21–3), which they, lacking the virtues, would not be able to engage in. But it is not only in their overall directedness, intellectually and practically, toward the good and the best that their virtues are crucial. It is also in the context of immediately prospective action.

Without the virtues the desires cannot be informed by reason, cannot be transformed into and be effective as desires for whatever reason prescribes. The very existence of *boulēsis,* rational wish, as practically effective depends upon the possession of the virtues, and it is the strength of the virtues which not merely excludes *epithumiai* from influence, as in the case of the *enkratic* person, but no longer lets them weigh at all with the fully rational agent. So the judgments in which *prohairesis* is expressed are true, well-founded, and effective only because of the part played by the virtues both in their genesis and in informing their content. It is the virtues which enable the desire which is *prohairesis* to be rational desire.

It is evident that each of the distinct virtues, or at least each of the more important of them, has its own highly specific part to play both in the initial formation of character and in guiding and informing *prohairesis* upon particular occasions. It is not difficult to discern what those parts must be from the accounts of each of the virtues which Aristotle supplies. What the account of justice in Book V of the *Nicomachean Ethics* makes clear is that without justice our judgments and actions in respect of others could not be informed by right principle, that is, by rationally justifiable principle, either generally or on particular occasions. We could not discharge our duties rightly within the *polis* either as holders of public office, as rulers, or as those ruled over. We could not discharge our duties rightly within the household or to our friends. For we would not in each case discern rightly what goods were at stake in particular situations and the relationship of those goods to the good and the best. So that, just as in the last chapter the conclusion could not be avoided that, on Aristotle's account, no one can be just without being practically rational, so the conclusion is equally and for correlative reasons inescapable that, on that account, one cannot be practically rational without being just—or indeed without the other central virtues.

What then is *prohairesis, prohairesis* informed by the virtues, of? For what is it a desire? "We take as the objects of *prohairesis* what we assuredly know to be goods" (*NE* 1112a7–8). The deliberation of a rational agent, that is to say, issues in a conclusion as to what good or goods is or are immediately to be achieved and in a rationally well-founded desire for just that good or those goods. In so doing it supplies an initial and motivating premise for a practical syllogism. In thus identifying the initial, the so-called major, premise of a practical syllogism with a conclusion issuing from deliberation I am of course once again following Cooper. But Cooper then presents the practical syllogism itself as though it were only a representation of stages through which the agent passes in generating action and not a piece of reasoning by the agent himself: "in fact such syllogisms ought not to be regarded as part of practical reasoning at all" (op. cit., p. 51). Were this correct, the agent whose practical syllogism is invalid would not have failed precisely as a reasoner, but this is in fact how Aristotle presents him. Consider more generally how on an Aristotelian view the agent whose practical syllogisms are valid acts in such a way that his actions *follow from* his conjoined judgments of principle and of perception. It follows that the inconsistency and unintelligibility of someone who affirms the premises of a valid practical syllogism, but who then fails to act when it is in his power to do so and the moment for such action is at hand, is the same inconsistency and unintelligibility which attaches to someone who affirms the premises of a valid theoretical syllogism and at the moment when it is appropriate for him to do so fails to affirm or even denies the conclusion. But none of this would follow if Cooper were correct. For Cooper would have to argue, as he does, that the language of syllogism is for Aristotle a mere *façon de parler*.

Moreover Cooper relies on those parts of Aristotle's analysis of action which apply to all animals and are not specific to rational animals, citing *De Motu Animalium* 701a 25–36. But what are common to both rational and nonrational animals are the desire and the perception which precede actions; what is specific to rational animals is the judgment informing the desire and the judgment of perception. Thus, when Cooper argues in effect that the practical syllogism is no more than a representation of the part played by desire and perception in generating action, he obscures the difference — crucial to Aristotle — between rational and nonrational animals.

The practical syllogism was then rightly so called. It *is* a syllogism. From a judgment or judgments as to what is good or needed or appropriate and from a judgment as to what is the case, supported by perception, a conclusion follows which is an action (*DMA* 701a 8–13, where the parallel is explicitly drawn between the utterance of a theoretical syllogism and the performance of a rational practical syllogism, a parallel incompatible with Cooper's interpretation, *DMA* 701a 20, *NE* 1147a 20–29). Anthony Kenny has argued that the conclusion of a practical syllogism is a decision to act, and not an action (*Aristotle's Theory of the Will,* London, 1979, pp. 142–143), relying in part on an example given by Aristotle at *DMA* 701a 18–22, where the conclusion seems to be a decision to make a cloak. But as Dahl has remarked (op. cit., pp. 160–161), the utterance "I should make a cloak" in the example can be treated as an intermediate conclusion within a complex argument rather than the final conclusion of a practical syllogism. Kenny also points out (op. cit., pp. 143–144) that Aristotle recognizes that one may be prevented from acting after affirming the premises of a practical syllogism (*DMA* 701a 15–16), and in such a case it might well seem that the agent could be prevented from acting, but not from drawing a conclusion in the form of a decision, a decision which the agent is hindered from implementing. To this it should be replied (and see also Dahl's reply, op. cit., pp. 161–162) that insofar as the agent who is prevented from acting does draw a conclusion, it will have to be the conclusion to a theoretical syllogism about what someone such as himself should do unless prevented from doing so. His completed syllogism will be about practice, but it will not be practical. For from Aristotle's reiteration of the thesis that the conclusion of a practical syllogism is an action it is clear that he holds this to be one of the identifying marks of this kind of syllogism.

One reason which some have had—this is no part of Kenny's case—for denying that Aristotle could possibly have been serious in asserting that the conclusion of the practical syllogism is an action is that it has seemed obvious to them that *only* a statement or a judgment could be the conclusion of an argument, while it has seemed equally plain to them that an action cannot be either a statement or a judgment. They are of course correct at least in supposing that if an action is the conclusion of an argument, it must be in virtue of its giving expression to a statement or a judgment. What such commentators have failed to notice is the character of the practical syllogism as a performance on a particular occasion in which the action which is the conclusion corresponds to the utterance of a statement as the conclusion of the recital of a theoretical syllogism. What such an action as utterance affirms in concluding a practical syllogism is that that selfsame action, answering as it does to the description of what is to be done furnished by the initial premise, is to be done.

The logical structure of a practical syllogism is then as follows. In the initial premise or premises the agent affirms of a given type of action a predicate which has gerundive force: such and such is to be done *qua* good. In the secondary premise or premises the agent affirms that circumstances are such as to provide the opportunity and the occasion for doing what is to be done. In the conclusion the agent in acting affirms that this action *qua* such and such is to be done. Someone who affirms the premises conjointly and refuses to affirm or denies the conclusion by doing something other than the required action contradicts himself, just as does someone who affirms the premises conjointly of a theoretical syllogism and refuses to affirm or denies its conclusion. Aristotle, as I noticed earlier, affirms the parallelism of the two kinds of syllogism in this respect (*DMA* 701a 8–13), and it is indeed the same concept of entailment which is being applied. Hence the concluding action does in the appropriate sense follow necessarily from the premises.

It follows that when the premises have been affirmed, if they are true and the inference is valid and the agent is fully rational, then the premises must afford sufficient reasons for the immediate performance of the action. There is no logical space for something else to intervene: a decision, for example. For the fully rational agent there is nothing remaining to be decided. So when an agent does affirm the true premises of a valid practical syllogism, when nothing occurs to hinder or to prevent that agent from acting and the agent does not at once act, it follows that in some respect the agent is not fully rational. *Something* contingent and accidental from the standpoint of rationality *must* have intervened.

This portrayal of the rational agent as acting immediately and necessarily upon affirming his reasons for action is once again one very much at odds with our characteristically modern ways of envisaging a rational agent. Someone, we are inclined to say, may rehearse the good reasons which he or she has for taking a particular course of action and then at the very least may hesitate without at all ceasing to be rational. The thought may cross his or her mind that there may be some other good to be pursued or that the promptings of some desire should be listened to. Or the person may just not feel like acting in the way dictated by good reasons. Indeed this is why we are apt to suppose that between the evaluation of our reasons for action and action itself some further act of decision is necessary. No set of practical reasons, however compelling, need, on this dominant modern view, be treated as conclusive.

What this shows of course is not that Aristotle was mistaken, but that he was describing a form of practical rational life both different from and in conflict with that at home in the social orders characteristic of modernity. But it may be instructive to consider those contemporary social contexts in which we do still find application for something very like Aristotelian conceptions of practical rationality. A hockey player in the closing seconds of a crucial game has an opportunity to pass to another member of his or her team better placed to score a needed goal. Necessarily, we may say, if he or she has perceived and judged the situation accurately, he or she must immediately pass. What is the force of this "necessarily" and this "must"? It exhibits the connection between the good of that person *qua* hockey player and member of that particular team and the action of passing, a connection such that were such a player not to pass, he or she must *either* have falsely denied that passing was for their good *qua* hockey player *or* have been guilty of inconsistency *or* have acted as one not caring for his or her good *qua* hockey player and member of that particular team. That is to say, we recognize the necessity and the immediacy of rational action by someone inhabiting a structured role in a context in which the goods of some systematic form of practice are unambiguously ordered. And in so doing we apply to one part of our social life a conception which Aristotle applies to rational social life as such.

It is thus only within those systematic forms of activity within which goods are unambiguously ordered and within which individuals occupy and move between well-defined roles that the standards of rational action directed toward the good and the best can be embodied. To be a rational individual is to participate in such a form of social life and to conform, so far as is possible, to those standards. It is because and insofar as the *polis* is an arena of systematic activity of just this kind that the *polis* is the locus of rationality. And it was because Aristotle judged that no form of state but the *polis* could integrate the different systematic activities of human beings into an overall form of activity in which the achievement of each kind of good was given its due that he also judged that *only* a *polis* could provide that locus. No practical rationality outside the *polis* is the Aristotelian counterpart to *extra ecclesiam nulla salus*.

There is yet another feature of Aristotle's conception of practical rationality which is equally or even more at odds with dominant modern conceptions. On a characteristically modern view the claims upon particular individuals of some good may be inconsistent with the claims of some other good, thus creating dilemmas for which on occasion there may be no mode of rational resolution. Precisely because Aristotle's logic in practical argument is the same deductive logic employed in theoretical argument, and precisely because there can only be at any one time one right action to perform, the premises of any Aristotelian practical argument must be consistent with all other truths. It cannot be true of someone on Aristotle's view that he or she is required by the claim upon him or her of some good to do such and such and by the claim of some other equal or incommensurable good not to do such and such. The difference between Aristotle and the modern view is perhaps most clearly apparent in the different interpretations of tragedy which each engenders. From the modern standpoint the incompatibility between the demands of one good and those of another can be real, and it is in terms of the reality of such dilemmas that tragedy is to be understood. It *can* therefore be held to be true of someone that he or she should do such and such (because one good requires it) and also that he or she should refrain from doing such and such (because some other good requires such refraining). But if these both can be held to be true, the concept of truth has been transformed: this is not truth as transmitted in valid deductive arguments. It is for this very reason that from Aristotle's point of view the apparent existence of a tragic dilemma must always rest upon one or more misconceptions or misunderstandings. The apparent and tragic conflict of right with right arises from the inadequacies of reason, not from the character of moral reality.

It would then be highly paradoxical if Aristotle's own writings confronted one with just such a dilemma. Yet something very like this has been claimed by some commentators. For, so they assert, in large parts of the *Nicomachean Ethics* Aristotle presents us with a conception of the highest good, of *eudaimonia,* as embodied in the life of civic duty, more especially in the life of the good ruler who is also a good man. But in Book X he argues that the perfect good is a type of theoretical activity in which the mind contemplates the unchanging and eternal aspects of things, an activity in which the mind, in virtue of that within it which is divine, contemplates in a way that reproduces the activity of God. The political life and the life of moral virtue are *eudaimon* only in inferior and secondary ways (*NE* 1177a 12–1178b 32). So here we have, according to some interpreters, two rival and conflicting views of the supreme good, both urged upon us by Aristotle.

That Aristotle understood there to be a problem about how to relate the life of political virtue to that of contemplative activity is clear. But he also makes it clear that the good life for human beings which constitutes their supreme good has a number of different types of constituent parts and that these parts each find due place within the whole (J.L. Ackrill *Aristotle on Eudaimonia,* London, 1974, reprinted in *Essays on Aristotle's Ethics,* ed. A.O. Rorty, Berkeley, 1980, is the best and most cogent exposition of Aristotle's view). How these parts find their place within that whole Aristotle discusses in summary fashion at the beginning of Book VII of the *Politics* in passages whose intended relevance to the discussion of contemplative, theoretical activity in Book

X of the *Nicomachean Ethics* is made clear by the way in which he repeats and amplifies certain points.

We need, so Aristotle argues in the opening passages of Book VII of the *Politics,* to pursue the external goods of the body in order to engage in those activities in which the soul perfects itself. So the life of moral and political virtue exists for the sake of and must be subordinated to the life of contemplative inquiry. But the latter is impossible for the individual, let alone for any group of individuals, without the former. Hence the two modes of life must be combined in the overall life of the *polis,* which itself has to be understood, in this light, as existing for the sake of that in human beings which links them to the divine. All rational practical activity has as its ultimate final cause the vision, so far as it is open to human beings, of what God sees.

So a story which began in Homer's poems with the justice of Zeus culminates in Aristotle's philosophy in an account of justice and the other virtues as serving a life moved in its activity toward and by the Unmoved Mover. In Book Alpha of the *Metaphysics* Aristotle gives us a history of his predecessors' successive investigations into the subject matter with which he is going to be concerned, presenting the *aporiai,* the difficulties which arise from their disagreements and from the unsolved problems of their enquiries, in such a way as to enable him to present his own system of thought as a more adequate way of dealing with these *aporiai.* The claim on behalf of his own standpoint is that it transcends the limitations of his predecessors. It is a parallel history of the same kind in respect of Aristotle's political and moral thought which I have tried to construct in my earlier chapters, in an attempt to show that the embodiment of the Homeric vision of action and justice in the life of Periclean Athens confronted Athenians, and to some degree Greeks in general, with a series of practical and theoretical *aporiai* successively confronted by Pericles, by Sophocles, by Thucydides, and by Plato. On the view which I am and have been taking, Aristotle's peculiar achievement was first to provide a framework of thought within which both the achievements and the limitations of his predecessors could be identified and evaluated and, second, in so doing, to transcend those limitations.

What Aristotle therefore had to provide the means for explaining was how the partial misconceptions of a Neoptolemus and an Odysseus, as presented by Sophocles, could be corrected—and this he did by providing the standard of the *phronimos;* how the actual failures of Greek states, as narrated by Thucydides, could be identified, defined, and explained as defections from a real possibility of the good and the best in the life of the *polis* — and this he did by contrasting justice and *pleonexia;* and how Plato's account of the relationship of justice and rationality to the structure of the *polis* could be both corrected and completed. And if Aristotle's well-founded claim against his predecessors is that he has by the use of dialectical enquiry overcome their limitations, his challenge to those who will subsequently attempt to displace his philosophical theses, either by extending and correcting or by rejecting them, will have to be that they too must situate themselves within the same history of dialectical enquiry and attempt to identify and to overcome his limitations in the same way, but now by standards which are of his setting.

Aristotle's achievement then is wrongly understood if it is supposed that he offered us an account of justice and of practical reasoning which can be shown to be superior to those advanced from other rival, fundamentally different standpoints, ancient or modern, by appeal to some neutral set of standards, equally available to and equally compelling for the rational adherents of every standpoint. As I argued earlier, in laying out the grounds for disagreement and conflict which divide those whose allegiance is to the goods of excellence from those whose allegiance is to the goods of effectiveness, the disagreements between fundamental standpoints are in key part over how to characterize those disagreements. There is at this level no neutral mode of stating the problems, let alone the solutions.

Progress in rationality is achieved only from a point of view. And it is achieved when the adherents of that point of view succeed to some significant degree in elaborating ever more comprehensive and adequate statements of their positions through the dialectical procedure of advancing objections which identify incoherences, omissions, explanatory failures, and other types of flaw and limitation in earlier statements of them, of finding the strongest arguments available for supporting those objections, and then of attempting to restate the position so that it is no longer vulnerable to those specific objections and arguments.

In precisely this way Plato identified the limitations of Socrates' procedure of *elenchus* and consequently of the Socratic treatment of the virtues, and what he consequently achieved in the *Republic* was a restatement of the Socratic position, enriched in respect both of the concept of *eidos* and of the theory of dialectic. And similarly, Aristotle, agreeing with Plato in Plato's self-criticism of the separation of the *eidos* from those particulars which exemplify it, was able to provide an account of justice and of practical reasoning — as also of other key philosophical issues — which enabled him to exhibit what it was for these to be at home in the institutionalized *polis* in a way that Plato had himself tried but failed to achieve convincingly in the *Laws*.

Any philosophical theory of any large degree of comprehensiveness has to include in what it explains the views of those intelligent, perceptive, and philosophically sophisticated persons who disagree with it, as Plato's account of what was wrong with Athenian education in the light of Socratic standards explained the attitudes, beliefs, and behavior of Thrasymachus. So Aristotle too, as I have already remarked, has a cogent and more comprehensive explanation for the varieties of error and disagreement. But it would be a mistake to suppose that it is the kind of explanation which could prove convincing to Aristotle's opponents and critics, ancient or modern. Aristotle's accounts of justice and of practical reasoning require it to be the case, if they are true, that those accounts shall be found erroneous and defective by a wide range of types of person, both philosophers and others. And in this respect too the truth of Aristotle's central theses has been impressively confirmed.

IX

The Augustinian Alternative

No sharper contrast exists between any characteristically fifth- or fourth-century Greek view of justice and any characteristically modern liberal view than in respect of the scope of justice, of the area defined as that to which the norms of justice are to apply. For a modern liberal the norms of justice are to govern the relationships of human beings as such; that the parties to a given transaction come from different political societies or are divided by other types of boundary does nothing to make justice irrelevant to that transaction. For Aristotle, by contrast, justice properly so-called is exercised between free and equal citizens of one and the same *polis,* and although justice may be at stake in certain limited ways in other relationships—in commercial or military treaties or in relationships to wives, children, and slaves—by and large the scope of justice is defined by the boundaries of this particular *polis.*

Nor was Aristotle in any way eccentric in this. Greek thinkers of very different kinds concurred. For example, Antiphon, the fifth-century sophist, advanced an account of justice which is at the opposite pole to Aristotle's: justice is contrary to nature and harmful to human beings. But he defines justice as consisting in not transgressing the laws and usages of one's own *polis* (844 DK), so agreeing that it is relationships within the *polis* to which justice is relevant. When in the ancient world justice was extended beyond the boundaries of the *polis,* it was always as a requirement of theology. The hospitality afforded to the stranger from outside the community was mandated by Zeus Xeinios. When Socrates acknowledged a justice whose scope extends beyond the frontier of the *polis* in a way that the written laws of the *polis* do not, it was to the unwritten laws made by God that he appealed (Xenophon *Memorabilia* IV, 4). And when later on in the Roman world a kind of justice over and beyond that of the justice of the *res publica* was once again recognized, it too was a divine justice. So it was from a solemn ritual invocation that treaties with alien peoples derived their binding force; to violate such a treaty would be to invoke the anger of Juppiter (Livy I, 24).

The god thus appealed to, however, was of course a Roman god. And such were the links between civic religion and the political community that characteristically, if not always, to extend the protection of the gods and of their justice to some alien or aliens was temporarily at least to bring such aliens within the boundaries of the political community. So it is unsurprising that in the ancient world the extension of the scope of justice beyond its original narrow bounds was generally not a matter of a rejection of the identification of the boundaries of justice with the boundaries of political community; it was rather that the conception of those latter boundaries was enlarged.

The most notable of such enlargements was that embodied in Stoic theory and practice. The Stoics were the first thinkers in the Greco-Roman world to assert systematically that the scope of justice is humanity as such, and they did so because they understood every human being, whether enfranchised as a citizen of some particular political society or not, whether slave or free, to be a member of one and the same community under one and the same law. This central Stoic thought was to be given memorable expression by Marcus Aurelius: "My *polis* and my *patris* is Rome *qua* Antonine, but *qua* human being is the cosmos" (*Quod sibi ipsi scripsit* VI, 44). But Marcus Aurelius was a comparative latecomer to the problem of what was involved in recognizing *both* a justice in respect of which all human beings are equal *and* the justice of one's own political community, ordered as was every ancient political community in terms of inegalitarian hierarchies, *both* the justice of the cosmos *and* the justice of Rome. The author who had provided what became the classical statement of that dual recognition, not only for the educated Roman world but also for many later thinkers in very different cultural situations, was of course Cicero, himself eclectic rather than Stoic, but expressing on this same issue at least some of the central theses of Stoicism.

Cicero's thought moves between two poles. On the one hand he asserts the universality for all rational beings of that one law which is both equally binding upon all and enjoins that all be treated in accordance with it. Justice and injustice (*ius* and *iniuria*) are to be defined in terms of obedience and disobedience to "that supreme law" which was in force "during all the centuries before any written law or any city-state (*civitas*) came to be" (*De Legibus* I, vi, 19). Human beings share this law because all have reason, and those who have reason have as a common possession right reason. And right reason *is* law, something shared with gods as well as with all human beings: "so that this whole world is one city to be conceived of as including gods and human beings" (I, vii, 23). Virtue in general (*virtus*) is nature perfected, and *ius* is defined as what accords with nature. So the achievement of justice is that for the sake of which we were born (I, x, 28).

In the way in which he understood this law Cicero faithfully reproduced the Stoic doctrine of *oikeiosis,* appropriation, making one's own. Each individual human being is a compound of appetite (*horme*) and of reason. Reason teaches and explains what is to be done and what is to be avoided. It is therefore the office of reason to command, of appetite to obey (*De Officiis* I, xxviii, 101). What reason instructs appetite about includes not only the preservation of the self but also the care of the self not merely *qua* individual self but also *qua* member of a family, *qua* member of other forms of association and ultimately *qua* member of the human race toward which the *caritas* of the individual will be directed (*De Finibus* III, v, 16, and III, xix, 62–63). So one has recognized humanity in oneself and as one's own; the progress of *oikeiosis* has been completed.

The word '*caritas*' may, however, mislead us if, for example, we project into its Ciceronian use a Christian meaning. How little it may involve becomes clear if we read Cicero's account of duties in *De Officiis.* Our highest duties are to parents and fatherland (*patria*), that state in which we have citizenship; next come children and the rest of the immediate family; then remoter kin; and finally those friends who deserve well of us (*De Officiis* I, xvii, 589 and 55–56). What then of the stranger, neither kin to us nor fellow citizen, someone to whom we owe whatever we do owe merely as a fellow member of the human race? What we owe to such a person is a share of what has not been defined as someone's property by the positive laws of states. Cicero quotes Ennius as saying that we ought to give directions to a traveler who has gone astray, and Cicero comments that what Ennius teaches is that what is owed to such a stranger is that which without loss to ourselves can be given from those things held in common, that is, not assigned as property (I, xvi, 51–52). So *caritas* does not extend very far.

What sets limits to it is in key part a conception of the life of duties as one of hierarchically ordered reciprocities in which each person owes and is owed in terms of fixed and coordinated expectations. Family, city, and universe are all examples of such hierarchically ordered systems of reciprocity, and to live in accordance with nature and reason is to act in such a way as not to breach or render defective those systems of which one is a component part. That the universe is such a system presupposes the truth of the Stoic metaphysics of the cosmos and of the divine ordering embodied in the cosmos, but, given that the universe is what the successive founders of Stoicism had taught that it was, it is plain why it is rational for each person to behave in accordance with the norms of systematic reciprocity; should he or she do otherwise, he or she will frustrate or disrupt his or her nature as a part of the system. When confronted by frustrations or disruptions of the system of ordered reciprocities by others, it will be the task of the virtuous human being to correct and repair that system by moral and political action. Hence justice itself requires the sustaining of justice by the defense of the *civitas*. It was in just such a defense that Cicero wrote *De Officiis* in the last months of his life after the death of Julius Caesar. And it was in just such a defense that M. Porcius Cato the Younger had defended the Roman republic against Caesar, preserving his sovereignty over his own life, in accordance with Stoic precept, by committing suicide after his defeat at Utica in 46 B.C.

The Stoic conceptions of law and justice are thus theologically grounded extensions of the conceptions of law and justice which inform the relationships of free citizens, first within the *polis* and later within the Roman republic and the Roman empire, when these are not disordered by tyranny. In this they resemble the precepts which in Roman law provided the content of the *ius gentium,* that part of the law which protected both treaties between states and commercial contracts between foreigners and Roman citizens. Yet the norms of the *ius gentium* were in fact no more than an extension of Roman law. What the Romans "thought of as *ius gentium* and applied to Romans as well as foreigners was in reality Roman law both by nature and by origin" (Wolfgang Kunkel *An Introduction to Roman Legal and Constitutional History,* trans. J.M. Kelly, Oxford, 1973, p. 77). In no fundamental way, therefore, do either the *ius gentium* or the Stoic accounts of law and justice provide any grounds for an appeal against the dominant practices or order of Greek and Roman polities. Any conception of a justice which not only had a scope which extended beyond the citizens of those polities to all mankind but also provided a standard for evaluating them independently had to come from elsewhere. When such a conception did emerge, it was one which had taken, not its origin, but its definitive form centuries earlier from the enactments of King Josiah of the kingdom of Judah in and after 622 B.C.

Just as Homer provides the horizon for one ultimate limit to the historical self-understanding of modern post-Christian cultures, so the history of the ancient Hebrews provides that for another. Jews and Christians of course look back to Abraham as the initiator of their own particular faith, but those who have rejected that faith also remain products of a distinctive history which begins with Abraham. That history was one which was retold again and again, so that the successive retellings themselves became part of the later history, the unity of that history being reestablished at each stage by some new reiteration of and some new reenactment of that obedience to divine commands in which Abraham, Isaac, and Jacob had been succeeded by Moses, Joshua, and David. When that whole history took what was to be its final canonical form in the reign of King Josiah, it was in the version of the book of *Deuteronomy* which was then produced—a remaking of a very much older book of the law given by Yahweh, found in the temple—that the whole history of Israel and Judah was framed and focused by the retelling and rehearing of that same law which had once long before been given by Yahweh to Moses on Mount Sinai. And it is of course Moses' final statement of the law which is the subject matter of *Deuteronomy*.

Some modern scholars (see for a summary Norman K. Gottwald 'Deuteronomy', in *The Pentateuch,* ed. Charles M. Layman, Nashville, 1983, pp. 280–284; the key work in the background is M. Noth *Uberlieferungsgeschichte des Pentateuchs,* Stuttgart, 1948) have understood the composition of *Deuteronomy* in its present form as emerging from "a liturgy of covenant renewal" in which the recitation of the law was a central part. This makes it all the more significant that the Yahweh who addresses Israel in terms of a special covenant between Himself and Israel does so as one who is not only the God of Israel but the God who made all the nations and laid down the boundaries of every people (Deuteronomy 26, 19, and 32, 8) and who has a peculiar care that justice should be extended to the resident alien non-Hebrew (14, 29; 24, 17; 27, 19). The law, the central precepts of which are the Ten Commandments, was delivered to Israel as God's chosen covenanted people, but that that law embodies wisdom and justice is recognized by other peoples (4, 6–9). And when Israel is warned that disobedience to the prohibition of idolatry will be punished by its destruction, the example of other peoples already punished for idolatry and therefore culpable under the same law is held up to them (8, 19–20). So what is enjoined by the Torah is, not a justice restricted to Israel, but justice as such, not only a law in much of its detail specific to Israel but also a law holding for all peoples.

The Ten Commandments are exceptionless precepts, enjoining and forbidding certain types of action independently of circumstance. To live according to them will be to act for one's own good at all times (6, 24–25). Justice consists in living in obedience to those laws which God has commanded. The judges who administer the law are to do so without showing favor or accepting bribes: "Justice and only justice you shall pursue . . ." (16, 20). The reward of justice will be the land which God has given to Israel. The core of injustice is thus disobedience to law, both to divine law and to human law insofar as it conforms to divine law.

The summons to conform to the requirements of justice thus conceived was to be continually reiterated throughout Israel's history. And that this summons extends beyond the people of Israel was to be proclaimed in a new way in the development of Jewish prophecy. The disciple of Isaiah who wrote the closing chapters of the book of *Isaiah,* in the period after the return from exile in Babylon which Cyrus permitted in 538, made it clear that it was part of the promise of God that the rewards of justice as well as its requirements were to be extended beyond Israel. The gentile peoples too will be summoned in obedience to Jerusalem (56, 7, and 66, 18). So the Deuteronomic sovereignty over Israel is extended to all human societies.

It had of course been specifically with Israel's own obedience to law and with the law as specified for Israel that *Deuteronomy* had been concerned. Some of the divine precepts, those of the Ten Commandments most notably, apply to the actions of every member of the Hebrew people in relation to every other person, Hebrew or not—and indeed, since justice as such is being defined, to the actions of every human being in relation to every other. But in the application of some laws a difference was made between the way in which the people of Israel were to treat an alien who was resident or a temporary sojourner, who was to be treated as a member of the community, and the alien who was completely outside the relationships of the community. So in the relationship of one member of the community with another, a brother (*l'ahika*), usury is completely and unconditionally prohibited, but "to a stranger (*nokri:* the Hebrew word is one used only of one quite outside the community; see B. Nelson *The Idea of Usury,* second edition, Chicago, 1969, pp. xix–xxi) you may charge interest on a loan . . ." (23, 20).

What was expressed in this and other such distinctions in *Deuteronomy* was of course an understanding of the giving of the divine law as part of the making of the covenant that Yahweh had made only with the people of Israel. So that when a group of Jews six and a half centuries later continued to understand themselves as members of the people addressed by Moses in the Deuteronomic narrative, but also understood themselves as the heirs of the transformation of that Deuteronomic community into the Christian *ekklēsia*—into which was summoned to redemption and to obedience the entirety of human kind, for all of whom, whether Jews or non-Jews, their relationship to the divine law was a crucial part of their relationship to Jesus Christ—the nature of that knowledge of God's law available to every human being, quite apart from its revelation on Mount Sinai, became a crucial question. It was a question addressed by St. Paul in his letter to the church in Rome.

Paul declared that all human beings have available to them the knowledge of the existence and attributes of God, to which human reason attests, and of the content of the divine law; it is in spite of this knowledge and by disregarding it that human beings disobey God's law (*Romans* 1, 18–23 and 32). "When the gentile peoples who do not have the law [i.e., the revealed Mosaic law] do what are by nature the requirements of the law, they, although not having the law, are law to themselves . . ." (2, 14–15). "Those who hear the law are not just before God, but those who do what the law requires are made just" (2, 13). So Paul, in the course of acknowledging just that divine sovereignty over all peoples proclaimed in the closing chapters of the Book of Isaiah, recognized also the existence of a natural law, promulgated by God as the creator and ruler of the universe, substantially identical in content to the Ten Commandments and equally binding upon all human beings.

Later Christian thinkers would identify Stoic and more particularly Ciceronian accounts of the law to which nature and reason require conformity as evidence of just that natural knowledge of God's law to which Paul had referred. The Deuteronomic and prophetic inheritance of Judaism and what were taken by Christians to be the greatest achievements in formulating the requirements of justice in the Greco-Roman world were from then on understood by Christians as speaking to them of one and the same divine law and divine justice. Therefore one of the central tasks of Christian theology became to provide a framework within which they could be so understood, a task to which many patristic writers contributed. But the full complexity of that task emerged only with the greatest achievement in discharging it, that of St. Augustine.

Augustine in his account of divine law and justice was able to draw upon the writings and translations of Marius Victorinus, who in the fourth century had translated part of Aristotle's *Organon* and a variety of Neoplatonic authors into Latin and produced commentaries upon both Cicero and Aristotle. After his conversion to Christianity he used the philosophical idiom of Platonism, especially in a Plotinian version, to defend the orthodoxy of St. Athanasius in Trinitarian theology. Victorinus made it possible for Augustine to integrate what he had learned from Cicero into a Platonic account of justice in such a way that he could then in turn integrate that Platonism into his Christian theology.

To know what justice is is to be acquainted with the form of justice, a truth about justice present within the mind which cannot have been derived from sense experience (*De Trinitate* VIII, vi). That Platonic claim is expressed by Augustine in a formulation familiar to him in Cicero's writings (*De Finibus* V, 63, and *De Inventione* II, 160) according to which justice consists in giving to each person what is due to each, a formulation which Justinian was to use as the definition of justice in the opening section of the *Institutes*. Thus what the mind enquiring within itself discovers is a conception of justice already exemplified in the theory and practice of Roman law, but inadequately exemplified in at least two central ways.

Cicero's formulation, as we noted earlier of his view of justice in general, presupposes that justice is exercised within a determinately structured form of community, in which there is a hierarchy of offices and in which the contributions made to the overall good of the community by the holders of those offices, as well as by the individual members of the community, determine what is owed to whom by whom, that is, they determine desert. Without the context of such a form of community, as we noticed earlier in the case of Aristotle and as we shall see once again in the case of Hume, any justice of desert has to lack coherent application. What then is the determinate form of community presupposed by Augustine's justice of desert?

It is very different indeed from that presupposed by Cicero, being nothing less than the *civitas Dei*, that divinely ordained form of community into which every human being is summoned to find his or her due place and within which every human being may finally receive, not his or her desert, but something far better. So as with the Stoics the scope of justice becomes universal, but that universality requires far more than had Stoic universality, particularly in relation to the poor and oppressed, so much more indeed that its requirements have from time to time been discovered to have yet further and more radical application throughout the subsequent history of the church. But it was not only in respect of scope of application and the content of its demands that Augustine's conception of justice differed from Cicero's.

Augustine goes on from quoting Cicero to quote Paul: we are to be just "so as to owe no one anything, but to love one another" (*De Trinitate* VIII, vi; *Romans* 13, 8). Augustine appealed to Paul at this point because he confronted a problem to which his Platonism offered no solution. Everyone can discover within his or her own mind that timeless form or conception of justice which is the measure of right action. But not only is it the case that many individuals do not exercise their ability to become intellectually aware of that standard, something for which Plato and the Neoplatonists did offer an explanation; it also is inescapable, so Augustine took himself to have discovered both in his own life as recorded in the *Confessions* and in the lives of others, that the full intellectual apprehension of the form of justice is not by itself sufficient to generate right action. And this from the standpoint of a Platonic or Neoplatonic psychology is unintelligible.

What more is needed? To direct our love (Augustine uses both '*amor*' and '*amare*' and '*diligere*' and '*dilectio*') toward that form is something which we are only able to achieve when our love is directed toward a life which perfectly embodies that form in its actions, the life of Jesus Christ. The particularities of that life alone can evoke from us a response of love which is both love directed toward that particular person and toward the form of justice. And Jesus points us toward that immutable form of justice in God which we first directly apprehended within our own minds, but toward a clearer apprehension of which we continually move, as we come to love God more and more, as He is revealed in Jesus Christ (*De Trinitate* IX, 13).

Love, as Augustine understands it, is not the Platonic *erōs*. It consists in the first instance of the sum total of our natural desires and our desires to achieve happiness in achieving the satisfaction of those desires. We have to learn, however, that the satisfaction of *all* our desires will not in itself achieve happiness. It is only the satisfaction of desire for what it is right to desire—here again Augustine is following Cicero—which is happiness (*De Beata Vita* 2, 10). So our desires need to be directed toward objects other than those to which we first find them directed and ordered hierarchically. The direction and ordering of human desires is the work of the will (*voluntas*), and because human desires are in whatever state they are because of either the direction of or the failure to direct the will, human desires unlike the desires of other animals are voluntary (*De Libero Arbitrio* III, 1, 2). This Augustinian psychology, which in the place that it assigns to the will is strikingly different not only from Neoplatonism but from any ancient psychology, provides a new account of the genesis of action. Before we consider that account, it is important to return to Augustine's discussion of justice in order to understand how his conception of the nature of just action presupposes his psychology.

The standard of justice, we have already seen, is provided by the form of justice; and just action in accordance with that standard is produced by a love of the just whose object is in fact the divine justice. But not all action which is in apparent accord with the standard of justice is genuinely just action. Human beings can be motivated to conformity with that standard, not from love of the just, which is possible only as a form of the love of God, but from pride, love of oneself. Augustine characterizes pride (*superbia*) as "the fault which arises from trust in oneself and from making the self the source of its own life" (*De Spiritu et Littera* vii), a fault which Augustine took to be exemplified in Pelagius' praise of self-reliance. He also saw it as the motive to apparent, but not real, virtue in the history of pagan Rome.

Pride is conceived of by Augustine as a love of self which aspires to self-glorification. And Augustine quotes Sallust (*Bellum Catilinae* vii) to show that the desire for glory was the overmastering passion of the Romans. This led them to curb their other desires in the interests of attaining and preserving their own liberty and subjugating others (*De Civitate Dei* V, 12). What the history of pagan Rome exemplified, therefore, was not justice even when the actions of the Romans outwardly conformed to what justice requires. For the pagan Romans were moved by pride, not by the love of God. And consequently when their self-glorification could only or better be achieved by outright injustice, they were led by pride to flout the requirements of justice, most notably in their conquest and oppression of other peoples.

Justice was therefore absent in fact from the history of pagan Rome, which can serve for Christians nonetheless as an example: "Let us consider how great things they despised, how great things they endured, what lusts they subdued for the sake of human glory . . . and let this be useful to us even in suppressing pride . . ."

In a discussion of Cicero's *De Re Publica* Augustine accepted the definition of a republic put into the mouth of Scipio in that dialogue, according to which a republic exists only where the citizens agree in recognizing a standard of right, the application of which in the affairs of the political community results in justice. But, so Augustine argued, since there was no justice in pagan Rome, "there never was a Roman republic" (XIX, 21).

Justice exists only in that republic which is the city of God, of which Christ is founder and in which Christ rules (II, 21). So there are two cities, each with its own history: the City of Man, whose first founder was Cain and whose final exemplification was in pagan Rome, and the City of God. The first of these was founded and refounded on perverse human willing which directs the desires to other than their true happiness; the second of these was founded on that gift of grace which enables the will to choose freely what in fact will lead to its true happiness. It was Augustine's conception of the will which underlay his political theory.

That conception of the will was Augustine's—invention? Or discovery? In his own eyes at least it was a discovery, but a discovery of what had always been the case. Albrecht Dihle in his paradoxically named *The Theory of Will in Classical Antiquity* (Berkeley, 1982) both has shown how the authors of classical antiquity prior to Augustine lacked any vocabulary and for the most part any conception of the will and has emphasized how it was Augustine's own moral experience, as portrayed in the *Confessions,* out of which he elaborated that concept. The difference between Augustine and his classical, as contrasted with his New Testament, predecessors can be described in two closely related ways. The first concerns how the failure of someone who knows what it is best for him or her to do, but nonetheless does not act accordingly, is to be explained. Within the framework successively sophisticated by Socrates, Plato, and Aristotle such failure must be explicable, as we noticed earlier, *either* by some imperfection in that particular person's knowledge at that particular time of what is good and best *or* by some imperfection in the education and disciplining of the passions. There is no third possibility. By contrast Augustine held that it is possible for someone to know unqualifiedly what it is best to do in a particular situation and for there to be no defect in the passions as such, except that they are misdirected by the will. The will, being anterior to reason, has at the most fundamental level no reason for its biddings. And this points to a second way of characterizing the difference between Augustine and his major classical predecessors.

For both Plato and Aristotle reason is independently motivating; it has its own ends and it inclines those who possess it toward them, even if it is also necessary that the higher desires be educated into rationality and that the bodily appetites be subordinated to it. For Augustine intellect itself needs to be moved to activity by will. It is will which guides attention in one direction rather than another. It is will which determines in key part what are made of the materials afforded by sense perception for cognition, both within memory and in the act of cognition itself (see for a summary of Augustine's view on these and the succeeding topics and for a comprehensive list of citations Dihle, op. cit., chapter VI and pp. 231–244, and R.A. Markus 'Human Action: Will and Virtue' Chapter 25 *The Cambridge History of Later Greek and Early Medieval Philosophy,* ed. A.H. Armstrong, Cambridge, 1967).

The human will is then the ultimate determinant of human action, and the human will is systematically misdirected and misdirected in such a way that it is not within its own power to redirect itself. Originally the will was directed to the love of God, but by the exercise of a freedom to choose between good and evil Adam chose to direct his will to the love of self rather than of God. In so doing Adam impaired his freedom to choose good, and because other human powers need direction from the will, Adam from then on lacked any resources to recover that freedom. Each individual human being reveals in the condition of his or her will, whether he or she recognizes it or not, his or her solidarity with Adam. It is only divine grace which can rescue the will from that condition.

Augustine affirms *both* the necessity of grace for the redirection of the will *and* the necessity of the will's freely assenting to the divine grace. How these affirmations are related to each other it is unnecessary for my present purposes to enquire. But it is important to remark that the fundamental human virtue is a virtue of the will in its returning to freedom, just as the fundamental human vice is the vice of the will in its self-enslaved condition. The fundamental human vice is of course pride; correspondingly the fundamental human virtue is humility (*humilitas*), fundamental in that without it one cannot have the love of God and so cannot possess any other virtue.

Justice, therefore, cannot inform an individual's character unless that character is also informed by humility, and the rootedness of injustice in pride entails that injustice consists in disobedience. It is not that injustice is not also, as Plato held, a failure in respect of metaphysical, political, and psychological order, and, as Aristotle held, *pleonexia,* but that willful disorder and *pleonexia* are both effects and signs of disobedience.

Because of the originality of his account of the will Augustine had to innovate linguistically as well as conceptually. In so doing, as Dihle has shown, he was able to draw upon changing uses of '*velle*' and '*voluntas*' in earlier Latin, particularly in legal contexts. And in writers as different as Philo and Seneca anticipations of the Augustinian conception of the will are certainly to be found. But such facts must not be allowed to obscure what is radically new in Augustine. Augustine of course was interpreting the scriptures in his accounts of human sinfulness and redemption, but his elucidation of them is distinctive in that he is able to give an account of Paul's doctrine in *Romans,* for example, using a vocabulary of a kind which was not available to Paul himself. In so doing there is no doubt that he captures Paul's meaning;

it is not a mistake, therefore, to impute to Paul a conception of the will which he himself could not have spelled out. But it would be a mistake to impute such a conception to the protagonists of any of the ancient philosophical schools, even to those Stoic writers who have sometimes been misunderstood in just this way.

Augustine thus does elaborate a genuinely new account both of the nature of justice and of the genesis of human action. The rationality of right action—and right action does indeed, on Augustine's view, conform to the rational standards provided by the forms which the intellect apprehends—is not its primary determinant, but a secondary consequence of right willing. Hence faith which initially moves and informs the will is prior to understanding; what understanding can provide is a rational justification for having initially believed or done what faith enjoined, but such justification must always be retrospective. Prospective rationality, understood very much as Plato had understood it, is then possible for the faith-informed intellect, further informing the will which had directed it into its state of faith (with the necessary work of grace) and continues so to direct it. This secondary character of practical rationality is something to which Augustine was necessarily committed by his psychology of the will.

The same psychology continued to be at work in alliance with the same theological doctrine throughout the Augustinian theologies of medieval Europe. New strands of doctrine, that of PseudoDionysius or that of Johannes Scotus Erigena, would be woven into the fabric of theological thought. And the realization of the institutional and other practical implications of the Augustinian standpoint was achieved often enough by those who were not themselves theorists, except in an *ad hoc* manner in the course of debates and struggles over practical issues, but whose words and actions emerge from a background of beliefs structured by Augustine's theology. Most notable of all in realizing the practical and especially the political dimensions of that theology was perhaps the monk Hildebrand, who became pope in 1073 as Gregory VII.

Gregory VII was by intention, insofar as he was a theorist at all, an entirely theological theorist. But within his theology, as A.J. Carlyle in his discussion of Gregory VII suggests with specific reference to Stoicism (*Medieval Political Theory in the West,* vol. III, Edinburgh, 1970, p. 97), there reappeared recognizable theses and strands of argument from ancient philosophy and from Roman law, transmitted through Augustine and through other patristic writers. And since Gregory VII was engaged in supplying answers to questions which few, if any, of his theological predecessors had had to frame in the same way, it is not surprising that his theology, while always returning to scripture and to tradition for its justification, drew upon conceptual resources of a kind whose use was uncharacteristic among theologians of his and of the immediately preceding centuries. Nor was he to find heirs of the same stature for many centuries to come. When Gregory VII's theocratic vision has reappeared, it has been in social, political, and theological circumstances so different from his that those heirs have not always been recognized as such. I think in this respect especially of Jean Calvin and of Pope Pius IX. What they shared with Gregory VII was above all his understanding that the nature of Christian community and of the virtues required for life in that community have to be spelled out in concrete institutional and organizational terms.

Gregory VII articulated his political theology in the course of discharging four distinct, but related, papal responsibilities in terms of which he defined the tasks of his papacy. The first was that of the internal reform of the church. Hence his immediate and necessary focus upon particular issues—such as those of enforcing the celibacy of priests, eliminating the sin of simony (the sin of purchasing ecclesiastical office for oneself or another by money or other wordly goods), improving the systematic application of canon law, and upholding the authority of the bishop of Rome over other bishops—must not be allowed to obscure his understanding of the church as a genuinely universal society. What Gregory expressed in the idiomatic and institutional forms of the eleventh century was a view of the place of the church expressed much earlier by Isidore of Seville, when he spoke of the church as *"universitas gentium"* (*De Fide Catholica* ii, 7) and as *"civitas regis magni"* (*Quaestiones in Vetus Testamentum: In Primum Regum* i). God reigns as king of a city with sovereignty over the entire universe, and the pope is God's viceroy.

Gregory's particular reforms were all aimed at enabling the concrete organizational forms of the church to express more adequately this universality and this sovereignty. The widespread breakdown in maintaining priestly celibacy and in preventing simony, and the tendency of bishops to value the favors conferred by princes rather than the authority of the papacy, were all understood by Gregory as ways in which sex, money, and political power were used to subvert the independence, the *libertas,* of the church. So that in his identification of the points at which he found himself compelled to enter into political conflict, most notably with the Emperor Henry IV, what is always in question is a vindication of the ability of the church to determine its own structure in a way that conforms to the sovereignty of God.

Libertas, therefore, is a condition for *iustitia,* and when both political societies and the universal church are ordered in accordance with justice, the appropriate *libertas* of each will also have been achieved. In affirming the order of *iustitia* against those ostensibly Christian secular rulers in the established powers of Europe, the Salian *Reich* and the France of the Capetian kings, whose aggrandizement violated that order, the second responsibility of Gregory VII's papacy was discharged. The order of *iustitia* is an order embodied in the universal church, an order in which each human being has his or her own allotted place and his or her own allotted duties. To occupy that place and to perform that function well is to be just. To refuse to occupy that place or to discharge its duties badly or to rebel against the order defining that place is to fail in respect of justice.

Injustice is *inoboedientia.* The vice to which disobedience gives expression is *superbia,* pride. The virtue underlying and required for justice is humility. It is at once clear that this is indeed Augustine's scheme of the virtues, presupposing Augustine's psychology, which is being expressed in political terms. And Gregory continued to use the Augustinian scheme in asserting that it is *iustitia* alone which ensures *concordia* and that when the ends of justice are not served, more particularly when kings act as tyrants, the outcome is discord. The concord which embodies justice is hierarchical. Kings and, above all, the Holy Roman Emperor do occupy supreme places, both of authority and of responsibility, but they are no more protected by *ius,* that law which expresses what *iustitia* demands, than is anyone else. Just because the scope of justice is universal, no human being lies beyond its protection, and the most basic forms of protection are extended to all. So equality before and under divine law belongs to human beings *qua* human beings, an equality which derives from membership in the universal, divinely ordained community.

Gregory VII's third papal responsibility was his formulation of the principles of justice, not in the course of his conflicts with the great powers which threatened the exercise of its proper authority by the papacy, but in the homilies which he sent to the rulers of the less well-established powers who looked to the papacy for guidance. Such rulers could expect from the papacy aid in their claims to *libertas.* Gregory VII's message to them was "that power entailed responsibilities" (K.J. Leyser 'The Polemics of the Papal Revolution' in *Trends in Medieval Political Thought,* ed. B. Smalley, Oxford, 1965, p. 55; this is the definitive statement of what was at issue between Gregory VII and his opponents and critics), and those responsibilities were to be expressed in a law to be acknowledged by all secular powers, a law spelled out with whatever detail law requires. Walter Ullmann spoke of "Hildebrand's clear perception of the need to have a law with which to govern the *societas christiana*. That law for which he repeatedly expressed his wish was to show the distillation of *iustitia* into *ius*, into generally binding rules of conduct. Hierocratic principles as evolved in times gone by and in historical events constitute in their totality *justitia*, and those detailed principles should be made available for the actual government of the *societas christiana*" (*The Growth of Papal Government in the Middle Ages*, London, 1955, pp. 274–275). Thus the fourth specific responsibility of Gregory VII's papacy was to give instructions for codifying the relevant parts of the law of the *ecclesia*, instructions which issued in the compilation of the *Dictatus Papae*, whose chapter headings, wrote Ullmann, "embody *iustitia* in the mould of *ius*" (loc. cit.).

The guardianship of the order of justice is one of the specific functions of the pope, and that guardianship imposes a duty of respect and obedience upon secular rulers. Gregory wrote to Toirrdelbach ua Briain, king of Munster and claimant to the high-kingship of Ireland, that the whole world must obey and revere the Roman Church (see A. Gwynn 'Gregory VII and the Irish Church' in *Studi Gregoriani*, vol. 3, Rome, 1948), and he reiterates similar claims to other princes. But it is important to emphasize both that the pope too is subject to the order of justice and that although he may judge, rebuke, and, if necessary, depose secular rulers, he could not assume their role. Nor did Gregory suggest that the authority of secular rulers derived from the pope or that the pope had the right to choose such rulers (Brian Tierney *The Crisis of Church and State 1050–1300*, Englewood Cliffs, 1964, pp. 53–57).

I am not here concerned with the arguments used by Gregory in support of these papal claims, some of which arguments were buttressed by anachronistic misinterpretations of precedents afforded by St. Ambrose and Pope Gelasius. What matters is rather Gregory VII's realization that the Augustinian theology of justice, like any substantive conception of justice, has not been fully articulated until its consequences for the theory of politics are rendered explicit. What Gregory supplies is thus a continuation of Augustine's thought in which the relationship of the two cities in a Christian society is understood in terms of the difference in both function and origin of the papacy and of ecclesiastical institutions generally from secular sovereignties.

The former are unambiguous in their import; they derive directly from divine institution. But secular rule has its roots *both* in original sin *and* in divine institution. So A.J. Carlyle first noted that in some passages Hildebrand "maintains that the origin of secular authority is related to the vicious or sinful character in human nature," while in others "he describes secular authority as being derived from God, and as finding its true character in the defence and maintenance of justice"; Carlyle then goes on to say that "these two conceptions may seem at first sight, especially to those who are unfamiliar with the Stoic and patristic tradition, inconsistent and irreconcilable, but this is merely a confusion. For, in this tradition, government, like the other great institutions of society, such as property and slavery, is the result of sin and represents sinful greed and ambition, and yet is also the necessary, and in the Christian conception the divine, remedy for sin. Men in a state of innocence would neither need coercive government, nor would they claim to rule over their fellow men, while in the state of sin and ambition, men desire lordship over each other, but also, in this condition, men need control and restraint if any measure of justice or peace is to be attained and preserved" (loc. cit.). Secular government is thus *both* the result of sin *and* divinely ordained. It is because of the way in which government is rooted in sin that secular rulers cannot be allowed to be the final judges in their own case. And for this reason God has provided the remedy of the papacy.

Gregory VII's theocratic development of the Augustinian conception of justice represented the highest achievement of the Augustinian tradition before the reintroduction of Aristotle's political and moral texts to Europe. Gregory's understanding of the virtue of justice was at two salient points at one with Aristotle's, even although he knew nothing of either the *Ethics* or the *Politics*. He conceived of justice in terms of what is owing to whom in respect of desert, and he evaluated that desert in terms of the discharge of the duties of one's assigned place within the institutions of a determinately structured community. Moreover, he conceived of the virtues in general and of justice in particular as dispositions whose exercise finds its point and purpose in leading human beings toward rather than away from their *telos*. But those points of agreement between an Aristotelian standpoint and a Gregorian are perhaps less significant than might at first appear, when we also consider the large disagreements between those two points of view. They concern at least four distinct, though related, issues.

First, according to Aristotle the institutionalization of justice is in the laws of a *polis,* and the best kind of Aristotelian *polis* is very different from the *civitas Dei.* The citizens of the *polis* are very different in moral capacity from those barbarians incapable of the life of a *polis,* barbarians who include in their number the vast majority of mankind;

and women and slaves are both excluded from citizenship. The law of the *civitas Dei* in all its versions, Deuteronomic, that of the Sermon on the Mount, Pauline, Augustinian, and Gregorian is by contrast a law for all mankind, for knowledge of whose basic tenets every human being can be held responsible. And no one is excluded from the *civitas Dei,* except by themselves.

Second, the Augustinian catalogue of the virtues and the content of the virtues as specified by Augustine and Gregory differ in significant ways from their Aristotelian counterparts. Aristotle finds no place among the virtues for either humility or charity. Augustine and Gregory assert that without humility and charity there can be no such virtue as justice. The law of the *civitas Dei* requires a kind of justice to the unborn which Aristotle's proposed measures for controlling the size of the population of a *polis* deny to them. The highest type of human being, according to Aristotle, is the magnanimous man. The highest type of human being on any Christian view, including the Augustinian, is the saint.

Third, the Aristotelian understanding of the relationship of human beings both to the good and the best and to the particular immediate good of each is specified in terms of a psychology of reason, passion, and appetite, within which there is no place for any conception of the will. But for Augustine's version of Christianity it is by bad will, *mala voluntas,* that we are kept from the good, and it is only by the redirection of the will that we can aim at achieving it.

Fourth, and finally, the keystone of the Augustinian conception of justice and of everything else is Augustine's biblical understanding of the relationship of the soul to God, as created by God, required by God to obey his just law and destined for eternal life in society with him. But within Aristotle's ethics and politics, as within his cosmology, there is no place for a divine creator or a divine lawgiver and no place for any human *telos* beyond that to be attained by mortals before death.

It is not to be wondered at, then, that when Aristotle's political and ethical texts were reintroduced into Europe, the protagonists of Augustinian theology often enough saw in Aristotle little but matter for condemnation. And it might well seem that from their own point of view they must have been right, given these large points of difference. What is surprising is rather that anyone should have conceived it as possible to bring together Aristotelian philosophy and Augustinian theology within a single scheme of thought, no matter how complex. Yet in the universities of the thirteenth century the project of rendering this possibility actual was to become central to intellectual and moral enquiry, particularly among Dominican teachers and scholars.

X

Overcoming a Conflict of Traditions

The late twentieth-century reader of St. Thomas Aquinas has to reckon with four characteristics of the *Summa Theologiae,* each of which has to be given its due weight (for the best general account see R. McInerny *St. Thomas Aquinas,* Notre Dame, 1982). The first is that, for all its length, it is a work presented to its readers, while and as still, in construction. I do not mean by this only or mainly that it was in fact unfinished at the time of Aquinas' death in 1274, some of the third part still remaining to be written and the earlier parts still open to revision. Even more important is the way in which each article, each question takes the argument as far as it needs to be taken in the light of what Aquinas knew of the discussions of each particular argument so far but leaves it open to be taken further. And this I shall suggest later is an important clue to Aquinas' method of enquiry.

Second, Aquinas' work of philosophical and theological construction is systematic, in a way and to a degree which surpasses even Plato, Aristotle, and Augustine. It is therefore important when one treats of Aquinas' developed views on particular topics or issues, as I shall be doing in discussing his accounts of justice and of practical rationality, not to abstract these in piecemeal fashion and treat them in too great isolation from the context supplied by his overall point of view and method. The degree of interdependence between Aquinas' treatment of one set of topics and issues and his treatment of others does of course vary, but sometimes the relationships are, to modern readers at least, unexpected, as, for example, in the way Aquinas developed his views on action, passion, and motion in relation to his treatment of the doctrines of creation and of actual grace (see B. Lonergan *Grace and Freedom,* New York, 1971, especially chapter 4).

Third, Aquinas avowedly writes out of a tradition, or rather out of at least two traditions, extending each as part of his task of integrating them into a single systematic mode of thought. He encountered those traditions, each with its own authoritative texts and its own standard commentaries, not only in those texts and commentaries but also in his day-to-day teaching and disputation in the University of Paris and in those questions which focused contemporary conflict both in the church and in secular society. For Aristotle the overall science within which enquiries about practical reasoning and justice find their place had been *politics,* and the necessary milieu for their experience in action had been the *polis;* for Aquinas the concerns of politics had to be understood in the framework of a rational theology, and the *civitas* had to be understood in relation to the *civitas Dei.* Modern nontheological readers of Aquinas at this point may be apt to suppose that their difficulties in coming to terms with Aquinas' relationship to tradition is a result of their alienation from his theology. In fact I suspect that it is characteristically the other way around. It is rather because the conception of tradition is so little at home in modern culture — and when it does seem to appear, it is usually in the bastardized form given to it by modern political conservatism — that they find it difficult to come to terms with Aquinas' metaphysical theology.

Fourth, Aquinas' readers have to reckon with his singleness of purpose. "Purity of heart is to will one thing," said Kierkegaard. Very differently John Rawls has written that "Although to subordinate all our aims to one end does not strictly speaking violate the principles of rational choice . . . , it still strikes us as irrational, or more likely as mad" (*A Theory of Justice,* Cambridge, Mass., 1971, p. 554). The examples which Rawls has just given of those who have in this way given their allegiance to one dominant end are those of St. Ignatius Loyola and of Aquinas. What Rawls says is an instructive measure of the cultural distance separating the protagonists of modernity from Aquinas. Interestingly, however, those protagonists often enough do not take Aristotle to be similarly alien or mad.

So Rawls generally quotes Aristotle with approval, and Martha Nussbaum has sharply contrasted Aristotle's account of practical judgment with Maritain's Thomist view (essay 4 in her commentary on *De Motu Animalium,* Princeton, 1978), emphasizing in subsequent work the variety and heterogeneity of the goods recognized by Aristotle (see *The Fragility of Goodness,* Cambridge, 1985, and 'The Discernment of Perception: an Aristotelian Conception of Private and Public Rationality,' in *Boston Area Colloquium in Ancient Philosophy,* vol. 1, ed. J.C. Cleary, Lanham, 1986). But Aquinas too recognized the variety and heterogeneity of goods and, no more and no less than Aristotle, understood them as goods insofar as they were and in virtue of their being constituents of the kind of life directed to *the* good and *the* best. What obscures recognition of the degree to which Aquinas and Aristotle are at one in this is in part at least a failure to recognize that it was through Aristotle's understanding of the integration of goods which the life of the best kind of *polis* affords and through his theology which specifies the teleological order of the cosmos, within which that political life finds its completion, that he came to understand the unity of the supreme human good in the way that he did. An Aristotle whose *Ethics* is read for the most part apart from his *Politics,* and both as though his theology did not exist, is much more unlike Aquinas than Aristotle in fact was.

Nonetheless Aquinas' work, especially in the *Summa Theologiae,* is informed by an overriding unity of purpose, expressed both in his conception of the ultimate unity of good and in the way he writes about it, which notably exceeds even that of Aristotle. And perhaps nothing less would have enabled him to confront the apparently incompatible and conflicting demands of two distinct and rival traditions, the Aristotelian and the Augustinian, both in their thirteenth-century versions deemed irremediably opposed to one another by many of his contemporaries, but to both of which he gave allegiance. How was he able to do so?

When two rival large-scale intellectual traditions confront one another, a central feature of the problem of deciding between their claims is characteristically that there is no neutral way of characterizing either the subject matter about which they give rival accounts or the standards by which their claims are to be evaluated. Each standpoint has its own account of truth and knowledge, its own mode of characterizing the relevant subject matter. And the attempt to discover a neutral, independent set of standards or mode of characterizing data which is *both* such as must be acceptable to all rational persons *and* is sufficient to determine the truth on the matters about which the two traditions are at variance has generally, and perhaps universally, proved to be a search for a chimera. How then can genuine controversy proceed? It does so characteristically in two stages.

The first is that in which each characterizes the contentions of its rival in its own terms, making explicit the grounds for rejecting what is incompatible with its own central theses, although sometimes allowing that from its own point of view and in the light of its own standards of judgment its rival has something to teach it on marginal and subordinate questions. A second stage is reached if and when the protagonists of each tradition, having considered in what ways their own tradition has by its own standards of achievement in enquiry found it difficult to develop its enquiries beyond a certain point, or has produced in some area insoluble antinomies, ask whether the alternative and rival tradition may not be able to provide resources to characterize and to explain the failings and defects of their own tradition more adequately than they, using the resources of that tradition, have been able to do.

Every such tradition, to some significant degree, stands or falls as a mode of enquiry and has within itself at each stage a more or less well-defined problematic, that set of issues, difficulties, and problems which have emerged from its previous achievements in enquiry. Characteristically, therefore, such traditions possess measures to evaluate their own progress or lack of it, even if such measures necessarily are framed in terms of and presuppose the truth of those central theses to which the tradition gives its allegiance.

In controversy between rival traditions the difficulty in passing from the first stage to the second is that it requires a rare gift of empathy as well as of intellectual insight for the protagonists of such a tradition to be able to understand the theses, arguments, and concepts of their rival in such a way that they are able to view themselves from such an alien standpoint and to recharacterize their own beliefs in an appropriate manner from the alien perspective of the rival tradition. Such rare gifts had not been evidenced in the earlier confrontations between the Augustinian and the Aristotelian traditions, and in the social and intellectual conditions of the late twelfth and early thirteenth centuries it would have been difficult for it to have been otherwise.

The late eleventh- and twelfth-century European culture was one in which philosophical enquiry was largely unsystematic and theological studies largely unphilosophical. There were of course exceptional philosophical figures, such as Anselm and Abelard, but the intellectual climate in the generations following is better represented by John of Salisbury. And when in the newly founded universities of the thirteenth century Aristotle's metaphysical, psychological, ethical, and political texts were made available, they were accompanied by Islamic interpretation and commentary, some of which seemed to place Aristotle in irreconcilable opposition to Christian doctrine, let alone to Augustinian theology, on such matters as the immortality of the soul and the eternity of the universe. So the followers of Ibn Roschd, Latinized as Averroes, in the University of Paris and elsewhere found themselves engaged in a philosophical enterprise which apparently generated conclusions incompatible with the theology to which they gave their allegiance. Their resulting predicament was one which was to strengthen the Augustinian opponents of Aristotelianism in their condemnation of it.

It was providential for Aquinas' intellectual development that after his early studies in Paris he was from 1248, when he was twenty-three years old, until 1252 the pupil of Albertus Magnus at the new Dominican *studium generale* in Cologne. He may indeed, although we do not know this, have studied under Albertus in Paris. Three aspects of Albertus' greatness were crucial for Aquinas' development. The first is the part which he played in reviving Augustinian theology by restoring its philosophical content, drawing as Augustine himself had done upon sources which were either Neoplatonic or themselves had been influenced by Neoplatonism. Thus he contributed to the revival of Augustinian philosophical theology, yet also — and this is the second aspect of his greatness which was important for Aquinas' education — insisted against some Augustinians on the relative autonomy of the natural sciences, in which enquiry begins from particulars.

In astronomy Albertus was a follower of Ptolemy, in biology of Galen. He himself made and recorded observations of plants, animals, and astronomical phenomena, pointing out, for example, Aristotle's error on the frequency of rainbows. Yet this willingness to correct Aristotle, both in the natural sciences and in metaphysics, was accompanied by another characteristic which was to prove seminal for Aquinas, a conviction that the first step in understanding Aristotle's texts so as to be able to respond to them, whether with assent or dissent, was to let Aristotle speak in his own voice, so far as possible undistorted by interpretative commentary. So Albertus in his major commentaries made it clear that he was expounding and clarifying Aristotle's views, reserving his own opinions for expression elsewhere (see J. A. Weisheipl *Friar Thomas D'Aquino,* Washington, DC, 1983, pp. 41–43).

When Aquinas was thus, as a result of his education by Albertus Magnus, confronted by the claims of two distinct and in important ways incompatible philosophical traditions, he had been trained to understand each from within. Perhaps no one else in the history of philosophy has ever been put into quite this situation, and the questions which he must have been in consequence led to formulate pointed toward a conception of truth, independent of either tradition, which he articulated in his earliest *Quaestiones Disputatae* in 1256–57, and a corresponding conception of reality, the essentials of which he propounded a little earlier in what very probably was the first treatise which he ever wrote, *De Ente et Essentia.* How Aquinas' initial intellectual situation bore upon his reasons for affirming those particular conceptions of truth and reality is perhaps best understood by considering why some modern writers have rejected them.

How can it be, such writers have asked, that our whole web of beliefs and concepts could be judged true or false, adequate or inadequate, in virtue of its and their relationship to some reality quite external to that web? For in order for us to compare our beliefs and concepts to that reality we should have to already have beliefs about it and have understood certain of our concepts as having application to it. So, they conclude, an understanding of any reality, in relation to which truth and falsity, adequacy and inadequacy are judged, must be internal to our web of concepts and beliefs; there can be no reference beyond that web to anything genuinely external to it. So runs an argumentative theme common to Hegel's criticism of what he took the Kantian *ding-an-sich* to be, to late nineteenth-century idealism and to Hilary Putnam's rejection of what he calls "external realism" (see *The Logic of Hegel,* Encyclopedia *Logic,* trans. W. Wallace, Oxford, 1873, sections 44 and 124; T. H. Green *Prolegomena to Ethics,* Oxford, 1893, chapter I; and H. Putnam *Reason, Truth and History*). It is characteristic of those who adopt this view that almost always in practice and often enough in avowed theory they treat the concept of truth as nothing more than an idealization of the concept of warranted assertibility. For on this view we can have no criterion of truth beyond the best warrants that we can offer for our assertions, and although the best warrants may not be those that we now adduce, they can only be those which will be invoked by the best rational enquirers among our successors in the long run.

So the concepts of truth and reality are defined internally to our scheme of concepts and beliefs. It is sometimes held to be one of the benefits of this point of view that from it any large skepticism ceases to be coherently formulable. For such skepticism presupposes that our scheme of concepts and beliefs could be largely, perhaps wholly, false and inadequate, and that in turn presupposes that it is not, as it is on this Hegel-Green-Putnam view, judge in its own case, finding its concept and its criteria of truth within itself and thus assured of the detection of no error which cannot, in principle as some like to say, be corrected by its own resources.

A key word in the formulation of this kind of internalism in respect to truth and reality is "we." The assumption underlying its use is that there is one and only one overall community of enquiry, sharing substantially one and the same set of concepts and beliefs. But what if there appears a second community whose tradition and procedures of enquiry are structured in terms of different, largely incompatible and largely incommensurable concepts and beliefs, defining warranted assertibility and truth in terms internal to its scheme of concepts and beliefs?

Each of these rival communities of enquiry is able to characterize the other as in error from its point of view, but in denying the claims of the other it can assert no more than that what the other asserts *is* in error from its point of view. But that after all is not in question; that at least is something upon which both parties can agree. What the protagonists of each rival tradition must at this point do is choose between two alternatives, that of abandoning *any* claim that truth-value can be attached to the fundamental judgments underpinning their mode of enquiry *or* that of making a claim to truth of a kind which appeals beyond their own particular scheme of concepts and beliefs, to something external to that scheme. The first of these alternatives would have evacuated the concept of enquiry embodied in both the Aristotelian and the Augustinian traditions of its distinctive content. For both had conceived of enquiry in terms of a directedness toward a truth independent of the enquiring mind. And indeed it is clear that the abandonment of the classical conception of truth in its entirety, rather than its modification and emendation, only becomes possible after and in the light of a particular post-Hegelian history in which the pragmatism of James and Dewey seemed to some to have opened up new possibilities.

The need in the thirteenth century for those confronted by the claims of the Aristotelian and Augustinian traditions to move in the direction in which Aquinas did in fact move is thus in retrospect plain. Aquinas' new account of truth challenged what had been the prevailing Augustinian view, so that it is not surprising that it was only Aquinas who at the time understood how to elaborate the conceptions which philosophy and theology alike required. P. F. Mandonnet, in a book whose central theses are now uniformly rejected (*Siger de Brabant et l'Averroisme latin an XIIIe siécle,* 2 vols., Louvain, 1908 and 1911), ascribed to the Latin Averroists and particularly to Siger of Brabant a rival solution to the problem confronting Aquinas, which invoked a theory according to which a particular thesis can be true in philosophy, while some logically incompatible thesis is true in theology. So on the view that Mandonnet ascribed to the Latin Averroists, the predicate 'true' would have been replaced by the predicate 'true in . . .' .

What would in any case have precluded most, but perhaps not all, Averroists from holding any such theory was the fact they shared with all other Aristotelians an unshakable adherence to the principle of noncontradiction as formulated and defended by Aristotle in Book Gamma of the *Metaphysics* (see F. Van Steenberghen *Thomas Aquinas and Radical Aristotelianism,* Washington, D.C., 1980, and, for an earlier rejection of Mandonnet's view of Siger, E. Gilson *Études de philosophie médiévale,* Strasbourg, 1921). But Mandonnet nonetheless had a genuine insight, that the major intellectual problems of the thirteenth century could only be resolved on the basis of a systematic conception of truth which enabled Aristotelian and Augustinian theses to be reformulated within one and the same framework. The position which Mandonnet foisted upon Siger is perhaps the only alternative to the position taken up by Aquinas for anyone who refused simply to reject either the Aristotelian or the Augustinian standpoint.

What Aquinas then does in the *De Ente et Essentia* and the opening discussions of the *Quaestiones Disputatae de Veritate* is to expound a set of distinctions concerning essence and existence on the one hand and truth on the other, distinctions whose justification lies in what they then enable him to achieve in reconstructing both Aristotelian and Augustinian positions within the framework of a unified metaphysical theology. With the major part of that achievement I shall not be concerned here. But given my present purposes, it is impossible to avoid taking note of the function of those distinctions in enabling Aquinas to give an account of that reality by reference to which the terminus of all intellectually adequate explanation and understanding, whether theoretical or practical, has to be specified and in relation to which the ordering of all subordinate explanation and understanding has to be carried through. That reality, providing, as it does, the terminus for all understanding *ex hypothesi,* cannot itself be explained in respect of its nature and characteristics by anything beyond itself. Nothing can make it be other than what it is; necessarily, therefore, it is whatever it is and in the necessity of its being and action contrasts with the contingency of all other being and action.

So it has to furnish a final *telos* for other beings in respect of their final causality. But that they must pursue this or that particular good here and now in order truly to enter into that relationship with it which constitutes their final good will always be a matter of how contingently things are. And enquiry into these contingencies, both as characterizable by unaided human reason and as revealed to faith by divine revelation, is a central part of the task of the metaphysician and of the philosophical theologian. How that enquiry is to proceed is exemplified in Aquinas' discussion of the specifically human *telos.* But it is illuminating first to consider more generally the structure of Aquinas' enquiries, particularly in the *Summa Theologiae,* remembering what was said earlier about its being a work still in the process of construction.

Every article in the *Summa* poses a question whose answer depends upon the outcome of an essentially uncompleted debate. For the set of often disparate and heterogeneous arguments against whatever position Aquinas' enquiries so far have led him to accept is always open to addition by some as yet unforeseen argument. And there is no way, therefore, of ruling out in advance the possibility that what has so far been accepted may yet have to be modified or even rejected. In this there is nothing peculiar to Aquinas' procedures. It is of the nature of all dialectic, understood as Aristotle understood it, to be essentially incomplete.

Nonetheless Aquinas' procedures entitled him, on many occasions at least, to place more rational confidence in the answers which he gave to particular questions than is provided by the particular arguments which he adduces, and this for two distinct reasons. First, Aquinas was engaged in an overall work of dialectical construction in the *Summa* in which every elementary part finds its place within some larger structure, which in turn contributes to the order of the whole. Thus conclusions in one part of the structure may and do confirm conclusions reached elsewhere. Second, Aquinas was careful in each discussion to summon up all the relevant contributions to argument and interpretation which had been preserved and transmitted within the two major traditions. So biblical sources are brought into conversation with Socrates, Plato, Aristotle, and Cicero, and all of them with Arab and Jewish thinkers, as well as with patristic writers and later Christian theologians. The length and detail of the *Summa* are not accidental features of it, but integral to its purpose and more particularly to providing both Aquinas himself and his readers with the assurance that the arguments adduced for particular articles were the strongest produced so far from any known point of view.

Aquinas then was engaged in a long series of constructive debates through whose arguments and conclusions he constructed or reconstructed a representation of the hierarchical order of the universe. What, so I have already suggested, justifies his fundamental theses in ontology and in the theory of truth is their indispensability for this work of representation. What justifies his representation of the order of things over against its Averroist, Neoplatonist, and Augustinian rivals is its ability to identify, to explain, and to transcend their limitations and defects, while preserving from them everything that survives dialectical questioning in a way which those rivals are unable from their philosophical resources to provide any counterpart.

At once the following objection will be made. Surely, it will be said, rational justification, according to both Aristotle and Aquinas, is a matter of deducibility from first principles, in the case of derived assertions, and of the self-evidentness as necessary truths of these same first principles. So that your account of the rational justification of Aquinas' overall view is quite inconsistent with Aquinas' own account of rational justification. What this objection fails to take account of is the difference between rational justification within a science, the rational justification of a science, and the rational justification required by an account of the sciences as a whole, hierarchically ordered system. Rational justification within a perfected science is indeed a matter of demonstrating how derivative truths follow from the first truths of that particular science, in some types of case supplemented by additional premises; and the justification of the principles of a subordinate science by some higher-order enquiry will be similarly demonstrative. First principles themselves will be dialectically justifiable; their evidentness consists in their recognizability, in the light of such dialectic, as concerning what is the case *per se,* what attributes, for example, belong to the essential nature of what constitutes the fundamental subject matter of the science in question (on first principles see *Commentary on the Ethics* I, lect. xi; *Commentary on the Posterior Analytics* II, lect. xx; and *S.T.* Ia, 85,8).

There are of course first principles concerning such basic conceptual relationships as those of parts to wholes such that any rational being must find them in some way or another undeniable. But even they are not necessarily immune to diversities of interpretation, and by themselves they cannot provide the first principles of any substantive science. The first principles which are able to provide the substance of such a science always have to include additional premises. And this is true at the most fundamental level. We do indeed, according to Aquinas, apprehend *being* as the most fundamental concept of theoretical enquiry and make explicit what we apprehend in the recognition which our judgments accord to the principle of noncontradiction. Similarly we apprehend *good* as the most fundamental concept in forming practical activity and make explicit what we apprehend in the recognition which our actions accord to the principle that good is to be done and evil to be avoided. But when each person assesses what it is good and best for him or her to do, more is needed.

Practical human activity is informed by different kinds of directedness (*inclinatio*). There is the directedness of each person *qua* being toward persisting in that being, toward self-preservation. There is the directedness of each person *qua* animal expressed in the purposiveness of the bearing and education of children to participate in the forms of human life. And there is the directedness of each person *qua* rational and social being expressed in the purposiveness of the pursuit of those rational goods which include the pursuit of knowledge and, above all, the pursuit of the knowledge of God. It is important that these *inclinationes* are ordered: we educate our children for the sake of their being able to participate in the pursuit of knowledge; we subordinate our need for self-preservation if the lives of our children or the security of our community are gravely endangered. It is not of course that everyone always orders their inclinations in this way, but that the general patterns of distinctively human behavior evince those directednesses in such a way that it is the ends toward which they are directed that provide our primary experiences of the pursuit of particularized goods (*S.T.* I–IIae, 94,2).

Each individual is thus initially confronted by such questions as: How am I to achieve those goods set before me? Which is it best for me to try to achieve now? Is such and such really good or does it only seem so to me? And this confrontation is initially not theoretical, but in the context of the immediacies of practice. There are, of course, as Aquinas was well aware, wrong ways of answering all these questions. Each individual has within him or herself, on Aquinas' view, a capacity for giving the right answers, but this capacity has to be elicited. To elicit that capacity successfully will involve the discovery of principles, formulated with varying degrees of explicitness in different cases, which will guide one toward what is good and best for one. That there is that which is best for one is something initially comprehended in articulating to oneself the bare apprehension of good, but the question of how one's end is to be understood in adequate detail requires for its answer an activity of dialectical questioning, of entertaining alternatives, and of deciding between them. What the individual person has to do here mirrors what as a theorist the moral philosopher has to do. And, as with the moral philosopher, there is no question of simply being able to *deduce* the truth either about the true end of human beings or as to what must be done to achieve it. Like the moral philosopher the individual person who poses the questions about his or her own good seriously is engaged in *constructing* a deductive system through which he or she can discover true answers to those questions. A fully perfected practical science will indeed, like other sciences, be a system of demonstrable truths, but the achievement either of that science or of such partial apprehension of its truths as is required by ordinary agents is a work of dialectical construction (*Commentary on the Ethics* I, lect. xii).

It is a Cartesian error, fostered by a misunderstanding of Euclidean geometry, to suppose that first by an initial act of apprehension we can comprehend the full meaning of the premises of a deductive system and then only secondly proceed to enquire what follows from them. In fact it is only insofar as we understand what follows from those premises that we understand the premises themselves. If and as we begin from the premises, our initial apprehension will characteristically be partial and incomplete, increasing as we understand what it is that these premises do and do not entail.

So in the construction of any demonstrative science we both argue *from* what we take, often rightly, to be subordinate truths *to* first principles (*Commentary on the Ethics* loc. cit.), as well as from first principles *to* subordinate truths (*Commentary on Boethius' De Trinitate* Qu. VI, 1 ad 3). And in this work of coming to understand which premises it is that state what is the case *per se,* in such a way as to function as first principles, we continually deepen our apprehension of the content of those first principles and correct those misapprehensions into which everyone tends to fall.

This account of how first principles are understood and of their place in enquiry is of course deeply at odds not only with Cartesian and other rationalist accounts of the structure of philosophical and scientific theory but also with the moral theories of thinkers as various as Hobbes, Hume, Bentham, and Kant, for each of whom there is a way of founding adequately the first principle or principles of right action by appeal to considerations which they take to be equally available at the commencement of enquiry to every rational person as such. By none of them is the moral life conceived of as a journey toward the discovery of first principles as an end, the full disclosure of which is, in both senses of "end," the end of that journey, so that it is in a strict sense only at the end that we know whether or not at the beginning we did in fact know what the true beginning was. It is, as Aristotle remarked, difficult to know that one knows.

Yet of course there have been notable Thomists in the last hundred years who would have disagreed with this account of first principles as strenuously as any Humean or Kantian, ascribing both to Aristotle and to Aquinas a belief in a set of necessarily true first principles which any truly rational person is able to evaluate as true. For this kind of Thomist the rational superiority of Aquinas' overall system of thought does not lie both in its having transcended the limitations of its predecessor traditions, while preserving from them what had withstood dialectical objection, and in its since then having not similarly been transcended by any successor system of thought, but instead in its argumentative ability to encounter its modern rivals on *their* chosen ground for debate and to exhibit the rational superiority of its claims concerning first principles to theirs. The outcome of these debates is, however, now clear.

In moral philosophy the central question which the participants in those debates had hoped to answer was: What are those principles governing action to which no rational human being can deny his or her assent? Hume's appeal to consensus concerning the passions, Kant's formulations of the categorical imperative and the principle of utility were all attempts to supply an answer to this question. Yet each one of these answers turned out to be susceptible of rejection by the adherents of rival answers, whose claims to rational justification were as much and as little contestable as those of its opponents. And it is no different with the contemporary heirs of Hume, Kant, and Mill; they too are engaged in a battle in which no one is finally defeated, only because no one is ever the victor. One interesting response to the recognition of this situation by those who are otherwise at one with the heirs of Hume, Kant, and Mill in their allegiance to the ideals of the Enlightenment has been the recent redefinition of the task of moral philosophy as that of rendering coherent and systematic "our" intuitions about what is right, just, and good, where "we" are the inhabitants of a particular social, moral, and political tradition, that of liberal individualism. So a concept of tradition is reintroduced as part of the necessary *de facto* background to normative enquiry.

Those Thomists who engaged in the earlier stages of this debate shared in its inconclusive and unsatisfactory outcome. They never on any major issue refuted their opponents in such a way as to persuade those opponents, and this was not only because they had accepted the terms of a debate with a predetermined outcome. What they had also failed to estimate was the extent to which Aquinas' portrait of human beings in a state of nature, at the very beginning of the project of moral enquiry, differs from the corresponding portraits in modern moral philosophy.

These modern portraits have been of a number of different kinds. What they have shared has been the assumption that the acquisition of an ability to make correct moral judgments (I speak of "correct" here rather than true, because of the unwillingness of some modern writers to allow that moral judgments can be either true or false, except perhaps in a Pickwickian sense) does not require the substantial acquisition of the virtues as a prerequisite. Aristotle, as we noticed earlier, had denied this assumption. The development of a capacity for sound practical reasoning which will guide one both to judge truly and to act rightly is, in his view, inseparable from an education in the exercise of the moral virtues. Hence the misdirected or the defectively educated are incapable of learning how to exercise sound practical reasoning. So that Aquinas, as an Aristotelian, could not have adopted the modern standpoint, and it is clear from his *Commentary on the Ethics* (VI, lect. 7) that he did not. But, as we have also already noticed, the biblical authors, from the writer of *Deuteronomy* to Paul, declare that every human being has a sufficient knowledge of the requirements of justice, as defined by God's law, to be held responsible in the light of that knowledge. So Aquinas confronted a problem: the acquisition of practical knowledge and the exercise of good practical reasoning cannot occur without some development of the moral virtues and that in turn cannot occur without education; yet it must be the case that those not yet educated and those deprived of the possibility of such education possess sufficient practical knowledge to do and be what justice and the divine law require.

We can best understand Aquinas' solution by first considering his account of how the young ought to be educated. All education is the actualization of some potentiality. Hence to be educable is already to have a potentiality for learning whatever it is, but it is more than this. It is also to have a potentiality for actualizing that first potentiality. All education is in part self-education (*Commentary on Posterior Analytics* II, lect. 20). Unsurprisingly in view of this "a teacher leads someone else to the knowledge of what was unknown in the same way that someone leads him or herself to the knowledge of what was unknown in the course of discovery" (*De Veritate* XI, 1). The order of good teaching is the order in which someone would learn by and for him or herself. What order is that?

Two considerations are involved. Generally in learning we ought to move from what is most easily apprehended in the light of what we already know toward what is more intelligible as such, but less easily apprehended by us immediately. But in some cases we cannot enter upon one type of enquiry until we have already mastered another, because the first has to draw upon the second. For this reason logic, although Aquinas thought it the most difficult of sciences, has to be studied first. For every other enquiry draws upon the resources of logic, including as it does on Aquinas' classification of the sciences everything about which Aristotle wrote in the *Organon* (*Commentary on Boethius' De Trinitate* loc. cit.).

After logic comes mathematics, and after that physics. Only by then will the student have reached a stage where the two conditions which were prerequisites for moral enquiry will have been satisfied: sufficient experience of action and judgment and a mind undistracted by the immediacies of passion (*Commentary on the Ethics* VI, lect. 7). What then will the course of introductory moral teaching be? It is outlined for us in the *Prima Secundae* of the *Summa,* in a way which directs us toward the ordering of the *Secunda Secundae.* Here the questions follow a sequence in which we begin by asking what the ultimate end or good of human beings is, a question on whose answer most of the subsequent answers depend. We then ask what human actions are, so that we can understand which types of human action are directed toward what is good and best for us and which direct us toward what is less and other than that. It turns out that this requires us to understand the nature of the passions and the different parts which they can play in the genesis of action, a discussion which is a prologue to an account of what a virtuous habit or disposition is and correspondingly what vices and sins are (see Mark Jordan 'Aquinas's Construction of a Moral Account of the Passions' *Freiburger Zeitschrift für Philosophie und Theologie* 33, 1–2, 1986). In all of this the conclusions of the *Prima Pars* are presupposed and at key points reintroduced into the argument. Most notably only by reference to the existence and goodness of God can the ultimate end of human beings be specified.

Why did Aquinas follow Aristotle in holding that only those with sufficient moral experience and training will be able to learn what is taught in the *Prima Secundae?* The answer is that the train of argument, broadly speaking, recapitulates at the level of theory the sequence of questions and answers which someone embarked on the moral life will find him or herself following through, as they make what they are doing and judging more and more intelligible to themselves, in the course of trying first to specify and then to achieve the kind of excellence appropriate to human beings. And it is only individuals thus embarked, educated into the making of certain kinds of discrimination that enable them to order the expression of the passions in the light of an ordering of goods—something which in the first instance they will have had to learn from their teachers—who will be able to understand that the arguments of the *Prima Secundae* are about themselves and amplify what they have already learned in a way that will enable them to learn further practically as well as theoretically.

Someone who lacked this initial moral training and experience could well be able in some sense to understand the account of the moral life conveyed by the sequential answers to questions of the *Prima Secundae,* but it would have to read to him or her as if it were an account of some partly alien and unknown form of human life. For someone who lacked altogether the kind of training and development which Aquinas—and Aristotle—takes to be required would develop the expression of their desires in a piecemeal, uncoordinated way so that they would come to have in adult life desires which appeared essentially heterogeneous, aimed at goods independent of one another and without any overall ordering. From the standpoint of such a person the unity of the goods aimed at in the moral life, as described by Aquinas, could only appear as a symptom of some kind of monomania. From that standpoint one would have to judge such a person "as irrational, or more likely as mad," just as Rawls does.

Aquinas' theory of human development is then open to the possibility that human beings may develop in more than one way. A particular culture may, relative to the essential nature of human beings and their ultimate end, miseducate and mislead them in particular ways, as Aquinas, on the authority of Julius Caesar, believed that the Germans had been misled in respect of theft (*S.T.* I–IIae, 94, 4). Nonetheless every human being has within him or herself the potentiality of formulating those principles which constitute the most fundamental precepts of divine law, as it is presented to human reason by human reason, and of rendering this knowledge actual in such a way and to such a degree as to make every individual responsible for not acting upon it (*S.T.* I–IIae, 94, 1, 3 and 6). This actualization of potentiality is part of the development of a natural aptitude for virtue, which needs to be trained (*S.T.* I–IIae, 95, 1). Such training is generally given to the young within the household; Aquinas calls it "paternal" (loc. cit.) since in the household and family structures of which he knew everyone else acted as the agent of the male head of household. What then are the resources of those deprived of such training, the many who may "fancy that if they do not keep the law [of nature], they may be excused on account of ignorance"? Their resource, Aquinas replies, lies in their intelligence "which shows us what we should do and what we should avoid" (Introduction *De Duobus Praeceptis Caritatis*). What then does intelligence bid such a person to do?

First it bids him or her to ask the question "What is my good?" and "What precepts must I follow in order to learn what it is?" in as persistent and searching a way as possible. The attempt to answer these questions will at the very least make it clear to such persons that they cannot pursue their good, whatever it is, in isolation and that the relationships into which they enter in order to secure their most obvious goods need to be such as will enable them to improve their knowledge of what their good is. Notice that internal to this process of questioning is a directedness deriving from the inclinations and a movement from those inclinations to satisfy physical and biological needs toward the directedness of social life (*S.T.* I–IIae, 94, 2). What the person deprived hitherto of adequate moral education has to discover is that what he or she needs is a friend who will also be a teacher in the approach to the virtues. For those who are still morally immature need friends anyway if they are to become virtuous (*Commentary upon the Ethics* VIII, lect. 1), and so the first enquiry of such a person must be how he or she is to constitute relationships of friendship with other persons, such that through those relationships he or she may learn what his or her good is.

We could not of course expect of such a person initially a full understanding of what the mutuality of friendship involves. But it has to be clear to anyone what the primary precepts which have to be obeyed in willing the good of the other person as friend are, so that he or she is secure, so far as one is concerned, from bodily danger, loss of possessions, the telling of lies about them, and the like. But to obey these precepts is to obey the primary precepts of the natural law and those other precepts which follow immediately from them, and so to embark upon that education in the virtues which is the necessary prologue to adequate practical enquiry. That is to say, those human relationships through which alone anyone can hope to learn the nature of their good are themselves defined in practice as well as in theory by the standards set by the natural law. So the natural law is discovered not only as one of the primary objects of practical enquiry but as the presupposition of any effective practical enquiry (compare what Aquinas says about the kind of friendship in which the other wills one's good, the only kind of friendship through which one could have any confidence of learning what one's true good is, in the *Commentary upon the Ethics* VIII, lect. 4, and at *S.T.* IIa–IIae, 23,1, with what he says about the need to be trained in virtue by another at *S.T.* I–IIae, 95,1, and how *caritas* requires us to participate in the training of others in the *Quaestiones Disputatae de Correctione Fraterna*).

In deriving from a variety of texts this account of the way in which confrontation with the natural law is inescapable for anyone who persists in the enquiry as to what his or her good is—and anyone who does not so persist will of course thereby have put him or herself in the wrong—I have of course offered an interpretation which goes beyond those texts, but I know of no cogent account of Aquinas on these matters which is not compelled to such an interpretation. What needs emphasizing is that on Aquinas' view the precepts of the natural law function in more than one way in the moral life. They are the expression of divine law as apprehended by human reason, and God in uttering those precepts to human beings is at once sovereign legislator and teacher. Aquinas follows Aristotle (*Commentary on the Nicomachean Ethics* I, lect. 1) in holding that we can only become just by performing just actions, so that we must have a way of identifying which actions are just prior to our acquisition of the virtue which enables us to judge and to act rightly in respect of justice. Among those who provide us with such an identification is the lawgiver insofar as the positive law conforms to the natural law. So such law also has a function in our moral education (*S.T.* I–IIae, 95,1) by answering the question "What actions is it bad for me to perform?" before we have through education in the virtues learned how to answer it more adequately. As on Aristotle's view the law stands to the citizen in the best kind of *polis,* so on Aquinas' view the natural law stands to every human being in the *civitas Dei.*

There is, however, a crucial difference between Aquinas and Aristotle. For Aquinas the single most important experience of human beings in relation to the divine law, whether in the form in which reason apprehends its precepts as the natural law or as revealed directly by God in the Ten Commandments, is that of disobedience to it, a disobedience ineradicable by even the best moral education in accordance with reason. Each particular act of disobedience is a consequence either of a corruption of reason by the force of some passion or of bad habit or of some undisciplined natural tendency (*S.T.* I–IIae, 94,4). But our inability to eradicate this tendency to disobedience out of our own natural and rational resources points toward the collusion of the will in moral evil, a will which being free to choose not only can choose to do evil but can give to that choice an endurance and a commitment which it would not otherwise possess (*S.T.* I–IIae, 20, 4).

The only remedy is divine grace, and it is no accident that the section of the Summa which deals with the divine law, both natural and revealed, is immediately followed by the section on grace. In this respect, although not only in this respect, the structure of the *Summa* is Pauline and Augustinian, and the treatment of the tendency to disobedience in human nature in terms of *mala voluntas* separates it radically from Aristotle's treatment of *akrasia.* Thus Aquinas is committed in a very particular way to giving an account of practical rationality which, even if Aristotelian in its general structure, integrates into that account the central themes of Augustine's psychology. And what is true of Aquinas' analysis of practical rationality holds also of his treatment of the virtues. The virtues understood only in Aristotelian terms are incapable of perfecting human beings in such a way that they can attain their *telos,* partly because of Aristotle's inadequate understanding of what that *telos* is and partly because the natural virtues themselves can only perfect when informed by that *caritas* which is a gift of grace.

Hence Aquinas' account of the virtues in general and of the virtue of justice in particular also have to synthesize Pauline and Augustinian with Aristotelian elements, although here it is necessary to speak of integrating what is Aristotelian into a Pauline and Augustinian framework rather than vice versa. It is therefore essential to understand Aquinas' particular theses about practical rationality and about justice in terms of the constraints imposed by his overall project. The evaluation of the truth or falsity of these claims is similarly dependent in key part upon the evaluation of that project, just as the evaluation of the project as a whole also depends in key part upon how successful the treatment of particular problems and issues is.

XI

Aquinas on Practical Rationality and Justice

How individuals understand their relationship to their own actions and how those actions are generated is in part a matter of the size and subtlety of the vocabulary available to them for that understanding and the range of the discriminations which their vocabulary enables them to make. The development of that vocabulary and of those discriminations depends upon the pressures of various aspects of practical life toward self-understanding and the understanding of others. It does not of course follow that before some particular set of words and concepts becomes available, enabling those who acquire them to understand their own minds and actions in new ways, those words and concepts did not already have application. So we may be justified in accusing ourselves or others in retrospect of having been hitherto blind to that of which we or they could have been aware. Augustine had in just this way used his discovery of the will to accuse his pagan Roman predecessors of having willfully concealed from themselves that *mala voluntas* which had underlain and corrupted their achievements.

Augustinian Christianity in consequence required of its adherents both a new degree of self-awareness and of responsibility for developing that self-awareness. It became impossible in both pastoral and theological contexts to discuss the ways in which bad will can occur without enquiring into what our knowledge of the badness of our wills consists. In the former, it was especially monastic writers who developed both an idiom and a doctrine of intention and of conscience designed to enable individuals and their confessors both to achieve self-awareness in action and to evaluate accountability for lack of it.

So three key words enter the medieval Latin moral vocabulary: *intentio, synderesis,* and *conscientia,* these being understood with a degree of specificity which is denied to their more loosely applied modern counterparts, if only because they are introduced as parts of theological and philosophical theories. Thus Abelard, impressed by the Augustinian view that what is one and the same action in outward respects may be in the case of one person an expression of pride but in the case of another an expression of humility, argued that actions themselves are morally indifferent and are to be called good or bad in virtue of whether or not the agent's *intentio* does or does not conform to divine law (see on this and more generally D. E. Luscombe 'Peter Abelard and Twelfth-Century Ethics' in his *Peter Abelard's Ethics,* Oxford, 1971). And when commentators discussed what became the standard theological textbook in the thirteenth-century University of Paris, Peter Lombard's *Sententiae* — the author had himself taught in the cathedral school at Paris and was archbishop there briefly before his death around 1160 — their discussions of his account of rival views of how the will can be bad often led on to discussions of *synderesis* and *conscientia*.

Originally '*conscientia*' was the Latin translation of '*syneidesis*.' The distinction between it and *synderesis* emerged in commentaries upon St. Jerome's interpretation of the biblical story of Cain in *Genesis* 4. Jerome held both that Cain throughout his evil deeds continued to have a conscience, that is, that he knew that what he was doing was wrong, and yet that in some cases evildoers are able in time to obliterate their awareness that what they are doing is wrong. So commentators wanted a word for what it is that is indelible, that survives in even the wickedest human being, to distinguish it from that consciousness of good and evil which can be extinguished, '*synderesis*' being used for the former, '*conscientia*' for the latter (Timothy C. Potts *Conscience in Medieval Philosophy,* Cambridge, 1980, pp. 9–11, and more generally throughout).

Different theologians understand and develop this distinction in different, not always compatible, ways, as they do also that between an *intentio* and the action or actions to which it is related. But from the twelfth century onward all these expressions are central both for practice and for theory. When therefore Aquinas, having accepted from Aristotle the latter's view of practical reasoning and from Augustine his development of the Pauline doctrine of the defective human will, has to integrate these into a single, unified, complex account of human action as such, he also could not escape the task — no teacher in the University of Paris could have escaped it — of showing to what use such expressions as *intentio* and *synderesis* and *conscientia* had to be put within his overall scheme of action concepts.

I discussed earlier Aquinas' view of the inescapability of the primary precepts of the natural law. *Synderesis* is, on his account, the natural disposition exhibited in our most basic apprehension of those precepts, which we do not comprehend as a result of enquiry if only because a knowledge of their truth is already presupposed in all practical activity. It is perhaps to be classified as a particular potentiality of reason (*Quaestiones Disputatae de Veritate* 16, 15; Aquinas reproduces his early discussion of *synderesis* in summary form in *S.T.* Ia,79,12). *Synderesis* is infallible (*Quaestiones* 16,2). Aquinas' claim here is that any moral or practical judgment which is false, which mistakes the good for the bad, will on sufficient examination turn out to be derivative, whether on the surface it initially appears so or not. He is not appealing to any psychological quality of evidentness, to any intuition. Nor does he deny that the operation of *synderesis* in determining one's action may be hindered either by physical damage or by the distracting force of some passion, which leads one to ignore what one in fact knows (16,3) (see Mark Jordan *Ordering Wisdom,* Notre Dame, 1986, pp. 139–141).

The application of fundamental principles to a particular situation requires an additional set of capacities, both that involved in deducing from the universal and general fundamental principles more specific principles, with more immediate application to specific types of situation, and that involved in deriving from both of these principles the particular practical judgments about what is to be done here and now or in some particular set of circumstances which may some day be, but is not yet, here and now. To these capacities the name '*conscientia*' is applied.

Conscientia can indeed be in error (16,2, and 17,2), either because its judgment was deduced from a true premise or from a set of true premises conjoined with a false premise, which happened in this case to yield a false conclusion, or because its judgment was derived from true premises by fallacious reasoning. There are, however, cases where *conscientia* cannot err, namely, when the deduction from a true principle affirmed by *synderesis* is so immediate that there is no room for error in moving from premise to conclusion, as when one infers from "God is to be loved by everyone" to "God is to be loved by me." Except in such cases our apprehension of basic true practical judgments as true does not involve that we understand what is involved in the living out of those judgments in the specifications and particularities of practical life. By coming to understand this we gradually enlarge our understanding of the fundamental judgments and of the entire system which they partially constitute. There are, therefore, even for those who do not avert their attention from the primary precepts of the natural law, radical possibilities of error, error which can assume tragic dimensions.

Aquinas held both that *conscientia* can be in error and that *conscientia* binds (17,3 and 4). So it must seem to be the case that it can be simultaneously true of someone that he or she ought to do such and such, because it is enjoined by *conscientia,* and true of that same person that it is not the case that he or she ought to perform that same action, because it is wrong, being expressly forbidden by divine law. But were this the case, we should be committed to asserting a contradiction, which is absurd. Aquinas' reply is that we can distinguish between the two "oughts." Someone is bound *per se* to do what *conscientia* enjoins when *conscientia* judges truly, but only *per accidens* to do what *conscientia* judges falsely (17,4). So of the person who judges what he or she ought to do on the basis of a false deliverance of *conscientia* it is true that he or she is bound and ought to act in such and such a way *per accidens,* but not true that he or she is bound and ought to act *per se.* There is no contradiction.

Timothy Potts has criticized Aquinas' conclusion that it is untrue that such a person is genuinely bound and that the solution for such a person is to give up his or her false belief, a belief for which, on any matter of moral substance, the person is in any case blameworthy, since he or she could have and ought to have known better (17,4). Potts replies that "the difficulty still remains that a man who believes that he is obliged to φ will not simultaneously recognize that he is obliged not to φ and so will not see *himself* as being in a dilemma . . ." (op. cit., p. 59). This is indeed true, but misses the point that Aquinas is not prescribing a way of recognizing and so eliminating dilemmas, but only explaining how someone may be in what is objectively a dilemma precisely because it is unrecognized. The importance of this can be brought out by considering its bearing upon certain modern criticisms of Aquinas.

On Aquinas' view someone who has accepted as true a false deliverance of *conscientia* must have admitted into his or her set of moral beliefs and judgments a contradiction, since the false judgment of *conscientia* will be inconsistent with some principle affirmed by *synderesis* or some consequence of such a principle. But we know from the theorem first enunciated by an anonymous pupil of Duns Scotus and later by C. I. Lewis that from a contradiction anything whatsoever follows. Such a person will therefore be liable to find him or herself affirming what he or she cannot fail to recognize as contradictory assertions, even if their original source is by its very nature, as Potts points out, unrecognized.

Such are often enough the persons who confront the dilemmas constitutive of tragedy. It follows from Aquinas' view that such dilemmas will always rest upon an underlying mistake, but nothing in Aquinas' view precludes it being the case that recognizing this may be for the moment out of the question. Martha Nussbaum has argued that Aquinas' view is incompatible with a type of situation portrayed in some Greek tragedy in which, so she suggests, full rationality is compatible with recognizing the genuine binding force, in Aquinas' terms, the *per se* binding force, of conflicting moral claims ('Practical Syllogisms and Practical Science,' Essay 4 in *Aristotle's De Motu Animalium,* Princeton, 1978, pp. 168–173). Nussbaum has developed her views further (*The Fragility of Goodness,* Cambridge, 1986) in a way that makes it clear that in so arguing she differs from Aquinas over at least two major issues.

First of all Nussbaum rejects and Aquinas accepts what she calls "the assimilation of practical conflict to disagreement and of practical claims to beliefs" (op. cit., p. 36). That is to say, Nussbaum seeks to avoid imputing contradiction either to tragic figures themselves or to our descriptions of them by denying truth-values to their assertions. Yet she goes on in the same work to argue that Aristotle provides an account of practical thinking which is open to the insights which she takes to be central to tragedy, understood as she understands it. But Aristotle, who takes practical and moral theses to be expressible as the major premises of syllogisms, could not have done so without ascribing either truth or falsity to them. And, indeed, more generally it is difficult to make much sense of Aristotle without such an assumption.

Second, Aquinas and Nussbaum agree that someone may seem to themselves to confront conflicting moral claims; the person bound by erroneous *conscientia* knows that he or she is bound by *conscientia* (*Quaestiones Quodlibetales* II, 27) and is liable therefore to be unable to avoid treating himself or herself as the subject of contradictory predicates, even although in fact he or she is not. What someone who followed Aquinas would have to affirm, and what Nussbaum, if she dissents from Aquinas, would have to deny, is that such a person *must* be guilty at some point of some error or flaw to which he or she is blind. Interestingly, in the unfolding of the dramatic action in some Greek tragedy just such error or flaw seems to be plain: Oedipus' arrogant insistence on his ability to learn and to deal with the truth and Neoptolemus' acceptance of Odysseus' unjust plan to defraud Philoctetes are examples. What Aquinas cannot allow is that it is, not human sinfulness, but the nature of things or the divine will which generates tragedy.

In treating Aquinas' accounts of *synderesis* and *conscientia* as integral to his account of practical knowledge in this way, I am already developing an interpretation of Aquinas that is at odds with that developed by some other commentators. M. B. Crowe has argued (*The Changing Profile of the Natural Law* Dordrecht, 1977, pp. 136–141) that Aquinas' early treatment of *synderesis* became redundant when his later reading of the *Nicomachean Ethics* allowed him to give due place to reasoning in the genesis of action and that this change represented a movement from "neo-Platonizing moral philosophy" toward a more Aristotelian position. Were this the case, it might be difficult to account for the identity of the views expressed on *synderesis* in the *Prima Pars* with Aquinas' earlier account. But more generally it is important to understand Aquinas as at every stage—and perhaps most notably in the years when he was at the same time writing his commentary on the *Nicomachean Ethics* and the *Secunda Secundae*—integrating Neoplatonic and Augustinian elements with Aristotelian rather than discarding one in favor of the other.

My account so far is also at variance with some modern Thomistic writers on natural law who hold that it is possible to construct a genuinely Thomistic account of natural law and of our knowledge of it "without needing to advert to the question of God's existence or nature or will," as John Finnis, for example, has argued against Kai Nielsen (*Natural Law and Natural Rights,* Oxford, 1980, pp. 48–49). What is instructive here is to notice the difference between Finnis' consequent treatment of the goods of religion (op. cit., pp. 89–90 and 371–410) and Aquinas' (*S.T.* II–IIae, 81). On Aquinas' view religion is a moral virtue, being that part of the cardinal virtue of justice concerned with what we owe to God in the way of honor, reverence, and worship. Since perfected obedience to the natural law requires the virtue of justice in full measure (*S.T.* IIa–IIae, 79,1), it is difficult to understand how someone who did not believe that God is and that his attributes make him worthy of honor, reverence, and worship could be perfectly obedient to the natural law. It is then important to my interpretation of Aquinas' positions that I understand his positions on practical knowledge and practical reasoning, let alone those on justice, as always presupposing the type of rational knowledge of God exemplified in the conclusions of the *Prima Pars*.

We have, therefore, a theological framework within which is presented a fundamentally Aristotelian account of the genesis of action, into which are integrated both an Augustinian conception of the will and such later concepts as those of *intentio* and *synderesis* and *conscientia*. How was this achieved? Aquinas accepted from Aristotle the substance of what Aristotle has to say on three central issues: the theoretical and practical relationship of subordinate goods to the supreme good; the process of deliberation, whereby argument proceeds as to how, given some good to be achieved, the best means to achieve it is identified; and the organization of that reasoning whereby the affirmation of the good to be achieved and the perceptual recognition of the agent's situation combine to provide the agent with premises which, in an agent acting in accordance with right reason, generate the right action as a conclusion of practical reasoning.

Aquinas' key discussions are in his *Commentary on the Ethics,* and it is in his use of certain Latin words as translations of Aristotelian expressions that we can most illuminatingly see his introduction of Augustinian elements into the Aristotelian scheme. The translation of the *Nicomachean Ethics* used by Aquinas was a revised version of Robert Grosseteste's translation, and he was, when he wrote his commentary in 1271–72, still at many points influenced by Albertus' teaching on the *Ethics.* Aquinas may well have written his commentary as an immediate prelude to writing the parts of the *Summa* concerned with moral theory; the parallels between the two works, especially in the *Secunda Secundae,* are striking (Georg Wieland 'The Reception and Interpretation of Aristotle's *Ethics,*' chapter 34 *The Cambridge History of Later Medieval Philosophy,* ed. N. Kretzmann, A. Kenny, J. Pinborg, and E. Stump, Cambridge, 1982).

From both Albertus and Grosseteste Aquinas takes the word '*electio*' as a translation of Aristotle's '*prohairesis*'. I remarked about '*prohairesis*' earlier that the word 'choice', if it is given its modern English connotations, is a misleading translation of '*prohairesis*'. But when '*prohairesis*' is translated by '*electio*', we are brought much nearer to the modern English 'choice'. '*Prohairesis*' names that which issues from deliberation and expresses the agent's conclusion as to what it is good for him or her now to do as an immediate means to the end to which, through deliberation, he or she has been considering which means to adopt. Aquinas follows Aristotle in characterizing it as either rational desire or desiring reason, emphasizing (*Commentary on the Ethics* VI, lect. 2) that it is only desire as disciplined and directed by right moral habit which accords with reason; the truth which the enquiring practical mind arrives at is that which corresponds to right desire in the judgment as to what is to be done. But Aquinas takes the component of action which expresses *prohairesis,* rational desire, to be an act of the will. And the will is always free, in this sense, that it acts on the basis of contingent judgments as to what is good or bad and is always open to some alternative contingent judgment proposed to it by, for example, some disordered passion, by which it may be moved rather than by the considered judgment of reason. The will is not moved to any end by necessity (*S.T.* Ia–IIae, 10,2).

So Augustine's *voluntas* is introduced into Aristotle's scheme, and not only at the point of *prohairesis*. Will is always moved to action by intellect; even its most wayward moments are at the bidding of some judgment. When intellect first judges some end good, an act of will toward that end is elicited (Ia–IIae, 8,2), that type of act of will Aquinas identifies by the name '*intentio*'; *intentio* may be directed either toward what is immediately to be chosen as an end or to it as means to some further end or indeed to a variety of ends. It is the presence of *intentio* which distinguishes a genuine act of will from a mere wish (*S.T.* Ia–IIae, 12,1–4). Will also has to consent to the means judged appropriate by the intellect through the process of deliberation (*S.T.* Ia–IIae, 15,1).

The deliberation which determines the means to be chosen to some end and which terminates in *electio* is always, if it is fully rational, directed toward that end only insofar as it is also a further means to the ultimate end of human beings, the only end which cannot also be a means and so is not subject to choice (*S.T.* Ia–IIae, 13,3). When the deliberation leading up to *electio* has determined the means, the will, itself a power commanded by the intellect (*S.T.* Ia–IIae, 17,2 and 5), consents to the means (*S.T.* Ia–IIae, 15,1) and commands an act which completes the action, implementing the choice by this act of command. The will may have to contrive devices to make itself effective, calling upon the resources of reasoning for such contrivances (*S.T.* Ia–IIae, 16,1); this Aquinas calls 'usus' by the will.

Alan Donagan ('Thomas Aquinas on Human Action,' chapter 33 *The Cambridge History of Later Medieval Philosophy:* this is the most useful and illuminating account provided from any standpoint; see also his 'Philosophical Progress and the Theory of Action,' *Proceedings and Addresses of the American Philosophical Association* 55,1, September 1981) both praises and reproaches Aquinas for his account of action. He praises him for "correcting Aristotle's mistake" of supposing that *prohairesis* is always of ends consistent with and adopted because of the agent's character ('Philosophical Progress and the Theory of Action,' p. 34). And he reproaches Aquinas for what he calls Aquinas' sheer blunder of supposing that when the will has exerted its executive, commanding power, there could be something further to be done to which the name 'usus' could be given ('Thomas Aquinas on Human Action,' p. 652). I am not sure that either the praise or the blame are merited, at least in the terms supplied by Donagan.

By his making *electio* an act of will and characterizing it as he does, Aquinas does not so much render *'prohairesis'* into Latin as offer instead an alternative concept. For Aristotle the person whose conclusions as to what means to adopt do not spring from that person's character is someone as yet morally uneducated, or at least not fully educated, open to *akratic* impulse; as such that person has not yet entered into the maturity of moral enquiry. Aquinas by contrast sees every human being as held responsible from a relatively early age for his or her choices; even before character is adequately formed I am to make those choices which will lead toward an adequate formation of character. Even an immature rationality is adequate to that task. So it is not just that Aristotle omitted something from his accounting of *prohairesis* and that Aquinas corrected that omission; it is rather that Aquinas affords a new and enlarged perspective on the relationship of choice, action, and character.

Moreover it is, so far as I can see, a mistake to suppose that *'usus'* names an act of will over and above that act in which will exerts its executive power; 'usus' names those components of that act of will which on occasion constitute its exertion, as, for example, when I will to get out of bed, I may exert that will by muttering abuse at myself, these mutterings being subordinate components of the overall act or subact of willing.

Aquinas' conception of the will follows Augustine's closely in connecting the will with love; what we will we enjoy, both in willing it and in achieving it, and Augustine's account of the enjoyment of something as "to cling to it with love for its own sake" (*De Doctrina Christiana* I,4) is quoted by Aquinas in the *Summa* (Ia–IIae, 11,1). The enjoyment of what is possessed or achieved exceeds that enjoyment of willing which is only at the stage of intending, and it is only with the possession of perfect good in the form of the beatific vision that the delight of the will is such that it is finally at rest (*S.T.* Ia–IIae, 11,3). The will will then have attained that ultimate end to which the rational intellect originally directed it, and the type of enjoyment which will supervene upon that end will be the highest of all pleasures.

A fully fledged, spelled-out account of human action according to Aquinas has then a beginning in a recognition of the ultimate end of human beings, a recognition itself often far from fully fledged and spelled out; the immediate terminus of reasoning and willing is in judgment and action by some particular individual about what particular action that individual ought to perform to achieve his or her particular good in some particular set of circumstances. On both the nature of the ultimate end of human beings, which provides the first premise of all fully rational practical reasoning, and on the relationship of knowledge of universal truths about human good to judgments about particularities and to particularized actions, Aquinas both extends Aristotle's account and at certain points expresses disagreements, sometimes radical disagreements, with Aristotle.

Aristotle had argued that a variety of particular goods cannot, for one reason or other, be the *telos* of human life as such. So neither money nor honor nor pleasure (as distinct from that enjoyment which is not itself the good but supervenes upon the achievement of the good, so as to be a part of that achievement) nor a life of moral virtue can be the *telos*. Aquinas extended Aristotle's arguments, not only so as to exclude other particular items such as worldly power (*Summa Contra Gentiles* III, 31), but also so as to exclude every finite state which can be achieved in this present life, even finding some confirmation of this in Aristotle himself (*S.T.* Ia–IIae, 5,4). For every such state will be less good than it might be; it will not adequately exemplify the universality of good or its self-sufficiency. So the ultimate end of human beings is outside and beyond this present life.

Nothing, so Thomas argues, can be the ultimate end of human beings except that state of perfect happiness which is the contemplation of God in the beatific vision, in which contemplation all of human nature finds its completion (*S.T.* I–IIae, 3,7). That completion will include the perfecting of the human body with which at the general resurrection souls will once again be united. Everyone desires perfect happiness, and everyone has as the true end of their nature, that for the sake of which they move toward all other goods in the way that they do, the goodness of God (*S.T.* Ia, 6,1). This latter movement toward their final cause human beings share with all other created beings, but nonrational beings cannot of course know or acknowledge this about themselves. Human beings can and before Adam's fall did. In their present state they often do not recognize, what nonetheless they possess all the means for recognizing, if only they would attend to them, that in being moved by a love of their own good, they are being moved by a love of and desire for God (*S.T.* Ia–IIae, 109,3).

It follows that human beings who fail to discover what their true good and happiness consist in will be perpetually balked and frustrated. That this is so throws important light on the relationship in which Aquinas' theory of the practical life stands to Aristotle's. For neither the life of the civic virtues lived out in the *polis* nor the contemplation of what is eternal which *theoria* affords is, on Aquinas' view, other than imperfect happiness. Subtract the goodness of God, as it is understood in the *Prima Pars,* from Aquinas' account, and what is left is not Aristotle, but a radically truncated version of the *Nicomachean Ethics* in which the knowledge that there is an ultimate end of human beings is unaccompanied by any achievement of knowledge as to what that end is. On Aquinas' account the Augustinian understanding of the Christian doctrine of human nature does not merely show that Aristotle's theory of practical life is incomplete, in the sense that it needs to be supplemented. It shows it to be incomplete in a way which involves radical defectiveness (see A. Donagan *Human Ends and Human Actions,* Milwaukee, 1985).

Aquinas follows Aristotle in holding that the knowledge of our ultimate end, so far as it is within our natural rational powers to achieve, belongs to the theoretical rather than the practical activity of the intellect: "It must be said therefore that the practical intellect indeed has its *principium* [the translation of *'archē'*] in a universal consideration and in this respect is the same in subject as the theoretical intellect, but its consideration reaches its terminus in a particular thing which can be done" (*Commentary on the Ethics* VI, lect. 2). That is to say, we reason theoretically *to* and *about* that ultimate end which is the *archē* of practical enquiry and reasoning, but *from* that *archē* it is by practical reasoning that we are led to particular conclusions as to how to act. Yet even the best theoretical enquiry yields an inadequate knowledge of our ultimate end, and even the revealed truth that that end is the enjoyment of the beatific vision involves a reference to aspects of the divine nature of which we can only have the most inadequate apprehension.

It is important, however, not to exaggerate this inadequacy (see David Burrell *Knowing the Unknowable God,* Notre Dame, 1986, and *Aquinas: God and Action,* Notre Dame, 1979); it is an inadequacy in respect of the nature of that which we shall enjoy if we achieve our ultimate end, not at all in respect of its sufficiency in specifying how we ought to act. The practical life, as Aquinas portrays it, is a life of enquiry by each of us into what our good is, and it is part of our present good so to enquire. The final discovery of what our good is will indeed reveal to us the inadequacy of all our earlier conceptions, an inadequacy strikingly expressed in Aquinas' verdict in his own work in the days immediately before his death. But at every stage in this practical enquiry we have a knowledge of our good adequate to guide us further, so that what *synderesis* and *conscientia* initially supply—if, but only if, we both ask the questions which actualize the knowledge which they afford and focus attention upon the answers—are the principles initially needed, principles whose content and application are more and more adequately understood in the course of our education and self-education into the virtues.

The moral life begins with rules designed to direct the will and the desires toward its and their good by providing a standard of right direction (*rectitudo*). This rectitude is valued, not for its own sake, but as leading to that perfected will and those perfected desires which happiness requires. Consequently the rules are to be valued as constituting the life which leads to perfect happiness, and they can only be understood insofar as their point and purpose is understood. Moreover the right kind of rule-following is not possible without education in the moral virtues, both because the actions which are rule-governed are only genuinely good insofar as they are expressions of the virtues and because rule-following itself requires the virtue of prudence.

It is important not to understand this education in too intellectualized a way. The practice of the moral virtues is central to our acquiring knowledge of them, and there is a kind of knowledge to be so acquired which is not at all that produced by intellectual enquiry. We can learn what a virtue is through the experience of having our will directed by that virtue (*per inclinationem;* Aquinas calls this knowledge by way of connaturality [*S.T.* IIa–IIae, 45, 2, and see also *S.T.* Ia, 1, 6, and the discussion in J. Maritain *Antimoderne,* Paris, 1922, pp. 32–35]). So the practice of the virtue of justice yields a knowledge of justice of this kind, including a knowledge of the precepts of the natural law.

Obeying the precepts of the natural law is more than simply refraining from doing what those precepts prohibit and doing what they enjoin. The precepts become effectively operative only as and when we find ourselves with motivating reasons for performing actions inconsistent with those precepts; what the precepts can then provide us with is a reason which can outweigh the motivating reasons for disobeying them, that is, they point us to a more perfect good than do the latter. And moreover they always do so in a context in which more than one aspect of our good is at stake. Consider in this respect someone who sets out to construct a house for his or her family. The first way in which he or she has to judge their activity good is in respect of the kind of activity it is: its goodness lies in its being good for human beings to live together commodiously in families, and this activity of construction is a good as a means directed by that fundamental *inclinatio.* Second, it is insofar as that person only uses land, materials, and labor which are genuinely his or her own to make use of that the action is morally good, by conforming to the primary precept of the natural law not to take what belongs to another, thus ensuring that the house is genuinely the builder's work and the family's possession. Third, the activity is good insofar as no harmful consequences ensue *per accidens,* as for example by excluding someone else's land from sunlight. And fourth, the activity is good insofar as its cause is the relevant kind of goodness in the individual or individuals carrying out the activity, in this case the virtue of justice.

Aquinas emphasizes that for an action to be good it needs to be good in all four ways; for it to be bad it need be defective in only one of them (*S.T.* Ia–IIae, 18,4). What I have wanted to emphasize is that obedience to the primary precepts of the natural law is only characteristically one ingredient of the goodness of actions and that the force of such precepts as reasons for actions is characteristically derived in key part from the contexts in which they are ingredient. 'Not killing someone else gratuitously' or 'Not taking what is not one's own' are not by themselves descriptions of actions.

Moreover, in understanding the relevance of the precepts of the natural law to any particular situation we have to identify the kind of relevance which those precepts have to that situation, and there are no universal rules for doing this. The precepts of the natural law are themselves divided into the genuinely universal exceptionless first principles and the secondary conclusions immediately following from these, which do not vary from culture to culture any more than do the first principles, except when vice and sin have obliterated awareness of them, but which do require on numerous particular types of occasion supplementation in order to have right application (*S.T.* Ia–IIae, 94,5). So we are enjoined *always* to respect the property of others—a primary precept—and this *generally* involves restoring to another what has been lent to us by him or her, but if in the meantime that other has become mentally incompetent, then what is involved in respect for that other is put in question (*S.T.* II–IIae, 47,2).

Aristotle in Book II of the *Nicomachean Ethics* had argued that since in ethics and politics we do not have the same degree of accuracy as in mathematics—his point, as I noticed earlier, was that relevant contingent premises have to be introduced into our arguments in ethics and politics in a way which is not itself rule-governed—we must not try to determine what is to be done in particular cases in a way which presupposes the necessary applicability of invariant rules. Aquinas agreed: "Since discourse on moral matters even in their universal aspects is subject to uncertainty and variation"—Aquinas refers here to there being no rules for applying rules—"it is all the more uncertain if one wishes to descend to bringing doctrine to bear on individual cases in specific detail, for this cannot be dealt with by either art or precedent, because the factors in individual cases are indeterminately variable. Therefore judgment concerning individual cases must be left to the *prudentia* of each person . . ." (*Commentary on the Ethics* II, lect. 2).

Aquinas goes on to make two further points. Lack of certainty in how the universal rule applies does not entail that judgment in particular cases cannot be unerringly correct; and *prudentia,* although its province is particularity, can be educated by generalized reflection on what ethics has to say. Nonetheless it is *prudentia (phronēsis)* which is the virtue without which judgment and action in particular occasions are resourceless beyond the bare level of what *synderesis* provides. It is by *prudentia* that we understand the relevance of the precepts of the natural law to particular situations (*S.T.* IIa–IIae, 47,3 and 6), and it is by *prudentia* that we are guided to right action in respect of all those other aspects of good and bad actions, good and bad projects, and good and bad character which are specified by the moral and intellectual virtues.

There is thus no sharp antithesis and certainly no contradiction between Aquinas' emphasis on the indispensability of rules as such and his equal, if not stronger, emphasis on the limitations of rules as such. Every particular practical situation has aspects which fall under rules and others which do not; in some cases the importance of the latter is minimal; in others it is maximal. Knowing which is which and how to act accordingly is the work of *prudentia.* Aquinas followed Aristotle in holding that the exercise of *prudentia* is required for the exercise of the other moral virtues (*Quaestiones Disputatae de Caritate* 3) and that it is the one moral virtue without which the intellectual virtues cannot be exercised (*S.T.* Ia–IIae, 57,5). And the *Commentary* on Book VI of the *Nicomachean Ethics* makes it clear how far Aquinas goes in reproducing the Aristotelian standpoint. Yet there is a dimension to Aquinas' discussion of *prudentia* which is not Aristotelian. *Prudentia* is exercised with a view to the ultimate end of human beings (*S.T.* II–IIae, 47,4), and it is the counterpart in human beings to that ordering of creatures to their ultimate end which is God's providence (*S.T.* Ia, 22,1). God creates and orders particulars and knows them precisely as what he has made and is making. We, if we act rightly, reproduce that ordering.

Aquinas once again follows Aristotle in classifying types of *prudentia* into that which is concerned with one's own good, that which is concerned with the goods of the household, and that which is concerned with common good of political and social community (*S.T.* IIa–IIae, 47,11). Just as according to Aristotle the good legislator has to exercise *phronēsis* in legislating for a *polis,* so that its relationships may be informed by justice, so according to Aquinas the good legislator needs *prudentia,* but that *prudentia* is exercised so that human law accords with the divine law, more especially in respect of the divinely ordained precepts of the natural law. Thus *prudentia* always has for Aquinas a theological dimension, even when it is exercised as an acquired natural virtue rather than as a supernatural virtue.

Prudentia perfects those who possess it by providing the kind of control over one's actions which is required for all the virtues (*Quaestiones Disputatae de Virtutibus Cardinalibus* 1). It is exhibited both in the carrying through of practical reasoning and in the actions which follow from right reasoning (*S.T.* IIa–IIae, 47,8). Its exercise is inconsistent with overhasty, unconsidered, inconstant, and negligent or careless action, and equally with those simulacra of the virtue of prudence —worldly good sense, caution, and cunning—which are vices and sins (*S.T.* IIa–IIae, 53–55).

Virtue, says Aristotle, makes *prohairesis* right; and it is clearly *prudentia* which directs *electio* rightly, but *prudentia* in association with and reinforced by the other virtues. Aquinas, interestingly, follows Plato and Cicero rather than Aristotle in using the scheme of the four cardinal virtues as a key to the relationship of the moral virtues to each other, and this is all the more notable since he adopted Aristotle's definition of a virtue (*Commentary on the Ethics* II, lect. 7), integrating it with Augustine's into a single account (*S.T.* I–IIae, 55,1,2 and 6). Aquinas expounds and explains the scheme of the four cardinal moral virtues by considering how the virtues may be classified first in terms of the formal principle of each, what each of them is, and second in terms of the subject matter with which they each deal. The two classifications turn out to coincide. Prudence is both an exercise of reason and concerned with how reason should operate in practice. Justice is an application of reason to conduct and is concerned with how the will may be rationally directed toward right conduct. Temperateness is the restraining of passions contrary to reason, and its subject matter is "the concupiscible appetite" which urges us to act contrary to reason, while courage is the holding fast of the passions to what reason requires, when fear of danger or hardship urges otherwise, and its subject matter is "the irascible appetite" which so urges (*S.T.* Ia–IIe, 61,2).

Someone whose reason and passions are rightly ordered will therefore exhibit each of the four cardinal virtues. What are accounted other virtues are all in some way parts or aspects of the cardinal virtues, and someone may possess one of the cardinal virtues while not yet having learned how it needs to be exercised in all of those particular areas which are each the province of some one of the subordinate virtues. Education into each of the cardinal virtues requires the others; Aquinas quotes St. Gregory (*S.T.* Ia–IIae, 61,4) on how one cannot, for example, be prudent unless one is also just, temperate, and courageous. But each cardinal virtue has to be developed as a distinct, habitual set of dispositions, and such education will, while it is in progress, be uneven, so that Aquinas' view does not rule out the possession of one virtue in markedly greater degree than that of some others. The unity of the virtues is exhibited in what is required to perfect each of them.

What, then, is the peculiar place of justice within this scheme? The right place to begin is not with Aquinas' discussions of the virtues, but with his metaphysical theology. For just as there is an inescapably theological dimension to prudence even as a natural virtue, so there is also such a dimension to justice. In its primary application 'Justice' is one of the names applied to God. Augustine had followed Plato in arguing that the standard of justice is afforded to the mind by an ideal form of justice which the human mind apprehends from within itself. Aquinas accepted Aristotle's criticisms—some of them being indeed also Plato's own criticisms—of the theory of forms as a theory of universals. But he also held that God not only conceives of justice perfectly, but is justice perfectly. Plato was wrong in supposing that 'justice' named a form existing independently and self-sufficiently; he was, on Aquinas' account, right in thinking that 'justice' names the *archē* to which all other attributions of justice have to be referred as their exemplar (Prologue to *Commentary on the Book of the Blessed Dionysius on the Divine Names; S.T.* Ia, 21,4). It is not of course that it is by reference to this divine exemplar that *we* acquire the concept of justice; Aquinas' theory of concept-acquisition was Aristotelian, not Platonist, in its starting point, although it moved beyond Aristotle. But that there is such a timeless standard of justice is a claim ultimately grounded on a theological understanding of the ordering of things (for discussion of Aristotle's use of Plato see Ralph McInerny *St. Thomas Aquinas,* Notre Dame, 1982, chapter 4).

Aquinas begins his discussion of the content of human *iustitia* by elucidating its relationship to *ius; ius* is what is rightly owed to another, either in accordance with the natural law or with positive law. '*Ius*', as in Roman law, is the word used of those norms which define the relationships of each person to others, and so '*iustitia*' names *both* the virtue of living by those norms and so exhibiting in one's dispositions a constant and perpetual will to render to each person what is due or owed to him or her *and* the standard of right required of each of us. To every human being every other human being thus owes, and of all the virtues *iustitia* is the one peculiarly concerned with relations to others. In so characterizing it Aquinas unified within a single complex account the definitions of justice provided by Aristotle, Cicero, and Augustine (*S.T.* IIa–IIae, 57 and 58).

The requirements of distributive justice are satisfied when each person receives in proportion to his or her contribution, that is, receives what is due in respect of their status, office, and function and how well they fill it and so contribute to the good of all. The requirements of commutative justice are satisfied when restitution is made, so far as is possible, for wrong, and when penalties for wrongdoing are proportional to offenses and administered for offenses committed. Justice itself of course requires that no wrong be committed: no murder, no other violence against the person, and no theft without or with violence (*S.T.* IIa–IIae, 61–66).

The condemnation of theft presupposes the legitimacy of private property. Aquinas, however, inherited from the patristic tradition a view of the limitation of the right to property which would have been as we shall see, vehemently rejected by some later writers, such as Hume and Blackstone. If someone is in desperate need, or has others for whom he or she is responsible who are in such need, then that person may treat as part of the common property of human beings anything otherwise belonging to someone else, which will save him or her, or those for whom he or she is responsible, from perishing, and which is not similarly required by the person hitherto owning that property, only provided that those who thus convert private into common property have no other resource (*S.T.* IIa–IIae, 66,7). Ownership is limited by the necessities of human need.

Aquinas next considers the justice of positive law. Justice in the administration of justice requires respect of jurisdiction, no irrelevant discrimination between persons, no unfounded accusations, truth-telling by everyone in court, that if a poor person has no one to defend him or her here and now but this particular lawyer, this particular lawyer defend that poor person, and that no lawyer defend knowingly an unjust cause. Exorbitant legal fees, like all other exorbitant prices—Aquinas, like Aristotle, held a version of the labor theory of value—are a form of theft (*S.T.* IIa–IIae, 67–71).

Justice prohibits open, angry speech which reviles another, and quiet, insidious speech which spreads calumny or detraction; it prohibits talebearing and gossip, using words to deride another by casting scorn upon him or her, and cursing another in a way that expresses a wish that they be harmed (*S.T.* IIa–IIae, 72–76).

In what would now be called the economic sphere Aquinas distinguishes between the value of a thing and what it is worth to a particular person, a distinction which lacks application in the modern economics of free markets. The justice of a price is not only a matter of the value of a thing but in most types of cases it is such. Trade is a legitimate activity when it is undertaken by someone "for the sake of public utility so that necessary things should not be lacking from the life of one's *patria,* and he seeks money, not as if an end, but as if a wage for labor" (*S.T.* II–IIae, 77,4). Deception and exorbitant pricing are prohibited unconditionally, and so is usury. Aquinas quotes the Deuteronomic prohibition, remarking that it was from their brethren that the Jews were forbidden to take usury, and then saying that we ought to treat everyone as brother and neighbor (*S.T.* IIa–IIae, 78,1). Aquinas could have made the distinction which later writers, interested in legitimating capitalism, were to make, between one person's lending money at interest to another in such a way, as Aristotle would have put it, as to expect to breed money from money, and one person's entering into a partnership with another, in which both parties invest and share the profits, the interest on the original investment being therefore to be regarded not as usury, but as a return on partnership. That he did not is not unimportant, for it is quite clear that any such return upon investment, which was not either a *stipendium laboris* or compensation for a need unmet because of that investment, would have been regarded by him as usury. The standard commercial and financial practices of capitalism are as incompatible with Aquinas' conception of justice as are the standard practices of the kind of adversarial system of legal justice in which lawyers often defend those whom they know to be guilty.

It is important to remember at this point not only that Aquinas held that unjust laws do not require obedience (if they require what is opposed to the divine good, they are to be disobeyed, whereas if they are only unnecessarily burdensome, there is no obligation to obey them, although it may be prudent to do so: *S.T.* Ia–IIae, 96,4), but also that he agreed with Augustine that unjust laws do not have the force of law and do not merit the name of 'law' (*S.T.* Ia–IIae, 95,2; *S.T.* IIa–IIae, 104,5 and 6). And so also insofar as unjust regimes approach the character of tyrannies, they lose all legitimate claim to our obedience (*S.T.* IIa–IIae, 42,2; compare *De Regno,* cap. 3). What is bad about tyranny is that it subverts the virtues of its subjects; the best regime is that whose order best conduces to education into the virtues in the interest of the good of all. Hence the modern liberal conception of government as securing a minimum order, within which individuals may pursue their own freely chosen ends, protected by and large from the moral interference of government, is also incompatible with Aquinas' account of a just order.

Aquinas brings to a close his argumentative summaries in the *Summa* of what distributive and commutative justice require by showing how these conclusions all exemplify the fundamental precepts of the natural law (*S.T.* IIa–IIae, 79,1–4). He then goes on to identify and to characterize those virtues so closely connected with justice that they share in its character, while they also have some special and distinctive characteristics of their own. Aquinas called these "potential parts" of justice.

First and most important among them is what is owed in justice to God by way of religious observance. Aquinas stresses that the specific virtue of religion is a moral and not a theological virtue (*S.T.* IIa–IIae, 81,4) requiring of us devotion, prayer, adoration, sacrifice, and offerings in support of the institutions of religious observance. We are also required to praise God in words and music. Superstition, dabbling in divination, tempting God, perjuring ourselves, committing acts of sacrilege, and trying to purchase spiritual goods with money are the vices which correspond to the virtue of religion.

What religion involves in a society in which the truth of the Christian religion has been recognized is also political acknowledgment; this Aquinas had noticed earlier: "Secular power is subject to spiritual power as the body is subject to the soul and therefore jurisdiction is not usurped if a spiritual prelate intervenes in temporal affairs in regard to those things in which secular power is subject to him or which secular power has relinquished to him" (*S.T.* IIa–IIae, 60,6). What this means Aquinas spelled out in other works: the Pope has legitimate authority over secular rulers; he is in this world "head of the *respublica* of Christ" (*Contra Errores Graecorum* ii, 32) in virtue of his position in the *ecclesia* (see also *Commentary on the Sententiae* II, 44, and *S.T.* IIIa, 8,1). In this Aquinas was clearly the heir of the political theology of Gregory VII, and unsurprisingly, therefore, he once again upheld a position strikingly at odds with that of liberal, secular modernity.

The discussion in the *Summa* of the virtue of religion is followed by a discussion of other potential parts of justice, beginning with the virtues of piety, observance, and the giving of honor. In each of these what we owe to God is accompanied by a duty to others: piety, for example, involves proper respect not only for God but also for parents, family, and *patria* and observance similarly requires respect for excellence in others. There follow accounts of the virtue of obedience to legitimate superiors, of gratitude to benefactors, of the vindication of justice to restore what has been violated by wrong-doing, of truthfulness, of friendliness, and of generosity (*S.T.* IIa–IIae, 101–119). Finally Aquinas reports the substance of what Aristotle had said about *epieikeia,* adds to what he had already said about piety as a natural virtue a short account of it as a supernatural virtue, and concludes his whole discussion of justice with a demonstration of how justice is completely specified by the Ten Commandments.

What differentiates Aquinas' account of justice from other philosophical and theological accounts, including those by his contemporaries and near contemporaries, is in part the extraordinary range of topics which it comprehends within its own scheme of rational ordering — something which I hope is at least suggested by my own bare catalogue — as well as the detailed treatment which each particular topic receives, something which can only be appreciated by going to the text itself. On one matter, however, it is necessary, for the sake of even limited comprehensiveness, to make an addition: it had been in the course of his earlier treatment of *caritas* in the *Summa* that Aquinas had treated of the justice and injustice of war, and that was presumably why he did not advert to it in the discussion of justice itself.

A just war requires that one's own political society be gravely wronged and that the enemy have refused to make amends or restitution; it requires that war be declared by a sovereign authority before hostilities may commence; and it requires stringent limitations upon the means which may be employed and upon the spirit in which the war may be fought. As with good and bad acts in general, the goodness of acts of war requires that they fulfill the condition of just action in every way, while defectiveness in any one way renders the war unjust and the actions of those who engage in it bad.

To whom was Aquinas addressing himself in his remarks upon war and for that matter in his discussion of justice in general? He was a teacher of teachers and an advisor of advisors. Both the comprehensiveness and the detail of his discussions reflect the range of persons and problems with whom and by whom those teachers and advisors were called upon for tasks requiring moral and political judgment. The Dominican order was, in the person of Aquinas and of others, a teaching presence not only in universities and *studia,* and not only in countless dioceses and parishes, but in the French court and at the papal court, and in the institutions administering law, both ecclesiastical and secular. Aquinas, like Aristotle before him, had the task of instructing some of the participants in the major institutional and political conflicts and divisions of his day, or at least of instructing their instructors.

I have stressed the extent to which his account of justice is at odds with the characteristic attitudes of contemporary liberal modernity. It is important to stress equally the degree to which the standards to which he tried to hold his thirteenth-century contemporaries involved a radical break with the conventional standards of the age and the arguments commonly employed in their justification. Consider in this respect Aquinas' rigorism with respect to truth-telling and lying. We are, on Aquinas' view, required *never* to assert anything except what we believe to be true. We are under no general obligation to tell all that we know; when to speak and when not to speak is a matter of other duties and obligations, of discretion and of the exercise of prudence. But we may never lie, not for profit, nor convenience, nor pleasure, nor to cause pain or trouble. Lying as such is evil, and lying with malice is a mortal sin (*S.T.* IIa–IIae, 109 and 110).

In the third article of *Quaestio* 110 Aquinas provides six arguments in favor of the view that lying is sometimes permissible, including the argument that a lie as a lesser evil may be used to prevent some greater evil such as killing or being killed. His rejection of these arguments embodies his conviction that the precepts of justice are not means designed to secure some external end, such as political success or worldly security, but are constitutive of those relationships through which and in which we live out that just life whose end is our true and ultimate end. Insofar as I lie I make myself into the sort of unjust person incapable of achieving my ultimate end. And to this immediate considerations must be subordinated. It follows that my responsibility for averting by some other means the greater evil in the face of which I am tempted to lie is all the greater and that even the sacrifice of my own life may be required of me to secure this, if the evil is sufficiently great.

The stock of arguments against this position, which Aquinas rejected, was of course that relied upon by many in contemporary thirteenth-century discussion. Telling those with power and authority that lying is prohibited to them was as unpopular an activity in the thirteenth century as in the twentieth. What, however, twentieth-century political society, unlike its thirteenth-century counterpart, characteristically lacks is the existence in its midst of any influential body of protagonists of an absolute prohibition upon lying, let alone the presentation of that prohibition as part of a body of thought claiming to merit both its intellectual and its moral allegiance.

That latter claim was also of course a presupposition of the comprehensiveness and detail of Aquinas' argumentative treatment of justice. Against contemporary Aristotelians Aquinas was committed to showing that both in what he accepted from Aristotle and in what he amended or dismissed he had genuinely come to terms with Aristotle's arguments. Similarly against contemporary Augustinians he was committed to a treatment of the patristic and Augustinian texts which gave them their due. And most fundamentally he could accept nothing from either which was irreconcilable with scripture.

Consider in this respect Aquinas' treatment of injustice. In agreeing with Aristotle that every virtue is exercised in conformity to a mean (*S.T.* Ia–IIae, 64,2), he nonetheless does not go on to understand justice as a virtue midway between two vices, as Aristotle does. Injustice is, so to speak, a single-minded vice, that of being disposed deliberately to oppose what justice requires (*S.T.* IIa–IIae, 59). Justice can be opposed by giving someone either more or less than what is his or her due, and herein the standard of the mean can be discerned. But the particular way in which justice is flouted is held to be less important than the will to flout it. And in this Aquinas is following Augustine rather than Aristotle.

Yet Augustine had seen injustice as fundamentally a sign of pride, the sin and vice lying in the pride. Against Augustine Aquinas argues that injustice is a distinctive vice and sin, not simply to be assimilated to pride. His reasons for so insisting concern pride as well as justice and express his concern for the detailed, differentiated structures of practical life. Pride (*superbia*) on his account is indeed related to injustice, since it is the vice which disposes one to make of and present oneself as more than one is. It is excessive self-esteem, informing the will so that one ascribes falsely to one's own powers all one's genuine excellences, pretends falsely to possess excellences which one does not, and takes oneself to be in a position to despise others, thus justifying one's malice toward them. It is above all a willful refusal to give God what is due to him and to be subject to God. St. Gregory understood it as present in all vices and not therefore specially to be connected with any one of them. And in this Aquinas followed Gregory (*S.T.* IIa–IIae, 162).

The importance of Aquinas' precise identification and characterization of vices is not only a matter of his theoretical scheme. The central human experience of the natural law, as I remarked earlier, is of our inability to live by it; and what we know of justice as or more often finds application in its flouting and disregard as in its observance. Hence it is, as I also said earlier, no accident that the discussion of law in Aquinas in the *Prima Secundae* leads straight into the treatment of grace, the only remedy for disobedience to law, and that the account of the natural virtues in the *Secunda Secundae* had to have as its prologue an inquiry into the supernatural virtues. For just as and because justice is continually the victim of the vice and sin of pride, so justice cannot flourish, cannot indeed, so it turns out, even exist as a natural virtue, unless and insofar as it is informed by the supernatural virtue of *caritas*. Charity is the form of all virtue; without charity the virtues would lack the specific kind of directedness which they require. And charity is not to be acquired by moral education; it is a gift of grace, flowing from the work of Christ through the office of the Holy Spirit (*S.T.* IIa–IIae, 23 to 44).

I also argued earlier that Aquinas does not merely supplement Aristotle, but that he shows Aristotle's account of the teleology of human life to be radically defective. That radical defectiveness in understanding turns out in the light of these sections of the *Summa* to be, on Aquinas' view, not only or so much a radical defectiveness in Aristotle's account as a radical defectiveness in that natural human order of which Aristotle gave his account. A strong thesis about the inadequacies and flaws of the natural human order emerges, so that the relationship of Aquinas' Aristotelianism to his allegiance to Augustine appears in a new light. The Augustinian understanding of fallen human nature is used to explain the limitations of Aristotle's arguments, just as the detail of Aristotle often corrects Augustine's generalizations.

What is clear nonetheless is that Aquinas' account is only fully intelligible, let alone defensible, as it emerges from an extended and complex tradition of argument and conflict that included far more than Aristotle and Augustine. The notion of detaching it from that tradition and presenting its claims in terms of some alleged neutral criteria of a rationality, understood in independence of any tradition of practice and theorizing, makes no sense, for it is an account of the criteria of rationality, and of the part played by the virtues in the exercise of rationality, which itself emerges from and is justified in terms of the background of the traditions to which Aquinas made himself the heir.

Aquinas' response to those traditions was very different either from that of his contemporaries or from that of his successors. There is a history, as yet only written in part, of the stages which had set the scene for Aquinas' enterprise. The revival of learning in the eleventh and twelfth centuries had simultaneously generated two different kinds of enterprise. One was the commentary, especially on sacred scripture, out of which were generated a set of theses about the different kinds of meaning and levels of meaning which could be found in a text along with a set of problems about how disagreements were to be resolved where authoritative writers conflicted or appeared to conflict. The first yielded the concept of the *distinctio;* the second, that of the *quaestio.* At the same time scholars were innovating, often drawing upon fragmentary or misunderstood inheritances from the past in logic, in dialectic, and in the understanding of law and of political authority. When the rediscovery of so much material by Aristotle which had been hitherto unavailable, along with his Islamic and Jewish interpreters, and the revival of Augustinian theology provided frameworks within which to try to understand the relationship between these enterprises, it was in the formal organization of the debates and disagreements recorded as *quaestiones disputatae* and *quaestiones quodlibetales,* and in the elaboration of both the theological and the secular *distinctiones* which these involved, that enquiry at last found the means to become simultaneously comprehensive and systematic. The past had provided a set of *auctoritates,* both sacred and secular. The former could be reinterpreted, although not rejected. The latter could only be rejected when there was sufficient reason to reject them. Enquiry, therefore, had to proceed by counterposing authority to authority, in respect of both theses and arguments.

Many of Aquinas' contemporaries and immediate successors responded either by rejecting some large part of their intellectual inheritance, in the interests of systematic coherence, or by turning to the piecemeal investigation of particular areas and elaborating solutions to particular problems on the basis of some sharply delimited set of perspectives. The former response characterized not only those Augustinians who rejected Aristotle, for fear of accepting Averroism, but also those other pupils of Albertus who developed this or that strand of Albertus' work in neglect of the rest. The latter response is exhibited by those who compartmentalized to greater or lesser degree their enquiries, so that the pursuit of logical studies proceeded in substantial part independently of enquiries in theology, and both in equal independence of writings about ethics and politics, in a way that foreshadows the compartmentalization of later enquiry.

Neither party fully understood the idiosyncrasy of Aquinas' project, that of developing the work of dialectical construction systematically, so as to integrate the whole previous history of enquiry, so far as he was aware of it, into his own. *His* counterposing of authority to authority was designed to exhibit what in each could withstand dialectical testing from every standpoint so far developed, with the aim of identifying both the limitations of each point of view and what in each could not be impugned by even the most rigorous of such tests. Hence the claim implicitly made by Aquinas against any rival out of the past is that the partiality, one-sidedness, and incoherences of that rival's standpoint will have already been overcome in the unfinished system portrayed in the *Summa,* while its strengths and successes will have been incorporated and perhaps reinforced. Against any similar rival from the future the corresponding claim would be that it too could be brought into the dialectical conversation at every relevant point and that the test of Aquinas' standpoint would lie in its ability to identify the limitations and to integrate the strengths and successes of each rival into its overall structure.

It is characteristic of intellectual, as well as of social, history, however, that it is always subject to a variety of unrelated contingencies. And so it was with Aquinas' standpoint, which, except within Roman Catholic theology, generated for the most part one more tradition of defensive commentary rather than an ability to engage with the greatest of its rivals. What effectively happened was that those rivals came to determine the terms of public fifteenth- and sixteenth-century philosophical debate, so that followers of Aquinas were confronted with a dilemma, albeit one which neither they nor their opponents generally recognized. *Either,* that is to say, they refused to accept the terms of contemporary debate and in so doing isolated themselves and were treated as irrelevant, *or* they made the mistake of accepting those terms of debate and on those terms seemed to have been defeated. Aquinas' thirteenth-century achievement had been to insist upon setting the terms for debate and enquiry. It was generally, even if not quite always, the misfortune of his fifteenth- and sixteenth-century heirs either not to perceive the need to do so or to fail in attempting to do so.

When, therefore, Aristotelianism had a dramatic revival of fortune in the universities of the sixteenth century, it was Aristotle without Aquinas who partially dominated the intellectual scene. The *Nicomachean Ethics* and the *Politics* once again became key educational texts. But Aristotle thus revived had to be vindicated in a milieu to which practically and theoretically his concepts came to seem increasingly irrelevant. The type of context of enquiry which the thirteenth-century university had made available and within which the relationship of Aristotle's texts to other texts had been elaborated lacked any adequate counterpart in the sixteenth and seventeenth centuries. In consequence it was not so much the revival of Aristotelianism as its rejection which was to produce new ways of theorizing about practical rationality and justice in an age when new modes of social life made such innovation once again practically important.

XII

The Augustinian and Aristotelian
Background to Scottish Enlightenment

The revival of Aristotelian studies, let alone of Aristotelian modes of thought and action, in the sixteenth century has so far been the subject of only preliminary historical enquiry (see especially Charles B. Schmitt *Aristotle and the Renaissance,* Cambridge, Mass., 1983). Their continued flourishing in Protestant as well as in Catholic circles during the seventeenth century is part of a history almost all of which still has to be written. The renewed use of the *Nicomachean Ethics* and the *Politics* in education taught young men to continue to think in terms of an *ultimus finis* of human life in the very same period in which teleological modes of thought were being systematically rejected in the ascendant physics and metaphysics. And the Aristotelian account of the virtues continued to provide them with a standard of natural excellence at the same time as Lutheran, Calvinist, and Jansenist theologians were teaching that the revealed supernatural chief end of human beings was one in the light of which the radical imperfection of all merely natural excellence could be discerned.

That this coexistence of Aristotelianism in the moral sphere with a variety of Augustinian theologies and with increasingly anti-Aristotelian modes of theorizing in the sciences should have proved fragile is scarcely surprising. But what most profoundly finally moved the largest part of Europe's educated classes to reject Aristotelianism as a framework for understanding their shared moral and social life was perhaps the gradual discovery during and after the savage and persistent conflicts of the age that no appeal to any agreed conception of *the* good for human beings, either at the level of practice or of theory, was now possible. It is no doubt true that for a very long time projects of religious and social reconciliation which had embodied such an appeal had had more of illusion than of reality about them. But even so great and perceptive a thinker as Leibniz was still able to envisage this practical outcome as one of the realistic goals not only of political negotiation but also of a rational theology which should embody a cogent shared conception of the good.

All such projects, including Leibniz's, did fail, and so had all attempts to impose by force of arms a type of agreement which rational moralists were unable even to formulate satisfactorily, let alone to sustain. The central practical tasks of moral enquiry and construction were in consequence transformed from the late seventeenth century onward. That a diversity of rival and incompatible conceptions of the good should obtain the allegiance of a variety of contending parties was from now on increasingly to be taken for granted. The practical question became rather: What kind of principles can require and secure allegiance in and to a form of social order in which individuals who are pursuing diverse and often incompatible conceptions of the good can live together without the disruptions of rebellion and internal war? The different and competing answers which were given to this question, like the question itself, presupposed the continued possession of a common, although changing, stock of concepts through the application of which human relationships were to be described, explained, and justified, along with a broadly shared understanding of the problems involved in such description, explanation, and justification. Certain aspects of this common stock of concepts and of this shared problematic emerged as peculiarly important.

One concerned the relationship of individuals to their social roles within an hierarchically structured social and political order. "The individual" was from now on conceived of as one of the fundamental, if not the most fundamental, categories of social thought and practice. Individuals are held to possess their identity and their essential human capacities apart from and prior to their membership in any particular social and political order. The central question posed about individuals so conceived is: What furnishes them with good reasons or at least adequate motivation for subjecting themselves to the constraints imposed by any particular social and political order? The very form of the question precluded those who asked it from even entertaining certain ancient and medieval conceptions, namely, those according to which it is only as the already self-identified inhabitant of some social role either within some institution, such as the *polis,* or within some teleologically understood, divinely legislated order that someone can come to have adequately good reasons for accepting and valuing the constraints imposed upon him or her by the social and political order within which he or she does whatever his or her role requires. For on such ancient and medieval views of the matter, as I have argued earlier, the goods which furnish me with such reasons are only to be apprehended in and through living out the type of human life which is structured by such roles.

It was not of course that such thoughts could not still be entertained. There continued to be Aristotelians and Thomists, and among them even the occasional eccentric political theorist who drew upon such ancient and medieval conceptions of polity. But their thought was marginalized and made to seem largely irrelevant just because it was at odds with the presuppositions of the dominant political question. The continuing dominance of that question was assured by the nature of the claims of the two dominant institutions, the emerging modern state and the growing market economy. The rulers of the modern state claimed to be able to justify their assumption of authority and their exercise of power insofar as they supplied the ruled with what could be identified as benefits and protection from harms, no matter what specific conception of *the* human good, if any, were held by rulers or ruled. The upholders of the market economy, whose new extended dominance was both consequence and cause of the way in which the household finally ceased to be the primary locus of production, claimed to be able to justify the transformation of land, labor, and money itself into commodities insofar as the market too supplied those who participated in it with benefits, which could be understood as such independently of specific conceptions of *the* good (see Karl Polanyi *The Great Transformation,* New York, 1944, still the single most illuminating account of the inception of institutionalized modernity; for more recent evaluations of that book see Charles P. Kindleberger '*The Great Transformation* by Karl Polanyi' *Daedalus* 103, 1, 1973, and Fred Block and Margaret R. Somers 'Beyond the Economistic Fallacy: The Holistic Social Science of Karl Polanyi' in *Vision and Method in Historical Sociology,* ed. Theda Skocpol, Cambridge, 1984).

Any answer to the dominant political question presupposed answers to two other closely related questions, and any systematic attempt to answer that dominant question could not avoid, implicitly or explicitly, furnishing answers to those other questions. The first of these concerned the nature of practical reasoning; the second, that of justice. If individuals were generally to accept as reasonable the constraints imposed by a social and political order upon their pursuit of a variety of heterogeneous aims, inspired by a range of different and incompatible conceptions of the human good, then these individuals must also generally share standards of practical reasoning by appeal to which two characteristics of their practical reasoning could be justified. For by their standards certain types of reason for acting—reasons which led them to accept, endorse, and enforce the constraints of the political and social order—must be accorded a status as good reasons independently of any relationship to any particular conception of *the* good. Disagreement, even radical disagreement, about *the* good had to be compatible with agreement in acknowledging the authority of such reasons. And this alone would be sufficient to render such a mode of practical reasoning incompatible with the Aristotelian mode.

Moreover, those reasons which were to be accounted adequately good reasons for accepting, endorsing, and enforcing the constraints of the social and political order must be such as generally to override, when they conflicted with, reasons for action whose authority and force derived from some particular conception of *the* good. So there had to be a way of rank-ordering reasons for action, which was once again not merely non-Aristotelian but anti-Aristotelian.

A second set of questions concerned the nature of justice. Any rationally defensible account of what had become or was to become the dominant type of social and political order had to confront the question of the respective parts to be played in the sustaining of that order by agreement on the one hand and coercion on the other. Most European states had secured internal order after the internal and external strife of the sixteenth and seventeenth centuries by enforced settlements. If an appeal to violence were not to be renewed, then the settlement had to be one found at least minimally acceptable, and its acceptability required an answer to such questions as: To what principle of social and political order is it reasonable to agree? To what degree can obedience to such principles be required? What kind of force may reasonably be employed in exacting such obedience when it is not yielded voluntarily?

These were versions of questions to which answers had hitherto been furnished by inherited beliefs about justice. And if now these questions were to be asked on the basis of new presuppositions, which conceptualized social realities in new ways, then either some older account of justice would have to be transformed sufficiently to serve the new purposes, or else some new account of justice, specifically devised for the new circumstances, would have to be elaborated. So any well-articulated understanding of those social and political orders which had emerged from the conflicts of the seventeenth century, framed in the concepts available to those who now in the eighteenth century inhabited them, had to provide a rationally defensible account of three central interrelated topics: political authority, practical rationality, and justice.

Any such account had to be constructed from three kinds of element: some conception of the passions and interests which motivate action, some conception of the principles comprehended by reason to which appeal can be made in political and moral matters, and some conception of the place of human action in the order of the universe, both the order of nature and that of divine providence, belief in which was still widely shared by those of otherwise conflicting theological views. About each of these elements and about their relationship, questions arise to which more than one type of answer can be given. Are the passions exclusively the motivating force of human action? When rational calculation shows someone that the expression of some passion presently felt in action will not be to their longer term interest, how is that passion to be inhibited? Can reason be an independently motivating force? What considerations advanced by reason can produce a sufficient motive for behaving justly when it is not in one's interest to be just? Is there an order of things, natural or providential, such that if individuals pursue their own interests, the interest of maintaining the social and political order will be served? (For an account of the background to the framing of these questions see Albert O. Hirschman *The Passions and the Interests,* Princeton, 1977.)

Two contrasting types of answer to these questions were to become particularly influential, and each of them was to present its own particular problems, its own *prima facie* vulnerability to objections. It was on the one hand possible to understand obedience to such principles as those of justice or those determining the legitimacy of political authority as a means to the promotion of the interests of groups and to understand interests as the collective expression of the passions of individuals. Principles thus serve the purposes of both interest and passion, and to recognize this is to recognize also that it is irrational to obey a principle when to do so would not or would no longer serve those purposes of interest and passion which provide that particular principle with its justification. Of course individuals sometimes make mistakes, either about the relationship of principles in general to passions and interests or about the purpose served by some particular principle, and when they do so, they fail to recognize and to respond to their own motivation. But those who are more clear-sighted will understand that human beings, whether they acknowledge it or not, are inescapably creatures of passion and interest.

Yet it also remained possible to understand principles in quite another way as having an authority independent of passions and interests, so that appeal to principle against one's passions and one's interests could not only be rationally justified but could be effective in moving one to do what would be at the levels of passion and interest to one's own detriment. The central problem confronting this latter view is obvious: How is it possible for the rational apprehension of principle to motivate, let alone to motivate in such a way that passion and interest are temporarily at least deprived of their power? The central problem confronting its rival is that of how anyone moved only by passion and interest could be motivated — as palpably some are motivated — to obey principles of justice, obedience to which on some occasions at least would deprive them of satisfaction at the level of passion and benefit at the level of interest.

Each of these rival conceptions of the relationship of principles to passions and to interests proved itself in the course of the eighteenth century capable of an alliance with some kind of theology, albeit often enough a vulgarized and attenuated theology. So even in the crudest versions of the view that human beings are moved only by their passions and interests, that according to which they are moved only by the prospect of self-interested advantage, it was possible to argue — and some did argue — that God had provided us with a view of the pleasures and pains to be enjoyed and suffered in an afterlife which afforded the rational calculator of self-interest good reason for obedience to the divine will. And some of those who held that reason apprehends principles independent of passion and interest found no difficulty in including among those principles some concerning the being and will of the deity. Nonetheless, the way in which each view was elaborated and defended was increasingly in terms of a purely secular rationality, a rationality by appeal to which theology was gradually excluded from any substantial part in the arenas of moral and political life.

These two rival modes of understanding the relationship of principles to passions and to interests confronted one another in the first half of the eighteenth century in two quite different ways, as rival philosophical theories contending in academic debate, but also and more fundamentally as alternative modes of shaping social existence, as beliefs systematically embodied in and presupposed by the actions and transactions of institutionalized social and political life. What type of social and political order exemplified each of these alternative modes?

A society in which the established principles could be understood as instruments in the service of passions and interests would have to be one in which passions and interests were, or rather were taken to be, organized so as to provide mutuality in satisfaction and benefit. Agreement on principle would have to presuppose a more fundamental concurrence of interests and passions, and a stable social and public order would require conscious and conscientious willing of that concurrence, on the part of many, if not all participants; it would also require the exercise of conformity-producing sanctions against actually or potentially disruptive individuals or groups. Actions and transactions would be characterized and evaluated as both produced by and conducing to either the satisfaction of or the frustration of desires and aversions, that is, of passions. The social classification of individuals would be in terms of what they consume and enjoy, or at least aspire to consume and enjoy, and of what they bring about in the way of consumption and enjoyment for others. The fundamental relationships of the social order would be defined in terms of who provides what for whom and of who threatens the prospects of enjoyment and satisfaction for whom by the ways in which they pursue their own enjoyment and satisfaction.

Examples of milieus in which some measure of such a form of social life was to be found were not rare in eighteenth-century Europe, but the prime example of such a social order was to be found in England. Roy Porter has written of the problems which confronted the great landowners of eighteenth-century England: "Magnates were on the horns of a self-created dilemma. Greed urged them to maximize agrarian profit, pride to bask in undisturbed private grandeur—both alienating the community. The richer they got, the more they cultivated tastes—Palladianism, French fashions, fine manners and connoisseurship of the arts—which elevated them above their natural right-hand men, homespun squires and freeholders. . . . And yet popularity was the kiss of life. Lacking private armies, in the end they had to rule by bluster and swank. Authority could be upheld only by consent, through tricky reciprocal negotiations of will and interests, give and take. . . . The fraternizing game, however nauseating, however phony, had to be played" (*English Society in the Eighteenth Century*, Hormondsworth, 1982, pp. 79–80).

The key to this type of social order lies in the reciprocal character of the passions from which behavior is understood to issue. If I am to be accorded, so far as is possible, what pleases me and to be protected, so far as is possible, from what pains me, it can only be insofar as it pleases others that I should be pleased and it pains those same others that I should be pained. This in turn can only be the case if it generally pleases me that these others should be pleased and generally pains me that they should be pained. But such reciprocity and mutuality of satisfaction and dissatisfaction can only be imperfectly embodied in actual social arrangements. Some individuals will find themselves omitted from the reciprocity of benefit, some who participate will be cheated, and the less power that individuals or groups have to supply satisfaction or to inflict pain, the less the consideration which need be given to pleasing them. Thus sanctions will be required to curb the rebellious and the deviant. And in eighteenth-century England the rules of justice provided just such sanctions. So, for example, "to cope with self-created rural polarization . . . grandees stage-managed a more studied theatre of power: conspicuous menace (and mercy) from the Judge's Bench; exemplary punishment tempered with silver linings of philanthropy, largesse and selective patronage; a grudging and calculating display of *noblesse oblige*" (Roy Porter, op. cit., p. 81).

The dominant standards to which appeal is made in such a type of social order will be such that to express them is to endorse the standpoint of mutual reciprocity in the exchange of benefits. To condemn an action or a transaction will be, and will be understood to be, to express toward it the negative response appropriate to failure in respect of such reciprocity. Thus the appeal to standards—moral, aesthetic, political standards of right judgment and action—will itself be a form of participation in the shared transactions of social exchange. The standards themselves will function within and as an expression of this form of political and social order. The utterance of a judgment that such and such is to be approved or disapproved will itself be one more action performed and understood from within the web of relationships constituted by those exchanges which express the interests and the passions of the participants in this form of social life. Among whom do these relationships hold?

They link, not individuals as such, but individuals identified in terms of the resources which they possess and upon which they can draw in contributing to the exchanges which constitute social life. So the individual as propertied, as property owner or as propertyless, is the unit of social life, and the rules governing the distribution and exchange of property are an integral part of the rules constituting the system of social exchanges. Status and power within the system depend upon the ownership of property; to be propertyless is to be eligible only to be a victim of the system, whether a victim of its oppression or of its charity. And simply because the rules of property are so integral to the functioning of the whole *and* because all appeals to standards of right judgment and action are internal to that same system, functioning as expressions of attitude within it, there cannot be from the standpoint of this form of social and political order any well-founded appeal against the property relations of the *status quo* to a standard of right external to that social and political order, to a standard expressed in principles whose truth would be independent of the attitudes and judgments of the participants in the order.

Any purported appeal to such a standard will be understood from the standpoint of the system itself to have two salient characteristics. It will mark those who make such an appeal as deviants, outsiders whose motivations are not in harmony with and are at least potentially disruptive of the established order of exchanges. But there will also have to be from the perspective afforded by that standpoint some intellectual confusion involved in any such appeal. For those who make it will be acting as if there could be a standard for practical judgment and action whose authority was independent of the purposes to be served by political and social institutions in maintaining the exchange of benefits and satisfactions. To put matters in another way: nothing is to be accounted a good reason for practical judgment or action, by the standards provided for the evaluation of reasons and practical reasoning established within this type of social and political order, unless it can motivate those whose only regard is for the type of satisfaction and benefit which that order provides. Hence it would be concluded by an adequately reflective adherent of such an established order that there can be no good reason for appealing to some standard external to the order.

The grandees and squires of eighteenth-century England were often enough sufficiently articulate, but rarely, if ever, sufficiently reflective to make this point for themselves. It was to be made on their behalf much later in the eighteenth century by Edmund Burke, whose rhetoric provided simultaneously a defense of the established order which appealed only to values already acknowledged within the exchanges of benefits and satisfactions which partially constituted that order as well as an attack upon any appeal to theoretically grounded principles purporting to have an authority independent of that conferred from within. Three features of Burke's stance are illuminating. The first is the way in which Burke had first to make himself into a member of the English established order in order to be able to speak from within it. It was not open to him to commend that order from without as an Irishman; he had to transform himself into an owner of English property, to imagine or reimagine himself as an English gentleman.

Second, Burke draws our attention to the fact that any stable and continuing example of this kind of order will have to have successfully been adaptive to changing circumstance, repressing this group, repelling that, coopting this other, so that one and the same system may at different times enlarge or diminish both the range of benefits conferred within it and the ranks of those who enjoy them. This history will also inevitably be a history of the adaptation of principle to circumstance. It will be one in which no principle will have been exempt from periodic reevaluation and revision in the light of its success or failure in serving the purposes of securing benefit and satisfaction within the exchanges of social life.

Third, Burke through his identification of his antagonists in England as well as in France reminds us that the appeal to principles claiming authority independent of that conferred upon them by the established political and social order had in fact defined the opposition of a number of groups to the established order throughout the eighteenth century. I have said that the type of established political and social order which I have been describing finds its fullest exemplification in England. But it is as important to note that in England it always had to coexist with a variety of dissenters, commonly dissenters with a theology less capable of complacent incorporation into the socially dominant scheme of things than was the religion, so agreeable to Burke, of the majority of Anglican dignitaries. Burke's own immediate antagonists had been nurtured in the meeting houses and academies of the kind of English Protestantism which claimed for itself the proud name of "Old Dissent." But the list of other present and past dissenters included as well Nonjuring and Roman Catholic Jacobites, and earlier still the English Republicans of the Commonwealth, and those even more radical puritans, the Levellers and the Diggers, who had attacked established property relations. From the standpoint of those principles of justice expressing the concordance of the interests and the passions of the participants in the established order, such dissent, if embodied in action, could only issue in the injustice either of crime or of rebellion.

It was perhaps no accident that the English established order of the eighteenth century could only finally find an effective rhetorical champion by recruiting a renegade Irishman. For if Burke was only able to express and endorse the evaluations internal to the established English and social order by having entered it and identified himself from within with the standpoint of its propertied participants, he also had had the advantage of first viewing it from without, the kind of view of the relationship of the parts of a social system to the whole which is often denied to those who inhabit that system. For they after all are themselves among the parts of that system, encountering other parts piecemeal in the encounters of everyday life, but characteristically being denied the opportunity of viewing the whole as a whole. So it was with those whose cause Burke championed. But Burke himself had been able to view the kind of life afforded by the dominant English social system as an alternative to that which he could have enjoyed had he chosen to live either by the principles of his Catholic mother's Irish kin or by those of his Quaker schoolmasters.

This ability to view the dominant English social system from without was not of course available only to those who were not English. Cobbett, for example, later on was to view it from the standpoint of an alternative England, an England still with pre-Reformation roots; and no one has been more successfully destructive of the ideological vision which Burke handed on to his successors than was Cobbett. Nonetheless, what England in fact was and what it required of those who gave their allegiance to its established order could especially perhaps in the earlier eighteenth century be seen with particular clarity by those for whom entry from without into that order as individuals, and indeed the possibility of the assimilation of their institutions to its institutions, represented one of the two alternative forms of social life confronting them. This was peculiarly the situation of young educated Scotsmen in the first half of the eighteenth century.

When in 1707 Scotland lost her sovereignty, nominally to a new entity, the United Kingdom, but in fact to a continuing English parliament at Westminster, augmented by only sixteen Scottish members out of two hundred and six in the House of Lords and by only forty-five Scottish members out of five hundred and sixty-eight in the House of Commons, politics itself became an arena closed to all but a few Scotsmen, and those ones who were willing to become almost, if not quite, totally subservient to the purposes of the English ruling elite. "The English Government ruled from the basis of a solid block of sycophantic votes organized by experienced managers dispensing safe seats with the one hand and lucrative positions of government office with the other. Their eye picked out the Scottish newcomers to the Westminster assembly as promising recruits: they organized them under one of their own number until, with a little training, they became almost as bovine in their passivity to the English administration as their forefathers had been to the Scottish Lords of the Articles" [who until 1689 had represented the Crown in the Scottish Parliament and for the most part controlled its activities] (T.C. Smout *A History of the Scottish People 1560–1830,* London, 1969, p. 218).

It was, therefore, in and through those distinctively Scottish institutions which survived the Treaty of Union, rather than in and through the formal structures of politics, that an alternative mode of civil and social existence, capable of resisting to some large degree and for some length of time the pressures toward the Anglicization of Scottish culture and society, was maintained and elaborated. Those institutions were of three kinds. There was the established Church of Scotland, presbyterian in order, Calvinist in its official documents, the Westminster Confession of Faith and the Larger and Shorter Catechisms. There were the institutions of Scottish law and of the legal profession, a law informed by an inheritance from Roman-Dutch law, especially in the area of municipal law, and very different in both theory and practice from the English Common Law. And there was the educational system, designed to implement the intention of the Reformers that there should be a school in every parish. This intention had been gradually, but unevenly, implemented, so that by the early eighteenth-century Lowland parishes commonly had a school, and grammar schools existed in the major burghs. At the apex of the system were the three pre-Reformation universities of St. Andrews, Glasgow, and King's College, Aberdeen, and the two post-Reformation foundations, Edinburgh and Marischal College, Aberdeen.

The system provided a homogeneous education for future ministers, lawyers, and schoolmasters. The habits of mind in which it trained them were the habits appropriate to a culture in which the tasks of rational justification by appeal to principles with an authority independent of the social order were central. Those tasks arose at three different levels. Most fundamentally the adherents of Scottish institutions were committed to claims that their institutions embodied principles which could be vindicated rationally against any alternative set of principles and institutions. Their indebtedness in theology to Geneva and in law and later in education to Holland in the view of most of those adherents showed only that their countrymen had been willing to learn the truth wheresoever it was taught. Thus it was part of the peculiarly Scottish ethos to envisage Scottish principles and institutions as those that could be rationally vindicated within an international community of Protestant civility, within which standards of rational justification were shared. It is unsurprising that the study of the foundations of international law became an important part of a university education.

Second, the particular tasks of rational justification for socially shared beliefs and socially approved actions and institutional arrangements had to be discharged within the Scottish legal system, the Scottish theological system, and the Scottish educational system, by showing in detail how particular subordinate conclusions could be derived by valid deductive inference from appropriate intermediate principles that could in turn be justified by deduction from first principles. And third, each individual, in making those decisions and embarking upon those projects which would determine the future course of his or her life, had also to confront a framework of theological, legal, and moral principles in terms of which such decisions and projects had to be justified.

The university-educated Scotsman also faced an even more fundamental type of decision: whether to continue to live in Scotland the kind of life shaped by Scotland's own peculiar cultural institutions and institutionalized beliefs or to live out an Anglicized life either by transforming, so far as possible, Scottish ways into English ones within Scotland or by emigrating to England. This involved a choice most obviously of what type of career to follow and where, but it also involved choices in modes of religious observance, in manners and in habits, and in how to talk and to write. Alexander Carlyle, minister of Inveresk, wrote that "to every man bred in Scotland the English language was a foreign tongue," and more than one group of young Scotsmen in Edinburgh joined together in order to learn to speak English in an Anglicized mode, so doing perhaps because they failed to consider that the question of who speaks standard or "the best" English and who a mere provincial dialect is always susceptible of more than one answer.

The attempt instead to preserve an independent un-Anglicized culture whose speech was still a version of English required distinguishing and upholding a viable Scottish identity in yet another way. Gaelic-speaking Scotland, in large part Roman Catholic, had also to be repudiated. The Gaelic language—as often referred to as 'Erse' as 'Gaelic' by English-speakers—was almost unknown outside the Highlands. The Church of Scotland treated large parts of the Highlands as missionary areas. The landholding and kin relations of the clan system were afforded no recognition by the law until they achieved that negative recognition afforded by the liquidation, so far as possible, of everything pertaining to clanship in the draconian legislation which followed the rising of 1745. The Gaelic Highlanders were valued only as soldiers, first when those drawn from the loyalist Protestant clans were used to contain and suppress the rest of the clans and from 1739 onward as troops to be used abroad on England's behalf.

It was not surprising, then, that many, if not all, young educated Scotsmen viewed the Highlanders as aliens and to some degree enemy aliens. When in November 1745 a largely Highland Jacobite army approached Edinburgh, the Edinburgh College Volunteers went out to enlist in the army of General Sir John Cope, arriving, however, only in time to witness that army's panic-stricken defeat. And if those young men saw in the Rising of 1745 nothing but a Roman Catholic Jacobite army threatening their Protestant cause rather than an expression of an older Scotland, this in itself was a symptom of the impoverishment of the Scottish identity. "Scotland" had now to be counterposed both to England and to the Gaelic Highlands. That the attempt to invent and sustain this "Scotland" finally failed—it was to be replaced by the conjunction of Sir Walter Scott's imaginative and romantic reinvention of "Scotland" with the brutal realities of industrial and landowning capitalism—is not surprising; what is remarkable is that it *was* sustained and enriched through so many decades, producing and produced by a culture and a social order quite other than that of England.

To be Anglicized, even to be thoroughly Anglicized, it was not, of course, necessary to go to England. Distinctively English modes of life were increasingly at home in Scotland politically, commercially, and socially. Politically the web of patronage, of mutual dependency, and of what was from one point of view corruption—from another, the adroit use of resources to prevent disorder—extended from Westminster, administered in Scotland for long periods by the second and third Dukes of Argyll. Commercially it was important that the reciprocities of interest and passion which were central to the dominant English mode fitted so well with the reciprocities of the market. And insofar as Scotland became to a growing extent a commercially successful country, especially among the Glasgow merchants, it fostered the same reciprocities and so became further Anglicized. English fashions, English manners, and, as we have already seen, English idioms and accents were more and more invasive. It is therefore unsurprising that within the internal Scottish debates and conflicts of the Scottish eighteenth century a variety of English and Anglicizing standpoints not only appear but appear as among the strongest contenders for Scottish allegiance.

It was indeed as debate and conflict that Scottish intellectual and social life was constituted in the eighteenth century. The starting-point for that debate was a variety of interpretations of the political and religious Settlement of 1690 and of the possibilities which had thereby been opened up. The framework for, as well as a key part of, the subject matter of those debates and conflicts were provided by Protestant Scotland's distinctive religious, legal, and educational institutionalized beliefs. The alternatives confronted in debate and conflict were gradually transformed during the century. But since it was the institutional framework and the beliefs embodied in it which determined the forms of debate, it is with these that we ought to begin.

The type of society which is understood by most of those who in-

habit it as exemplifying in its social and political order principles independent of and antecedent to the passions and interests of the individuals and groups who compose that society requires for its maintenance the generally shared possession—not necessarily universally
shared—of some account of the knowledge of such principles and a
set of institutionalized means for bringing those principles to bear upon
the issues of practical life. In seventeenth- and eighteenth-century
Scotland it was almost an intellectual commonplace that those first principles, by deduction from which subordinate judgments were rationally justified, had a quality of evidentness that made them recognizable
truths by everyone of sound mind who understood the terms in which
they were stated and whose understanding had not been subverted by
false doctrine. This was, of course, in no way a commonplace only in
Scotland. When we encounter philosophically sophisticated versions
of this view in the context of the philosophical theories of Locke or
Leibniz or in the philosophical antitheory of Shaftesbury, we do not
always recognize that we are encountering at the level of philosophy
a type of belief widely credited in everyday nonphilosophical social life.
What differentiated Scotland was the degree to which social life was
organized around types of justification which presupposed just this
belief.

This shared belief in a stock of evident substantive truths had at least
two distinct sources, one of which was indeed a matter of the influence
of philosophy upon the rest of life, the other of which had little to do
with philosophy. This latter is to be found in most, perhaps in all, premodern societies, where there was and is a common stock of beliefs
whose expression in language was and is treated as the utterance of
evident truth. Such beliefs provide a touchstone for other claims. And
if in our society we find it difficult to imagine ourselves back into the
state of mind for which evidentness is an important epistemological
property, it is not only because of the relative paucity of such beliefs
in our own time and place, at least among those who take themselves
to be sophisticated, but also because we are well aware how different
and incompatible sets of beliefs have had the same property of evidentness ascribed to them in different cultures. The problem which this variety and incompatibility presents to believers in evidentness was one
of which educated Scotsmen became aware during the eighteenth century, and Dugald Stewart, as we shall see later, was to propose an ingenious solution to it.

What happened in some premodern European societies, such as Scotland, was that socially shared beliefs in evident truths were both re-

inforced by, and partially organized in terms derived from, philosophy. It had of course been crucial to the whole Platonic-Aristotelian tradition to affirm that there are first principles and that the human mind can be educated to see their truth. But the first principles of those structured hierarchies of demonstrative argument which, on an Aristotelian view, constitute the sciences, although they cannot be *demonstrated*— for then they would not be first principles of demonstration—are not therefore independent of all rational support. As I noticed a good deal earlier, they are arrived at, on Aristotle's own view, a view reaffirmed by Aquinas in his commentary on the *Posterior Analytics,* by the methods of dialectic, including both *epagōgē* from particulars and the refutation of alternative, rival theses. Just because, however, the move from premises asserted in a dialectical mode to a conclusion concerning some particular first principle is not a deductive inference, something other than logical acumen is required to complete that move successfully, something which provides a grasp of the relevant first principle and which is a "seeing that," something to be named "intuition" perhaps or "insight." But it is crucial that such insight is unwarranted apart from the outcome of the previous dialectical arguments, not only with respect to rational support for the first principle in question but also in respect of its content, since the meaning of the key terms used in formulating it was given to those terms in part by the distinctions and clarifications which emerged from the process of dialectical argument. Aristotelian science, both on Aristotle's own account and also on Aquinas', had thus been an inseparable blend of demonstration and dialectic. But from late medieval Aristotelianism onward they were split apart in a way that first diminished the importance of Aristotle's discussions of the *Topics,* either by downgrading the importance of dialectical argument or else by assimilating the study of dialectic to the study of *consequentiae* (see Eleonore Stump 'Topics: their development and absorption into consequences' chapter 14 *The Cambridge History of Later Medieval Philosophy,* ed. N. Kretzmann, A. Kenny, J. Pinborg, and E. Stump, Cambridge, 1982), and then during the Renaissance permitted the presentation of dialectic, or rather what then became represented as dialectic, as a rhetorical rival alternative to the Aristotelian logic of demonstration.

What matters to my present argument in this history, however, is not the rise and fall of Ramist dialectic as a challenge to Aristotelianism. In Scotland the reformer Andrew Melville had introduced Ramist methods at Glasgow after he became principal there in 1574. But quite early on in the seventeenth century the influence of Ramus had become negligible. What matters to the present narrative is not so much the history of the fate of dialectic—crucially important as that history is for its own sake—as the way in which the first principles of the sciences, conceived in a mode that was still in large measure Aristotelian, came to be treated as evident and undeniable in their own right, without dialectical or any other rational support.

Ernan McMullin in noting how Galileo himself retained the idiom of Aristotelian demonstration has pointed to the way in which "Some of the principles of mechanics may easily seem so plausible as almost to take on the status of necessary truths" ('The Conception of Science in Galileo's Work' in *New Perspectives on Galileo,* ed. R.E. Butts and J.C. Pitts, Dordrecht, 1978, p. 229). And if by a necessary truth we understand only a truth which it is not possible for any reasonable person to deny—rather than defining "necessary truth" in terms of some philosophical theory of necessity and contingency—then we may remove McMullin's qualifying "almost" and say that for many in the seventeenth century the first principles of mechanics, as of every other science, were assigned the status of necessary truths.

This conception of each science, of each mode of knowledge and understanding, as deriving from some set of evident first principles, principles whose evidentness is such that they have no need of further rational support of any kind and whose status as first principles is such that they cannot have further rational support, reinforces then in some early modern European societies popular belief in the evidentness of certain truths. And this belief was sustained by the version of scholastic Aristotelianism which dominated the universities in mid-seventeenth-century Scotland. The most notable protagonist of what I characterized earlier as an ultimately unstable alliance of Calvinism and Aristotelianism was perhaps Robert Baillie, who taught philosophy as a regent at Glasgow University from 1625–31, later became professor of Divinity, and, after the restoration of Charles II, principal of the university. Among Baillie's papers is a draft of an 'Overture' from the university which was probably presented to the General Assembly of the Church of Scotland in August 1641 (*The Letters and Journals of Robert Baillie MDCXXXVII–MDCXLII A.M.,* ed. D. Laing, vol. 2, Edinburgh, 1842, pp. 463–465).

In the Overture Baillie argues that divinity students should be taught to respond "first *axiomaticè* and then by syllogistik objections." Thus the referring back of subordinate theses to first principles is explicitly made part of the training of a minister. The foundation for this practice would have been laid earlier in the teaching of Aristotelian logic, both in Aristotle's own texts—the *De Interpretatione* and the *Prior Analytics* are to be prescribed—and in the Scholastic textbooks which were used. Baillie was influenced by the blend of Aristotle and Calvin which had come to prevail in parts at least of Holland. He corresponded with Gisbert Voet, professor of theology at Utrecht and from 1641 rector of that university, and defender of Plato and Aristotle against Descartes. The authors of the textbooks which he prescribed included Franco Burgersdijk, professor at Leyden, whose *Institutionum Logicarum Duo Libri* had been made a prescribed text in Holland by the Estates in 1636, thus stemming the influence of Ramism (E.J. Ashworth *Language and Logic in the Post-Medieval Period,* Dordrecht/Boston, 1974, p. 18), and whose expositions of Aristotle's ethics and physics were reprinted at Oxford (F.C. Lohr 'Renaissance Latin Aristotle Commentaries: A–B' *Studies in The Renaissance,* vol. 21, 1974).

The teaching of Aristotelianism continued in the senior undergraduate years (Baillie, op. cit., p. 464). In the third year "the rest of the Logick, Ethick and Politick" was to be taught, and the fourth year was to include both metaphysics and a study of the *De Anima.* Great emphasis was laid on the teaching of Greek at the outset of an undergraduate career, so that "Aristotle's text would be read in Greek," Baillie anticipated the later history of the Scottish curriculum, both in his willingness to draw upon the intellectual resources afforded by Protestant Holland and in his view of the effects of Anglicization upon Scotland, something about which he learned at first hand under Cromwellian rule (Hugh Kearney *Scholars and Gentlemen,* Ithaca, 1970, p. 130). And in helping to furnish Scotland with a systematic, even if unstable, blend of Calvinism and Aristotelianism he also helped to provide the intellectual climate within which classic definition could be given to certain attitudes of mind which were to be the legacy of the Scholasticism of the seventeenth century to the Scotland that was to be reinvented in the early eighteenth century.

That definition was in fact given by *The Institutions of the Law of Scotland* by Sir James Dalrymple of Stair, afterward created Viscount Stair by William III, first published in 1681 in Stair's first period as Lord President of the Court of Session, an office of which he was deprived by his refusal to take the oath required by the Test Act of 1681 and to which, after exile in Holland, and the overthrow of King James VII and II by William of Orange, he was restored. During this second period as Lord President, Stair published a revised second edition of his *Institutions* in 1693. What Stair's *Institutions* provided was a comprehensive statement of the nature of justice, of law, and of rational and right conduct, which articulated the presuppositions of what were to be distinctively Scottish attitudes. No one in the Scottish eighteenth century could engage with these topics without in one way or another confronting Stair's theoretical and conceptual scheme, a scheme which expressed in terms of the law of Scotland not only the legal but also the key theological and philosophical doctrines concerning justice, law, and rational and right conduct.

As a comprehensive exposition of the law of Scotland Stair's book was without predecessors. Justinian's *Institutions* provided his most fundamental model, and Stair makes many references to commentators on Roman law. The modern European jurist most often cited is Grotius, and Stair also shows knowledge of Gudelinus' treatise on the law of the Netherlands, evidence of the continuing intellectual influence of Dutch writers and Dutch institutions. No English legal commentator is ever mentioned, nor is any English statute or case. Law is defined at the outset as "the dictate of reason, determining every rational being to that which is congruous and convenient for the nature and condition thereof. . . . Even God Almighty, though he be accountable to, and controllable by none, and so hath the absolute freedom of his choice, yet doth he unchangeably determine himself by his goodness, righteousness, and truth; which therefore make the absolute sovereign divine law" (*Institutions* I, 1, 1). Insofar as human beings share in the divine attributes, the law which it is rational for them to observe is that which expresses God's nature; insofar as they have attributes which distance them from divinity, reason directs them accordingly. "And reason doth determine mankind yet further, from the convenience of his nature and state, to be humble, penitent, careful and diligent for the preservation of himself and his kind; and therefore, to be sociable and helpful, and to do only that which is convenient for mankind to be done by everyone in the same condition" (loc. cit.).

What human beings apprehend by reason are the common principles of law: "The principles of law are such as are known without arguing, and to which the judgment, upon apprehension thereof, will give it ready and fully assent; such as, God is to be adored and obeyed, parents to be obeyed and honoured, children to be loved and entertained. And such are these common precepts which are set forth in the civil law, to live honestly, to wrong no man, to give every man his right (Justinian's *Institutions* 1,1,3; *Digest* 1,1,10)" (I,1,18). Reason apprehends first principles of law of two kinds, those of equity or right and those of the good, useful or expedient. Had it not been for the fall of man, the principles of equity alone would have sufficed. But because human beings are in rebellion against God and the principles of equity, it is profitable for human beings "to find out expedients and helps to make equity effectual; and therefore to make up societies of men, that they may mutually defend one another and procure to one another their rights . . ." (loc. cit.).

The primary obligations of human beings are those required by obedience to God and his law. Those secondary obligations which arise from merely human conventions and institutions serve the end of securing the rights which obedience to divine law would assure, and in this lies their utility. Hence the useful, the expedient, and the profitable are defined in terms of what is just, equitable, and right. They in no way provide independent standards for right action.

Stair explicitly departs from and quarrels with Justinian's ordering of the subject matter of law in the place which he assigns to the discussion of obligations. Where Justinian and Roman law generally had categorized the concerns of law in terms of persons, things, and actions, Stair argues that "the proper object" of law "is the right itself, whether it concerns persons, things or actions . . ." (I,1,23). Hence the foundation of rights, in the character of the primary obligations which human beings have, has to precede as a topic the exposition of the particular rights of persons, in which the more fundamental principles are applied.

It is instructive to contrast Stair's method of argument with that which was to be followed a good deal later in England by Sir William Blackstone, the first Vinerian Professor at Oxford University, who published the substance of his lectures on the laws of England in 1765 under the title *Commentaries on the Laws of England*. Blackstone had in his inaugural lecture, which he reprinted at the beginning of the *Commentaries,* asserted the superiority of English to Roman law, and in the early sections of the *Commentaries* he gives a very different account to that provided by Stair both of the first principles of the law and of their relationship to subordinate principles. Three central points of contrast obtrude. Blackstone begins by writing as if he too is going to deduce the first principles of the law from theological or metaphysical doctrine. But he at once declares such an appeal redundant by declaring of God that "he has been pleased so to contrive the constitution and frame of humanity, that we should want no other prompter to inquire after and pursue the rule of right, but only our own self-love, that universal principle of action. . . . he has not perplexed the law of nature with a multitude of abstracted rules and precepts . . . but has graciously reduced the rule of obedience to this one paternal precept 'that man should pursue his own true and substantial happiness'. This is the foundation of what we call ethics or natural law . . ." (*Commentaries,* Introduction, Section 2).

God has on Blackstone's view so constituted human beings that we effectively neither possess nor need any standard external to our passions, for "The only true and natural foundations of society are the wants and the fears of individuals" (Introduction, Section 2). Some few of the principles which express and guide our self-love are immutable because of the unchanging character of our desires; such is the prohibition of murder. And such principles are reinforced by divine revelation. But apart from such principles, which, being natural to all human beings, compose the natural law, Englishmen are to be guided by the past practice of their own society: "And it hath been an antient observation in the laws of England, that whenever a standing rule of law, of which the reason perhaps could not be remembered or discerned, hath been wantonly broken in upon by statutes or new resolutions, the wisdom of the rule hath in the end appeared from the inconveniences that have followed the innovation. The doctrine of the law then is this: that precedents and rules must be followed, unless flatly absurd or unjust: for though their reason be not obvious at first view, yet we owe such a deference to former times as not to suppose that they acted wholly without consideration" (Introduction, Section 3). Edward Christian, professor of the laws of England at Cambridge, who edited the twelfth edition of the *Commentaries* (1793–95), asserted that the qualification "unless flatly absurd or unjust" ought to be omitted. But since the standards by which absurdity and injustice were to be judged were in fact derived from the practices whose rules and precedents were in question, what divided Christian from Blackstone was perhaps less than might appear at first sight.

Blackstone was, of course, the legal counterpart of Burke. In the *Reflections on the Revolution in France* Blackstone is praised as the latest in a line of succession from Coke. And, like Burke, what Blackstone provides is an account of the dominant English social structures according to which the justification of those structures is internal to them. The standards by which established practice is to be judged are, with minimal qualification, the standards already embodied in established practice. The contrast with Stair could not be sharper, and it emerges clearly on three particular topics.

The first of these is the place allotted to appeals to equity. For Blackstone such appeals are in place only where a case arises which the established rules do not cover and where precedent is silent. But for Stair the rules of equity are among the first principles of justice, and to them appeal *against* established rule and precedent may always be made. Appeal to precedent has for Scottish law, on Stair's account, no force except as evidence of how the rules of justice have been applied and of the view taken by the author or authors of the particular precedent as to how in this kind of case they ought to be applied. We ought, on Stair's view, to treat what is established custom and precedent with some deference as providing such evidence, but with no more than this. So the rules of justice according to Stair provide a fundamental standard external to all established practice, even including the practice of the legislator, whose work may be found defective and corrected by a judge on the basis of an appeal to the first principles of justice.

A second key difference between Stair and Blackstone is apparent in their understanding of property. I have already emphasized how within the dominant social structures of the English eighteenth century it is the individual as propertied or propertyless who participates in the mutuality and reciprocity of social exchange. And Blackstone unsurprisingly absolutizes the rights of property. What obligations individuals have depends almost, if not quite entirely, upon their place within established property relationships. Stair by contrast makes the treatment and the status of obligations prior to the treatment and the status of property. So obligations are imposed upon and constrain the property owner. Peter Stein has summarized Stair's view: "God granted the dominion of the creatures of the earth to man. This dominion was originally held in common, but the fruits of the creatures and the products of art and industry were proper to individuals. Normally they could be disposed of at will; but there was an implied obligation of commerce and exchange in cases of necessity and even, where there was nothing to receive in exchange, an obligation to give. . . . Thus property, in Stair's eyes, was subject to definite restrictions in the public interest" ('Law and Society in Eighteenth-Century Scottish Thought' in *Scotland in the Age of Improvement,* ed. N. T. Phillipson and R. Mitchison, Edinburgh, 1970, p. 151).

A third contrast between Stair and Blackstone concerns the relationship between theology and law. Both of Blackstone's brothers who survived to adult life became Church of England clergymen, and there is no reason to doubt the importance which Blackstone himself attached to the theological prolegomena to the *Commentaries.* Nonetheless, with the assertion that the foundation of ethics and of law resides in the precept "that man should pursue his own true and substantial happiness," the theology becomes redundant, at most reinforcement, at least decoration, for what is asserted and argued for on entirely nontheological grounds. But in Stair's *Institutions* the theology cannot be excised without irreparable damage to the whole. Scottish seventeenth- and eighteenth-century law, like Scottish seventeenth- and eighteenth-century life, is pervasively and ineliminably theological.

The theology, of course, is that of the presbyterian formulas: the Westminster Confession of Faith, along with the Larger and Shorter Catechisms, which were composed by the assembly of divines which began its work at Westminster in 1643. The General Assembly of the Church of Scotland had adopted these in 1649, and from then on they provided the standard of both doctrine and teaching. Like any theological document they are susceptible of alternative interpretations. And it is perhaps typical of Calvinist theological texts, such as those authored by the Westminster divines, that they should be peculiarly open to rival interpretations in two particular areas. The first of these concerns the relationship of the powers with which God had originally endowed human beings at the Creation, and especially their reason and their free will, to the corrupting effects of sin and the work of grace. In Calvinist versions of Augustine's theology human beings are characterized in two ways. They are on the one hand viewed as having in some sense totally lost both their freedom to respond to God, to His commands, and to the offer of His grace, and any rational ability to discern the true nature of God and His law, so that all good is lost to them except by the operation of divine grace acting upon human beings, independently of their will. But on the other hand they are held to be guilty before God and accountable to Him in a way that presupposes both a knowledge of God's law and responsibility for disobedience to it. And both of these stances are affirmed in the Westminster Confession and in the Catechisms.

Alternative and rival interpretations of this type of theology arise when one of these two stances is emphasized at the expense of the other. When it is the former which is thus emphasized, the Christian revelation, which is itself to be received only by grace, is made to appear the sole possible source either of any knowledge of the divine law or of any detailed specification of how it is to be implemented. Philosophical or other rational enquiry into the foundations and content of the moral law appears in this light as a vain and sinful enterprise. There were not lacking presbyterians in seventeenth-century Scotland who took this view, and they were to have their eighteenth-century heirs. But Stair, of course, was not among them. And he was also to be found among the opposing party on a second key issue of theological interpretation, distinct from but closely related to the first.

If the revealed Word of God, expressed in the Bible, and preached in accordance with the formulations of the church by the ordained ministers of the church, is the sole trustworthy source of enlightenment on right action, then the church has to be supreme over the state, and the magistrates subservient to the courts of the church. Theocracy requires ecclesiocracy. From this standpoint the independence of the secular state and of its law courts is always at best a threat to the Christian religion, and any attempt on the part of the state or its courts to control the church is intolerable. This was the view of those presbyterians who rebelled against Charles II, while Stair was still one of his judges. Stair, and presbyterians like him, although they disapproved of several facets of the royal policy and more especially of the reintroduction of episcopacy into the Church of Scotland, saw nothing inconsistent in their combination of loyalty to the Westminster formularies with service both to the state and its courts and to secular learning in matters of law and morals. For as to the former the section in the Westminster Confession entitled "Of the Civil Magistrate" declares that it is God who has "ordained civil magistrates to be under him over the people, for his own glory and the public good. . . ." And as to the latter, although reason cannot supply us with the kind of knowledge of God which is necessary for salvation, nonetheless not only is it the case that "the light of nature and the work of creation and providence, do so far manifest the goodness, wisdom and power of God as to leave men inexcusable . . ." (*Westminster Confession* I, 1), but "The moral law is the declaration of the will of God to mankind, directing and binding everyone to personal, perfect and perpetual conformity thereunto . . ." (*Larger Catechism,* Answer to Question 93).

The compatibility of Stair's *Institutions* with the *Confessions* and the *Catechisms* is much more than a matter of general principles. Stair on many particular points adduces scripture as confirmation of the moral law. And in his use of scripture on points of moral detail he follows the practice of the *Larger Catechism,* which subsumes under each of the Ten Commandments a numerous set of more particular duties, obligations, and injunctions to virtues, followed by an equally numerous set of prohibitions. It is important to notice that the appeal to scripture is essential to Stair's legal argument and not merely a piece of pious superstructure. Divine revelation in the scriptures not only is the source in which God affords us knowledge of "these sacred mysteries which could only be known by revelation, as having no principle in nature from whence they are deducible; but also, because through sin and evil custom the natural law in man's heart was much defaced, disordered, and erroneously deduced, he hath therefore re-printed the law of nature in a viver character in the Scripture, not only having the moral principles, but many conclusions thence flowing, particularly set forth" (*Institutions* I,1,7). The scripture is therefore necessary to correct error, both confusion as to what first principles are in fact evident and also failures in deduction.

Stair's fundamental philosophical theses both in the *Institutions* and in his book on physics, *Physiologia Nova Experimentalis,* published at Leyden in 1686 while he was in exile in Holland, are stated rather than defended. Stair was more interested in arguing from his first principles than in arguing about them. He writes before Locke's *Essay* and therefore is able to treat our knowledge of first principles as innate without adverting to the objections which Locke advanced against innate ideas. Stair's philosophy had first been learned when he was a student at Glasgow, where he was placed first on the list of arts graduates in 1637, and he later taught logic, moral, and political philosophy and the elements of mathematics as a regent at Glasgow from 1641 to 1647. And it is all too tempting to regard him as a philosophically naive author (see the remark by Duncan Forbes *Hume's Philosophical Politics,* Cambridge, 1975, p. 7). But this would be a mistake which may obscure the extent of Stair's threefold philosophical achievement.

This consists first of all in the comprehensiveness and generality of the deductive structure which he constructed. To have provided such a structure for the laws of Scotland was in itself a considerable achievement; to have done so in such a way that not only the fundamental principles of Calvinist theology, but also what Stair took to be the truths of astronomy and physics could be incorporated into the same structure was a much greater one. Few readers of the *Institutions* have also read the *Physiologia Nova Experimentalis,* and this was doubtless true from the very beginning. For Stair had the misfortune to publish his geocentric astronomical and physical system, in which he attempted to take account of all the major experimental and observational findings of the sixteenth and seventeenth centuries, one year before Newton published his *Principia.* Stair had dedicated his book to the Royal Society, and Bayle, who must have seen it before publication, gave it a short notice in *Nouvelles de la République des Lettres* for December 1685.

It seems to have made no further impact on the learned world, so that it came not to be recognized that it had been Stair's view that one and the same set of first principles could, with more specialized additional premises in each particular area, provide the foundations for all human knowledge. The structure of *Physiologia Nova Experimentalis* mirrors very precisely that of the *Institutions,* and this is scarcely surprising when one reads there Stair's assertion that the study of nature is subordinate to natural theology, to the metaphysical disciplines which supply it with the *"principia per se evidentia"* which it needs for its own first principles, and also to moral philosophy "insofar as that shows to what extent we are bound to assent to the truth of our cognitions from which moral certitude arises" (Section 20, p. 11). So the first and second postulates of natural science derive the trustworthiness of that wherein the senses and reason agree in their findings from the divine perfections, just as in the opening arguments of the *Institutions* Stair had derived the unchangeableness of natural law from the unchangeable character of the divine will. The *Institutions'* first sections are entitled 'Common Principles of Law'; the first of the four 'Explorations' into which the *Physiologia Nova Experimentalis* is divided is entitled 'De Communibus Principiis naturalibus.' So the different branches of study are integrated into a unified deductive hierarchy with a certain elegance as well as a certain generality. And on the keystone of the whole, our natural and revealed knowledge of God's nature, Stair published his *A Vindication of the Divine Perfections* in 1695.

Stair's second philosophical achievement is to have understood at least in germ one of the key problems which confronts any doctrine which appeals to self-evident first principles. To *whom* must these first principles be evident? What Stair appeals to is the consensus of philosophers, and at first sight this may seem a hopeless appeal. For about the divine perfections, for example, which provide the subject matter for key first principles for both the *Institutions* and the *Physiologia Nova Experimentalis,* philosophers have notoriously been in sharp disagreement with each other. Indeed, Stair shows himself aware of the difficulties posed by the doctrines of three such dissenters: Epicurus, Hobbes, and Spinoza.

Stair's thesis (*PNE* Section 25) is that when philosophers hold doctrines incompatible with what he takes to be a true doctrine of the divine perfections, it is either because of a misperception on their part of the incompatibility or else because of pretense. That is, we shall be able to identify in any philosopher who is at odds with what would otherwise be a consensus either some intellectual or some moral failure. Stair never provides us with any good reasons to accept this claim, but even his making it shows that he is aware of what any doctrine of self-evident first principles requires in order to be rationally vindicated. It is a necessary condition for the truth of any such doctrine that of any allegedly self-evident first principle identified by that doctrine it is the case that *either* every intelligent and adequately reflective human being assents to it *or* those intelligent and adequately reflective individuals who withhold their assent can be shown by adequately good reasons to be guilty either of intellectual error or of bad faith. How to satisfy this requirement is the central problem for any doctrine such as Stair's.

Stair's failure to confront this problem except in a grossly inadequate way does not diminish his achievement in showing how the principles which are fundamental to peculiarly Scottish cultural and social modes, especially in the sphere of law but also elsewhere, require for their upholding their vindication in the arena of specifically philosophical debate. That is to say, it is Stair's third achievement to have shown that if the sphere of public belief is to be understood in the way that it is understood in the *Institutions,* then philosophical debate will have to become central to social and cultural life.

That Stair was in his fundamental attitudes not expressing a private or eccentric point of view is made clear, not only by the reception of his book almost from first publication as an authoritative text, both for legal theory and for actual practice in the Scottish courts—two centuries later Lord Benholme was to say, "When on any point of law I find Stair's opinion uncontradicted I look upon that opinion as ascertaining the law of Scotland"—but also by the way in which the same attitudes were repeatedly expressed by others. The most notable recognition of the centrality of philosophical debate and argument to Scottish national life was in the work of a Commission appointed by the Scottish parliament to examine the state of the universities during the same period in which Stair was Lord President.

This Commission's work was part of the general settlement of Scottish affairs in the period following the overthrow of King James VII by William of Orange and his presbyterian allies in Scotland. It was appointed in July 1690, with the primary immediate task of ensuring loyalty to the new regime and of purging from the universities any teacher who could be identified as an opponent of it. Both an oath of political allegiance and subscription to the Westminster Confession were required. But William Carstares, Secretary of State for Scotland to King William, and King William himself favored a policy of moderation and inclusiveness, designed to make the settlement of 1689–90 as widely acceptable as possible. So that not only was a wide range of different Presbyterian views permitted, but Episcopalians, who were permitted by their bishops to take the requisite oath, continued to be tolerated if they did so. The Commission therefore concentrated its attention not so much upon enforced conformity as upon producing a curriculum in philosophy which would educate Scotland's teachers, lawyers, ministers, and gentry into belief in the appropriate principles. They therefore invited the university teachers of philosophy to give them their considered opinion upon the content which a standard set of philosophy courses ought to have and the texts which ought to be employed in such courses. What the teachers replied they reported to the Parliament in 1695 as follows: "They tell the commissioners of parliament that it is altogether dishonorable to the universities, and the famed learning of the nation, that a course of philosophy should be made the standard of authority, which none belonging to the universities have composed. They criticise the existing books and systems of logic and philosophy. The existing courses of philosophy are either not intended and suited for students, or they are in themselves objectionable. The course that the fairest is, 'Philosophia Vetus et Nova', which is done by a popish author, and bears marks of that religion; but therein the logics are barren, the ethics erroneous, and the physics too prolix. Henry Moir's ethics cannot be admitted; they are grossly Armenian, particularly in his opinion 'de libro arbitrio'. The determination and pneumatology of De Vries are too short. Le Clerc is merely sceptical and Socinian. For Cartesius, Rohault, and others of his gang, besides what may be said against their doctrine, they all labor under this inconvenience — that they give not any sufficient account of the other hypotheses, and the old philosophy, which must not be ejected." (Quoted from vol. 37 of *Parliamentary Papers*, 1837, the report on St. Andrews University of the *Report of the Universities Commission*, 1826–30; the other parts of this rich source for the history of the Scottish universities are the *General Report*, vol. 12, 1831, and those on Edinburgh, vol. 35; on Glasgow, vol. 36; and on Aberdeen, vol. 38, 1837.)

An initial attempt by the commissioners to get the teachers of philosophy in all four universities to agree to a common syllabus and a common text so that "in tyme coming the students shall not spend ther time in wryting ther courses of philosophie in ther class, but in place thereof that there be one printed course" broke down as a result of the disputatiousness of the philosophers. The commissioners therefore adopted the device of setting the teachers in each university to write a textbook on one section of the discipline, thus avoiding the need of reaching prior agreement with their colleagues elsewhere. It is noteworthy that the preservation of a fundamentally Aristotelian approach to philosophy was still taken for granted, in spite of the recognition of the existence of a variety of competing views. So in the rules which were agreed by the universities as a preliminary to writing the four textbooks it was laid down, "That in the didactic part on every head the notion and definition of everything to be agitated be clearly laid down, with an example given thereof, which examples in the logic and metaphysics especially will be most fitly taken from the peripatetic philosophy . . ." The textbook on logic and general metaphysics was assigned to St. Andrews, that on general and specific physics to the two colleges in Aberdeen, that on pneumatology to Edinburgh, and that on general and special ethics to Glasgow. The texts were submitted to the commission in 1697, but only that on metaphysics and that on logic appeared in print, both published in London in 1701. And it is clear that the two aims of the commissioners, to raise the standard of teaching in philosophy and to secure uniformity of content in courses, went unrealized. It was left to the Town Council of Edinburgh, the governing body of the University of Edinburgh, to take the first decisive and effective action.

In seventeenth-century Scotland almost all university teaching and all teaching of philosophy was carried out by regents, young men appointed soon after graduating. An undergraduate was taught by the same regent throughout his university career, and the regent characteristically taught the entire arts curriculum. Regents were, therefore, not specialists, seldom outstanding in any one area, and lacked authority in the community at large. They taught a curriculum laid down for them by others. It was, therefore, a transformation of the position of the university teacher both within the university and in the larger community when regents were replaced by professors, who specialized in their enquiries, enjoyed autonomy in devising their own curriculum and developing their discipline, and were invested with a new kind of prestige. By replacing the regents in philosophy with professors the Town Council of Edinburgh in 1708 took a fundamental step in making philosophy even more central to the national life than it had already been.

In both Glasgow and Edinburgh there had of course been some professorships in the seventeenth century. Andrew Melville would have liked to replace regents by professors in the 1580s. In 1620, for example, a professorship of Mathematics was founded at Glasgow, and one of Humanity was endowed at St. Andrews, but the first lapsed and the second had a chequered history for a quarter of the century. It was only with the growing importance of Continental Protestant influence, and by the end of the century more especially of Utrecht and Leyden, that the role of the professor was given its due in Scotland. The great James Gregory was first professor of mathematics at St. Andrews and then at Edinburgh in 1674. The Edinburgh physician Archibald Pitcairne, who was professor at Leyden in 1692–93—John Pringle received his M.D. from Leyden—had with two other teachers of medicine been given the title of professor at Edinburgh in 1685.

The creation of professorships in philosophy at Edinburgh followed hard upon a similar change in the teaching of Greek. One year's Greek was indeed required before proceeding to philosophy, although by as early as 1731 this requirement had in effect lapsed, and undergraduates would move into the logic class immediately on entering the university. In philosophy there were to be three professors, each with responsibility for a single part of the discipline. Pneumatology and moral philosophy were classed together, and the senior regent, William Law of Elvington, became professor of moral philosophy and pneumatology. The other two regents became the professor of logic and the professor of natural philosophy. When Law died in 1729, the chair was claimed in virtue of his seniority by William Scott, who had been Professor of Greek since 1708. The basis for Scott's claim is easily surmised. In 1708 the philosophy regents seem to have had their choice of professorships in order of seniority; Scott's assumption was that when a professor died or retired—professors were appointed "*ad vitam aut culpam*"—the rule of choice of professorship in order of seniority revived. The Town Council at once made it clear that this was not so. They did appoint Scott, but only after examining him privately as to his fitness in the subject—Scott had published as long ago as 1707 an annotated compendium of Grotius—and one member of the Council, Bailie Fenton, thought that even that was inadequate.

It is not surprising that when in 1734 Scott asked for the professorship to be shared with John Pringle, so that Pringle could perform the teaching duties which Scott's ill health prevented him from carrying out, the Town Council took the appointment of Pringle with great seriousness. Rules were laid down to ensure that lectures on both pneumatology and moral philosophy were delivered. In addition, weekly on Mondays Pringle had to lecture on the truth of the Christian religion. After Scott's death Pringle continued to hold the chair.

Glasgow followed Edinburgh's example in 1727, although only after the intrusion of a Committee of Visitation, dominated by representatives of Edinburgh. Once again the regents chose which chair of philosophy to occupy in order of seniority. Gerschom Carmichael, a regent since 1694 and himself educated at Edinburgh, who had not only edited Pufendorf but also published a manual of logic, chose the professorship of moral philosophy. When Carmichael died in 1729, after publishing his *Synopsis Theologiae Naturalis* in that year, his son, a minister later well-known for his sermons, was a candidate for his father's chair, but Francis Hutcheson was appointed. It was still sufficiently unclear, however, whether or not the rule of choice by seniority might not be revived for Hutcheson to be required to show fitness for any of the three philosophy chairs. Hence he had to defend a thesis in logic and a thesis in physics as well as a thesis in moral philosophy. In physics his discourse was entitled *De Gravitatione Corporum versus se mutua;* in logic it was *De Scientia, Fide et Opinione inter se Collatis;* and in moral philosophy it was *An sit una tantum Morum Lex Fundamentalis, vel si sint plures, quaenam sint?* All three discourses were delivered on February 20, 1730.

It is no accident that Hutcheson began his career as a professor of moral philosophy at Glasgow with an enquiry into the conception of a fundamental moral law, an enquiry sustained throughout his teaching and his writing. For the task of a professor of moral philosophy in eighteenth-century Scotland came to be that of providing a defense of just those fundamental moral principles, conceived of as antecedent to both all positive law and all particular forms of social organization, which defined peculiarly Scottish institutions and attitudes. And in providing this kind of defense philosophy and especially moral philosophy assumed a kind of authority in Scottish culture which it has rarely enjoyed in other times and places.

It was therefore necessary in eighteenth-century Scotland for a professor of philosophy to hold a certain kind of view on questions of justice and on questions about the nature of practical reasoning. Justice must be definable in terms of the kind of fundamental principle which I have characterized; fully rational agents must be motivated by such principles in acting and must appeal to them to justify their actions, both prospectively and retrospectively. This association between the occupation of a certain institutionalized position, that of a professor of moral philosophy, and the espousing of a particular kind of standpoint appears first and paradigmatically in the career of Francis Hutcheson. But Hutcheson's importance as a role model emerges also in the work of his successors not only at Glasgow and Edinburgh but also later in the century at Aberdeen and St. Andrews, which were much slower in changing from regents to professors.

To understand what the role of a professor of moral philosophy was is then a necessary preliminary to understanding the Scottish conflicts and debates about justice and practical reasoning. And this requires in turn some account of the way in which the discharge of the duties of a professor of philosophy was related to the changing balance of authority and power between ecclesiastical and secular institutions in eighteenth-century Scotland. (For the history of Edinburgh University Sir Alexander Grant's *The Story of the University of Edinburgh,* 2 vols., London, 1844, has not been displaced, although it needs correction at some points, and James Coutts' *A History of the University of Glasgow,* Glasgow, 1909, is similarly valuable and more reliable; for the developing history of the Scottish eighteenth-century professoriate see Roger L. Emerson 'Scottish universities in the eighteenth century, 1690–1800' *Studies on Voltaire and the Eighteenth Century,* vol. 167, Oxford, 1977, and for a sometimes idiosyncratic, but always brilliant, overview of the intellectual history of the Scottish eighteenth century see G. E. Davie *The Scottish Enlightenment,* London, 1981.)

XIII

Philosophy in the Scottish Social Order

Any society in which practical life is both professedly and to some large degree in fact governed by appeal to some set of fundamental principles must possess institutionalized ways in which those who deviate from, rebel against, or put in question those principles are called to account. In seventeenth-century Scotland that function was discharged for the most part, so far as both belief and action were concerned, by the courts of the established church, especially by local kirk sessions, backed up where necessary by the secular courts.

The local kirk sessions, in which the elders of each parish sat in judgment, were courts of morals as well as of law, exacting fines for fornication and adultery, enforcing the keeping of the Sabbath, and exerting a high degree of general social control. It was they who appointed the parish schoolmaster. And it was a mark of the growing secularization of eighteenth-century Scotland that the power of these ecclesiastical courts gradually declined, while the secular legal system correspondingly functioned decreasingly as a reinforcement of the power and authority of the established church, but rather as an independent institution (see B. Lenman and G. Parker 'Crime and Control in Scotland 1500–1800' *History To-Day,* vol. 30, January 1980).

It was of course essential to the functioning of the church courts that they were able to hold accountable not only those who infringed or were suspected of infringing the standards of conduct laid down in the Confession and the Catechisms but also and especially those who questioned the doctrines from which those standards were derived. Heresy and skepticism were as crucial and more fundamental than adultery and sabbath-breaking. And in tracing the changing patterns of accusations of heresy and of heresy trials the growingly important place of philosophy in Scottish life is illuminated. What emerges is a confrontation between those members and officers of the church who assert that the only remedy for doubt and unbelief is saving faith and that the powers of natural reason fall short of offering adequate grounds for belief in any of the central tenets of the Christian religion and those by contrast who hold that the Christian religion is not merely congruent with authentic, uncorrupted rationality, but that its central tenets are among the conclusions supported by rational enquiry.

It was not, of course, the case that from the outset there were two clearly defined, antagonistic positions held by opposing parties. There was at least through the first half of the eighteenth century a spectrum of positions. But from the late 1740s onward the divisions within the church have become those between two more or less organized, if shifting, factions, the so-called Moderate party and the so-called Evangelicals, names that it is all too easy to use anachronistically in the preceding period, but which, so used, have a certain justification. The process through which this division emerged and hardened was one in which conflict on a number of issues reinforced earlier lines of division. How far was it important that ministers of the church should participate in the cultural achievements of the age, as mathematicians or historians or philosophers? Should the statutes against witchcraft have been repealed? Was the theater a place for Christians or a work of the devil? And most important of all: Was the continuing existence of a right of patronage which allowed the government and a handful of great landowning nobles to appoint the minister in many parishes tolerable, and, if not, with what was it to be replaced?

The indirect relationship of divisions over this last question to disagreements about the status of philosophy is important. Those ministers who were later to become the Evangelical party, who looked back not only to the Westminster Confession and the Catechisms but to the Solemn League and Covenant of 1643 and to those who in the reigns of Charles II and James II had suffered martyrdom for their continuing allegiance to the Covenant, wished to rest the right to name ministers in each parish congregation. Such congregations were composed for the most part of those who, being unpropertied, were among the less educated and who tended to be responsive to Evangelical preaching.

The ministers who were to become the Moderate party were by both interest and standpoint bound to resist this. They could agree with the Evangelicals in condemning the status quo of patronage, as established in 1711. But if they were to retain or advance their position not only as preachers but as teachers of as yet often unenlightened congregations, then the right of patronage must be vested in members of the educated classes, in those gentry, lawyers, and professors whom Francis Hutcheson invited to agreement on this issue in 1735 in his *Considerations on Patronages Addressed to the Gentlemen of Scotland*.

In so writing Hutcheson was defending the interests of philosophy both within the church and within Scottish culture at large. For what the right of patronage in the end determined was the membership of those courts of the church—the local parish kirk session, the presbytery, the synod, and finally the General Assembly—through which discipline was imposed upon dissenters, deviants, and heretics and by which it was decided who was a dissenter, a deviant, and a heretic. The outcome of heresy trials and the issue of patronage were thus directly related, and it was in a crucial way in heresy trials that the claims made on behalf of philosophy and especially moral philosophy become apparent.

It is important of course to recognize upon how much the controversialists within the late seventeenth- and eighteenth-century Church of Scotland agreed. About the fundamental Christian doctrines embodied in the Confession and the Catechisms there was no dispute within the ranks of ministers and elders. When in 1696 a divinity student at Edinburgh, Thomas Aikenhead, was accused of a number of heresies, including denials both of the authority of the scriptures and of the divinity of Christ, he was put to trial and in January 1697 publicly hanged by the civil authority (*State Trials,* vol. xiii); and this last execution for heresy in Scotland was defended in subsequent debate by clergy of all views. What was divisively at issue was the degree to which and the way in which the doctrines of the Christian religion either could be or needed to be presented as supported by the conclusions of philosophical enquiry. And in asserting the impotence of natural reason in general and of philosophy in particular the proto-Evangelicals forged a tacit alliance between their theology and philosophical skepticism in metaphysical and moral matters. The first definitive Evangelical statement framed in terms of that alliance was made by Thomas Halyburton, who became professor of divinity at St. Andrews in 1710.

Halyburton's father had been deposed from his parish ministry for refusing to acknowledge the royal supremacy in 1662, and he had been denounced to the Privy Council for his part in illegal conventicles in 1682. Thomas Halyburton had been educated in exile in Holland as a boy, and he represented by family connection and upbringing, as well as by conviction, that covenanting strain in the Church of Scotland which, if it had been successful in asserting its claim to represent the orthodoxy of the Confession and the Catechisms, would have prevented the rise of the Moderate party. But Halyburton's convictions were very much his own, appropriated in his response to crises of doubt which afflicted him as late as 1696, the year in which he graduated from St. Andrews. What Halyburton took himself to have discovered in these crises was twofold: before the onslaught of skeptical doubt only a scriptural faith in the revelation of Christ's saving work was effective, and appeal to rational argument was not only ineffective but a delusive snare.

One of Halyburton's specific targets was Aikenhead. Another was Archibald Pitcairne, the physician and teacher of medicine, whose deism Halyburton attacked in his inaugural lecture "A Modest Enquiry whether Regeneration or Justification has the Precedency in the Order of Nature." Pitcairne was a Jacobite and an enemy of Calvinism of any kind. He never attended public worship, and, worst of all, he assailed his opponents with jokes as much as with arguments. He was reputed to be the author of an anonymously published Latin pamphlet, the *Epistola Archimedis,* which appeared in 1688, and it was this that Halyburton attacked. But Halyburton treated those of his contemporaries whom he assailed as mere local exemplifications of universal forms of sin and error. It was the recurring unwarranted pretension of philosophical reasoning which now exhibited itself in a variety of local forms. Thus in his major work *Natural Religion Insufficient and Revealed necessary to Man's Happiness* (Edinburgh, 1714) Locke, Hobbes, and Spinoza are cited, but even more importantly Greek philosophy is impugned as exhibiting the arrogance of natural reason in the absence of the Christian revelation. The admiration of Socrates is condemned, and in so condemning it, Halyburton sounds a note which is reiterated in later controversy. When much later the Evangelical John Witherspoon sought to counteract what he took to be the baneful influence of Hutcheson in his satirical pamphlet of 1753 *Ecclesiastical Characteristics* — a pamphlet which unites the mocking style of Pitcairne with the substance of Halyburton — it was not only Hutcheson's admiration for Shaftesbury but also his praise of Socrates, Plato, Aristotle, and Marcus Aurelius which were held up to scorn.

It is worth remarking the difference in attitude between Halyburton and Robert Baillie. Halyburton's theology was intended to represent the same allegiance to the theocratic theology not only of the Westminster Confession and the Catechisms but also of the Solemn League and Covenant as Baillie's. But whereas the strict Calvinist orthodoxy of a Baillie, as of a Voet, issued in a conviction that erroneous philosophical argument had to be confronted by sound philosophical argument, as well as by preaching, the same strict Calvinist orthodoxy in Halyburton's version leads not only to an attack upon philosophy as such, but more especially upon just that type of ancient philosophy to which Baillie had appealed. The view of themselves taken by Halyburton and by his later theological heirs as the authentic defenders of that for which the

Church of Scotland had stood in the midseventeenth century involved, therefore, a misconception of what orthodoxy had been and a new way of attempting to draw the line between orthodoxy and heresy.

It is unsurprising, then, that we discover in the first part of the eighteenth century a sequence of heresy trials in which, although sometimes the orthodoxy of the accused in respect of some central Christian doctrine, such as that of the Trinity or of the intercessory work of Christ, is in question, the central issues are the relationship of rational enquiry in general, and more particularly of the enquiries of the moral philosopher to the Christian revelation within theological study. These are the trials for heresy of John Simson, professor of Divinity at Glasgow, in 1717 and in 1727; of Archibald Campbell, professor of Church History at St. Andrews and Simson's pupil, in 1735–36; of Francis Hutcheson, also Simson's pupil, in 1738; and of William Leechman, professor of Divinity at Glasgow, close friend of Hutcheson and pupil of William Law, the first holder of the chair of moral philosophy at Edinburgh, in 1744. The first three of these trials were before specially constituted Commissions of the General Assembly, while the last two never proceeded beyond presbytery or synod level.

At issue in both of Simson's trials was his contention that it was from a prospect of future happiness that human beings were brought to obey God, but even more fundamental was his avowed guiding maxim in theology that reason is its principle and foundation. When Simson was acquitted at his first trial, the commissioners enjoined him to take care to distinguish what could be known by reason from what could only be apprehended by faith. At his second trial Simson was convicted, but the measure of sympathy for his views is the fact that although suspended from teaching thereafter, he was allowed to continue to occupy his chair and to draw its salary until his death in 1740.

Archibald Campbell's reply to the General Assembly's Commission which handled his case is instructive. Campbell had no hesitation in allowing that revelation is necessary for any sufficient knowledge of God's nature and will. But human beings have to judge the claims of revelation "by the nature of things, or from the common maxims or principles of common sense that are self-evident notions or propositions which need no proof . . ." Here we find the same appeal which Stair made to the evidentness of first principles, although the author whom Campbell cited was the English deist Matthew Tindal (see James K. Cameron 'Theological Controversy: A Factor in the Origins of the Scottish Enlightenment' in *The Origin and Nature of the Scottish Enlightenment*, ed. R.H. Campbell and A.S. Skinner, Edinburgh, 1982).

Among the utterances on the basis of which Campbell was accused was his reiteration of Simson's view that it is the prospect of future happiness which is the ground for Christian obedience, a view which Campbell advanced on the basis of a theory of self-love as the sole motive for virtue; and when Hutcheson was later accused of heresy, it was for "teaching to his students in contravention to the Westminster Confession the following two false and dangerous doctrines, first that the standard of moral goodness was the promotion of the happiness of others; and second that we could have a knowledge of good and evil, without, and prior to a knowledge of God" (quoted by W.R. Scott *Francis Hutcheson,* Cambridge, 1900). The attack on Leechman, which was part of an attempt to prevent him from taking up his chair, seems to have been motivated by fear of an increase in Hutcheson's influence, which Hutcheson's critics quite correctly thought would be a consequence of Leechman's appointment.

All three—Campbell, Hutcheson, and Leechman—were acquitted, and their acquittal coincided in time with the separation from the church of the so-called Seceders, most notably the Evangelical ministers Alexander Moncrieff, a trenchant critic of Archibald Campbell's theory of self-love, and the brothers Ebenezer and Ralph Erskine, who claimed that the Church of Scotland had defected in a variety of crucial ways from its Confession of Faith. One ground for that claim was the failure of the Church, as they perceived it, to deal adequately with heresy. And in an important way the Seceders were right. I do not mean by saying this to take sides on the issues raised in these particular heresy trials. I want to point rather to the way in which the growing ascendancy of philosophy marked a radical transformation in the way in which fundamental principles were upheld and appealed to in the culture of Scottish presbyterianism. What emerged was a period in which it was by the standards of philosophical debate and enquiry that claims concerning first principles were evaluated, justified, and impugned. To some significant degree the judgments which were vindicated in the arenas of philosophical controversy usurped the place of the judgments delivered by the courts of the church if only because those clergy and laymen who were to become the Moderate party acted and voted in those courts in accordance with what they took to be the conclusions of philosophical reasoning. "I dread mightily that a rational sort of religion is coming in among us," Thomas Halyburton had prophesied. But by 1729 Robert Wallace, the minister of Moffat, could preach to the Synod of Dumfries a sermon which could not but have been interpreted by his hearers as a rejoinder to the outcome of Simson's second trial, in which he told those hearers to examine in the light of reason every claim to revelation, old or new. Reason is indeed insufficient in religious matters; revelation is provided by God to remedy that insufficiency. But it is for us to scrutinize, criticize, and interpret all claims to revelation by rational enquiry. So Wallace endorsed Campbell's defense of rational enquiry (Cameron, op. cit., p. 123). And it was philosophy which was and was to be the principal instrument of such rational enquiry.

How did philosophy come to have this kind of cultural hegemony and what were the characteristics of the role of the professors of moral philosophy, in virtue of which they played such a key part in their society? It is important first to notice how philosophical discussion extended beyond university classes. Professors on occasion gave private classes for those not attending the university. Hutcheson's were attended by "tradesmen and youths from the town" (Scott, op. cit., p. 63). More importantly a gift for philosophical debate was nurtured by the way in which in the university teaching of philosophy the professor's lectures were supplemented by periods of discussion, by the oral interrogation of students by the professor, and even on occasion by debate. Opportunity to exercise the capacities thus developed for those who had completed their undergraduate studies were provided by the societies wholly or partly devoted to philosophical discussion which came to exist in the major university cities.

The most important of these, the Rankenian club at Edinburgh, which was founded by students in law and divinity about 1718, became a forum in which the central theses of Locke and Berkeley were introduced into the Scottish debate, in a way parallel to that in which Tindal's deistic writings were a little later to be introduced into the theological controversies. At Glasgow a student society similar to the Rankenian was founded at about the same time. And although the Literary Society of Glasgow College was only founded in 1752 after Hutcheson's death, it had its predecessors in his lifetime (Smout, *A History of the Scottish People*, p. 390). Most seminal of all was to be the way in which, when philosophical discussion started to flourish in the colleges of Aberdeen later in the century, the Philosophical Society there, which was founded in 1758, brought together George Campbell, Thomas Reid, John Gregory, and others in what turned out to be a systematic refounding and reformulation of the Scottish philosophical tradition.

The activities of the members of these societies were both cause and consequence of a widened readership for philosophical writing, not only on what would now be taken to be philosophical subjects, but also in those areas of natural theology, of the sciences, of law, and of social enquiry which were still treated as parts of philosophy. Hutcheson aided his former pupil, Robert Foulis, to become first a bookseller and in 1741 a publisher in Glasgow. The effect was to create that very rare phenomenon, an educated public, in this case a philosophically educated public, with shared standards of rational justification and a shared deference to a teaching authority, that of the professors of philosophy and especially of moral philosophy. To be called to account for one's beliefs and judgments, in respect either of their justification by deduction from first principles or of the evidentness of those first principles themselves, was a matter from about 1730 onward of being called upon to defend oneself in the forums of philosophically educated opinion rather than in the courts of the church.

The role of the professor of moral philosophy was therefore a crucial one. He was the official defender of the rational foundations of Christian theology, of morals, and of law. And he was also and necessarily the defender, together with his academic colleagues, both in philosophy and elsewhere, of a particular view of what rational justification and rational methods of enquiry consist in and of the conclusions which they provide. William Wishart, principal of Edinburgh University and, like Leechman, a pupil of William Law—when at Glasgow he had helped to appoint Hutcheson—asserted that because the holder of the moral philosophy chair was required to teach "the principles of Natural Religion and Morality and the Truth of the Christian Religion" he "could not but look upon this as a Professorship of Divinity" (see M.A.C. Stewart 'Hume, Wishart and the Edinburgh Chair' *Journal of the History of Philosophy,* forthcoming). And of the candidates whom Hutcheson suggested for the Edinburgh chair of moral philosophy in 1744, when he had become aware that there was a prospect of it falling vacant by the resignation of Law's successor, John Pringle, one, Robert Pollock, became a professor of divinity shortly afterward. It is clear that professors of moral philosophy were and were expected to be as committed to a particular standpoint as were their colleagues in divinity.

They were, however, in their view of rational justification and methods also able to draw upon resources deriving from large agreements between the philosophers and the exponents of other secular disciplines. With them—the professors of law, of mathematics, and of physics—they shared their inherited conception of rational justification as consisting in the deductive derivation of subordinate conclusions from evident first principles, a conception embodied in paradigmatic form in Euclidean geometry. The teachers of geometry and of mathematics in general were expected to present their subject matter in a way which made its general relevance clear. When in the nineteenth century Sir William Hamilton looked back in order to characterize the past holders of the Edinburgh chair of mathematics, he described it as one "which has hitherto always owed the celebrity it has enjoyed not certainly more to the mathematical skill than to the philosophical ability and varied learning of its Professors" (quoted in G.E. Davie *The Democratic Intellect,* Edinburgh, 1961, p. 120). And Glasgow was no different from Edinburgh.

Robert Simson, who became professor there in 1711, edited both Pappus and Euclid and defended the superiority of ancient geometry against the Cartesians. At Edinburgh Colin Maclaurin, son of a parish minister in Glendaruel, who had graduated from Glasgow University when he was fifteen years old, had won the mathematics chair at Marischal College, Aberdeen, at the age of nineteen and had been appointed at Edinburgh in 1725 on Newton's recommendation, made geometry the foundation of mathematical teaching. The introductory mathematical class proceeded through Books I–VI of Euclid. It was Maclaurin who in 1742 refuted Berkeley in his *Treatise of Fluccions* by giving Newton's mathematics a geometrical basis and thus provided a classical example of what counted as a rational justification for a particular set of beliefs in eighteenth-century Scotland.

One of Maclaurin's central concerns in the summary of his book, which he presented in two communications to the *Philosophical Transactions* of the Royal Society, was to emphasize that a return to the standards of rigor of the ancient geometricians was necessary in order to avoid philosophical as well as mathematical confusions. "Unbounded Liberties have been introduced of late, by which Geometry (wherein everything ought to be clear) is filled with Mysteries, and Philosophy is likewise perplexed. . . . Geometry has always been considered as our surest Bulwark against the Subtleties of the Sceptics, who are ready to make any use of any Advantages that may be given them against it [here Maclaurin has a footnote referring his readers to the article on Zeno in Bayle's *Dictionary*]; and it is important, not only that the Conclusions in Geometry be true, but likewise that their Evidence [that is, evidentness] be unexceptionable . . ." (*Philosophical Transactions,* no. 468, vol. 42, January 20–February 3, 1742–43, p. 327).

That adequate rational justification is always deductive in form does not entail of course that rational enquiry is similarly deductive, and neither Maclaurin nor his academic colleagues, earlier or later, held that it was. The contingent historical particularities of divine revelation invoked by the divines, the physical experiments catalogued by

Stair, and the solutions of particular mathematical problems advanced by Maclaurin provide us with a knowledge of truths which we then confirm by discovering their place within the overall hierarchy of deductive explanation. In Maclaurin's view (*An Account of Sir Isaac Newton's Philosophical Discoveries,* London, 1748) a central aspect of Newton's achievement was that he had eschewed the methodologically deductive ambitions of Descartes, Leibniz, and Spinoza. It is crucial "that we should begin with the phenomena, or effects, and from them investigate the powers or causes that operate in nature. . . . Being once possest of these causes, we should then descend in a contrary order; and from them, as established principles, explain all the phaenomena that are their consequences, and prove our explications . . ." (pp. 8–9).

It is this method which defines the relationship of physics to theology. "We are to endeavour to rise, from the effects thro' the intermediate causes, to the supreme cause. We are, from his works, to seek to know God, and not to pretend to mark out the scheme of his conduct, in nature, from the very deficient ideas we are able to form of that great mysterious Being. Thus natural philosophy may become a sure basis to natural religion, but it is very preposterous to deduce natural philosophy from any hypothesis, 'tho invented to make us imagine ourselves possest of a more complete system of metaphysics, or contrived perhaps with a view to obviate more easily some difficulties in natural theology" (p. 90).

Moral philosophy was thus a form of enquiry and a set of conclusions closely related to other forms of enquiry and to their conclusions. The established scheme of human knowledge in the Scottish seventeenth and eighteenth centuries was—and to some limited degree this persisted into the nineteenth century—a unitary and more or less integrated scheme, the articulated disciplinary parts of which involved continuous reference to each other. And both the unity and the differentiation of that scheme were replicated in the curriculum. The professors who taught that curriculum, therefore, had to be widely knowledgeable outside their own special discipline, and none more so than the professors of moral philosophy whose teaching and enquiries provided the curriculum to a significant extent with its central focus. I have already noticed how the professor of moral philosophy was a secularized professor of divinity, but he had also to be knowledgeable elsewhere. Thomas Craigie, whose name was also on the list of candidates originally suggested by Hutcheson to succeed Pringle as professor of moral philosophy at Edinburgh, was at that time professor of Hebrew at St. Andrews, and later before he finally succeeded Hutcheson at Glasgow, he was a candidate for the Edinburgh chair of mathematics (Stewart, op. cit.). Nor was Craigie in any way unique as a polymath. Both Hutcheson and Reid, for example, were deeply interested in contemporary mathematics.

The institutionalized role of the professor of moral philosophy, therefore, made him one of the most important bearers of a distinctively Scottish intellectual and cultural tradition, which defined itself in terms of just those comprehensive conceptions of rational justification and explanation which I have described. It was a tradition which drew upon certain medieval precedents and doctrines, transmitted through the scholastic commentators on Aristotle both inside and outside Scotland. But it was only fully articulated in the seventeenth century. From then on it developed through confronting a series of challenges posed by both internal and external conflict. Like all traditions, it vindicated itself from the standpoint of its adherents insofar as it was able *both* to recognize and to give due weight to objections and difficulties posed for it either by encounters with rival points of view or by conflicts over its own interpretation by its own adherents *and* to discover within itself the resources for evaluating such objections and difficulties and responding to them, when cogent, by revisions or extensions of its own doctrines.

From a standpoint external to such a tradition it is all too easy to isolate each of its particular theses and require a justification of each in isolation from the others. So it has often been, for example, in respect of the contention that there are evident first conceptions and principles, whether as advanced within the Scottish seventeenth- and eighteenth-century tradition from an Aristotelian standpoint or otherwise. There are in fact no nontrivial statements which have appeared evidently true to *all* human beings of moderate intelligence. Even the law of noncontradiction as formulated by Aristotle has encountered thinkers both sufficiently ingenious and sufficiently wrongheaded to deny it. This fact alone has seemed to many thinkers to provide sufficient grounds for denying Scottish or Aristotelian or indeed any claims that there are evident first conceptions and principles. To this denial the adherents of different traditions and standpoints have replied in somewhat different ways. I have already noticed, for example, how from the seventeenth century onward Scottish versions of this claim are supported by a further claim to be able to produce cogent explanations — cogent, that is, from the standpoint of the tradition — of why particular persons or classes of persons fail to find evident what is in fact evident. Evidentness, that is, is held to be not equally apparent to all perceivers.

It is important at this point that there is available a more general form of defense of the appeal to evident first conceptions and principles than those actually invoked. That defense involves three contentions. The first is that it is only in the context of a coherent tradition, which supplies a shared conceptual framework, a shared conception of what constitutes a central problem, and a shared view of how data are to be identified that competing theories which are organized as deductive structures dependent upon first principles can be evaluated. Without these prerequisites there can be no procedure by which one such theory can be justified or fail to be justified over against its rivals. The second contention is that it is indeed only relative to some competing theory or set of competing theories that any particular theory can be held to be justified or unjustified. There is no such thing as justification as such, just as there is no such thing as justification independent of the context of any tradition. And third, the first principles of such a theory are not justified or unjustified independently of the theory as a whole. It is the success or failure of the theory as a whole in meeting objections posed either from its own or rival points of view which vindicates or fails to vindicate the first principles to which that theory appeals. And the evidentness of those principles is always relative to the conceptual scheme which that particular theory embodies and by its success or failure vindicates or fails to vindicate. It is in this way that large-scale theories in the physical sciences are justified, and there is no other way to justify them. So it was in fact with the metaphysical and theological theories of the Scottish seventeenth and eighteenth centuries.

This was not of course how the defenders of those theories understood themselves and their own intellectual work. That they did not perceive the particularity, the historicity, or even the reality of their own intellectual tradition is unsurprising for two quite different types of reason. First, the kind of historical understanding which would have enabled them to do so did not yet exist and would not exist until the German philosophers of history of the nineteenth century had at last enabled us to come to terms with Vico. And second, it was as central to the thinkers of the Scottish tradition as it had been to those of an earlier Aristotelianism and to Aristotle himself to assert from their particular standpoint the uniformity and universality of human nature. Walter Bagehot was to joke about Adam Smith that in his lectures at Glasgow, as well as in *The Wealth of Nations,* he had undertaken "the immense design . . . of saying how, from being a savage, man rose to be a Scotchman" (*Collected Works,* vol. 3, ed. N. St. John-Stevas, Cam-

bridge, Mass., 1968, p. 91). But this was *mutatis mutandis* the enterprise of almost every Scottish thinker of the seventeenth and eighteenth
century: it is, on this general view of things, the distinctive peculiarity
of Scottish modes of thought and culture that in their particularity universality is manifest. All human beings share the same human nature
not only in respect of reasoning powers and passions but also in respect of at least the bases of moral judgment. Scottish thinkers of otherwise widely different views share this belief, unsurprisingly in view of
the Christian doctrine of human nature which they inherit. Consequently
such thinkers also, as I suggested earlier, share the problem of how to
account for the obvious diversities of culture and the plain disagreements concerning morality of which in the late seventeenth- and early
eighteenth-century Europeans were becoming increasingly aware. And
one way of evaluating rival standpoints within the Scottish debates
will be to ask what resources they are able to employ in the attempt
to advance anything like a cogent solution to this problem.

The salient characteristics of the developing Scottish intellectual tradition should by now be plain. They were fourfold, and each of them
defined both an area of socially shared agreement and a set of issues
for actual or potential controversy. It was first of all an essentially theological tradition with the Calvinist version of Augustinian theology providing it with its classical texts. A certain knowledge of the nature and
will of God was held to be the keystone of all enquiry, no matter how
secular. Initially the problems were those posed by deism rather than
by atheism. How far was it possible to move toward agreement with
the deists on the character of a rationally founded religion without putting in question the required kind of knowledge of God? Later more
radical forms of unbelief had to be confronted. The Moderate theologians had to identify themselves as contending against two opposing
positions, which George Campbell, who became principal of Marischal
College in 1754, characterized when he warned his niece, "The two
extremes to be guarded against are libertinism and bigotry" (quoted
by J. McCosh *The Scottish Philosophy,* London, 1875, p. 244). The
libertine disregarded the legitimate claims of religion. And the intellectually dangerous libertine was the one who underpinned his disregard
for obedience to God in everyday life by the construction of skeptical
philosophical arguments. Bigotry by contrast was marked by sectarian
attachments, by enthusiasm, a too great reliance upon feeling rather
than reason, and by fanaticism.

The prototypical bigots, in the eyes of the Moderate clergy and their
predecessors, were the Seceding ministers and laity who were finally

expelled from the Church of Scotland in 1740, but who had for a number of years made it plain that they regarded the leading clergy of that church as having apostasized. Ebenezer Erskine, perhaps the greatest Seceder preacher, attacked what he called "empty harangues of morality" and reliance upon obedience to the moral law. "The strong bias and current of nature must be altered, and reason (which sits king in the soul) deposed from its sovereignty and lie down as a servant at the feet of sovereign grace . . ." ('The law of faith issuing forth from Mount Zion' in *The Whole Works of Mr. Ebenezer Erskine,* Edinburgh, 1785, vol. I, p. 531). Another Seceder had contended that "as little of Christ was to be found in most of the discourses of many Ministers and preachers, as in the moral writings of heathen philosophers . . ." (Adam Gib *The Present Truth,* Edinburgh, 1774, vol. I, pp. 44–45, quoted and discussed in B.J. Bullert *Ethical Individualism and Religious Divisions in Enlightenment Scotland,* Oxford University M. Litt. dissertation, 1980).

Against this extreme distrust of reason and of the moral law the adherents of the central Scottish intellectual tradition were committed to providing both arguments in defense of the central tenets of their metaphysics, theology, and ethics and arguments in favor of arguments. This latter commitment was a matter of interpreting the requirements of their theology; the former involved them in confronting all those counterarguments which entailed conclusions either actually or apparently incompatible with their stance, so that they had to review the whole range of philosophical positions which required apologetic rebuttal. What these were was determined by the nature of a second area in which intellectual agreement among the adherents of the tradition also required intellectual conflict.

The type of hierarchical deductive scheme and the view of how it was to be constructed and understood which were central to this tradition put its adherents at odds both with what they held to be the overambitious rationalist metaphysical constructions of Descartes, Leibniz, and Spinoza and with the empiricism of Locke. Indeed it was in part the need to find adequate grounds for rejecting rationalist metaphysics which led to some measure of agreement with Locke (Cleghorn at his graduation in 1739 defended a dissertation in which he denied the innateness of any idea, but asserted the existence of an innate aptitude for forming ideas), but Locke's nominalism was in crucial respects incompatible with the claim to a knowledge of universal principles so central to this Scottish tradition. So we do find Hutcheson including Locke among the modern authors whom he recommended to the attention of students, but we also find him recommending Plato, Aristotle, and Cicero.

What Locke did force upon the Scottish academics was a consciousness of a need to supplement their metaphysics and philosophy of science by an epistemology. It was Hutcheson's project to supply that epistemology insofar as it was necessary for carrying through the tasks of the philosophy of morals and politics. The nature of those tasks derived from a third salient characteristic of the Scottish intellectual tradition, its conception of justice as not to be founded upon, and binding independently of, either the passions or the interests. So Hobbes, Mandeville, and the other exponents of versions of the view that human beings are motivated wholly by self-love had to be rejected. But so also did the views of such theologians as Archibald Campbell, who had argued that self-love and the prospect of eternal happiness were the true motivations of Christian obedience. Hutcheson therefore could only defend the morality to which he is committed by defending some account of justice which makes both our knowledge of what is just and our reasons for doing what is just independent of whatever is supplied by our passions and our interests.

In so doing he could not escape confronting the issues raised by the fourth salient characteristic of the Scottish tradition, its belief that reason ought to be the master of the passions and that reason itself was capable of motivating human beings to obedience to general principles. The individual who was called to account for failure to master his or her passions was presumed to have had the power to summon up good reasons for mastering them, and the prospect of discipline by the courts of the church as well as by the civil courts was intended to enhance and reinforce those good reasons. Thus in the legal as well as in the moral realm the individual was held to be accountable for not abiding by sound principles, even when those principles were at odds with that individual's passions and interests.

Anyone, therefore, who was committed to sustaining the moral standpoint of this Scottish presbyterian tradition, as Hutcheson was, was also committed thereby to formulating and justifying a particular type of view of justice and a related congruent view of what practical reasoning consists in. It was Hutcheson's task to attempt to achieve this not only for a philosophical audience whose reading included Descartes and Malebranche, and Locke and Berkeley, but also for a theological audience whose standards of belief were still defined by the Westminster Confession and the catechisms. In so doing he could not escape defining his position in terms of two controversies whose significance has already emerged and a third whose importance grew as the eighteenth century progressed.

Of the first of these, the theological debate internal to Scottish presbyterianism, all that remains to be stressed is its inseparability from philosophical enquiry. The implications of each and every thesis in philosophy for theological assertions and denials were central and not marginal aspects of those theses, not so much because of the particular religious beliefs of individual philosophers and of members of their audience, as because on the one hand of the presupposed unity of enquiry and the crucial place of beliefs about God in the structure of claims to knowledge and on the other hand of the specific doctrines of Scottish Calvinist theology. An example of the bearing of the latter on philosophy is the way in which the Westminster Confession affirms both predestination and the freedom of the human will, affirmations to which almost any philosophical theory of the causality exerted by and upon human agency are bound to be relevant.

A second debate was that which concerned the preservation of the distinctiveness of Scottish institutions and culture. Almost noone of Hutcheson's generation had any inclination to campaign for repeal of the Act of Union, and understandably so. For one thing the defense of the established United Kingdom government had come to coincide with the defense of the Protestant Succession and what the Church of Scotland took to be its rights. Hutcheson was as hostile to Jacobitism as Cleghorn. Moreover, in the debates over the issue of Scottish independence the single fully articulate and principled defender of that independence, Andrew Fletcher of Saltoun, had linked the issue of political independence to a social and intellectual program which had been decisively rejected.

"Andrew Fletcher of Salton," wrote George Lockhart of Carnwath (*Memoirs Concerning the Affairs of Scotland from Queen Anne's Accession to the Commencement of the Union of the Two Kingdoms of Scotland and England in May, 1707,* London, 1714, p. 68), "in the first part of his Life, did improve himself to a great Degree by Reading and Travelling; He was always a great Admirer of both Ancient and Modern Republicks . . ." The principles derived from that admiration led him to fall out successively with the governments of Charles II, James VII, and William III. Even when he shared what were widely held positions, as in his opposition to standing armies as potential instruments of royal despotism, his distinctive principles emerged in the alternatives which he advocated. So instead of a standing army Fletcher argued in *A Discourse of Government with relation to Militias* (published in two versions, one in London addressed to the English in 1697, one in Edinburgh addressed to the Scots in 1698) that universal military service for young men should be provided through training in a type of camp which would be "as great a school of virtue as of military discipline" (*Selected Political Writings and Speeches,* ed. D. Daiches, Edinburgh, 1979, p. 24). It would make use of "a severe discipline, and a right method of disposing the minds of men, as well as forming their bodies, for military and virtuous actions . . ." And in so doing it would emulate the ancient republics.

Fletcher's opposition to the Act of Union united an appeal to principle with an appeal to experience. Since the union of the crowns under James VI and I, Scotland, so Fletcher contended in the Scottish parliament, had been ruled only by those subservient to England, with the result "that we have from that time appeared to the rest of the world more like a conquered province than a free independent people" (op. cit., p. 70). Fletcher was therefore not arguing for a continuation of the political status quo. What then did he advocate? In Fletcher's view—and it clearly derives from his reading both of Plato and Aristotle and of the history of Rome's expansion—no large-scale state or government can escape corruption. "Cities of a moderate extent are easily governed, and the example and authority of one virtuous man is often sufficient to keep up good order and discipline, of which we have divers instances in the history of the Grecian republics; whereas great multitudes of men are always deaf to all remonstrances, and the frequency of ill example is more powerful than laws" (op. cit., p. 134). From which Fletcher concluded that both England and Scotland should be dissolved as nations and replaced by twelve city states, each self-governing, but joined in a federation for purposes of mutual defense.

The place of ancient authors in Fletcher's ideal curriculum corresponds to that of ancient republics in his political theory (see G.E. Davie, op. cit., p. 8, for an account of Fletcher's *Proposals for Schools and Colleges,* Edinburgh, 1704). Modern science was to be studied, but not the contending voices of contemporary philosophy. Ancient philosophy would be taught in the context of ancient literary studies and to a relatively small student body, for Fletcher disapproved of the democratizing effect of the bursaries by means of which the presbyterians had opened the universities to a wider range of students.

Fletcher's political proposals were so obviously Utopian and offensive to all would-be practical people that we, like his contemporaries, may miss the thesis of real substance which those proposals masked. Almost alone among his contemporaries Fletcher understood the dilemma confronting Scotland as involving more radical exclusive alternatives than they were prepared to entertain. For on his view at the level of political action either Scotland moved into the world of the modern large-scale state and large-scale economy and ceased thereby to be Scotland or it had to recreate itself within a form of government more local and more morally homogeneous than even the midseventeenth-century Calvinist Aristotelians had envisaged. And at the level of philosophy either the contending voices of the moderns could be studied, thereby producing institutionalized lack of agreement, or there could be a return to an education which relied upon Aristotle's *Ethics* and *Politics*. But neither at the level of political action nor at that of philosophy was there any third set of possibilities.

By contrast it was the presupposition of those who were the continuing bearers of a distinctively Scottish cultural tradition that there was a third way which was that neither of Fletcher nor of the Anglicizers. The sustaining of the role of the professor of moral philosophy became central to their enterprise just because the peculiar and distinctive principles of Scottish law, Scottish education, and Scottish theology depended for their survival on the elaboration of philosophical theories and theses which could underpin those principles and provide for their defense in public debate within Scotland as effectively as the Calvinist Aristotelianism of Baillie had done, but which had also come to terms with the philosophical debates of late seventeenth-century and early eighteenth-century modernity. And it was Hutcheson who made the importance of that role socially and culturally visible outside Scotland as well as within it, in a way that such predecessors as Law and Carmichael had not themselves done, although they had played an essential part in carrying the tradition forward to the point at which Hutcheson became its central figure.

Hutcheson's work then has to be understood in terms of its place both in a continuing set of theological controversies and in a cultural debate in which the philosophical presupposition of distinctively Scottish institutions were at stake. As the eighteenth century continued, a third closely related set of issues became more central. For Scotland this was an age both of agricultural improvement and of commercial expansion. The values of the market and of growing wealth were to prevail increasingly, and those of kinship and of local community were to be correspondingly eroded. The distinctive values of the Scottish educational system were to be challenged in the name of commercial utility. So from 1762 onward William Thom, the minister of Govan, published a series of pamphlets whose subject matter was specified in the title of the first as "The Defects of an University Education and its Unsuitableness to a Commercial People." Logic and metaphysics waste the students time; moral philosophy as taught should give way to the teaching of "practical morality." And Thom spoke for a growing class, especially in Glasgow (see Donald J. Withrington 'Education and Society in the Eighteenth Century' in *Scotland in the Age of Improvement,* ed. N.T. Phillipson and R. Mitchison, Edinburgh, 1970). The question thus became inescapable: What is the effect of an expanding economy upon the moral and intellectual life? The relationship of this question to the question of whether in entering upon enlarged relationships of trade and commerce Scotland could avoid a rupture with its inherited culture is clear and was clear in the eighteenth century. But Hutcheson wrote before this question had become as pressing it was to be for Hume, Smith, and Ferguson. Nonetheless his work cannot escape having implications for this controversy too.

The question to be posed about Hutcheson's work is then this: What philosophical resources does it afford for sustaining the tradition once carried forward by Baillie and Stair, in face both of the challenges of the newer philosophies and of the need for the tradition to preserve its theology, its legal and moral principles, its account of justice, and its view of what it is for individuals to be practically rational? It is part of Hutcheson's genuine greatness that when we understand his philosophy in this perspective, we also come to understand the extraordinary way in which he summoned up all the available resources relevant for his work. What has appeared to some commentators as mere eclecticism was in fact a remarkable, even if unsuccessful, project of synthesis.

XIV

Hutcheson on Justice
and Practical Rationality

Frances Hutcheson as an Irish presbyterian, the son and grandson of ministers—his grandfather from Ayrshire was among those lowland Scots settled in eastern Ulster in the seventeenth century in the course of the forcible expropriation of the native Irish—was brought up on the periphery of Scottish presbyterian culture. And as is commonly the case, the culture of the periphery was what the culture of the metropolitan centers had been a generation or two earlier. So Hutcheson in his presbyterian Academy in Ulster had the advantage of an initial training in the kind of scholastic Aristotelianism which was no longer taught in Scotland: "he was taught there," wrote Leechman in his account of Hutcheson's life, "the ordinary Scholastic Philosophy which was in vogue in those days, and to which he applied himself with uncommon assiduity and diligence." The effect of this upon his later philosophical writing is notable.

His education at Glasgow University, from 1710 onward, where he was taught philosophy by Gerschom Carmichael and divinity by John Simson, is also evident in his later writing. From Carmichael he acquired more than his knowledge of Pufendorf; he says in the introduction to his *Philosophiae Moralis Institutio Compendaria* (Glasgow, 1747) that Carmichael in his commentary on Pufendorf "has so supplied and corrected that the notes are of much more value than the text," and later in the same book he cited, not Locke's own account of government, but Carmichael's account of that account (III, 7).

What Hutcheson owed to Simson is also plain. Hutcheson's philosophy does not merely include, it *is,* a rational theology of the type which Simson taught. Revelation by God in the scriptures has a place, but a very restricted place, according to Hutcheson. Speaking of God as governor of the universe, Hutcheson wrote that "The sole use of words, or writing, in laws, is to discover the will of the governor. In positive laws it must by such means be discovered. But there is another and primary way by which God discovers his will concerning our conduct, and likewise proposes the most interesting motives, even by the constitution of nature, and the powers of reason, and moral perception, which he has given to mankind, and thus reveals a law with its functions, as effectually as by words, or writing; and in a manner more noble and divine" (*A System of Moral Philosophy,* London, 1755, vol. I, pp. 268–269). Notice that the contrast drawn is, not between reason and revelation, but between the modes of divine revelation. Moreover, even in the sphere of nature the imperfection of human reasoning, especially in "the bulk of mankind," is such that the perfection of the system of laws of nature "does not supersede the usefulness of the revelation of laws to mankind by words or writing . . ." (op. cit., pp. 271–272).

Hutcheson was bound to the doctrines of the Westminster Confession by oath as one licensed to preach by a presbytery, quite apart from his role as a professor. And his success in rebutting the charge of heresy against him, unlike Simson, shows that his philosophy was capable of being understood as at least reasonably congruent with the doctrines of the Confession. But it is difficult to resist the inference that it was not so much that Hutcheson was more orthodox than Simson as that the dominant conception of orthodoxy had somewhat changed. It is crucial to note, however, that Hutcheson frequently cited scripture as well as reasoning in support of his arguments, and there can be no doubt that he believed in a perfect agreement between scripture, rightly understood, and the conclusions of reason concerning the system of nature, rightly understood. Belief, for example, in miracles Hutcheson held to be rationally justified. And in the Introduction to the *Institutio* he declared that "the holy Scriptures . . . alone give to sinful mortals any sure hopes of a happy immortality."

The knowledge of nature and the knowledge of God are on Hutcheson's view inseparable. And since on Hutcheson's view the knowledge of God is in large and primary part impossible without the knowledge of nature, any purely *a priori* reasoning to God's existence and nature is precluded. Leechman tells us that around 1717 Hutcheson had written a letter to Samuel Clarke objecting to such reasoning. And indeed Hutcheson's theory of knowledge, from the moment that he had one, left no place for such reasoning.

It is important that Hutcheson does not approach the theory of knowledge, especially of knowledge in moral matters, with any measure of Cartesian doubt. He took Descartes' importance to reside entirely in his physics, and he had no sympathy with any other form of skepticism. The nature of law and morality Hutcheson never seems to have found in the least problematic. The part of morality which had the form of law was what Carmichael and Pufendorf and above all Grotius, from whom Carmichael and Pufendorf had derived their thought, had said that it was. Moreover, the attempt to demonstrate that obedience to such law is wholly an expression of self-love, an attempt ascribed by Hutcheson chiefly to Hobbes, had already, on Hutcheson's view, been shown to fail by Richard Cumberland in his book on the laws of nature. And these modern writers had been in significant measure anticipated by Cicero in *De Officiis.*

That part of morality which is constituted by the virtues was what Hutcheson understood Plato and Aristotle to have said that it was. In the *Institutio,* addressed primarily to his students, this was made explicit. So in Book I, chapter III, Hutcheson sets out the Platonic and Ciceronian scheme of the cardinal virtues, ascribing it to "the Antients," and in succeeding chapters discusses particular virtues under the heads of duties to God, to others, and to ourselves. These discussions often follow Aristotle closely, and Hutcheson refers his readers to "Aristotle and his followers" for a more "copious explication," but there are significant differences in the list of virtues, in the delineation of some particular virtues, and in the understanding of what a virtue is. Hutcheson believed that it is sometimes the case that excess and defect in respect of a mean are the marks of vice, and that accord with such a mean is the mark of a virtue, but only in respect of some of our affections. There are affections such that the more extremely they operate in us, the more virtuous we are: such are those affections which are the love of God, benevolence or "extensive good-will toward all," and "the love of moral excellence" (*Institutio* I, iii, 4). And this brings out one of Hutcheson's major differences from Aristotle: a virtue is taken to be, not primarily a disposition to act in certain ways, but a natural affection, and insofar as it is a disposition, a "disposition of heart" (I,iii,3). The idiom of affection was taken, of course, from Shaftesbury, and it is one of the two key notions which Hutcheson used in order to show how morality is grounded in our nature. But before we examine the use that Hutcheson made of it, it is illuminating to consider two other parts of his account of the virtues in which Hutcheson departs not only from Aristotle but also from the ancients in general.

The first concerns veracity, where Hutcheson's discussion shows the impact of seventeenth-century casuistry as well as of scholastic discussions of the natural law (II, x, and II, xvi). We are required to use our powers of reason and speech "in such manner as is most conducive to the general good, and suitable to our several obligations in life." Hutcheson proceeds to distinguish between those cases in which veracity is not required of us, because they do not genuinely fall under the rule requiring veracity, and those cases in which we ought for the sake of the general good to make an exception to the rule. An example of the former is "If 'tis known to all concerned that in some affairs certain persons are allowed to deceive . . ." (II,x,3). Such is the case with "many diversions," and it is also this understanding which allows physicians to withhold the truth from patients.

Examples of the latter are when "higher laws give way to singular necessities. . . . Tullius Hostilius is renowned to all ages for presence of mind in delivering a false account, by which the Roman people were preserved" (II,xvi,2). It is important both that Hutcheson thought that such singular necessities were of rare occurrence and that he was not in any way or sense a utilitarian. As will appear, "right" is not definable in terms of the general good, although it is contrived by the providence of God that it is to the general good that each person do what is right. Two features of Hutcheson's treatment of veracity are thereby brought to our attention. The first is the relative complexity of the considerations which must, on Hutcheson's view, inform correct judgment on occasions when veracity is at stake. The second is the way in which Hutcheson's discussion is indebted to a variety of moral traditions out of which he constructs his complex amalgam.

An even more illuminating topic for understanding Hutcheson's general position is his account of justice. Hutcheson, as with the other cardinal virtues, followed what he took to be the view of the ancients in his initial definition of justice: "an habit constantly regarding the common interest, and in subserviency to it, giving or performing to each one whatever is due to him upon any natural claim" (I,iii,3). This habit comprises those "kind dispositions of heart by which a friendly intercourse is maintained among men, or which leads us to contribute any thing to the common interest." But what justice principally requires of us is respect for and obedience to the law of nature, for it is the law of nature which provides grounds for us making "any natural claim" upon one another. The *Institutio* is divided into three books. The whole of Book II is devoted to the law of nature, and Book III is concerned with the detailed application of that law to the management of households and the government of states. Almost five-sevenths of the text are therefore concerned with the content of justice. In *A System of Moral Philosophy,* which is more than twice as long and addressed to the general reading public rather than to Hutcheson's Glasgow students, almost six-sevenths of the text is so devoted. These parts of Hutcheson's work are almost entirely neglected by modern moral philosophers who write about Hutcheson, but they are clearly that for the sake of which the moral epistemology of the earlier parts of these two texts—and it is of course that epistemology upon which modern writers concentrate—was provided. What then was Hutcheson doing in those parts of his work which concern the natural law and the detail of its application?

The answer is that he is in some measure doing over again for his own generation and in a new way the work which had been done for an earlier generation by the opening sections—and indeed parts of the subsequent text—of Stair's *Institutes*. There is the same appeal to Justinian and to the tradition of commentary upon Roman law, the same substantial agreement with Grotius, and there is the same method of citing the scriptures in confirmation of independently argued theses. There is the same kind of indebtedness to Dutch sources. Hutcheson included in a list of authorities, along with the names of Grotius, Pufendorf, Locke, and Harrington, that of Cornelius van Bynkershoek, whose *Observationes Juris Romani* (Leyden, 1710) was part of Bynkershoek's project of restoring system and coherence to the laws of the Netherlands by refounding them on the principles of Roman law. Moreover, along with Carmichael's commentary on Pufendorf, Hutcheson used that of Jean Barbeyrac as a source for the opinions of other authors (see the note to students introducing the *Institutio*). Barbeyrac, although of French parentage—his father was a Calvinist minister expelled from France after the Edict of Nantes—was professor of public law at Groningen.

Absent from Hutcheson, of course, is any discussion of particular legal cases and any mention of Stair. But this is unsurprising if we remember that what Stair had presented as the laws of Scotland, albeit as a rationally justifiable system of law, Hutcheson was presenting as the law of humankind. And he was presenting it, moreover, particularly in his works in English, to an audience who were presumed by their reading to be part of an international public.

Four aspects of this coincidence of views (far of course from complete, but far too substantial to be passed over) between Hutcheson and Stair deserve special emphasis. Each signals their shared allegiance to the same tradition. The first is the way in which the requirements of the law of nature, and therefore the requirements which the just person must satisfy, involve in many cases actions which are not to the interest or advantage of the individuals from whom they are required and which cannot give expression to the particular sympathies of such individuals nor indeed to any passion which occurs independently of moral approval and commitment. Hence our concept of justice and our obedience to the rules of justice cannot be explained in terms of interest, advantage, or such passions. Indeed, "As far as any views of one's own advantage have excited a man to such actions as are in their own nature good, so far the moral beauty is abated" (*Institutio* II,iii,6; compare *A System of Moral Philosophy,* I,iv). That is to say, it is just insofar as actions are explicable by interests or advantage that they cease to have moral worth. Stair had said: "This law of the rational nature of man is not framed or fitted for the interest of any, as many laws of men's choice be . . ." (*Institutions*, I,6).

Second, Hutcheson and Stair agree in their fundamental attitudes to property rights. Human beings have rights independently of and prior to the institution of property, and the exercise of property rights may be justly limited on occasion (Hutcheson *System* II,vii,9; *Institutions* II,i,34); where, for example, famine or other disaster threatens, needy citizens may take the property of others by force, if that is the only way to avert such disaster (*System* II,xvii,5; *Institutions* II,i,6). Justice is antecedent to property, something that Hume was to deny; property rights are not what Blackstone was to describe them as: "that sole and despotic dominion which one man claims and exercises over the external things of the world, in total exclusion of the right of any other individual in the universe" (*Commentaries* II,1,2). So Hutcheson and Stair agree in disagreeing with the dominant English eighteenth-century view, upholding instead a part of the Scottish tradition ultimately derived through the scholastic post-Reformation texts from the social theory of Aquinas.

Third, both Stair and Hutcheson agree in holding that government is instituted to remedy the injuries to rights which arise from breaches of the law of nature, a law which, were human beings less prone to violate each other's rights and more apt to be impartial in their judgments about such violations, would be sufficient by itself (*System* III,iv; *Institutions* I,i,15 and 18). Hutcheson in his view of the nature of government was indebted to both Locke and Grotius, and Stair to Grotius, and no more than a congruence between Stair and Hutcheson can be claimed. But it is worth noticing that Hutcheson in his account of government gives evidence of attention to peculiarly Scottish concerns by considering how after "the coalition of two independent states into one" (*System* III,vii,1), "where there are fundamental laws reserving certain rights as unalterable, nothing but a manifest necessity can justify any steps beyond the limits of these laws; otherwise all faith in such treaties of coalition is gone." Hutcheson was here replying to Fletcher of Saltoun, whether or not that was his intention. Scotland is not a conquered province, he may be read as saying, but a breach of the key articles in the treaty of Union, those reserving the rights of the Church of Scotland and of the Scottish legal system as unalterable, could make it one. And if this were to occur, those conditions which on Hutcheson's view make it right for the governed to resist and to overthrow their governors (*System* III,vii,3–6) would be satisfied.

Finally, in spite of the large differences which arise both from the different nature of the projects of the two writers and from the different types of audience whom they were addressing, there are remarkable similarities in the deductive structures constructed by Stair and Hutcheson. Both at a variety of points supplement their fundamental first principles with additional empirically grounded premises in order to show the detailed application of the fundamental principles of right (*ius*) in particular kinds of social relationship and circumstances. Both invoke a conception of utility to justify their conclusions about those detailed applications, but in both cases it is a conception which defines utility in terms of right rather than vice versa, so that the general happiness is to be promoted by each person fulfilling their independently defined obligations and duties and securing their own rights, as well as by their pursuit of other sources of happiness.

Hutcheson was fully aware of the importance of the deductive character of his arguments. In his first published work *An Inquiry into the Original of our Ideas of Beauty and Virtue* (London, 1725) he wrote of "Sciences, or universal Theorems" (III,6), and he noted the particular pleasure which we experience "when one Theorem shall contain a vast multitude of Corollarys easily deducible from it . . ." He was a critic of the particular uses of deductive methods made by Descartes, by Pufendorf, and by Cumberland, but what he criticized was, not the use of deduction as such, but the attempt to be overparsimonious in respect of first principles, that is, the attempt to deduce too much from too little. It is unsurprising that his letters show a keen interest in and an admiration for the work of his colleague Robert Simson in geometry.

Where, of course, Hutcheson could not have agreed with Stair was in Stair's doctrine of the intellectual apprehension of first principles, and this for at least two reasons. The first was that the only philosophically sophisticated version of such a doctrine of which Hutcheson was aware was that formulated by Samuel Clarke and others, according to which the conjunction of certain ideas reveals to rational scrutiny either their necessary congruity or their necessary incongruity, both in mathematics and in morality. But Hutcheson had already rejected such apriorism in respect of natural theology in his youthful letter to Clarke, and when his first book was criticized by Gilbert Burnet—whose father, as minister of Saltoun, had been responsible for the upbringing and education of Andrew Fletcher after his father's death—he explained his grounds for rejection once more. Just as what it is reasonable to believe about the first cause of the universe depends upon what we take the constitution of nature to be—something that Hutcheson made clear in his discussion of what he took to be the evidently designed properties of nature—and never simply upon the concept of that first cause, so what it is reasonable to believe about the end or ends to be pursued by human beings turns out to depend, on Hutcheson's view, upon what on empirical grounds—or grounds conceived as empirical—we take the constitution of human nature to be.

Gilbert Burnet, using a pseudonym, had defended Clarke's view and criticized Hutcheson's in the *London Journal* (April 10, 1725). Hutcheson, also writing pseudonymously, argued in reply (June 12, 1725) that what someone who believed that human beings capable of pursuing only the ends proposed to them by self-love took to be reasonable would be very different from what someone who believed human beings capable of pursuing the general good for its own sake took to be reasonable. What it is reasonable for us to do depends upon the nature of our motivation. Hence Hutcheson concluded that reason as such can provide no independent standard for action, and there is no principle of morality of whose truth we can be assured merely by inspecting it, without examining the empirical facts about human nature. What did Hutcheson believe those facts to be? His view fell into two parts.

One part derived from Shaftesbury. What Hutcheson learned from Shaftesbury was first that actions are expressions of and produced by affections or passions and second that no natural affection or passion is of itself bad. When we judge an action to be virtuous or vicious, we judge it as the expression and product of some passion; when we make such a moral judgment about our own affections, we do so insofar as we judge them liable to produce certain types of action rather than others. Actions viewed in detachment from affections or passions may be convenient or inconvenient, advantageous or harmful to particular persons, but they have no moral significance as virtuous or vicious apart from passions. What makes an action vicious is its deriving from some passion which has been given excessive importance relative to some other passion or set or sets of passions. We in our judgments of virtue and vice afford expression to our own passions as favoring or disfavoring those passions expressed in the actions about which we judge. The task of the moral philosopher becomes principally that of constructing an accurate introspective psychology or phenomenology of the passions in order to judge of them more accurately. The chief finding of such a psychology or phenomenology is that there are—at least and perhaps at most—two central passions or affections which produce action, self-love and "a social feeling or sense of partnership with mankind."

What was it about Shaftesbury's writings that so impressed Hutcheson and indeed so many others of Shaftesbury's own and the succeeding generation? That Hutcheson *was* greatly impressed is plain. His first book was a systematic defense of Shaftesbury's ideas, and it was from Shaftesbury that he took the expression "moral sense," although he was to give to it a precise meaning which Shaftesbury never did. Moreover, some of Shaftesbury's doctrines fitted well with what Hutcheson already believed upon other grounds, most notably Shaftesbury's claim that all plain persons are well able, without education in moral theory, to discern the distinction between virtue and vice. But in two respects at least Shaftesbury's ideas, as I have outlined them, were new to Hutcheson: Shaftesbury was one of the first moral philosophers— he had been preceded by Malebranche—to understand human nature as informed by two great competing principles, one egoistic, one altruistic; and Shaftesbury shifted the central focus of moral philosophy away from the intellectualism of most seventeenth-century writers, an intellectualism of which Clarke was the principal eighteenth-century heir, to a new attention to the passions.

Henry Sidgwick declared that this new view of what he called "the duality of the regulative principles in human nature"—a clear statement of which he believed was first provided by Butler (whom Hutcheson also read and admired), although he recognized that Butler had been foreshadowed by Shaftesbury—marked "the most fundamental difference between the ethical thought of modern England and that of the old Greco-Roman world" (*Outlines of the History of Ethics,* London, 1886, pp. 197–198). Sidgwick also noted how striking this was, since so much of Butler's thought was in fact derived from Greco-Roman sources. And the same anomaly confronts us with Hutcheson. For Hutcheson inherited from Shaftesbury, just as Butler did, the distinctively modern conception of the two contrasting and often conflicting passions of self-love and of benevolence toward others and yet published his first exposition of it in the first of the two treatises which compose the *Inquiry,* the second of which was a defense of ideas of good and evil "according to the Sentiments of the Antient Moralists." And in *An Essay on the Nature and Conduct of the Passions and Affections* (London, 1728) Hutcheson asserts in his opening paragraph that "the main practical Principles, which are inculcated in this Treatise, have this Prejudice in their Favour, that they have been taught and propagated by the best of Men in all Ages . . ."

Hutcheson then, like Butler, was blind to the differences between the ancients and Shaftesbury, more specifically between Aristotle and Shaftesbury. And this illuminates his partial, but very important, misreadings of Aristotle's text. These misreadings played a key part in separating him both from the scholasticism of his early education and from some central beliefs of the Scottish tradition represented by, for example, Stair. The single most important of these is the belief that reason, unless corrupted by sin, prescribes to the passions in the light of the knowledge which it affords concerning the true end of human beings. That belief had been sustained by the Aristotelian intellectualism of the seventeenth century. But it received no support apparently from Aristotle as read or misread by Hutcheson, who seems only to have seen in Aristotle's text what eyes informed by Shaftesbury's vision of the moral life allowed him to see. How did his reading eyes come to be so informed? Any reader of Shaftesbury knows that it cannot have been either by rigor of argument or by precise, detailed, or systematic exposition of any kind that Shaftesbury impressed, as he so plainly did, the readers of his own day. Shaftesbury's style and substance make no pretense to those qualities. What made Shaftesbury convincing was rather that he articulated for his readers an understanding of themselves which they already possessed, but for which no one else had as yet provided a conceptualization or the elements of a theoretical understanding.

I have already remarked that Shaftesbury's thought exhibits a break with and a rejection of the intellectualism of seventeenth-century moral theory, whether Calvinist or Thomist, Aristotelian or Platonist. But that intellectualism had already been rejected to a significant degree at quite another level, that of the practices of seventeenth-century religion. Both preaching and devotional literature were characteristically presented in styles well calculated to arouse, stimulate, and guide passions, affections, and sentiments. Both exhorted to introspective self-examination and required a cataloging of those inner states of feeling by attention to which the individual could gauge the moral and religious condition of mind and heart. Both required for such cataloging the elaboration of a new idiom of the passions, affections, and sentiments. And it was to the inner consciousness of those whose self-understanding had come to be informed by an originally religious idiom that Shaftesbury's secular voice spoke with such effectiveness (see for an account of related developments in a New England context Norman Fiering *Moral Philosophy at Seventeenth-Century Harvard,* Chapel Hill, 1981, chapters 6 and 7).

Hutcheson then saw no problem in conjoining what he took himself to have learned from Greek moral philosophy with what he had learned from Shaftesbury. But I remarked earlier that only one part of what Hutcheson believed to be the truth about the constitution of our human nature was derived from Shaftesbury. The other, quite as important, Hutcheson learned from the protagonists of what was to be called "the way of ideas." "These two powers of perception, *sensation* and *consciousness,* introduce into the mind all its materials of knowledge. All our primary or direct ideas or notions are derived from one or other of these sources" (*System* I,i,4). So Hutcheson affiliated himself with Descartes, Malebranche, Arnauld, Locke, and their less eminent followers. What was central to the way of ideas was, of course, the primacy which its adherents assigned to an epistemological stance embodying a first-person point of view. What-is is to be constructed from, inferred from, or otherwise derived from or represented by—depending upon the particular version of the theory—what-is-immediately-presented-to-me-as-idea.

One crux is the same for all these different versions of the way of ideas. How is it possible for anyone to derive from particular immediate perceptions, and nothing but particular and immediate perceptions, any knowledge of or any justification for asserting any claim that is universal in form and general in content? This crux arises in a variety of forms, in one of them as a problem about ordinary sense perception: someone who utters a judgment of the form "This is red" makes a claim which is subject to correction by others in the light of socially shared standards governing judgments of color, yet if all perceptual judgments refer only to and derive their content from what-is-immediately-presented-as-idea-to-particular-individuals, how can such socially shared standards be possible?

The problem which arises for Hutcheson as a consequence of his allegiance to the way of ideas is analogous. Hutcheson was, we have already seen, deeply committed to the belief that human beings possess socially shared standards governing what is right and just. These standards are, on his view, embodied in rules of justice, comprising the law of nature, which are universal in form and more or less general in content. Yet our knowledge of these standards and rules is derived from and in the end unjustifiable apart from, so he asserted in his moral epistemology, an appeal to what is discriminated on particular occasions by a moral sense, a mode of perception *sui generis,* but in certain key respects resembling all other modes of perception. Is there some coherent, let alone rationally justifiable, way in which Hutcheson can combine his beliefs about justice and his beliefs about the moral sense? Any well-founded answer to this question requires on account of what Hutcheson means by the moral sense and of its place within the structure of his overall theory.

Hutcheson's first introduction of the moral sense, both in the *Institutio* and in the *System,* has three main features. First, it is a sense, and it is that sense to which we apply the name 'conscience'. As a sense it makes us immediately aware of its particular objects, objects which elicit a specific type of approval or disapproval. Second, in being moved by that of which the moral sense makes us aware we are delivered from a kind of difficulty which the rest of our nature would otherwise impose upon us. For we are creatures moved both by self-love and by generous affections, and without a moral sense we should have no way of adjudicating between the claims of what Hutcheson called "a calm self-love" and the claims of altruistic benevolence. There would be no answer to the question, either generally or on particular occasions, by which motive it is better for us to be guided. And it is just to this question that the moral sense is said to supply answers.

Third, the objects of the moral sense are qualities specific to that sense, detected and discriminated only by its exercise. The perception of those objects causes pleasure and pain, but the objects themselves are not to be identified with those pleasures and pains: "we are pleased in the contemplation because the object is excellent, and the object is not judged to be therefore excellent because it gives us pleasure" (*System* I,iv,1). Moreover, "the notion under which one approves virtue, is neither its tendency to obtain any benefit or reward to the agent or approver. . . . 'Tis also obvious that the notion under which we approve virtue is not its tendency to procure honour . . ." (I,iv,2).

To be moved by the objects and distinctions disclosed by the moral sense is then to have a way of ordering those other affections which move us to action, and by reflecting upon that ordering we discover that if we allow to self-love and to benevolent generosity that and only that which a regard for moral excellence would allot to them, we shall be pursuing that way of life best designed to ensure our happiness. It will be a way of life, so Hutcheson believed, marked by just those dispositions to affection, the exercise of which exhibit those virtues which

Aristotle had cataloged in the *Nicomachean Ethics.* So beginning from Shaftesbury and the way of ideas, we do indeed, on Hutcheson's view, arrive at concordance with the ancients and more especially with Aristotle. But about this Hutcheson was of course in large error, an error which becomes most obvious if we consider the difference between Hutcheson's and Aristotle's views of the place of reason in practical life.

Where Aristotle had said that we do not deliberate about ends, but only about what conduces to the achievement of ends (*NE* 1112b 11–12), although we do indeed *reason* about ends, including our ultimate *telos,* Hutcheson's view was that "the *Understanding,* or the power of reflecting, comparing, judging" judges about the means or the subordinate ends; but about the ultimate ends there is no reasoning. "We prosecute them by some immediate disposition or determination of soul, which in the order of action is always prior to all reasoning; as no opinion or judgment can move to action, where there is no prior desire of some end" (*System* I,iii,1). Our ends then are immediately given by our natural propensities and desires, and it is not by reference to their tendency to promote our higher good that we are to decide which of them to encourage and strengthen, which to weaken or to extirpate. It is rather that those ends toward which they move us compose our highest good.

Notice that what is natural to human nature is what is empirically given; Hutcheson's conception of nature had, under Shaftesbury's influence, become very different from Aristotle's. But it was a Christian conception. God has ordered nature and our nature providentially, so that our supreme happiness will in fact result from the pursuit of those ends proposed to us by the moral sense. And the discovery that this is so is indeed a work of reason, as is that demonstration of the existence and nature of God which is essential to our understanding of the relationship between the immediate ends proposed to us by the moral sense, our supreme happiness and our obedience to the laws of nature. Plain persons, endowed as they are with the moral sense, need not fear that the particular moral judgments which they make on the basis of its deliverance may be put in question by the conclusions of rational argument. For the moral sense is capable of being corrected and improved only by its own more extensive exercise, not by reasoning. Hutcheson compares this correction and improvement to that of our musical tastes. "We indulge ourselves in musick; we meet with finer and more complex compositions. In these we find a pleasure much higher, and begin to despise what formerly pleased us." And similarly, as we enlarge our experience of moral judgment, "we correct any apparent disorders in this moral faculty . . ." (*System* I,iv,5).

What the moral sense thus provides are a set of reliable judgments, but not only judgments as to what is the case in particular instances of action and affection. We apprehend, it is quite clear from Hutcheson's discussion, the action and more fundamentally the affection as being morally excellent or otherwise insofar as it is of some particular kind. So we apprehend affections as virtuous or vicious in respect of possessing some quality which is also to be approved in other instances. The moral sense thus supplies us not merely with singular moral judgments but also with those singular moral judgments as expressions of principles which, just because they are not either justifiable or corrigible by a rational appeal to any other principles, are necessarily first principles for moral reasoning and practical reasoning in general.

The deductive structure of Hutcheson's thought and the place of such fundamental principles within it are mirrored in the organization of his books, not only, but most clearly, in *A System of Moral Philosophy*. First, the existence of and nature of the moral sense are presented in the context of an outline of the constitution of moral nature. Both in the course of this account and subsequent to it the content of the principles warranted by the moral sense is expounded. Then, second, these principles in conjunction with other assertions about human nature and what generally pleases and pains provide the premises from which an account of the supreme happiness of human beings is deduced. This account in turn provides additional premises, which, conjoined both with those derived from the moral sense and with certain empirical truths, yield what Hutcheson in the title of Book II of the *System* called "a Deduction of the more special Laws of Nature, and Duties of Life, previous to Civil Government, and other adventitious States." Third and finally, with the addition of further premises the rights and duties constituting and governing families, households, government, and states of war are deduced.

Within this deductive structure beliefs about God and about the divine nature have a crucial place. We discover in God a being to whom we owe duties of veneration and obedience. Reason assures us of God's existence and nature, and in arguing to the divine excellence we employ an analogy drawn from our own moral sense. God must discriminate in a way which is analogous to ours. It was doubtless Hutcheson's argument on this point which led—very understandably—to the accusation of heresy in that he seemed to appeal to a standard of moral goodness independent of our knowledge of God. For Hutcheson did indeed assert that we are aware of the deliverances of the moral sense independently of any reasoning or any other beliefs, including theological beliefs. Nonetheless, what rational argument discloses to us concerning the divine nature is, on Hutcheson's view, that we judge morally as we do only because God so created us that our moral judgments should not be discrepant with his. And in this way we have no moral standard independent of the divine standard (*System* I,ix,5).

Moreover, without a knowledge of what we owe to God and of his providential ordering of the universe we should not, on Hutcheson's view, be able to arrive at a correct view of what the supreme happiness of human beings is, and hence we should fail in many of our subsequent deductions concerning right action and the laws of nature. So much is this the case that "As to direct Atheism, or denial of a moral providence, or of the obligations of the moral or social virtues, these indeed directly tend to hurt the state in its most important interests: and the persons who directly publish such tenets cannot well pretend any obligation in conscience to do so. The magistrate may therefore justly restrain them by force, as he might any deluded fool or enthusiasts who pretended conscience in invading the rights or properties of others" (*System* III,ix,2). Such persons cannot appeal to conscience, for 'conscience' is one more name of the moral sense, and it is the moral sense which is affronted by such persons.

Notice that although the moral sense does not provide us with any of the rational arguments for the existence of God, it warrants, when we are confronted with an adequate conception of such a being, his veneration as morally excellent. So plain persons do not need to be skilled in rational argument in order to judge truly that they ought to venerate God. Were this not so, the atheist would in this respect at least be guilty only of intellectual, not of moral, error. But in other respects the intellectual errors of the atheist may themselves be a cause of further moral error. For much which we deduce concerning the supreme happiness of human beings and much which we further deduce concerning the law of nature, in respectful obedience to which the virtue of justice is exhibited, cannot be validly derived if the truths which concern God's existence and nature are withdrawn from the deductive system. On these matters reasoning is indispensable, and the atheist is bound to be guilty of inadequate reasoning.

This double failure of the atheist, in respect first of the moral sense and then of reasoning, exhibits clearly the division of moral judgments into two classes by Hutcheson. We are motivated only by the affections, and we are rightly motivated only when affected by the moral sense in a way that gives to it its due and chief place among the affections. So far reason is impotent. But where it is a matter of our knowledge of those duties and rights which are secondary and derivative from the primary duties and rights of which the moral sense informs us, reason has an essential place in the moral life. Thus we have a two-tiered structure of duties and rights, and reason has a place only at the second level. To understand this is to understand how far his moral epistemology had removed Hutcheson from the Aristotle with whom he falsely believed that he was agreeing, particularly in respect of the nature and function of practical reasoning.

For Aristotle, as was clear in the earlier discussion of his views, all right practical judgment has to be in accordance with right reason, and every particular right judgment involves knowing how to bring *this* particular set of alternative courses of action under the relevant concept of good *qua* such and such in the formation of right practical judgment. So intellectual as well as moral virtue is involved in every exercise of *phronēsis*. Appeal to established rules of justice in particular cases, if and when it is warranted, is an appeal to those rules which in the light of right reasoning generally yield right judgment in such cases. Hence for Aristotle there was not and could not be any entirely prerational and nonrational warrant for true moral judgment such as Hutcheson took the moral sense to afford. Indeed for Aristotle there was not and could not be any such thing as the moral sense.

It follows that to some large degree the relationship of moral character to the capacity for making true practical judgments has to be different in the two systems of thought. For Aristotle the capacity for making true judgments is inseparable from the possession of the virtues, and education in that capacity proceeds *pari passu* with education in the virtues. For Hutcheson there is an ability to make true judgments which can be exercised prior to the education of moral habits and character. One can know, in some measure at least, what is just without actually being just. For the deliverances of the moral sense are in the first instance equally available to all, although human beings significantly differ from each other in how far they attend to these deliverances.

In describing Hutcheson's ostensibly Aristotelian catalog of the virtues I already noticed some ways in which Hutcheson revised or departed from Aristotle and I later pointed out how Hutcheson circumscribes the role of reason in respect of ends more narrowly than Aristotle does. To these differences we now have to add the corresponding, but perhaps more fundamental, difference embodied in and deriving from Hutcheson's disagreement with Aristotle over practical reasoning. For there is no place within Hutcheson's scheme for the virtue of *phronēsis,* that virtue according to Aristotle which is exercised in exercising all other virtues. *Phronēsis* had reappeared in medieval Christian Aristotelianism under the name '*prudentia*', and as such it is the first of the four cardinal virtues listed by Aquinas (*S.T.* I–IIae, 61,1). When William Dunbar, the Scottish renaissance poet and moralist (1465–c.1520), reproduced Aquinas' scheme of the cardinal and theological virtues in his poem *The Tabill of Confession,* 'prudentia' became 'prowdence'. And 'prudence' retained this meaning in both Scotland and England well into the seventeenth century, although alongside it there appears the modern meaning, which was in time to supersede the older entirely, where 'prudence' names the "ability to discern the most suitable, politic or profitable course of action" (*Oxford English Dictionary,* Oxford, 1933).

Hutcheson ascribes to "the Antients" a definition of 'prudence' as a cardinal virtue: "a cautious habit of consideration and forethought, discerning what may be advantageous or hurtful in life" (*Institutio* I,iii,3). Prudence thus defined requires for its exercise, according to Hutcheson, a prior and independent acquisition of what he describes as "an high sense of moral excellence," so that we may know what is truly to our advantage. Thus we have to learn what is right from the moral sense prior to learning how to be prudent rather than having to first acquire *phronēsis* or *prudentia* in order to judge rightly. *Phronēsis* has indeed been displaced, and what Hutcheson refers to by 'prudence' is no more than its ghost.

Hutcheson's overall moral scheme thus depends for its content in key part, as well as for its justification, upon the claims which he made for the moral sense. And it is therefore of the first importance to ask how precisely Hutcheson understood the concept of such a sense. A spectrum of rival interpretations has been advanced. At one end of that spectrum is the view of Hutcheson as a cognitivist, even although an antirationalist, for whom the moral sense discriminates the virtuous and the vicious, just as visual perception discriminates the light and the dark. The inwardness of the moral sense does not on this view render it a sensation rather than a perception. At the opposite end of the spectrum lie those noncognitivist interpretations according to which the moral sense is a feeling of approbation, albeit a distinctive feeling and one which responds uniformly—except in deviant cases—to the objects offered to its attention (for a recent illuminating extension of the debate between those standpoints see David Fate Norton 'Hutcheson's moral realism' chapter 2 of *David Hume,* Princeton, 1982; Kenneth Winkler 'Hutcheson's Alleged Moral Realism' *Journal of the History of Philosophy* 23, 2, 1985, and David Fate Norton 'Hutcheson's Moral Realism' ibid. 23, 3, 1985).

What I wish to do is not so much to participate in the debate between the protagonists of these opposing standpoints as to suggest that Hutcheson's conception of the moral sense was bound to present interpretative difficulties. For it is a conception within which incompatibles are united in at least two distinct ways. Hutcheson wanted the moral sense to supply us with the kind of certitude which is grounded in sensory immediacy, but, as I noted earlier, that of which we are to be thus apprised is, not some mere particularity, but the exemplification of some universal and general moral truth on a particular occasion. And in this claim to discover in particular perceptions or sensations a warrant for universal and general truths Hutcheson was in the same predicament as other adherents of the way of ideas. But the peculiar character of the morality which he wished to uphold by means of his epistemology confronted him with a second kind of difficulty.

The moral truths which Hutcheson had inherited, partly from scholastic Aristotelianism and partly from Calvinism, embodied a view of the content of justice as specifiable only by principles whose truth and whose claim to our allegiance are independent of the interest or advantage of any particular person or group of persons. To pursue justice one must be able, therefore, to transcend both whatever moves one to pursue one's own self-interest and also whatever moves one to consult the interest of any group of others, no matter how enlarged. To distribute justly is to distribute according to desert, not according to interest, and justice thus conceived cannot be shown to be to the interest of anyone and everyone, whether on a Hobbesian view or even on one derived from Shaftesbury's more generous conception of human nature. Hutcheson, as I have already indicated, preserved a great deal of the content of this traditional conception of justice, in a form closely related to the peculiarly Scottish version elaborated by Stair. But he wished to find some type of motivating reason available to anyone and everyone as both ground and motive for allegiance to a conception of right from which rules of justice of this kind might be derived, and, moreover, a type of motivating reasoning which could be characterized in terms basically consonant with Shaftesbury's understanding of the constitution of human nature.

So Hutcheson had to invent something *sui generis* in which these mutually incompatible aspirations could all seem to have been realized. The conception of the moral sense could not thus escape internal incoherence; it was a philosophical artefact whose function was to serve too many purposes. But this of course was not how it was viewed by Hutcheson himself or by that very large body of readers and students among his contemporaries who so often found his central theses illuminating and persuasive. Their response makes it clear that Hutcheson had succeeded in identifying and providing a philosophical account of a type of moral experience which was central to their practical lives.

What Hutcheson's account of the moral sense supplied for those contemporaries was a rationale for their reliance upon the felt evidentness of what were taken to be moral truths. By drawing upon psychological materials furnished by Shaftesbury Hutcheson provided a secular counterpart to the appeal to inward feeling so characteristic of the doctrines of Evangelical conversion. This appeal and the social consensus which embodied it were of course vulnerable to moral change and to moral conflict. Agreement in feeling and agreement as to what feeling showed to be evident were necessary conditions for sustaining the attitudes and beliefs of those who found Hutcheson's moral philosophy immediately credible. For were it to be the case that what one person or one society on the basis of his or her feeling finds to be evidently true, another person or society on the very same basis finds to be evidently false, then both the testimony of feeling and the very conception of evidentness in moral matters would be put in question. It was therefore crucial that Hutcheson should be able to show that what appeared to be examples of just such disagreement and conflict were in fact not what they appeared to be. Hutcheson identified three sources of apparent moral disagreement. Most such disagreements, he argued, "arise from opposite conclusions of reason about the effects of action upon the publick, or the affections from which they flowed. The *moral sense* seems ever to approve and condemn uniformly the same immediate objects, the same affections and dispositions . . ." (*System* I,v,7). It is thus from faulty reasoning either about the effects of actions or about their causes that disagreements for the most part arise. A second contributing factor is the tendency to regard one's own social group as the only one in which morally deserving individuals are to be found. "The different approbations here arise again from different opinions about a matter of fact." And so it is also with the third cause of moral disagreement: "the different opinions about what God has commanded," opinions which from hope of divine reward or fear of divine punishment may lead human beings to "counteract their moral sense. . . ."

It is then only from the inability of human beings always to reason correctly and uniformly that disagreements are engendered; the moral sense produces only agreement, and if human beings were to reason correctly from the premises provided by the approbations of the moral sense, they would agree upon the law of nature and therefore upon what it is that justice requires. The arguments which supported this conclusion clearly had for many of Hutcheson's contemporaries among the educated classes in Scotland, and indeed to some degree elsewhere, a force sufficient to explain and so to discredit disagreement with Hutcheson. His particular articulation of the role of the professor of moral philosophy thus became in some measure a paradigm for later professors, although none of them were to rival him in the degree to which his personal qualities seemed to exemplify and so to reinforce his intellectual stance.

By the time of his death he was recognized, in Leechman's words, as "one of the most masterly and engaging teachers that has appeared in our age. . . ." Students continued to attend his lectures after they had already completed their course in moral philosophy. When on Sunday evenings Hutcheson lectured upon the evidences of the truth of the Christian religion, he attracted an even wider audience. When his son published *A System of Moral Philosophy* posthumously in 1755, the list of subscribers included not only numerous ministers of the Church of Scotland but a significant number of merchants, advocates, and gentry.

Yet Hutcheson's remarkable achievement in providing new foundations both for moral theology and for the philosophy of law and justice, and in so doing preserving the distinctive characteristics of the Scottish presbyterian social and intellectual tradition, was and could only have been short-lived. Hutcheson turned out to be a transitional figure whose philosophy had an inherent instability. By founding his in many respects traditional account of the law of nature and of our duties to God upon a version of the new way of ideas, which drew so largely upon the idiom and the arguments of Malebranche, Shaftesbury, and Locke, Hutcheson appeared for the moment to have successfully vindicated the Scottish philosophical tradition against *both* the criticisms of those English students educated in modern philosophy by the English nonconformist academies, numbers of whom came to Scotland for their university education from the early eighteenth century onward, *and* those of the Calvinist clergy who had followed Halyburton in condemning the use of philosophy in theological matters. What he had in fact prepared was, if not its demise, at the very least the grounds for its radical transformation.

The moral sense ceased very quickly to be credible as a philosophical artefact; or rather it came to be recognized as merely a philosophical artefact rather than a feature of human nature. And those who recognized it as such and who set themselves to remove the incoherences within Hutcheson's philosophy were faced with a choice. *Either* they could retain Hutcheson's moral epistemology, amending it where necessary, and reject his view of moral principles, of the law of nature, of justice, and of our duties to God; *or* they could retain Hutcheson's central moral and theological position and reject the epistemology. David Hume and Adam Smith represent the first of these alternatives; Thomas Reid and Dugald Stewart, the second. All four were agreed, implicitly or explicitly, that it was possible to agree with Hutcheson *either* about justice *or* about practical reasoning, but not about both.

Hutcheson therefore engendered a new type of conflict within Scottish intellectual life, and it is a mark of his importance that he set the terms of debate for that conflict. Just because he did so, it is all too easy in retrospect to view that conflict as a continuation of the debates internal to the Scottish tradition. The participants after all were all Scotsmen. But it was in fact a conflict in which the continuing existence of the Scottish tradition was put in question. What Hume represented in almost every important respect, what indeed Smith too was to represent, even although he was Hutcheson's most distinguished and well-regarded pupil, was the abandonment of peculiarly Scottish modes of thought in favor of a distinctively English and Anglicizing way of understanding social life and its moral fabric.

XV

Hume's Anglicizing Subversion

David Hume's relationship to his Scottish upbringing and education was one in which throughout his life (1711–1776) he consistently discarded everything distinctively Scottish in matters of intellectual attitude and belief, while with equal consistency he retained and developed the warmest personal ties with his family, with early friends, and with a variety of figures prominent in Scottish life. His published work presented a series of the profoundest challenges to and ruptures with the fundamental convictions which had been embodied in the dominant Scottish tradition. But at any point at which this fact might have had an impact upon Hume's personal life, he tried so far as possible to minimize and to disguise the facts of challenge and rupture. This double aspect of Hume's life continually presents itself in a variety of contexts. Consider some of them.

Hume at the family estate of Ninewells had been brought up in the parish of Chirnside where standards of Calvinist orthodoxy were sustained in preaching and teaching. The father of Ebenezer and Ralph Erskine, Henry Erskine had been minister of that parish from 1689 to 1704. He was succeeded by Hume's uncle by marriage, George Home, whose father had been hanged for his activities as a covenanter in 1682. And Hume's mother, who, because of his father's death in 1713, was entirely responsible for his childhood upbringing, was herself a devout and undoubting believer. So was Hume as a child. "I asked him if he was not religious when he was young," wrote Boswell in his account of his conversation with Hume when Hume was dying. "He said he was, and he used to read the *Whole Duty of Man;* that he made an abstract from the Catalogue of vices at the end of it, and examined himself by this, leaving out Murder and Theft and such vices as he had no chance of committing, having no inclination to commit them. This, he said, was strange Work; for instance, to try if, notwithstanding his excelling his school-fellows, he had no pride or vanity."

It was in part at least as a result of reading and reflecting upon the arguments of Locke and Clarke that Hume had by the time that he was twenty abandoned the Christian religion altogether. But Hume went much further than mere rejection. He told Boswell "that the Morality of every Religion was bad," and he exhibits in many of his writings an ironic and measured scorn for religious observance. In 1739 he wrote in a letter to Hutcheson, "Upon the whole, I desire to take my catalogue of Virtues from *Cicero's Offices,* not from the *Whole Duty of Man.*" Thus Hume's youthful Calvinism had been thoroughly repudiated, as well as the maturer and more sophisticated theologies of his learned presbyterian contemporaries. This is not, of course, to deny that Hume's religious upbringing had a significant effect upon his views, but it was an effect which he himself recognized only in its negative aspects.

In private then, as well as in his published writings, Hume had no hesitation in avowing his hostility to religion. He said on his deathbed, according to William Cullen (Thomson-Cullen Papers, 161, Glasgow University Library, quoted by Peter Jones *Hume's Sentiments,* Edinburgh, 1982, p. 2), that he was leaving unfinished "the great work" of liberating Scotland "from the Christian superstition." But in social life he presented a different front. When in 1762 George Campbell sent Hume through their mutual friend, Hugh Blair, his shortly to be published manuscript criticizing Hume's argument against the credibility of reports of the occurrence of miracles, Hume complained in a letter to Blair: "I could wish your friend had not denominated me an infidel writer, on account of ten or twelve pages which seem to him to prove that tendency: while I have wrote so many volumes on history, literature, politics, trade, morals, which, in that particular at least, are entirely inoffensive. Is a man to be called a drunkard, because he has been seen fuddled once in his lifetime?"

Just as these uncandid protestations should not conceal from us the fact that Hume had at an early stage broken with the dominant Scottish intellectual and moral tradition insofar as it was a theological tradition, so Hume's personal links to the social world of Scottish law must not be allowed to disguise the extent to which Hume had very early repudiated yet another strand central to that tradition, its affiliation to Roman law and its inheritance from the commentators upon Roman law. The personal links were real enough. Hume's maternal grandfather, Sir David Falconer of Newton, had succeeded Stair as President of the Court of Session in 1682 and made one of the collections of that Court's decisions of which Stair made use in his *Institutions.* Hume's father had been admitted as an advocate in 1705, after having been a student at Utrecht, where he may have studied law. Hume himself in 1752 succeeded Thomas Ruddiman as Keeper of the Library of the Faculty of Advocates in Edinburgh and held that office until 1757. He held a commission as Judge-Advocate on an expedition against the French in 1746. And when he finished his undergraduate studies at Edinburgh University in 1725 or 1726, he had been set by his family to the study of law. But none of this gave Hume any but the most superficial knowledge of Scots law or of its roots in the tradition of the commentators upon Roman law.

Of his period of study after his university career he was to write: "My studious Disposition, my Sobriety and my Industry gave my Family a Notion that the Law was a proper Profession for me: But I found an unsurmountable Aversion to every thing but the pursuit of Philosophy and general Learning; and while they fancyed I was poring over Voet and Vinnius, Cicero and Virgil were the Authors whom I was secretly devouring." In 1729 he finally abandoned even the pretense of studying law: "The Law . . . appear'd nauseous to me," and set himself to become instead "a Scholar and Philosopher."

Hume's view of the study of law as quite other than that of philosophy marks a second type of break with the dominant Scottish tradition, one made obvious by the contrast between Hutcheson and Hume in this regard. Hutcheson in his moral philosophy refers his readers at a wide variety of points to Justinian's *Institutions*. Hume never so refers. Vinnius, of whom Hume spoke so cavalierly, was Arnold Vinnen, professor of civil law at Leyden, whose commentary on Justinian's *Institutions,* published in 1642, Hutcheson cites (*System* III,viii,4). And it was not merely that Hume flouted the study of the Roman and the Roman-Dutch jurists—Jan Voet, the other object of Hume's avoidance behavior, had been professor of civil law at Leyden at the time when Stair went into exile there in 1682 and was the grandson of Robert Baillie's correspondent, Gisbert Voet; his *Commentarius ad Pandectos* (1698–1704) was the single most important work on Roman law of that age—but also that in his account of justice in the *Treatise* he was summarily dismissive of their and, that is to say, of the traditional Scottish view of justice (III,ii,6). In 1759 he was to write to Adam Smith in a criticism of Henry Home, Lord Kames: "A man might as well think of making a fine sauce by a mixture of wormwood and aloes, as an agreeable composition by joining metaphysics and Scottish law."

When Hume left Edinburgh and Ninewells for England, he adopted, so far as he was capable of doing, the manners of an Englishman. Later on he was to write that "Scotland is too narrow a Place for me" and that "London is the Capital of my own Country." But more immediately in Bristol he changed the spelling of his name from 'Home' to 'Hume', presumably so that it would be correctly pronounced by the English, whose ignorance of the name 'Home' was after all only part of a larger ignorance about Scotland. And he made a friend of John Peach, an educated linen-draper, whose advice he later sought in order to eliminate every distinctively Scottish turn of phrase and mode of expression from his *History of England*. In 1757 in a letter to Gilbert Elliot he called the Scots idiom "a very corrupt Dialect of the Tongue which we make use of. . . ."

The effects of this intended Anglicization of the self were not in every respect what Hume intended. Walter Bagehot wrote of the prose style which resulted from Hume's self-conscious elimination of Scots idioms: "Hume is always idiomatic, but his idioms are consistently wrong; many of his best passages are, on that account, curiously grating and puzzling: you feel that they are very like what an Englishman would say, but yet that after all, somehow or other, they are what he would never say . . ." (op. cit., pp. 105–106). Moreover, Hume never succeeded in making the English recognize him as an Englishman. His surviving Scottish traits were sufficient for him to incur from time to time that hatred of the Scots which was so common at a variety of levels of English society in the eighteenth century. Hume therefore came to reidentify himself as a Scot, to take pride in the poetry of such inferior Scottish writers as Blacklock and Wilkie, and finally, upon his return to Edinburgh in 1769, to have a house built for himself there, writing to his publisher, William Strahan, that "I have abjurd London forever." But he did so only when he had "done with all Ambition." The life in which he lived out his scholarly and philosophical ambition was by design to a large degree an English life, even when lived out in France.

Most striking and important of all in this respect is the 'Introduction' to the anonymously published *A Treatise of Human Nature*. In it Hume first refers to "some late philosophers in *England,* who have begun to put the science of man on a new footing," and then says that while other nations may rival "us" in poetry and the agreeable arts, "the improvements in reason and philosophy can only be owing to a land of toleration and of liberty," and he speaks finally of the "honour to our native country" thereby accruing. No contemporary reader could have done other than suppose that the anonymous writer was an Englishman, and such a reader would also have had to suppose from the footnote, in which in a list of "the late philosophers in England" the misspelled name of "Hutchinson" is included, that this was an Englishman curiously insensitive to the very existence of Scotland.

It is of course in part because of the obvious indebtedness of Hume's thought to Hutcheson's that Hume has been commonly taken to be a thinker belonging to—indeed the greatest thinker of—the Scottish Enlightenment. But what Hume derived from Hutcheson was that in Hutcheson which belonged to "the way of ideas" and not at all that which Hutcheson had derived from that Scottish tradition in which the fundamental concerns of philosophy, Scots law, and presbyterian theology were inseparable. What Hume took from Hutcheson was fourfold.

He accepted from Hutcheson first and most fundamentally the view that reason is practically inert. It cannot by its very nature move us to action. As I remarked earlier, in discussing Hutcheson's acceptance of Shaftesbury's rather than Aristotle's account of the role of reason in practical life, this was a key point in respect of which Hutcheson himself had moved radically away from what had been a central thesis of the seventeenth-century Scottish tradition. So that in following Hutcheson here Hume also set himself against that tradition.

Hume also drew upon Hutcheson in three other closely related ways. His catalog of the passions at the beginning of Book II of *A Treatise of Human Nature,* although it moves further away from Aristotle than Hutcheson does, seems to depend upon Hutcheson quite as much as it does upon introspection. Hume, like everyone else, learned what a great many passions are and are like, not in the first instance by having them, but by reading about them. Moreover, Hume followed Hutcheson in dividing moral judgments into two classes: those prior to all reasoning—according to Hutcheson the immediate deliverances of the moral sense, according to Hume the expression of the natural virtues —and those secondary moral judgments derived as conclusions from a conjunction of primary moral judgments and judgments dependent upon reasoning concerning matters of fact—according to Hutcheson those judgments which tell us what the law of nature is, according to Hume the expression of the artificial virtues—although Hume had no objection to speaking in similar fashion of "laws of nature" (*Treatise* III,ii,1).

Finally Hume followed Hutcheson in founding his account of morality upon a view of the constitution of human nature as everywhere and in all societies uniform and invariant. Anyone holding such a view is confronted by the problem of how to explain apparent moral variation between cultures and apparent moral disagreement within them. Hutcheson scarcely adverted to the former problem but had, as we have already noticed, his own solution to the latter. Hume was well aware of both problems, and insofar as he responded to them, he did so within the framework of those beliefs about human nature which to a large degree he shared with Hutcheson.

Even however in those areas in which there is a large coincidence of standpoint between Hume and Hutcheson, the result in part of Hume's reading of those works of Hutcheson published before 1730 and in part of their common allegiance to the way of ideas, there are important differences. Hutcheson's account of the moral sense, as I argued earlier, is susceptible of a range of interpretations. It can be plausibly represented as cognitivist: we discriminate the virtuous from the vicious as we discriminate the light from the dark. And it can be plausibly represented as noncognitivist: we discriminate the virtuous from the vicious by responding to causal stimuli with one kind of feeling rather than another. Hume not only unambiguously adopted the latter standpoint as his own, but in so doing he also supposed himself to be doing no more than repeating what Hutcheson had said. So in treating "the Propositions of Morality" as giving expression to "the feelings of our internal *Tastes* and *Sentiments*" Hume claimed that "in this Opinion he concurs with all the antient Moralists, as well as with Mr. Hutcheson. . . ."

The occasion for this claim was the controversy which arose over Hume's candidacy for the chair of moral philosophy at Edinburgh in 1745 (for a full account of this episode the one indispensable work is M.A.C. Stewart, op. cit.). In April 1745 the Edinburgh Town Council had elected Hutcheson to the vacant chair, only to discover afterward that his unwillingness to leave Glasgow prevented him from accepting. Hutcheson had already expressed this unwillingness privately in a letter in July 1744 to Lord Minto, a letter which I cited earlier in discussing the characteristics required in a professor of moral philosophy. The list of eligible candidates suggested by Hutcheson in that letter included William Cleghorn, who was in fact to be appointed, but it did not include Hume. And Hutcheson, when Hume's candidacy was proposed, seems to have used his influence against Hume, to Hume's surprise, dismay, and indignation.

Of Hume's unfitness to hold a chair which, for example, required its holder to give instruction in the truths of rational religion in a way that would be at least congruent with and supportive of the Christian revelation there can in retrospect be little doubt. Robert Wallace, minister of the New North Church in Edinburgh, who supported Hume's candidacy, argued that the *Treatise* as an anonymous and juvenile performance should not be admitted as evidence of Hume's beliefs. The implication is clear: if Hume's beliefs at the time of his candidacy had been certainly known to be those of the *Treatise,* then his supporters would have had to agree with his opponents. But if in this respect Hume's professed surprise at the opposition to him provides further evidence of his lack of candor in his presentation of himself in Scottish society, this is not the case with his clearly genuine reaction of astonishment upon learning of Hutcheson's opposition. And it was in his anonymous defense of his candidacy and of the views expressed in the *Treatise,* published in May 1745 as *A Letter from a Gentleman to his Friend in Edinburgh,* that Hume asserted the concurrence of his moral philosophy, as expressed in the *Treatise,* with Hutcheson's.

We may at least suspect, therefore, that Hutcheson believed that Hume's belief in their fundamental agreement rested upon Hume's having in part misunderstood Hutcheson's standpoint. It is illuminating to consider their very different attitude to Cicero and more particularly to the *De Officiis.* Cicero's writings were canonical texts for Scottish seventeenth- and eighteenth-century education. Hume would have encountered Cicero at Edinburgh, first in his first-year rhetoric course and then, if William Law followed common Scottish practice, in Law's moral philosophy classes. And he exhibited throughout his life and throughout his published work an extensive knowledge of and agreement with Cicero's philosophical writings. So did Hutcheson, and their disagreement in the construal of the *De Officiis* is therefore all the more notable.

Hume in his letter of 1739 to Hutcheson had treated the *De Officiis* as presenting a catalog of the virtues preferable to that presented by the puritan author of *The Whole Duty of Man.* He was to reiterate this preference in *An Enquiry Concerning the Principles of Morals* (appendix IV, footnote to para. 266). And it is clear, therefore, that Hume understood Cicero in *De Officiis* to have claimed to provide the same kind of complete practical specification of the moral life which the author of *The Whole Duty of Man* had also claimed to supply. Indeed Hume's complaint in the *Enquiry* was precisely that the latter had constrained the expression of the moral sentiments within too narrow a system.

That Hutcheson took a quite different view of *De Officiis* Hume almost certainly did not know. For Hutcheson published nothing on this topic in his lifetime. It was only in the posthumously published Latin and English versions of the *Institutio,* in which are to be found the essentials of the lectures which he gave at Glasgow, that he warned against the misinterpretation of *De Officiis.* And perhaps indeed it was Hume's view of Cicero which occasioned this warning: "The design of Cicero's books *de officiis* which are so very justly admired by all, has been mistaken inconsiderately by some very ingenious men, who speak of these books as intended for a compleat system of morals or ethics. . . ." But, so Hutcheson points out, Cicero was avowedly in this work following "the *Stoicks*" who "made such difference between *virtue,* which they counted the sole good, and the *officia,* or external duties of life, that they counted these duties among the *things indifferent,* neither morally good nor evil." *De Officiis* is thus not, according to Hutcheson, about virtue or the virtues; it is intended for those persons in higher stations, already instructed in virtue, to teach them how to "so conduct themselves in life, that in perfect consistence with virtue they may obtain great interest, power, popularity, high offices and glory" (Introduction, *Institutio*).

That Hume and Hutcheson should have understood Cicero somewhat differently from each other is scarcely surprising. Cicero had proved through a long history that his writings could be put to a variety of purposes by authors of very different and incompatible standpoints. Augustine, first inspired to his lifelong pursuit of philosophical enquiry by Cicero's *Hortensius,* had used his reading of Cicero in so many ways that Cicero became one of the relatively small number of ancient authors indispensable to medieval scholars. But in the renaissance of the fifteenth and sixteenth centuries Cicero became a source for a type of humanism antagonistic to the Augustinian tradition, although his writings remained part of the shared stock of accepted texts for scholars of every standpoint, including those whose Augustinianism was of the Calvinist kind.

Hume's presbyterian upbringing, particularly as a student in Edinburgh, had thus, as we have already seen, familiarized him with the appeal to Cicero, and Peter Jones has identified the range of philosophical topics in his treatment of which Hume either certainly did or may have drawn upon theses or arguments of Cicero (*Hume's Sentiments: Their Ciceronian and French Context,* Edinburgh, 1982, pp. 29–41). But although it is clear that Hume had read widely in Cicero, his firsthand reading of the texts was supplemented and influenced by the account of Cicero in Pierre Bayle's *Dictionnaire historique et critique* (2 vols., Rotterdam, 1695 and 1697), that sourcebook—especially in its enlarged second edition (Rotterdam, 1702)—for so many eighteenth-century writers. Cicero had of course understood the law of nature as promulgated entirely by a reason which instructs and commands the passions of the virtuous person, and this view is so much at odds with Hutcheson's theory of the moral sense that it was only to be expected

that Hutcheson would have to discriminate between the practical advice to actual and potential officeholders of *De Officiis,* which he accepted, and Cicero's moral epistemology, which he would have had
to reject.

Yet since Hume's moral epistemology was, if anything, more at odds
with Cicero's than was Hutcheson's, we might have expected Hume to
repudiate Cicero in this area too. Hume, however, was almost certainly
following Bayle, who in his remarks about Cicero's views in his dictionary article on Ovid (I owe this insight to Peter Jones, op. cit., p. 5)
describes Cicero as referring to "l'esclavage de la raison" to the passions in a sentence which became in the 1739 English translation: "reason had become the slave of the passions," a striking anticipation of
Hume's own view. It is Bayle, then, rather than Cicero whom Hume
is influenced by at this point, and in the perspective afforded by Bayle,
the sharp contrast between Cicero's view of reason and Hume's may
well have seemed less important than it is.

Hume thus draws upon Cicero in ways very different from those who
in the eighteenth century continued or revised the Stoic tradition. In
the four essays representing ancient philosophical standpoints—'The
Epicurean,' 'The Stoic,' 'The Platonist,' and 'The Skeptic'—which he
published in 1742, it is clearly the skeptic, a skeptic about conclusions
of metaphysical debate, not about the fundamentals of morality, who
most clearly represents Hume's own attitudes. And in this revival of
Academic skepticism Hume was once again genuinely close to Cicero,
a good deal closer indeed than Hutcheson ever was. For it was in the
way in which Hume was able to combine a mitigated metaphysical skepticism with a lack of skepticism in moral matters that the largest difference between Hume and Hutcheson appeared. This difference was due
at least in part to the differing extent to which each was influenced by
his allegiance to the way of ideas. Hume's allegiance was at once more
thoroughgoing, more philosophically sophisticated, and derived from
a much wider course of reading than was Hutcheson's. It was of course
not only a matter of wide reading, but it was at first that and at least
that. Where Hutcheson had used not only Shaftesbury but also Locke
and Malebranche for his own purposes, Hume immersed himself in
both these latter authors in a way that Hutcheson had never done, as
also in both Descartes and Berkeley. He also made himself familiar with
both the original Port-Royal writers and with J.P. Crousaz's attempted
modernization of the Port-Royal logic in his *La logique, ou système
de réflexions qui peuvent contribuer à la netteté et à l'étendue de nos
connaissances* (1712). His view of the history of philosophy, whatever

it may have been at the time when he completed his undergraduate studies, became in general, and not only in relation to Cicero, that supplied by Bayle.

Peter Jones, noting how few of the authors upon whose resources Hume drew were actually named by Hume (op. cit., p. 10), points out that both Locke and Descartes name even fewer names. What Jones does not add, but might have, is that consistent allegiance to the way of ideas by its very nature excluded acknowledgment of fundamental intellectual indebtedness to philosophical writing. All the materials for any particular author's account of perception, thought, knowledge, the passions, the will, and the beliefs giving expression to these have to be drawn, whether the particular author's version of the way of ideas is Cartesian or empiricist, from the stock of impressions and ideas present to and in the consciousness of one single individual mind, that of the author. The first-person point of view is not only that with which, from the standpoint of the way of ideas, we have to begin, but that within which everything, including what we know of others, has to be comprehended as no more than some presented aspect of my impressions and ideas.

It was this radically first-person point of view which Hutcheson in fact had never adopted. Hume assumed it systematically with the opening sentences of Book I of the *Treatise*. The author of the only review of the *Treatise* of any length, that which appeared in a London magazine, the *History of the Works of the Learned* (November and December 1739) complained, "This work abounds throughout with *Egotisms*. The Author would scarcely use that Form of Speech more frequently if he had written his own Memoirs." What had escaped the notice of the generally obtuse author of that review was the fact that every philosophical work by a consistent adherent of the way of ideas cannot be anything but his or her own memoir.

Hume's central problem in structuring the *Treatise* must then have been that of how to move from the egotisms of Book I to the social relationships of the moral arena of Book III, which are susceptible of characterization and explanation only in the terms available and specific to a third-person observer. Hume's solution to this problem is provided by the doctrine of the passions in Book II, but in order to understand that doctrine as a solution to this particular problem, it is necessary to say a little more about the dimensions of the problem. One way of doing so is in terms of the issue posed for Hume by the concept of personal identity.

Identity is socially ascribed. To be one and the same person is to satisfy the criteria by which others impute identity, and their criteria of identity govern and are embodied in their ascriptions of responsibility and accountability. The responsibility of each person is what can be imputed to that person as an originating cause, extending through the time during which there is a true first-person account of his or her doings and sufferings to be given, and he or she can be held answerable in respect of such an account. Since the moral and practical life of societies always requires such responsibility and such accountability, and since the moral and practical concepts of a society are always articulated as members of a more or less coherent set in which the use of a variety of evaluative and practical judgments presupposes the applicability of the concepts of responsibility and accountability, there is no society in which the possession of a publicly usable, third-person, more or less complex conception of personal identity is not presupposed in everyday discourse. But if we shift our point of view from this third-person standpoint to the first-person standpoint espoused by the adherents of the way of ideas, matters are quite otherwise.

Since from the standpoint of the way of ideas my account of myself can draw only upon what is presented to and from a first-person standpoint, *my* impressions and *my* ideas, and therefore all socially ascribed conceptions disappear from view, anything which could constitute my personal identity necessarily also disappears from view. Between the different states and episodes of the self a variety of relationships can be discerned, but nothing other than or over and above these. Hence any belief in personal identity which is more than a belief in such relationships comes to seem a philosophically unwarranted fiction, as it does to Hume in Section VI of Part IV of Book I of the *Treatise*. So the account of social and moral judgments and relationships in Book III evidently and inevitably presupposes, although it never provides explicit statement of, a belief in personal identity; and yet belief in personal identity has apparently been deprived of rational justification by the argument of Book I. How then is the transition to be made?

It is made by and in the theory of the passions propounded in Book II. Book II begins where Book I begins, with a reassertion that "all the impressions of the mind may be divided into *impressions* and *ideas*" and the identification of "the passions and other emotions resembling them" as "secondary, or reflective impressions," which "proceed from some of these original ones, either immediately or by the interposition of its idea." Passions, however, have a property which differentiate them from primary impressions. They are not only states and occurrences, which as such have causes, but some of them also have a directedness internal to them, a directedness upon intentional objects—Hume does not use the idiom of intentionality, but it is entirely appropriate—which are ideas specific to particular types of passion. Those passions in which an idea is an essential component of the passion Hume calls the indirect passions, and it is these which play a central part in generating those actions which constitute the exchanges and transactions of social life.

Central to these are on Hume's account the passions of pride and humility, which, "tho' directly contrary, have yet the same object. This is self . . ." (*Treatise* II,i,2). It is true that Hume at the first introduction of the concept characterizes the self in terms drawn from Book I and thus from the way of ideas: "that succession of related ideas and impressions, of which we have an intimate memory and consciousness." But this self as an intentional object of the regard of pride and humility is from this point onward treated as a unitary and unified object. Yet this self, *my* self, which is that of which my idea informs my passions of pride and humility, is not the only self standing in a crucial relationship to those passions.

It is on Hume's view the actions of others, understood as signs or symptoms of their characters (III,iii,1), which are among the principal causes of each particular person feeling pride or humility. For pride is closely linked to the desire for a good reputation (II,ii,1). And the qualities in which we take pride are the very same as those for which we seek the admiration of others and they ours. So pride elicits, or at least seeks to elicit, what Hume calls love. And humility correspondingly elicits hatred. What we prize in ourselves is the object of our pride; what we prize in ourselves when presented as the same quality belonging to another is the object of our love. Hume's conceptions of love and hatred are thus not independent of his conceptions of pride and humility. Love and hatred therefore require the same conception of personal identity as that required by pride and humility: "As the immediate *object* of pride and humility is self or that identical person, of whose thoughts, actions, and sensations we are intimately conscious; so the *object* of love and hatred is some other person, of whose thoughts, actions and sensations we are not conscious" (II,ii,1).

The passions of each person are therefore inescapably characterized in part as responses to others who are in turn responding to us. So in the reciprocities and mutualities of passion, whether harmonious or antagonistic, each self conceives itself as part of a community of selves, each with an identity ascribed by others. Personal identity as socially imputed has emerged from the characterization of the passions, and to that extent the way of ideas has been left behind. And it was by way of this treatment of the passions and his consequent adoption of a standpoint which the way of ideas could not itself provide that Hume moved from the metaphysical skepticism, even if a mitigated skepticism, of Book I to the nonskeptical moral positions of Book III, a contrast with which it is now clear (largely because of David Fate Norton *David Hume: Common-Sense Moralist, Sceptical Metaphysician,* Princeton, 1982) every interpretation of Hume must come to terms.

In restoring the self to its social identity in Book II, by means of his account of the complex intentionality and causality of the passions, Hume believed himself to be following Hobbes, Shaftesbury, Mandeville, and Hutcheson in giving an account of the constitution of universal human nature and of human society as such, although of course he also believed—and rightly—that his account was superior to any of theirs. But in fact the social relationships, whose characterization emerges in the discussion of the passions, and which is then extended and sustained in the discussions of moral judgment and of the virtues and vices of Book III, are specific to one particular type of social and cultural order, and perhaps it could not have been otherwise. For the directedness of the passions within social life has generally to be toward objects particularized in some specific cultural and social idiom. What humiliates is never insult in general, but always an insult of some particular type having some particular significance for the inhabitants of some particular culture; what causes pride is never some good quality in general, but always some particular example of this quality developed, educated, exhibited, and valued in culturally specific ways and socially specific circumstances. In not perceiving that what he took to be universal was to a significant degree local and particular, Hume was at one with most of his contemporaries, perhaps indeed at one with most human beings most of the time. The interest lies not so much in the type of error which Hume made as in the consequences for his own specific doctrines. What then were the highly specific social and cultural forms and attitudes which the Hume of the *Treatise* falsely identified with human nature as such? To what type of social and cultural order did they belong?

It was first of all and most obviously a type of social order to which the expression of pride and its obverse was central. What according to Hume, as we have already noticed, moves us in others to either love or hatred is able to do so only because and insofar as it moves us to pride or humility regarding ourselves. And, moreover, our primary judgments of virtue and vice, those which depend in no way upon reasoning, but which express those pleasures and pains which have taken the place of Hutcheson's moral sense, are no more and no less than expressions of pride and love, humility and hatred. So Hume declares "that these two particulars are to be consider'd as equivalent, with regard to our mental qualities, *virtue* and the power of producing love or pride, *vice* and the power of producing humility or hatred" (III,iii,1).

We confront then a type of social order in which persons are evaluated by reference to those of their qualities which are the objects of pride and humility both in themselves and in others. Which qualities are the objects of pride? They are very various, and Hume finds no unifying principle among them except their relationship to pride. So that it is simply a surd fact about the type of social order which Hume is portraying, both that pride—and its cognate passions—fixes value and that the particular qualities which Hume catalogs are the objects and causes of pride. They include mental qualities: "wit, good-sense, learning, courage, justice, integrity"; bodily qualities: "beauty, strength, agility, good mein, address in dancing, riding, fencing, and . . . dexterity in any manual business or manufacture"; and also "Our country, family, children, relations, riches, houses, gardens, horses, dogs, cloaths . . ." (II,i,2).

Yet simply as objects of pride, when these qualities are our own, or of love, when they belong to others, these qualities are not valued in independence of each other. Men take pride in the qualities of friends and relatives, but not if they are poor. "As we are proud of riches in ourselves, so to satisfy our variety we desire that every one, who has any connexion with us, shou'd likewise be possest of them, and are ashamed of any one, that is mean or poor, among our friends and relations" (II,i,9). Men take pride not only in their persons but also in "houses, equipage or furniture" (II,i,5), insofar as they are both beautiful and minister to utility: "The order and convenience of a palace are no less essential to its beauty, than its mere figure and appearance" (II,i,8). Men take pride in the antiquity of their families but prefer to do so when "their ancestors for many generations have been uninterrupted proprietors of the same portion of land . . ." (ibid.) and when inheritance has been wholly in the male line. Men may take pride in "dexterity in any manual business or manufacture," but as between the maker and the owner of something it is the owner whose pride receives attention, as when Hume remarks that "the first mechanic, that invented a fine scritoire, produc'd pride in him, who became possest of it . . ." (II,i,3), and that unsurprisingly, since "the relation, which is esteem'd the closest, and which of all others produces most commonly the passion of pride, is that of *property*" (II,i,10).

Property and the rules for its safeguarding and transmission—the rules which on Hume's view specify the content of justice—thus are made the focus for pride, love, hatred, and humility. Our passions according to Hume are such that they produce in us a definition of our interests in terms of our relationship to property, and it is as propertied or unpropertied in particular ways and to particular degrees that we participate in those social exchanges and transactions whose outcome is either the increase or diminution, or at least the sustaining or the undermining, of the pride and love felt by particular individuals. The rights of property are absolute. There is and can be no standard external to them in the light of which some particular distribution of property could be evaluated as just or unjust (III,ii,6). Justice on this view serves the ends of property and not vice versa.

A system in which pride in houses and other such possessions, and in one's place within a hierarchy, is the keystone of a structure of reciprocity and mutuality, in which property determines rank, and in which law and justice have as their distinctive function the protection of the propertied, so that principles of justice provide no recognizable ground for appeals against the social order: this is the type of social and cultural order portrayed by Hume in the *Treatise* as exhibiting the characteristics of universal human nature, but it is also of course the type of social and cultural order described by Roy Porter as constituting the highly specific way of life of the eighteenth-century English landowning class and its clients and dependents. What Hume presents as human nature as such turns out to be eighteenth-century English human nature, and indeed only one variant of that, even if the dominant one (see the references to Roy Porter *English Society in the Eighteenth Century,* in chapter XI above).

Hume in the *Treatise* thus used materials provided by his own development and transformation of the way of ideas, in the most philosophically sophisticated version of that way which was ever to be achieved, to articulate in philosophical terms the concepts and theses embodied in the thought and practice of the dominant English social and cultural order. It was from the standpoint afforded by this articulation that he entered into two separate debates, that in the wider international philosophical arena in which he challenged positions as various as those of Locke, Clarke, and Wollaston in England, of Pascal and Malebranche in France, and of Berkeley in Ireland, and that internal Scottish debate between the remaining protagonists of the Scottish traditions of thought still rooted in the seventeenth century and those for whom Scotland had no viable future except by integration into and assimilation to the commercial, financial, political, social, and cultural

ways of a wider and essentially English world. Hume in his theory as
well as in his own life was a thoroughgoing assimilationist, second
only in influence perhaps to Adam Smith. Important light is thrown
on this not only by the essays in which Hume advocated particular
policies in the spheres of economics and politics but also by two other
later expressions of Hume's fundamental point of view: his literary
judgments and his *The History of England.*

E. C. Mossner (*The Life of David Hume,* second edition, Oxford,
1980, p. 386) speaks of Hume's motive in defending the Scottish poet
William Wilkie as springing from "patriotic impulses." But in fact the
work of Wilkie—who was the minister of the parish of Ratho in Midlothian—which Hume praised and defended against a hostile review
was the nine books of the *Epigoniad,* a poem based on the fourth book
of the *Iliad,* which was nothing but an inferior imitation of Pope. And
the poetry of the blind Thomas Blacklock, also praised by Hume as
a Scottish poet, comprised nothing but facile echoes of the English poets
read to him in his childhood, among whom Addison and Pope figured
largely. Hume showed no interest at all in quite another side of Wilkie's
work, that which was to issue in 'The Hare and the Partan,' published
in a book of fables a number of years after Hume's death, in which
Wilkie wrote in the Scots vernacular of Midlothian. And that is to say,
Hume praised Scottish poets only for becoming as like English poets
as possible.

In parallel fashion in *The History of England* he condemned Scottish actions and institutions for being unlike English actions and institutions, or rather for being unlike those English actions and institutions which either in their spirit or their efforts could be understood
as precursors of the social order whose dominance was finally established by the Williamite revolution of 1688, that same social order whose
key aspects reappear in Hume's moral and political philosophy as properties of universal human nature. From the vantage point afforded by
a narrative constructed to exhibit the progress toward that social order,
the affairs of Scotland necessarily appeared as a set of marginal episodes, episodes characteristically exhibiting deviant passions reinforced
by systematic misunderstandings of the relation of passion and interest
to principle. The presbyterians of the 1640s appear in Hume's most
favorable comment as "rigid churchmen," the covenanting rebels as
"fanatics" and "enthusiasts." Stair's extraordinary achievement in jurisprudence is invisible to Hume, doubtless because it had no effect on
English history.

What is manifest in the judgments of the *History* is latent in those of the *Treatise*. The standpoint which underlies and informs both Hume's own particular judgments in the *Treatise* and the type of evaluative judgment which he describes as expressive of the passions is the standpoint presupposed by the shared evaluative vocabulary of the dominant English social order. And it is crucial to Hume's account of evaluative and practical judgments that individuals within such a social order are able to make use of one and the same shared evaluative vocabulary. How is such a vocabulary made possible?

Every particular evaluative and practical judgment is of course the expression of some one particular individual's particular passion or passions. But the common vocabulary in which such judgments are framed, and which enables us to respond to the judgments as well as to the actions of others in our own judgments and actions, depends upon and is itself an expression of the agreement and concurrence of the passions of each with those of others in those patterns of reciprocity and mutuality which constitute the transactions of a society. Judgments deviant from the socially established norms are the outcome of deviant passions, passions which tend to disrupt the harmonies of social exchange. Every one of us is upon occasion liable to have somewhat deviant passions, by reason of our particular interests and our partiality for our own persons, property, and kin. In consequence we are apt to give expression to the interested partiality of our own passionate attachments rather than to that impersonal standpoint from which each individual expresses in his or her judgments allegiance to the ordered mutuality and reciprocity of the passions. Were this tendency to be unchecked, it would dissolve those agreements in passion and action which are presupposed by the shared idiom of evaluation, by the language of the virtues and the vices. But this tendency is in fact checked generally, although not always, by the influence of general rules which correct our evaluations, so that we speak from just such an impersonal standpoint in respect of time, place, and attachment and not from our own partial and limited perspective (*Treatise* III, 3, 1). The word 'perspective' is in place here, since the general rules governing our evaluations function much as do those perceptual rules, such as the rules of perspective, by means of which we make judgments of shape, size, and distance in such a way that everyone can agree in their judgments, rather than merely judging how shape, size, and distance appear to each individual from his or her particular point of view.

So practical judgments on Hume's account presuppose a socially ordered reciprocity of the passions, a reciprocity in which the key moments are to be characterized in terms of pride, humility, love, and hatred and those relationships to property, kinship, and hierarchy which play such a large part in providing the objects and causes of those passions. The characteristics of one very specific type of social order are thereby presupposed by those judgments, and to defend Hume's account it would be necessary to show of every actual social order that either it is of that type or it deviates from that type only in ways which can be explained by Hume's own principles. Hume's philosophical psychology does not provide foundations for Hume's political philosophy, independent of that political philosophy. The fundamental theses of the political philosophy are themselves presupposed by the account of the ordered interrelationship of the passions. It is worth in this respect comparing Hume to Aristotle.

Aristotle's accounts of practical reasoning and of justice require, so I argued earlier, one specific type of context, that of a society structured in terms of systematic forms of activity, within each of which specific goods are acknowledged and pursued, while within the overall social order the activity of politics provides for the inhabitants of the *polis* ways of understanding and pursuing those goods in an integrated way, so that the good and the best may be achieved. Hume's accounts, by contrast, require, so I have suggested, a very different type of context, that of a society structured in terms of modes of satisfaction of desire, within which transactions and exchanges for mutual benefit are organized, while the overall social order provides formally and informally for the sustaining and enforcement of the relationships embodied in such transactions and exchanges. Aristotle's presupposed social context is one in which evaluation is primarily in terms of the achievement of the ends of activity; Hume's is one in which evaluation is primarily in terms of the satisfaction of consumers. The individual envisaged by Aristotle engages in practical reasoning not just *qua* individual, but *qua* citizen, of a *polis;* the individual as envisaged by Hume engages in practical reasoning *qua* member of a type of society in which rank, property, and pride structure social exchanges.

The parallel between the relationship of Aristotle's theorizing to its social context and of Hume's to its may be carried one stage further. Each was arguing in a situation in which the members of his society confronted large-scale alternatives. Aristotle confronted both Isocrates' simpleminded renewal of the Periclean vision and the impact of Persian ways upon Macedonians and Greek alike. Hume similarly had to argue against conceptions of the social order and its potentialities derived from seventeenth-century Scottish theology and law. The *Treatise* was thus a political document, and not only in those parts where issues of government and allegiance are explicitly discussed. Had it upon publication been read widely and accepted within Scotland—as it was not—it would have subverted among that country's educated classes some of the central loyalties essential to maintaining a distinctive Scottish cultural identity. And it would have done so by means of an account of justice and of the place of reasoning in the genesis of action deeply at odds not only with that of the Calvinist Aristotelians of the Scottish seventeenth century but even more so with that of Aristotle himself. To the details of that account I therefore now turn.

XVI

Hume on Practical Rationality
and Justice

The materials out of which Hume constructed his account of the place of reasoning in the genesis of action were in very large part derived from his Hutchesonian inheritance. What immediately precedes action is an exertion of the will (*Treatise* I, i, 4). Hutcheson had accepted what he called, referring to the third and fourth books of Cicero's *Tusculan Orations,* "the old division of motions of the will into four general species, Desire, Aversion, Joy and Sorrow" (*System* I, i, 5). And for Hume an exertion of the will is nothing other than an effect of that pain or that pleasure which gives rise immediately to the direct passions: "Of this kind are, *desire and aversion, grief and joy, hope and fear* (*Treatise* III,iii,i).

It is then impressions of a certain kind which constitute the passions, direct or indirect, and it is these which generate action. Just as nothing but a passion or passions can produce an action, so nothing can inhibit the operation of a passion except some other passion. The most important type of conflict which can occur between passions is that between a calm passion and a violent passion. The calm passions are of two kinds: "either certain instincts originally implanted in our natures, such as benevolence and resentment, the love of life, and kindness to children; or the general appetite to good, and aversion to evil, consider'd merely as such" (*Treatise* II,iii,3). That is to say, they are passions directed to certain highly general types of good, of a kind which human beings tend to pursue recurrently throughout their lives. The violent passions by contrast are expressed in immediate strong reactions to particular situations, such as the receiving of injury from another or the immediate threat of any grievous ill. They make me heedless of "all consideration of pleasure and advantage to myself." Hence we count it a virtue, the virtue of strength of mind, to cultivate and encourage the calm passions in the interests of inhibiting the violent. For the violent passions run counter to our interests.

It is thus clear that we can and do reason *about* the passions. But no reasoning, including that reasoning, can ever move us to act. Reason is able, when exercised, to pronounce upon whether ideas do or do not have corresponding impressions—that is, to inform us as to matters of fact—and to exhibit the relationship of one idea to another— that is, to inform us as to mathematical truth and the validity of inferences. But even its exercise in these latter respects has to be motivated by some passion. From a Platonic or an Aristotelian point of view, as we observed earlier, rationality is exercised in its own specific forms of activity with its own goods, its own ends internal to that activity. From that point of view the passions must indeed be educated and redirected so that the human being *qua* rational being may pursue those ends specific to that rationality. But according to Hume there are and can be no such ends. The ends to which rational activity of any kind whatsoever is directed are and must be set before it by some passion.

Truth in itself according to Hume, apart from the utility of our knowing particular truths or the satisfaction of curiosity in particular circumstances, is not an object of desire. But how then are we to explain the pursuit of truth in philosophy? Hume's answer is that the pleasure of philosophy and of intellectual enquiry more generally "consists chiefly in the action of the mind, and the exercise of the genius and understanding in the discovery or comprehension of any truth" (*Treatise* II,iii,x). Philosophy, so it turns out, is like the hunting of woodcocks or plovers; in both activities the passion finds its satisfaction in the pleasures of the chase. And this view of philosophy accords very well with the place which we have seen accorded to it within the dominant English and Anglicizing social and cultural order. Philosophy is a delightful avocation for those whose talents and tastes happen to be of the requisite kind, just as hunting is a delightful avocation for those whose talents and tastes are of *that* kind. What philosophy cannot have on this view is anything resembling the place accorded to it within the older Scottish tradition, for which it is—in conjunction with theology— the discipline whose enquires provide the rational justification for the metaphysical and moral principles constitutive of the political and social order. It is a commonplace that Hume aspired to deprive theology of its traditional centrality. It is less often remarked that philosophy, on a Humean view, itself becomes a less than central activity.

Reason then cannot motivate us. And the passions, which do motivate us, are themselves neither reasonable nor unreasonable. "A passion is an original existence, or, if you will, modification of existence, and contains not any representative quality, which renders it a copy of any other existence or modification" (*Treatise* II, iii, 3). Passions are thus incapable of truth or falsity. They can neither have nor lack rational warrant, can neither be congruent nor inconsistent with the requirements of reason. Eighteenth-century English readers of Hume did not quarrel with *this* thesis, presumably because they recognized in Hume's account of the passions the structure of their own modes of feeling. Modern critics of Hume have, however, often attacked him on just this point, arguing that emotions presuppose or embody judgments or beliefs in a way which is excluded by Hume's account (see, for example, Jerome Neu *Emotion, Thought and Therapy*, Berkeley, 1977, especially pp. 36–45). The mistake here is to suppose that what Hume or other eighteenth-century writers meant by "passion" is what twentieth-century writers mean by "emotion."

Passions are on Hume's view preconceptual and prelinguistic. This is what enables him to speak of "the correspondence of *passions* in men and animals" (*Treatise* II, i, 12). Judgments or beliefs may of course be contingently conjoined to and associated with passions, but the passion is, as I have already noted, quite distinct from the judgment or belief and has quite different properties. By contrast what *we* call an emotion is a complex patterned regularity of dispositional and occurrent feeling, judgment, and expression in action, such that each element is a necessary part of the whole. Hence the relationship of judgment or belief to emotion is not the purely contingent association of judgment and passion which Hume described. The transition from the idiom of the passions to that of the emotions in the course of the two centuries which divide us from Hume required a set of transformations in the conceptualization of the relationship of feelings to action which were in part a condition of and in part a result of the work of the great novelists. It was they who helped to move us from the society of Humean sentiments—sentiments are simple conjunctions of judgment and passion, whether calm or violent—inhabited by the characters of Sterne, Fielding, and Henry Mackenzie through the patterned integration of feeling, judgment, and action achieved both in the descriptions of the great nineteenth-century novelists and in the type of person who actually inhabited the social world which they described, into that even more complex world of emotion about emotion which, by making the elements of those patterns into intentional objects, disintegrated patterned emotion into moments or segments of consciousness, in one way in the work of Joyce, in another in that of Virginia Woolf.

To understand that history is to distance ourselves in one way both from Hume's world and from Hume. It enables us indeed to discern a possible Humean thesis about modernity according to which the complexities of post-Humean feeling are held to conceal those elements of mental life so much more clearly introspectible by the seventeenth- or eighteenth-century adherent of the way of ideas. And it rescues Hume's account of the passions from anachronistic criticism. But it is also important not to misunderstand Hume's account in another way.

Anthony Kenny has asserted that "Hume denies very explicitly the intentionality of the passions," citing the passage from *Treatise* III, iii, 3, which I quoted earlier (*Action, Emotion and Will,* London, 1963, p. 25). Were this so, the passions could not have, as on Hume's account they clearly do, intentional objects. The vocabulary of intentionality was, as I remarked earlier, not available to Hume, but he understands the objects of particular passions on particular occasions as internal to those passions in just the way that intentionality requires. The passion itself is not a representation, but it contains a representation of its object, one which we may characterize, although the possessor of the passion need not, by such phrases as "to get such and such" or "to have such and such" or "to do such and such" or "to be such and such." Passions are directed toward objects, and it is only because and insofar as they are so directed that they motivate human actions in one way rather than another.

Commentators who have recognized the intentionality of Humean passions have, however, sometimes wrongly ascribed to Hume the view that internal to passions there are judgments. But not only is there nothing in Hume's text to warrant this, it runs clean contrary to the whole tenor of his account. A passion is not any kind of reason for action, and it affords or provides no kind of reason for action (for an example of the type of view with which I am disagreeing see Donald Davidson 'Hume's Cognitive Theory of Pride' in *Essays on Actions and Events,* Oxford, 1980, p. 286; for a discussion of Davidson's views for their own sake, rather than as exegesis of Hume, see Annette Baier 'Actions, Passions and Reasons' in *Postures of the Mind,* Minneapolis, 1985). So a passion cannot provide a premise for a piece of practical reasoning. How then are the passions related to the utterance of moral or other evaluative or practical judgments?

Such judgments afford expression to some passion. In judging this or that action to be virtuous or vicious, for example, I give expression to my response to that which caused in me pride or love in the one case, hatred or humility in the other. That response expresses a passion which, unless either some other more powerful passion inhibits it or external circumstances prevent the appropriate bodily movements, will move me to action. My judgment is not therefore a reason on the basis of which I act. The passion and not the judgment moves me. Thus my action, on Hume's view, stands in no logical or quasilogical relationship to either my evaluative judgment or my passion. Passions stand to actions as nonrational causes to effects, and insofar as reasoning does play a part in the genesis of action, it is a part quite distinct from that of any passion, calm or violent, direct or indirect. What part then is left for reasoning to play?

Reason's first practical role is to answer a type of question which the passions provide motives for asking and answering. These questions concern the existence and nature of those things which the passions move human beings to get or to have and the possibility of those actions or characteristics which the passions move human beings to want to do or to be. Second, reason prescribes means for the achievement of such ends set by the passions and judges those means as more or less efficient in terms not only of the particular end in view but also in terms of other ends which the agent is or may be moved to pursue.

In the genesis of those actions in which reasoning plays a part the sequence of events must then be as follows if Hume's account is correct. Some particular passion moves someone to get or have or do or be something or other. That person reasons: I shall get or have or do or be such and such, if, or if and only if, or only if so and so comes to be the case; acting in the following way will make it the case that so and so. The person then acts, the passion having been guided by this type of reasoning, so that it produces an action answering to the action-description in the conclusion of the reasoning. In the initial premise the description of what will satisfy the passion is of course supplied by the passion itself and the appropriate set of conditionals will be determined by the agent's beliefs about the relevant class of causal regularities. The conclusion specifies the action required if the passion is to be satisfied, but it is not itself productive of that action. It is the originally motivating passion, now more adequately informed by the reason of what it must do to satisfy itself, which alone produces the action. Moreover it must be the case, if we are to follow Hume's account, that what moved the reason itself to action in such a type of case, thus giving reason a practical function, was itself passion. So reason acts only at the command of passion, and the conclusions to which reason thus moved leads have force only so far as force is given to them by passion. It was no rhetorical exaggeration of his own view when Hume asserted, "Reason is, and ought only to be the slave of the passions and can never pretend to any other office than to serve and obey them" (*Treatise* II, iii, 3).

Such reasoning—and I have of course been constructing the overall pattern of reasoning put to the service of practice from the passages in the *Treatise* which I cited earlier—will have the same logical form as any other reasoning. Practical reasoning is distinguished from theoretical reasoning on Hume's view, neither by its content nor its form but only by the purpose to which it is put. So a piece of Humean practical reasoning—and here interestingly Hume is for once at one with Aristotle—will always be a performance on a particular occasion. Moreover Hume agrees with Aristotle in one other way. In Humean reasoning, just as much as in Aristotelian, there is no place for a premise of the form "I want such and such." Why not?

It is of course for very different reasons from those adduced by Aristotle. It is on Aristotle's view the case that my taking pleasure or pain in something is never by itself a reason, let alone a good reason, for action, even when I may in fact be moved to action by the prospect of either pleasure or pain. It is only insofar as I take it that the achievement of some pleasure or the avoidance of some pain will provide me with some good that I am afforded a reason for action, and then my reason is of the form "Achieving such and such is good for such and such persons." On Hume's view, although it is indeed the case that the prospect of pleasure or pain moves me to action, what moves me is the relevant passion—in modern idiom the relevant desire—and not its expression in an utterance of the form "I want such and such." I may indeed give expression to my passion by such a type of utterance, but the utterance in and by itself, as I noted earlier, plays no part in generating action. So we must understand such utterances as having an expressive rather than an assertive function. They are, in another modern idiom, emotive utterances.

Just because they are such, and therefore provide signs for others of passions of kinds which regularly produce certain types of action, they may and commonly do provide occasion for response by others, by moving those others to judgment and to action. But here it is crucial to emphasize the difference between modern emotivist moral philosophies, which often and with some degree of justification declare themselves Hume's heirs, and Hume's own standpoint. For it is crucial to Hume's account of practice and of the respective places of passion and reasoning within it—and this makes Hume's account very different from that of either Stevenson or Ayer—that the vocabulary of evaluation, approbation, and disapprobation is a shared vocabulary by means of which agreement in the content of evaluative judgment gives expression to that concurrence, those reciprocities, that harmonization of the passions without which there would be neither morality nor social order. To be moved by a desire or any other passion which is discrepant with or disruptive of that harmonization is to warrant the ascription to myself, by myself as well as by others, of some type of vice. And insofar as I am so moved, I shall render myself the more liable to the frustration of my passions by the actions of others.

Hence the person who aspires to success in satisfying passion and desire will have to include in his or her reasoning about means and ends reasoning about his or her own passions and the regularities which relate those passions to each other and to actions, and in similar fashion about the passions of others and the regularities which relate their passions and actions to our own. Such reasoning informs us that, as we saw earlier, we shall be more and more often frustrated if we do not develop the calm passions at the expense of the violent. And just as in so strengthening the calm passions we become more sociable, so the practice of sociability in turn strengthens the calm passions. In understanding this we understand how in Hume's portrait of human nature reasonableness, the attribute of the person whose reason serves his or her calm passions, sociability, and amiability go together. The same social and psychological experiences teach us both that we have, as creatures of our passions, an interest in social reciprocity and harmony and that the development of amiability toward and sympathy with the other members of our society serves that interest. This is true of all societies in all times and in all places. Hence on Hume's view my regard for ancient Roman virtue expresses the same approbation which I also express in respect of modern English virtue; the qualities which I approve in past and alien societies are those which in my own world serve my interest.

Yet when we examine what it is of which we approve, a problem appears concerning, not our natural first-order responses to each other's actions and attitude, but our approbation of those artificially contrived and constructed institutions which constitute and enforce the rules of justice and those concerning allegiance to government. For at first sight neither interest nor sympathy seems able to explain why each one of us should approve of the rules of justice or of the administration of those rules by government. It cannot be private interest or self-love which leads us to treat justice as a virtue: "For shou'd we say, that a concern for our private interest or reputation is the legitimate motive to all honest actions; it wou'd follow, that wherever that concern ceases, honesty can no longer have a place. But 'tis certain, that self-love, when it acts at its liberty, instead of engaging us to honest actions, is the source of all injustice and violence; nor can a man ever correct those vices, without correcting and restraining the *natural* movements of that appetite" (*Treatise* III, ii, 1). Thus the kind of connection between the passions and adherence to a rule or principle, which the Humean account requires, cannot be established by way of any conception of self-interest.

A regard for the public interest cannot supply the requisite type of connection either. Only after our regard for justice is established, and in the light of that regard, is a connection between justice and the public interest established. Moreover, on occasion a violation of the rules of justice may do no damage to the public interest; yet we condemn such violations as unjust as much as we do any others. And third, most of us act out of regard for the public interest on relatively infrequent occasions in our lives, while a concern for justice and injustice is part of the fabric of everyday experience.

The sympathy which we do indeed feel for particular others on occasion will not furnish a motive for a regard for the rules of justice whomsoever they may protect. "In general it may be affirm'd, that there is no such passion in human minds, as the love of mankind, merely as such, independent of personal qualities, of services, or of relation to ourself" (*Treatise* III, ii, 1). Yet, so Hume reminds us, I am required to obey the rules of justice even when it is my enemy or a vicious or useless person who will benefit.

Hume in setting his problem in this way had successfully separated himself from all those accounts of justice which had connected human allegiance to justice too directly to individual self-interest. But both by the way in which he set his problem, and by the way in which he provided the materials for its solution, he achieved a good deal more than this. The problem of justice was according to Hume centrally a problem about the rules of property and their enforcement, and as I have already suggested, it was property conceived of in one highly particular way. For what the rules of justice are taken to enforce is a right to property unmodified by the necessities of human need. The rules of justice are to be enforced in every particular instance not only in the face of violations of public and private interest, but also in the face of that traditional figure, the person who can only succor his family, those for whom he or she has immediate responsibility, by doing what would otherwise be an act of theft. The tradition of moral thinking which was shared both by Aquinas and by the characteristically Scottish thinkers saw in such an act no violation of justice, but Hume, asking the rhetorical question "What if I be in necessity, and have urgent motives to acquire something to my family?' sees such a person as one who may look to the generosity of "a rich man," but not one who provides an example in the light of which he ought to modify his conception of justice. Thus Hume, as I pointed out earlier, anticipates Blackstone and shows himself no follower of Stair. But this was not the only way in which he defined his attitude to property.

The origin and fundamental justification of the enforcement of such rules of property lies, according to Hume, in the effects upon social life of the absence or lack of such rules and of means for their enforcement. For it is the goods of property, "the enjoyment of such possessions as we have acquir'd by our industry and good future," which by their very existence create social instability, exposing us "to the violence of others" who seek them for themselves. For in respect of such goods "there is not a sufficient quantity of them to supply every one's desires and necessities" (*Treatise* III,ii,2). Hume is clearly here speaking not only of those human situations in which sheer scarcity engenders competition for goods necessary for bare survival. For he treats this ground for the justification of the rules of property and this explanation of them as holding for all times and places, prosperous as well as unprosperous, ever since the rules were first artificially contrived. And it is in this light that we must consider his thesis that enforceable rules of property function to effect social stability. For social instability and disruption might seem to arise in certain circumstances precisely from the enforcement of the rules of property

A central thesis of the tradition of political theory which derived from Plato and Aristotle was that too great inequalities in property characteristically generate social conflict, that injustice in the form of acquisitiveness characteristically produces such inequalities, and that the enforcement of rules of property protecting such inequalities and such injustice may in consequence cause disruption and even revolution. Hume was of course well aware of this tradition and of the examples in ancient Greek and Roman society to which its defenders appealed. His account of those examples was to appear in the essay "Of Commerce," published in 1752. Hume recognized that "their want of commerce and luxury" and "the great equality of fortunes among the inhabitants of the ancient republics" contributed to the strength of such republics, and he even recognized that although according to his own standards the inhabitants of those republics were deprived of the happiness which he supposed to be the outcome of economic growth, what is felt to be burdensome and what is not might be differently evaluated by "a people addicted to arms, who fight for honour and revenge more than pay, and are unacquainted with gain and industry as well as pleasure." But when in the light of these considerations Hume posed the question of whether an eighteenth-century ruler might not "return to the maxims of ancient policy," he replied "that it appears to me, almost impossible; and that because ancient policy was violent, and contrary to the more natural and usual course of things."

The natural and usual course of things is that in which the passions achieve their most extensive and most enduring satisfaction. Reasoning about the passions — reasoning which must of course itself be motivated by some passion — enables us to identify the types of occasions on which by satisfying some passion or passions immediately, I may in fact prevent myself from achieving the more extensive and enduring satisfaction of my passions of which I am in fact capable. Putting the conclusions of such reasoning to the service of the calm passions will enable me to calculate where my long-run interest and the long-run interest of those with whom I interact lie. It is just such reasoning which on Hume's view informs us of the advantages of policies of economic growth over "the maxims of ancient policy," whether as advanced in the ancient world or by the seventeenth- and eighteenth-century admirers of the ancient world, such as Fletcher of Saltoun; and it is just such reasoning which Hume advanced both to explain and to justify the rules of justice, conceived as he conceived them, and the obligations imposed by those rules, understood as he understood them.

The passions which underlie the contrivance of the artificially constructed institutions of justice and property — and these two according to Hume are so intertwined that one cannot have the one without the other — are of two kinds. We and everyone else want on the one hand to be able to prosecute our ends, whatever they are, within a framework which provides peace, order, and stability in the transactions and exchanges of social reciprocity; we and everyone else are, however, also on occasion moved by the immediacies of particularity and self-interest to disrupt that peace, order, and stability. We suffer, that is, from contrary passions. Nevertheless, reason assures us that it is by giving the primacy to the former set of passions and by controlling and, if necessary, frustrating the latter that our and everyone else's most extensive and enduring satisfaction will be achieved. So Hume concludes that "however single acts of justice may be contrary, either to public or private interest, 'tis certain, that the whole plan or scheme is highly conducive, or indeed absolutely requisite, both to the support of society, and the well-being of every individual" (*Treatise* III, ii, 2).

When therefore someone condemns an action as unjust, they are expressing that in themselves which is in key part the outcome of their reasoning. A regard for justice is not among "the natural sentiments of humanity" (*Treatise* III, ii, 5), and "those impressions, which give rise to this sense of justice, are not natural to the mind of man, but arise from artifice and human conventions" (*Treatise* III, ii, 2). How then do such impressions arise? The factual conclusion of our reasoning, that justice serves an interest, the service of which will provide the most extensive and enduring satisfaction of our passion, can move us according to Hume's psychology only if and insofar as there is annexed to it a sentiment of the rightness of justice and the wrongness of injustice. This sentiment is awakened and reinforced in us by the way in which our displeasure at acts of injustice in which we ourselves are the wronged party extends through sympathy to an "uneasiness" at acts of injustice in which others, even distant and unrelated others, are wronged. If we look back to the arguments of Book I of the *Treatise,* we shall understand that it is sympathetic imagination which is at work here in associating the verdict of reason with an impression of the kind which moves to action and expresses itself in judgments concerning virtue and vice. So Hume explains both what he calls "the *natural* obligation to justice, *viz.* interest" and what he calls "the moral obligation" (*Treatise* III, ii, 2).

It was perhaps Hume's recognition of these two species of obligation which engendered a controversy among Hume's modern readers about the interpretation of the remarks with which he brings the first section of Book III of the *Treatise* to a conclusion: "In every system of morality, which I have hitherto met with, I have always remark'd, that the author proceeds for some time in the ordinary way of reasoning, and establishes the being of a God, or makes observations concerning human affairs; when of a sudden I am surpriz'd to find, that instead of the usual copulations of propositions, *is,* and *is not,* I meet with no proposition that is not connected with an *ought,* or an *ought not.* This change is imperceptible; but is, however, of the last consequence. For as this *ought,* or *ought not,* expresses some new relation or affirmation, 'tis necessary that it should be observ'd and explain'd; and at the same time that a reason should be given, for what seems altogether inconceivable, how this new relation can be a deduction from others, which are entirely different from it" (*Treatise* III, i, 1). Hume adds that attention to this point "wou'd subvert all the vulgar systems of morality, and let us see, that the distinction of vice and virtue is not founded merely on the relations of objects, nor is perceiv'd by reason."

Controversy over the interpretation of this passage has focused upon two issues. The first concerned the substance of Hume's thesis. Was Hume here denying that *any* conclusion requiring an "ought" for its statement could be deduced from premises whose copula is "is"? Or was he only asserting that extreme care must be taken not to locate such inferences at points in moral argument at which they have no justifiable place? Those who argued in favor of the former position had recognized correctly that conclusions concerning what Hume calls "moral obligation" could not be validly deduced or otherwise inferred from entirely nonmoral premises. Those who argued in favor of the latter had recognized with equal correctness that Hume's conclusion about what he calls "the natural obligation to justice" not only can be inferred but was inferred by Hume himself from factual premises, including premises stating facts about human passions (see for a selection of articles on both sides *The Is-Ought Question,* ed. by W. D. Hudson, London, 1964).

A second issue concerned the target of Hume's barbs. Was he here attacking rationalist philosophers, as he clearly was elsewhere in the same section of the *Treatise?* Or was he also attacking as "the vulgar systems of morality" those systems of Christian precepts for which he had come to have such distaste? I have elsewhere suggested that the latter was the case ('Hume on "is" and "ought"' *Philosophical Review* 48, 1959, reprinted in Hudson, op. cit.), and I am still inclined to believe that Hume had *The Whole Duty of Man* in mind. But the arguments of Professor D. D. Raphael ('Hume's Critique of Ethical Rationalism' in *Hume and the Enlightenment,* ed. W. B. Todd, Edinburgh, 1974, especially pp. 26–27) that Hume's principal intention here was to express agreement with Hutcheson's attack on Samuel Clarke (compare section II of the *Illustration on the Moral Sense* printed together with the *Essay,* London, 1728, especially p. 246, where Hutcheson calls "ought" "another unlucky word in morals") are compelling. Yet this should not distract us from recognizing the crucial place that factual reasoning about the passions and the way to satisfy them in extensive and enduring fashion has in the construction and sustaining both of the artificial virtues themselves and of the secondary artifice by which these primary artifices are reinforced.

This secondary artifice is government. What makes government necessary is that the virtue of justice and the closely allied virtue exhibited in the keeping of promises—the institution of promising is also of course an artifice—are not by themselves sufficient to ensure adequate obedience to what Hume calls the "three fundamental laws of nature" (*Treatise* III,ii,8), that which prescribes stability in the possession of property, that which prescribes its transfer from one person or persons to another or others by consent, and that which prescribes the keeping of promises. Such obedience is endangered because human beings "are always much inclin'd to prefer present interest to distant and remote; nor is it easy for them to resist the temptation of any advantage, that they may immediately enjoy. . . ." The threat that this presents is only considerable, however, when once possessions have multiplied. So long as "possessions, and the pleasures of life are few"— and Hume always takes it for granted that the multiplication of possessions and the multiplication of pleasures go together, as indeed they must for those whose culture teaches them to take pleasure above all in possession—the laws of nature which human beings have invented will generally be observed. But where possibilities for the exercise of acquisitiveness open up, the threat to the observance of the fundamental laws of nature becomes such that the invention of government is required in order to ensure it. Government of whatever form justifies itself insofar as it protects life and property and provides for the enforcing of contracts. A well-contrived government is one in which these purposes are served, no matter what its constitutional form. But "nothing is more essential to public interest than the preservation of public liberty" (*Treatise* III, ii, x), and it is in a "mix't government," such as that of the United Kingdom, where power is shared among king, lords, and commons that public liberty is preserved, for each part of the constitutional whole has an interest in protecting certain rights and privileges against any encroachment by the others.

"It may now be affirmed of civilized monarchies," Hume was to write in an essay published in 1741, "what was formerly said in praise of republics alone, *that they are a Government of Laws, not of Men.* They are found susceptible of order, method, and constancy, to a surprising degree. Property is there secure; industry encouraged; the arts flourish; and the prince lives secure among his subjects, like a father among his children" ("Of Liberty and Despotism," retitled "Of Civil Liberty" from its 1758 republication onward). Moreover, although it is not unqualifiedly true "that commerce can never flourish but in a free government," commerce is more apt to decay in conditions of unfreedom "not because it is there less *secure,* but because it is less *honourable.*" But those who eschew commerce eschew riches and in so doing diminish the range of satisfactions of the passions. Hence Hume argues in favor of whatever will lead to economic growth within the framework of an anglicized Great Britain and in so doing returns us to some of the central theses of his practical psychology: "In general, we may remark, that the minds of men are mirrors to one another, not only because they reflect each other's emotions, but also because those rays of passions, sentiments and opinions may be often reverberated, and may decay away by insensible degrees. Thus the pleasure, which a rich man receives from his possessions being thrown upon the beholder, causes a pleasure and esteem; which sentiments again, being perceiv'd and sympathiz'd with, encrease the pleasure of the possessor; and being once more reflected, become a new foundation for pleasure and esteem in the beholder. There is certainly an original satisfaction in riches deriv'd from that power, which they bestow, of enjoying all the pleasures of life. . . . But the possessor has also a secondary satisfaction in riches arising from the love and esteem he acquires by them, and this satisfaction is nothing but a second reflexion of that original pleasure, which proceeded from himself. This secondary satisfaction or vanity becomes one of the principal recommendations of riches, and is the chief reason why we either desire them for ourselves or esteem them in others" (*Treatise* II, ii, 5).

Pleonexia has at last made a social world for itself to be at home in, acquiring for itself that esteem which *time* once conferred. Hume's values and the values of that English and anglicizing society for which Hume speaks represent a striking reversal of what as recently as the latter part of the seventeenth century has been inculcated in Scottish universities through the reading of the *Nicomachean Ethics* and the *Politics*. And that reversal could not have occurred without the social and economic changes of Karl Polanyi's "great transformation." But it could not have been presented in an intellectually cogent manner without Hume's elaboration of a radically new way of conceiving both the relationship of reason to the passions and the nature of the passions. What Hume's discussion of government and of economic matters make clear is how, although reason does indeed always serve the ends of some passion or passions, that fact itself provides premises for a type of extended reasoning without the assistance of which the passions would be continually balked and frustrated in their search for satisfaction.

This reasoning, in its most elaborated and extended form, *is* the reasoning of the second and third books of the *Treatise*. It is because of this that Hume was able to claim for his work that to read it and to assimilate its conclusions would be not merely to enhance one's theoretical understanding but also to improve oneself practically and morally. So he concludes his work by asserting that the relationship of the philosopher to the practical person resembles that of the anatomist to the painter. The anatomist by his accurate dissections and accounts of the parts of the body enables the painter to design more elegantly and correctly. So too "the most abstract speculations concerning human nature, however cold and unentertaining, become subservient to *practical morality;* and may render this latter science more correct in its precepts, and more persuasive in its exhortations" (*Treatise* III, iii, 6).

Yet it is important to Hume's argument as a whole that although the *Treatise* extends and elaborates that reasoning about the relationship of means to ends which informs artificial virtues such as justice and institutions such as government, in so doing what it extends and elaborates, what at its core it replicates, is a structure of reasoning which informs the actions and allegiances of ordinary nonphilosophical practical persons. That such persons cannot usually articulate the relevant chain of reasoning for themselves is, on Hume's account, no objection to imputing it to them. "Few persons can carry on this chain of reasoning: 'Government is a mere human invention for the interest of society. Where the tyranny of the governor removes this interest, it also removes the natural obligation to obedience. The moral obligation is founded on the natural, and therefore must cease where *that* ceases; especially where the subject is such as makes us foresee very many occasions wherein the natural obligation may cease, and causes us to form a kind of general rule for the regulation of our conduct in such occurrences.' But tho' this train of reasoning be too subtle for the vulgar, 'tis certain, that all men have an implicit notion of it, and are sensible, that they owe obedience to government merely on account of the public interest; and at the same time, that human nature is so subject to frailties and passions, as may easily pervert this institution, and change their governors into tyrants and public enemies" (*Treatise* III, ii, x).

So Hume imputes to the unsubtle vulgar a prior, even if inexplicit, comprehension of reasoning identical with his own in the preceding section of the *Treatise,* concerning first the nature of the obligations to government and second the conditions under which such obligations no longer obtain. The vulgar agree with one another and with Hume in reasoning thus, but this agreement in reasoning presupposes and derives from a deeper agreement at the level of those fundamental and natural approbations and disapprobations which give expression to the passions of those who participate in the ordered interchanges and exchanges of social life. Agreement in passion and sentiment underlies and issues in agreement in reasoning, and consequently in still further agreement in the identification of interests. These agreements find expression in habits of judgment informed by those general rules noticed earlier, which are at work in correcting idiosyncratic particularities in our moral and practical judgments, just as the rules of perspective are at work in correcting idiosyncracies of perception. So that a will to and a habit of agreement with others within the dominant social framework itself is a motivating factor. Such a will and habit require the adoption by each person of one and the same impartial point of view in his or her use of the idioms of the virtues and the vices, so that instead of giving expression to the differing and variable partialities of each person, it serves rather to express certain constant, socially approved attitudes. "Experience soon teaches us this method of correcting our sentiments, or at least of correcting our language . . ." (*Treatise* III, iii, 1).

Hume's statement of the extent of these agreements is very striking; he does indeed go so far as to commit himself to an assertion of the general infallibility of moral judgment. In the section of the *Treatise* where he is arguing that "the obligation of submission to government is not deriv'd from any promise of the subjects" he declares that he will prove it "from the universal consent of mankind . . ." (*Treatise* III, ii, 8). He goes on to assert that "it must be observ'd, that the opinions of men, in this case, carry with them a peculiar authority, and are, in a great measure, infallible. The distinction of moral good and evil is founded on the pleasure or pain, which results from the view of any sentiment, or character; and as that pleasure or pain cannot be unknown to the person who feels it, it follows, that there is just so much vice or virtue in any character, as every one places in it, and that 'tis impossible in this particular we can ever be mistaken." In this of course Hume once again echoed Hutcheson; and, like Hutcheson, he had thereby set himself the task of explaining what at least appear to be large moral and practical disagreements. But the problem was somewhat more acute for Hume than it had been for Hutcheson, since both in the political parts of the *Treatise* and in those which have a bearing upon religious issues Hume's avowed purpose is to confute the erroneous views advanced by the protagonists of what either are or have been significantly and even in some cases dangerously influential standpoints. Hume thus has to dissipate any impression that his own writings provide an important set of counterexamples to his claim that there exists a universal moral and practical consensus.

At first sight Hume has a simple and straightforward reply to this accusation. Those who apparently dissent from the universal consensus are those who have made some philosophical mistake in understanding what virtue or vice are, or what the nature and function of government is, or what the truth in religious matters is. After all, Hume immediately before the passage just quoted says that no one need "wonder, that . . . I should now appeal to popular authority, and oppose the sentiments of the rabble to any philosophical reasoning." And later on in "A Dialogue," published together with *An Enquiry Concerning the Principles of Morals* in 1752, Hume extended his thesis from philosophers to whole cultures: "You see then . . . that the principles upon which men reason in morals are always the same; though the conclusions which they draw are often very different. That they all reason aright with regard to this subject, more than with regard to any other, it is not incumbent on any moralist to show. It is sufficient that the original principles of censure or blame are uniform, and that erroneous conclusions can be corrected by sounder reasoning and larger experience." How adequate is this as a diagnosis of the source of dissent of those whom Hume had classified as deviant and argued against in the *Treatise?*

They were in fact adherents of a number of very different standpoints, and if we look beyond the *Treatise* to the *Enquiry,* to "A Dialogue" and elsewhere, their number was to be extended still further. In the case of some of them the source of their dissent in what Hume took to be a philosophical mistake is quite clear. So it was with his rejection of the definition of justice advanced by the adherents of Roman and Roman-Dutch jurisprudence (*Treatise* III, ii, 6)—that is, among others, the protagonists of the Scottish legal system—and so it was with his attack upon those Whigs who wished to base legitimate obedience to government upon some original act of consent (*Treatise* III, ii, 8, and "Of the Original Contract," published in 1748). So it was also with his attack upon Jacobite views of the right of succession to the throne. For the legitimacy of a particular ruler has, on Hume's view, nothing whatsoever to do with the origins of the form of government which gives power to the ruler. What makes government legitimate is most of all "long possession": "we shall find that there scarce is any race of kings, or form of commonwealth, that is not primarily founded on usurpation and rebellion . . ." (*Treatise* III, ii, 10), but time legitimates. Yet long possession, although sufficient, is not necessary. "When there is no form of government establish'd by *long* possession, the *present* possession is sufficient to supply its place. . . ." To these Hume added as sources of legitimacy the right of conquest, the right of succession, usually by male primogeniture, and the right conferred by positive laws. But it was present and immediately past possession to which he appealed in justifying the revolution of 1688: "Tho' the accession of the *Prince of Orange* to the throne might at first give occasion to many disputes, and his title be contested, it ought not now to appear doubtful, but must have acquir'd a sufficient authority from those three princes, who have succeeded him upon the same title."

Hume thus rested the legitimacy of King William III's accession to power in 1688 more solidly upon the right conferred by possession of power than he did upon the right of the governed to rebel against intolerable tyranny, the kind of tyranny which represents a failure of government to respect that public liberty which is a safeguard against government's functioning otherwise than in the interests of the "mutual advantage and security," which provides government with its sole justification. For Hume, although he spoke of the revolution of 1688 as having "had such happy influence upon our constitution," declared also that it was not his purpose to show that the right of resistance to tyranny was in fact justly exercised in 1688. What I take it that he wished thereby to emphasize was that whether this latter justification be invoked or not, the right of present and immediately past possession was by itself sufficient to show that Jacobite claims were erroneous.

What was the source of the Jacobite error? It was in essence the same as that of the protagonists of Roman law. Just as the latter supposed, on Hume's view erroneously, that there are principles of justice which hold independently of and antecedently to any established *status quo* distribution of property, so the Jacobites supposed that there are principles of dynastic right which could hold independently of and antecedently to any established *status quo* possession of the power to govern. Such alleged principles cannot be derived from the interest that everyone has in the *status quo* of property and the *status quo* of power, and principles which cannot be so derived cannot furnish human passions with motives for action.

That, by the standards afforded by Hume's moral philosophy, the Jacobites had indeed made a philosophical mistake is clear. Its dangerous practical consequences, however, arose from the passions attaching themselves to their mistaken principle, so that the Jacobites *were* moved to act in a way inimical to the general interest in the institutions of property and government. That they were so moved does at first sight create a still further problem for Hume's account, more specifically, for his account of the relationship of reason to the passions. For it now appears that Hume has to allow that the passions of those intellectually convinced of the truth of a particular philosophical theory, albeit in the Jacobite case a mistaken one, may be redirected and reordered in accordance with that theory. Must we therefore conclude that reason has turned master and the passions slaves?

Moreover the question may be raised: What if the philosophical theory in question is not as easily to be shown to be in error from Hume's own premises as was Jacobite political theory? Hume raised this question himself in the closing passages of "A Dialogue," where he considers the examples of Pascal and of Diogenes the Cynic, both of whom lived by a rule of life incompatible with what Hume had declared to be the universal judgment of mankind concerning virtue and vice. Pascal exemplified what a scornful Hume, agreeing at least in this with the presbyterian clergy, was to castigate in the *Enquiry* (section IX, part I) as "the monkish virtues": "celibacy, fasting, penance, mortification, self-denial, humility, silence, solitude. . . ." These alleged virtues — they are in fact, according to Hume, vices — Pascal justified by an appeal to Augustinian theology. It is true that what Hume calls Pascal's "most ridiculous superstitions" were regarded by Pascal himself as rationally indemonstrable and held only by faith. Yet in Book I of the *Treatise* Hume had after all written that "all probable reasoning is nothing but a species of sensation. 'Tis not solely in poetry and music, we must follow our taste and sentiment, but likewise in philosophy. When I am convinc'd of any principle, 'tis only an idea, which strikes more strongly upon me" (I, iii, 8). And he had further argued that more than one universally held belief is indemonstrable. Thus Pascal's religious dissent both from what Hume takes to be his own worldly good sense and from the social consensus for which Hume has constituted himself the spokesman may seem to be one to which Hume can make no effective reply. Hume's objection to Pascal, it may seem, can be no more than the voicing of one sentiment in opposition to another. Yet from Hume's own standpoint this is not so; for quite apart from and in addition to any philosophical mistakes which a dissenter such as Pascal may have made, the dissenter has additionally condemned him or herself by the very fact of his or her dissent.

Consider the argument deployed by Hume in the essay in which he finally fulfilled the promise made in a footnote in the *Treatise* (III, ii, 8) to explain "In what sense we can talk either of a *right* or a *wrong* taste in morals, eloquence or beauty. . . ." That essay, "Of the Standard of Taste," published in 1757, advanced two central theses: that the principles of taste are "universal, and nearly, if not entirely the same in all men . . ." *and* "that the taste of all individuals is not upon an equal footing, and that some men in general, however difficult to be particularly pitched upon, will be acknowledged by universal sentiment to have a preference above others."

The arbiter of taste is he or she who articulates that to which in the longer run the majority assent, expressing in their consensus the concurrence of their sentiments and passions. And the dissenter is he or she who violates this consensus, even if winning immediately some short-lived approbation. "Authority or prejudice may give a temporary vogue to a bad poet or orator; but his reputation will never be durable or general." The rough and the barbarous, the bigot and the superstitious, all fail by this standard, and Corneille's art is rejected on the same ground as Pascal's morality. That ground is consensus.

A consensus of sentiment and passion, and a consensus of reasoning about justice and about government, which both presupposes and derives from the consensus of sentiment and passion, is thus established historically over time. And the norms of both passion and reasoning are exhibited by writing the history of that establishment. Such a history will have to show how certain forms of the expression of passion, in both belief and action, are relatively local and temporary phenomena, so differing from the relatively universal and enduring forms of expression of the consensus; and characteristically such local and temporary phenomena will also be exhibited not only as aberrant relative to the consensus but also as threatening to its stability. This is the task which Hume set out to perform in *The Natural History of Religion,* where he recounted the development of religion from the barbarous ignorance of early religion, through "the adulation and fears of the most vulgar superstition" which generate theism, to the modern enmity to the reasonable of the dominant forms of religion.

This history of aberration is, however, only the negative counterpart of that development in which the invention of government — it sprang originally, so Hume believed, from the exercise of military authority: "Camps are the true mothers of cities (*Treatise* III,ii, 8) — promotes not only the very consensus of passion, sentiment, and reasoning which provides its own justification but the material wealth which enables the society embodying that consensus to flourish. "Thus bridges are built; harbours open'd; ramparts rais'd; canals form'd; fleets equip'd; and armies disciplin'd; everywhere, by the care of government, which, tho' composed of men subject to all human infirmities, becomes by one of the finest and most subtle inventions imaginable, a composition, that is, in some measure exempted from all these infirmities" (*Treatise* III, ii, 7). It was what he took to be the political history of just such a consensus, progressing unsteadily toward just such an outcome, threatened from time to time by a variety of aberrant religious passions, but surviving so far at least those threats, which Hume narrated in *The History of England.*

In *The History of England* Hume's vocabulary of approbation and disapprobation presupposes a shared community of sentiment and reasoning in which both the author and his readers participate. The norms to be vindicated by the writing of the history inform the mode of its writing. Hume's history is not, does not even entertain the possibility of being, evaluatively neutral. The evaluative standpoint of the history is of course that of the dominant order inaugurated in England after 1688. Hume as author no longer pretends, as he did under cover of the anonymity of the *Treatise,* to be English; he merely writes of Scotland as if it were a foreign country. It is instructive to consider the way in which Hume's judgments on seventeenth-century Scotland in chapter LIII of the *History* echo his judgments on the inhabitants of pre-Roman Britain in his first chapter.

The key adjective in chapter I is "barbarous" as contrasted to "civilized"; and when Hume speaks in chapter LIII of the mode of preaching of the presbyterian clergy, he calls it "the rhetoric, however barbarous, of religious lectures and discourses," having earlier characterized the Scottish audience which was receptive to that rhetoric as "uncultivated and uncivilized." The disorderly political life of the ancient Britons sprang from "a relish of liberty" and expressed itself in the way in which "Each state was divided into factions within itself . . ."; the rebelliousness of seventeenth-century Scotland exemplified "fanaticism mingling with faction" and "private interest with the spirit of liberty." The ancient Britons were subdued by "the terrors of their superstition"; the seventeenth-century Scots were aroused to rebellion because they were "inflamed with religious prejudices."

Hume's narrative, his judgments of approbation and disapprobation, and his reasoning about the prudence or imprudence, justice or injustice, of the various characters in his narrative thus express the standpoint of a social order which has excluded from itself so far as possible both the barbarous turbulence which attended its origins and the disruptions which have threatened its later stability. In so narrating, judging, and reasoning Hume narrates, judges, and reasons as a member of that self-same type of social order. And it is now possible to understand how from a Humean standpoint there is no other way to narrate, judge, or reason (for an extended discussion of and a different perspective upon Hume's commitments in this respect see Donald W. Livington *Hume's Philosophy of Common Life,* Chicago, 1984).

What on Hume's view makes reasoning about justice sound reasoning is, in key part, that it is reasoning shared by at least the vast majority of members of the community to which one belongs. What makes the utterance of judgments about virtue and vice effective is that they express not merely one's own individual responses but the responses shared and reciprocated by the same vast majority. So one reasons and judges in all moral and practical matters as a member both of a particular community and of a type of social order characteristic of all civilized peoples. Withdraw from human beings that reciprocity of shared responses and the consequent possibilities of shared reasoning and you withdraw also that type of social order in which the calm passions and the habits of response which express them restrain and overcome the violent passions. You thereby surrender the social order either to the superstitions of ancient barbarians or to the enthusiasms of the barbarous of modern times. The parallel at this point between Hume and Aristotle is notable.

Both present an account of practical rationality according to which the individual who reasons rightly does so *qua* member of a particular type of political society and not just *qua* individual human being. Both recognize of course that the kind of reasoning which merely matches means efficiently to ends can be exercised apart from membership in such a society. But to reason apart from any such a society is to have no standard available by which to correct the passions. On such central issues as the relationship of reason to the passions, the nature of the standards by appeal to which the passions are to be corrected, and the structure of practical reasoning, Aristotle and Hume have of course very different and largely incompatible views. But this incompatibility ought not to be allowed to obscure either the resemblances between their views or what those resemblances at least suggest: that practical rationality with a determinate structure is always informed by and itself informs the practices of some distinctive form of social order and that it is *qua* member of such a form of social order and not merely *qua* individual that someone exercises determinate practical rationality.

If this hypothesis is correct, then the fact that to each determinate form of practical rationality there corresponds a determinate conception of justice—and Hume's theorizing exhibits this connection as clearly as Aristotle's does—assumes added significance. Some differences and disagreements over justice and some differences and disagreements over practical rationality will, if this hypothesis is correct, be inseparable. The two will express one and the same conflict between rival social allegiances. So those who disagree with each other radically about justice will not be able to look to some neutral conception of rationality, by appeal to which they will be able to decide which of them is in the right. For the same or similar disagreements can generally be expected to appear on questions about the nature of practical rationality. And the political and social character of such disagreements will emerge clearly into view.

In eighteenth-century Scotland it had never been lost sight of. That

Hume in his account of the relationship of reason to the passions, quite as much as in his account of justice and of government, had assumed a socially and politically controversial stance which aligned him with some parties and tendencies in both Scottish and English affairs and set him immediately at odds with others was as patent to his readers, both of the *Treatise* and of his later works, as it was to Hume himself. And in a number of cases the response which Hume's stance invited was an unambiguous one. But in the case of the clergy and the educated laity of what became the Moderate party in Scottish Presbyterianism what was elicited was a large degree of ambivalence.

Hume on the one hand represented for them a challenge to and a subversion of their views of law and morality. Some modern commentators upon Hume have argued that the charge of skepticism about morality, leveled against Hume at times by ministers of the Moderate as well as of the Evangelical standpoint, must have rested upon a misreading of the *Treatise* in which the mitigated skepticism of Book I had been mistakenly ascribed to Book III also. And perhaps there was some degree of such misunderstanding. But it is much more to the point that Hume's account of morality was in fact deeply incompatible with the traditional Scottish view, according to which justice was precisely what Hume said it could not be, antecedent to all rules of property, and according to which it is theology which provides the most adequate understanding of morality. Hence Hume did indeed have to be excluded from any part in educating the young. And when he was a second time a candidate for a university chair, that of Logic at Glasgow in 1752, it was once again the ministers who played a key part in preventing Hume's appointment.

Yet Hume was also one of the most articulate and cogent spokesmen for the political and economic policies with which the moderate clergy and laity had identified themselves. He excelled in the kind of literary art which they valued so highly. And he had strong friendships among them, some dating from his younger days, some of later origin, friendships which as Hume, disappointed by his reception among the English, reidentified himself in greater and greater degree as a Scotsman made Hume a highly valued member of Moderate society. The outcome was to cast Hume in a role which he had not designed for himself. He was identified, and rightly so, as the antagonist *par excellence,* the philosopher whose views had to be defeated in open philosophical debate. He became the one thinker in opposition to whom decade after continuing decade Scottish philosophers had to frame their enquiries.

The earliest responses to Hume were not always of great merit. The anonymous publication in 1751 by Henry Home—who was to take the title of Lord Kames as a judge of the Court of Sessions a year later—of *Essays on the Principles of Morality and Natural Religion* was the first of any length. It was followed in 1753 by James Balfour of Pilrig's also anonymously published work *The Delineation of the Nature and Obligation of Morality,* which was a reply to the *Inquiry.* Balfour shortly afterward succeeded Cleghorn as Professor of Moral Philosophy at Edinburgh. At Aberdeen the foundation of the Philosophical Society in 1758 provided a forum for the discussion of Hume's philosophy. Thomas Reid wrote to Hume that "A little Philosophical Society here . . . is much indebted to you for its entertainment. Your company would, although we are all good Christians, be more acceptable than that of Saint Athanasius. And since we cannot have you upon the bench, you are brought oftener than any other man to the bar, accused and defended with great zeal but without bitterness." From those debates there emerged two major books, Principal George Campbell's *Dissertation on Miracles* in 1762 and Thomas Reid's *Inquiry into the Human Mind on the Principles of Common Sense* in 1764. Part of the importance of Reid's work was that it decisively changed the nature of the debate.

Two rival modes of social and cultural life had confronted each other in early eighteenth-century Scotland: one prizing the seventeenth-century Scottish past but recognizing the need to transform it so that the distinctively Scottish inheritance in religion, in law, and in education might be renewed as well as preserved; the other seeing no prosperous future for Scotland except as an increasingly anglicized part of the United Kingdom and repudiating in consequence, so far as might be necessary, the seventeenth-century past. Both parties accepted the revolution of 1688–90 and the Act of Union as happy events; both repudiated the alternatives represented by those heirs of the covenanters, the Cameronians and the Seceders. The crucial question which had confronted them was whether a philosophical justification for distinctively Scottish conceptions of theology, of law, of morality, and of education could replace the impoverished Aristotelianism of the seventeenth century which had been universally rejected.

It had been Hutcheson's task to undertake this task of justification by replacing the resources of the scholastic Aristotelianism in which he had first been educated with those afforded by Shaftesbury and by the way of ideas. It had been Hume's genius to understand that if once the fundamental principles and conceptions of the way of ideas are adopted, then what emerge are conclusions deeply incompatible with the central theses of Scottish theology and law, and with any conception of morality which embodies them. And in so doing, Hume, a philosopher eccentric in terms of the Scottish past, found himself articulating the principles of the dominant English social and cultural order, an order itself deeply inhospitable to philosophy, but inhospitable to philosophy in a way which Hume's philosophical theorizing had led him to applaud.

So Hume had declared "that there are in *England,* in particular, many honest gentlemen, who being always employ'd in their domestic affairs, or amusing themselves in common recreations, have carried their thoughts very little beyond those objects, which are every day expos'd to their senses. And indeed, of such as these I pretend not to make philosophers. . . . They do well to keep themselves in their present situation; and instead of refining them into philosophers, I wish we cou'd communicate to our founders of systems, a share of this gross earthy mixture . . ." (*Treatise* I,iv,7).

Hume thus constituted himself the philosophical champion of an essentially unphilosophical culture. There is, therefore, no paradox in the fact that his philosophy was much debated among those whose beliefs he aspired to refute and to subvert, but for a very long time little discussed — apart from some intellectually third-rate grumbling by Anglican theologians such as Warburton — among those whose beliefs and way of life he upheld and whose history he wrote.

Part of Reid's originality lay in his challenging Hume by appealing against Hume's philosophy to the principles of just those plain, unphilosophical persons who were so highly valued by Hume himself. Moreover, he appealed to that in those plain persons which is independent of the particularities of their history, their institutions, or the ordering of their passions, for he appealed to that in them which he claimed to be both constant and unvarying in all human nature and prior to all theorizing. So Reid never appealed to the Roman law tradition or to the scriptures in the way in which Hutcheson had done, and his prose style was one well designed to address an audience of any and every nationality, religion, politics, or culture. He does not speak in terms of the standards of some particular type of community either in the way in which Hume had done or in the way in which Aristotle had done. For agreement in fundamental principles does not on Reid's view derive either from agreement in passion and sentiment embodied in institutionalized exchanges or from an education in the virtues only to be provided by some one particular type of community; such agreement is not in fact derivative. All plain persons of sound

mind assent to one and the same set of fundamental truths as unde-
rived first principles, the truths of common sense, as soon as these truths
are elicited from the mind by experience. Those stigmatized as barbarians either from a Humean or an Aristotelian standpoint are on
Reid's view as much possessors of this set of fundamental truths as
anyone else, and indeed may be the more secure in that possession, in
that their grasp of those truths has not been endangered by misleading philosophical theorizing.

I have argued that on Hume's account, as on Aristotle's, the exercise of practical rationality—very different as their two accounts are—
requires a particular type of social setting. And I have also argued that
in each case the characterization of the relevant type of setting embodied a particular conception of justice. With Reid it was quite otherwise: the exercise of fundamental rationality, practical or theoretical,
was taken to require no particular type of social setting. Reid thus confronts us with what is a radical alternative to both Aristotle and Hume.
He was of course not the first to do so, and his books appeared in a
period in which a number of other such philosophical conceptions of
practical rationality as a property of individuals apart from and prior
to their entry into social relations were being elaborated, most notably
by Bentham in England and by Kant in Prussia. The multiplicity of
such conceptions is itself not unimportant. For in moving from the Scottish debates of the seventeenth and eighteenth centuries to the discussions of practical reasoning and justice in twentieth-century modernity
we not only move away from theories according to which the exercise
of practical rationality presupposes some kind of social setting, but we
move into a world in which the exercise of practical rationality, if it
is to occur at all, has to be embodied in social contexts of fundamental
disagreement and conflict.

XVII

Liberalism Transformed into a Tradition

The previous chapters have told parts of the history of three distinct traditions: that which runs from Homer to Aristotle and later passes through Arab and Jewish writers to Albertus Magnus and Aquinas; that which is transmitted from the Bible through Augustine to Aquinas; and that which carries the Scottish moral tradition from Calvinist Aristotelianism to its encounter with Hume. A tradition of enquiry is more than a coherent movement of thought. It is such a movement in the course of which those engaging in that movement become aware of it and of its direction and in self-aware fashion attempt to engage in its debates and to carry its enquiries forward. The relationships which can hold between individuals and a tradition are very various, ranging from unproblematic allegiance through attempts to amend or redirect the tradition to large opposition to what have hitherto been its central contentions. But this last may indeed be as formative and important a relation to a tradition as any other. Such was Hume's relationship to that Scottish tradition which emerged from the seventeenth-century alliance of a Calvinist version of Augustinian theology and a rereading of Aristotle. And when the Scottish tradition moved into its later stages —a tale not to be told here—its responsiveness to Hume was one of its key features. Nor can Hume himself be rightly understood except as someone defining himself in part through that opposition.

This Scottish tradition in its origins had reenacted, although in a very different way from the medieval, the relationship of Augustinianism to Aristotelianism. But it is important to reemphasize that for most of their history these two traditions of enquiry were not only distinct traditions but traditions in conflict. Aristotle after all had stood in a very different relationship to Plato than did Augustine with his debt to Plotinus, as Plato's heir, rather than to Aristotle. And the Aristotelian understanding of the human agent and of practical reasoning had no way of admitting into itself out of its own resources the Hebraic concepts of the Bible, let alone Augustine's concept of the will. It required Aquinas' constructive discovery of a mode of understanding more comprehensive than either tradition had possessed for it to be possible to integrate those two traditions. And it is a measure of their potentiality for conflict that very few indeed of the adherents of either tradition in the thirteenth century could see the point of Aquinas' enterprise.

These three traditions of enquiry all merit that description not just because of the continuities of debate and enquiry which they embodied but also because of the transmutations and translations which they were able to undergo at and through points of conflict and difference. A tradition becomes mature just insofar as its adherents confront and find a rational way through or around those encounters with radically different and incompatible positions which pose the problems of incommensurability and untranslatability. An ability to recognize when one's conceptual resources are inadequate in such an encounter, or when one is unable to frame satisfactorily what others have to say to one in criticism and rebuttal, and a sensitivity to the distortions which may arise in trying to capture within one's own framework theses originally at home in another are all essential to the growth of a tradition whose conflicts are of any complexity or whose mutations involve transitions from one kind of social and cultural order to another and from one language to another.

It is also part of the nature of traditions that their adherents cannot know in advance, whatever their own convictions or pretensions may be, how and in what condition their tradition will emerge from such conflicts and encounters. Their warranted confidence in their own tradition will of course increase as their tradition shows itself in successive encounters able to furnish the necessary resources and achieve the necessary transformations. But the perspective of a tradition originally rooted in contingent circumstance, arising out of problems, perplexities, and disagreements in some particular social order, articulated in terms of the particularities of the language and culture of that order, does not permit of any generalized confidence about the potential hospitality of other languages and cultures to the articulated statement of, let alone to allegiance to, that particular tradition. And that is to say that the standpoint of traditions is necessarily at odds with one of the central characteristics of cosmopolitan modernity: the confident belief that all cultural phenomena must be potentially translucent to understanding, that all texts must be capable of being translated into the language which the adherents of modernity speak to each other.

At one level this belief informs a variety of activities: the confident teaching of texts from past and alien cultures in translation not only to students who do not know the original languages but by teachers who do not know them either; the conducting of negotiations, commercial, political, and military, by those who suppose that not knowing each other's languages cannot debar them from understanding each other adequately; and the willingness to allow internationalized versions of such languages as English, Spanish, and Chinese to displace both the languages of minority cultures and those variants of themselves which are local, dialecticized languages-in-use. At another level this same belief appears in the form of philosophical theses about universal translatability.

Why and in what ways the standpoint of a tradition-constituted enquiry involves the rejection of all such theses will have to be made clear at a later point in the argument. But it will be important to bear in mind from the outset that there is always the possibility of one tradition of action and enquiry encountering another in such a way that neither can, for some considerable stretch of time at least, exhibit to the justified satisfaction of its own adherents, let alone to that of the adherents of its rival, its rational superiority. And this possibility will arise when and if the two traditions, whether embodied in the same language and culture or not, cannot find from the standpoint of either an adequate set of standards or measures to evaluate their relationship rationally.

We can begin to approach the problems involved in the evaluation of one tradition of enquiry by another by first considering the difference between the task of rationally evaluating rival and competing claims within one and the same tradition and that of evaluating similar claims when each has been developed within one of two very different and competing traditions. Consider in this light the difference between comparing in respect of their accounts of practical reasoning and of justice Aquinas with Aristotle or Aristotle with Plato or Hume with Hutcheson, on the one hand, and comparing Aristotle's or Aquinas' accounts of these matters with Hume's. In the first type of case we have a set of relatively unproblematic standards to which to appeal in making the comparison: How far does the later thinker solve either the problems posed by or the problems found insoluble by the earlier thinker? How far is the later thinker able to resolve incoherences in the work of the earlier? How far does the later thinker make available conceptual or theoretical resources which do not have the limitations of those of his predecessor? But with the latter type of case it is quite otherwise. Hume and Aristotle, for example, simply do not stand in the kind of relationship to each other in which later and earlier adherents of the same tradition stand.

Here instead we have accounts of practical reasoning and of justice which are advanced within very different conceptual frameworks, which employ quite different modes of characterization and argument, and which yet are clearly incompatible. What Hume takes to be just would on an Aristotelian view often be unjust; the conception of desert has a place in Aristotle's account which is denied to it in Hume's; on Aristotle's view reason conceived in one way is capable of governing and educating the passions, while on Hume's view reason conceived in quite another way can only be their servant. There are certainly coherent alternatives to being either an Aristotelian or a Humean, but anyone who is an Aristotelian is thereby committed to denying Hume's central claims and vice versa. How then are we to decide between these rival and mutually exclusive claims? Is there some neutral tradition-independent standard of a rationally justifiable kind to which we may appeal?

Two possible answers to this question reveal their inadequacy after a tolerably brief scrutiny. The first is that proposed by Thomas Reid and Dugald Stewart. Thomas Reid had argued against Hume that there are certain truths evident to almost every human being, denied only by those who are either of unsound mind or in the grip of some unsound philosophical theory. Our awareness of these truths is elicited by experience but is not derived from experience. In so arguing Reid had attempted to restore the appeal to evident first principles, so characteristic of the Scottish seventeenth-century tradition, but in the form in which Reid appeals to such principles tradition itself becomes fundamentally irrelevant. For if each of us, by him or herself out of our own inner resources, can know the truth of and cannot indeed acquire knowledge in any other way of those fundamental principles, knowledge of which is presupposed in all other knowledge, theoretical or practical, then tradition, at least in this regard, becomes functionless.

Stated as squarely and as boldly as Reid stated it, his thesis confronted an immediate charge of implausibility. Reid had asserted over against Hume an account of duty and obligation which makes our regard for them independent of desire, passion, or interest; there are on Reid's view two independent rational principles, one of which bids us to do what duty and obligation require and the other to do what will produce our own happiness, principles which, if rightly understood, coincide in their instructions. But while Reid could ascribe Hume's failure to recognize the independence of these two principles to Hume's having been misled by his unsound philosophical theorizing, it was more difficult for Reid to explain in the light of his own theory how plain people, innocent of philosophy, could apparently disagree upon the fundamentals of morality. For all such were held to be equally aware of the basic principles of morality.

This was one of the types of consideration which led Dugald Stewart, while accepting the core of Reid's doctrine, to substitute for Reid's phrase "the principles of common sense" his own "the fundamental laws of human belief." Stewart agreed with Reid that the uniformity of those laws and the underlying uniformity of the human mind is such that all human beings do indeed agree on the same basic moral principles, which are not inferred from or are reducible to anything more fundamental than themselves. This agreement would be manifest in their actual moral judgments were it not for the large differences in the physical and social environment of different societies which are such that one and the same set of moral principles require very different practical judgments. Other factors producing justifiable diversity of judgment are differences in "speculative opinions" and differences in what constitutes polite or deferential or friendly behavior in different societies (*Philosophy of the Active and Moral Powers,* in *Collected Works,* vol. I, Edinburgh, 1855, pp. 235–248).

Stewart thus followed Hutcheson, and such other followers of Hutcheson as Smith, Beattie, and indeed Hume himself, in holding that the appearance of variation and disagreement in moral judgment between different cultural and social orders is an illusion. On morality human beings in fact agree, and were we all similarly circumstanced in respect of culture, intellectual capacity, and our physical and social environments, this universal agreement would be manifest. Stewart's peculiar merit was to state this position more clearly, at greater length, and with more examples than had any of those predecessors.

His thesis was a factual thesis. If it is true, then the moral and practical judgments of every culture will exhibit a conjunction of universal and invariant moral and prudential (in the modern sense of "prudential") elements on the one hand and local, variable elements on the other. One is reminded inescapably in reading these parts of Stewart's work of what Aquinas says about *synderesis* and *conscientia* and about the primary and secondary precepts of the natural law. And this is presumably no accident. In looking back to Hutcheson — and while Stewart, like Reid, dissented from Hutcheson's moral epistemology, he, also like Reid, agreed with Hutcheson upon the substance of morality — Stewart unknowingly looked back also to some elements of the Scholasticism from which Hutcheson had inherited so much. But there are crucial differences.

What make *synderesis* and *conscientia,* when the latter is not in error, an expression of the principles of right reason, according to Aquinas, is that they are constitutive of that form of human life which alone is directed toward our *ultimus finis.* And in the virtuous person whose *prudentia* ("prudence" in the older, not in Stewart's, sense) has guided him or her toward that end, we have both a vindication of our identification of the content of the precepts of *synderesis* and an authority on how to discriminate them. For Stewart there is and can be no such secondary test available, and the importance of this becomes clear when we consider one crucial issue upon which Stewart disagrees with Aquinas. It concerns the extent to which our consciousness of even fundamental precepts may be subverted by the distractions and corruptions of evil, so that the wrongness of a whole class of actions may cease to be evident to us. Thus, according to Aquinas there are absolute and unconditional prohibitions which a whole culture may infringe without recognizing that it is so doing. Stewart was committed to denying this. His Baconian inductivism does not allow for this kind of error in those who are to supply the data for his generalizations. So if infanticide (an example which Stewart takes from Smith) or the killing of parents (an example which he takes from Locke) is sanctioned in some culture, this is for Stewart clear evidence that in some circumstances it is permissible or even obligatory to kill the very young or the very old. But the allegedly universal basic principles, as such examples accumulate, lose more and more of their specificity and turn out in the end to enjoin whatever in any culture people in the circumstances of that culture generally do. There is no room for widespread moral error. But in committing himself to this Stewart has not solved, but merely shifted, the problem of radical disagreement.

For now he has to account for the problem of such disagreement between those whose moral judgments are framed and tested on the assumption that large moral error is possible, such as Aquinas and indeed Aquinas' whole culture, and those whose mode of moral judgments does not allow for this possibility, such as Stewart and his own culture. This is to say, Stewart has to vindicate his theory of moral variation against at least one rival theory, and in so doing he confronts two distinct kinds of difficulty.

The first is that what was to have been an appeal against philosophical theories to the deliverances of reason to the consciousness of plain persons has now turned out to depend for its force on the outcome of a theoretical debate, and so has been deprived of what was seen by Reid as its distinctive merit. A second is that the empirical facts of moral disagreement are incompatible with Stewart's claims, not only because his counterfactual explanations are not adequate to account for the data concerning disagreement and variation between cultures (on both the empirical and the conceptual questions see R. Needham 'Remarks on the Analysis of Kinship and Marriage' *Remarks and Inventions,* London, 1976, and C. Geertz 'The Impact of the Concept of Culture on the Concept of Man' *New Views on the Nature of Man,* ed. J.R. Platt, Chicago, 1965) but also because his view, like Reid's, cannot account for the existence of radical moral disagreement within one and the same cultural and social order. It was in fact the inability of the philosophy of Reid and Stewart in the versions then current in the United States either to explain the disagreement between those holding proslavery views and those holding antislavery views or to provide grounds drawn from the alleged fundamental moral principles to vindicate one side rather than the other which was a major factor in discrediting the moral philosophy of Reid and Stewart in the United States in the decades immediately preceding the War between the States.

The attempt to decide between the claims of rival and competing traditions concerning both the genesis of action and the content of morality by appealing to a set of fundamental deliverances of what Reid called common sense thus fails both in less and in more sophisticated versions. What alternative is there? Another possibility is that if we are to discover what the form of practical reasoning is or what the nature of justice is, we ought not to begin from any theory, whether the tradition-informed theories of writers such as Aristotle and Hume, who are responding in part to earlier thinkers, or those theories which attempt to make an entirely new beginning, such as those of Reid and Stewart, but rather in the case of practical reasoning from *the facts themselves* about the genesis of human action and in the case of justice with the most elementary apprehensions of what right conduct is. Yet this project also, so it turns out, founders.

Consider what is involved in the attempt to evaluate rival claims about practical reasoning by comparing each with what are taken to be the basic facts about practical reasoning. Hume, for example, claims that reason can be nothing but the servant of the passions. Aristotle and Aquinas claim that reason can direct the passions. Should we then proceed by considering as wide a range as we can of examples of human action, in which both reasoning and passion are present and play some part in generating action, and in the light of those examples decide between the two rival claims? The problem is: how to describe the relevant examples. When individuals articulate to and for themselves the processes through which they proceed to action or when observers describe those processes in others, they cannot do so except by employing some particular theory-informed or theory-presupposing scheme of concepts, by conceptualizing that which they do or undergo or observe in a way which accords with one theory rather than another. There are no preconceptual or even pretheoretical data, and this entails that no set of examples of action, no matter how comprehensive, can provide a neutral court of appeal for decision between rival theories. I do not of course mean to say, and it would be absurd to say, that the empirical facts about action and its generation are not such as to impose constraints upon what can constitute a plausible or workable conceptualization. But those constraints are, unsurprisingly, consistent with a range of theories at least as wide as, and possibly a good deal wider than, the set of rival, mutually incompatible theories which emerged from the histories of the previous chapters.

Consequently, if any attempt were made to judge between competing theories by appealing to empirical examples, one of two outcomes would occur. If the examples were drawn from the particular culture whose practice was being articulated by one of the theorists in question, then that theorist would doubtless emerge from the test substantially vindicated—perhaps of course corrected or supplemented on points of detail —since the examples would be of just the kind which that theorist had pondered in elaborating his theory. If the examples were, however, drawn from some culture alien to and different from that of either of the competing theorists, then those examples would instantiate the conceptualization required by some third, perhaps not-yet-articulated type of theory. In neither case would there be any genuinely neutral examples. To put the same point in another way: each theory of practical reasoning is, among other things, a theory as to how examples are to be described, and how we describe any particular example will depend, therefore, upon which theory we have adopted. Hence the appeal to examples must be in vain.

Related and parallel points arise for similar proposals concerning how we should adjudicate between the different and incompatible accounts of justice advanced by rival and competing traditions. Insofar of course as such accounts of justice are either derived from or justified in terms of particular conceptions of practical rationality, the impossibility of identifying a neutral standard by which to judge between competing theories in the case of the latter entails a like impossibility in the case of the former. But even if this consideration were to be waived, such proposals encounter other formidable difficulties.

Just because they involve the attempted identification of some ground for or content of justice which is to be independent of the competing traditions, what is found must be some feature or features of a human moral stance which hold of human beings independently of and apart from those characteristics which belong to them as members of any particular social or culture tradition. It is to some kind of universality and impersonality, which can be conceived of as specifying and furnishing a tradition-independent moral standpoint, that resort must be had. A first difficulty is that those conceptions of universality and impersonality which survive this kind of abstraction from the concreteness of traditional or even nontraditional conventional modes of moral thought and action are far too thin and meager to supply what is needed.

There have of course been recurrent attempts, of which certainly the greatest was Kant's, to deny this. But the history of attempts to construct a morality for tradition-free individuals, whether by an appeal to one out of several conceptions of universalizability or to one out of equally multifarious conceptions of utility or to shared intuitions or to some combination of these, has in its outcome, as we noticed at the very outset of this enquiry, been a history of continuously unresolved disputes, so that there emerges no uncontested and incontestable account of what tradition-independent morality consists in and consequently no neutral set of criteria by means of which the claims of rival and contending traditions could be adjudicated. The evidence for the failure of Kant's heirs in these constructive enterprises is contained in the reviews of the books expounding them in the professional philosophical journals. The book review pages of those journals are the graveyards of constructive academic philosophy, and any doubts as to whether rational consensus might not after all be achievable in modern academic moral philosophy can be put to rest by reading them through regularly. Nor is this only or even primarily because the realm of practical life is one of moral, political, and religious controversy. In key part it is a consequence of the kind of philosophy which has been put to work in such attempts at construction. For a condition of the success of any one such attempt is that its rival should fail. No particular thesis can be conclusively established unless incompatible points of view are conclusively refuted.

Yet what the kind of philosophy which has been put to work in the history of post-Enlightenment academic philosophy reveals is that although very, very occasionally some particular thesis is conclusively refuted or at least rendered utterly implausible, and although a good deal more often the relationship of one argument to another or of one set of affirmations to another is clarified in respect of entailment, implication, or other logical and conceptual relations, disagreement upon major issues seems to be ineradicable. The outcome of almost any attempted refutation of a philosophical theory, so David Lewis has put it, is that the "theory survives its refutation—at a price. Our 'intuitions' are simply opinions, our philosophical theories are the same. . . . Once the menu of well-worked out theories is before us, philosophy is a matter of opinion . . ." (*Philosophical Papers,* vol. I, Oxford, 1983, pp. x–xi). What this kind of philosophy does achieve is to show what other commitments we logically or conceptually incur when we assert or deny some particular thesis. But it possesses no general shared standards by which to judge whether or not it is rational to incur them. The metaphor of "price" which Lewis uses is apt. We are provided with no philosophical standard of value in the light of which we can discover whether the cost of a particular commitment is too high relative to the philosophical benefits which it confers. For this reason we have to fall back upon the deliverances of prephilosophical opinion and to acknowledge that this kind of philosophy is, when conducted in self-aware fashion, what some of its most acute exponents always said that it was, a way of clarifying issues and alternatives but not of providing grounds for conviction on matters of any substance. We should also note that in respect of the ineradicability of disagreement so-called continental philosophy does not differ significantly from analytic philosophy.

Yet it is of the first importance to remember that the project of founding a form of social order in which individuals could emancipate themselves from the contingency and particularity of tradition by appealing to genuinely universal, tradition-independent norms was and is not only, and not principally, a project of philosophers. It was and is the project of modern liberal, individualist society, and the most cogent reasons that we have for believing that the hope of a tradition-independent rational universality is an illusion derive from the history of that project. For in the course of that history liberalism, which began as an appeal to alleged principles of shared rationality against what was felt to be the tyranny of tradition, has itself been transformed into a tradition whose continuities are partly defined by the interminability of the debate over such principles. An interminability which was from the standpoint of an earlier liberalism a grave defect to be remedied as soon as possible has become, in the eyes of some liberals at least, a kind of virtue.

Initially the liberal claim was to provide a political, legal, and economic framework in which assent to one and the same set of rationally justifiable principles would enable those who espouse widely different and incompatible conceptions of the good life for human beings to live together peaceably within the same society, enjoying the same political status and engaging in the same economic relationships. Every individual is to be equally free to propose and to live by whatever conception of the good he or she pleases, derived from whatever theory or tradition he or she may adhere to, unless that conception of the good involves reshaping the life of the rest of the community in accordance with it. Any conception of the human good according to which, for example, it is the duty of government to educate the members of the community morally, so that they come to live out that conception of the good, may up to a point be held as a private theory by individuals or groups, but any serious attempt to embody it in public life will be proscribed. And this qualification of course entails not only that liberal individualism does indeed have its own broad conception of the good, which it is engaged in imposing politically, legally, socially, and culturally wherever it has the power to do so, but also that in so doing its toleration of rival conceptions of the good in the public arena is severely limited.

What is permitted in that arena is the expression of preferences, either the preferences of individuals or the preferences of groups, the latter being understood as the preferences of the individuals who make up those groups, summed in some way or other. It may well be that in some cases it is some nonliberal theory or conception of the human good which leads individuals to express the preferences that they do. But only in the guise of such expressions of preference are such theories and conceptions allowed to receive expression.

The parallels between this understanding of the relationship of human beings in the social and political realm and the institution of the market, the dominant institution in a liberal economy, are clear. In markets too it is only through the expression of individual preferences that a heterogeneous variety of needs, desires, and goods conceived in one way or another are given a voice. The weight given to an individual preference in the market is a matter of the cost which the individual is able and willing to pay; only so far as an individual has the means to bargain with those who can supply what he or she needs does the individual have an effective voice. So also in the political and social realm it is the ability to bargain that is crucial. The preferences of some are accorded weight by others only insofar as the satisfaction of those preferences will lead to the satisfaction of their own preferences. Only those who have something to give get. The disadvantaged in a liberal society are those without the means to bargain.

Against this background two central features of the liberal system of evaluation become intelligible. The first concerns the way in which the liberal is committed to there being no one overriding good. The recognition of a range of goods is accompanied by a recognition of a range of compartmentalized spheres within each of which some good is pursued: political, economic, familial, artistic, athletic, scientific. So it is within a variety of distinct groups that each individual pursues his or her good, and the preferences which he or she expresses will express this variety of social relationships (see John Rawls 'The Idea of Social Union' chapter 79, op. cit.).

The liberal norm is characteristically, therefore, one according to which different kinds of evaluation, each independent of the other, are exercised in these different types of social environment. The heterogeneity is such that no overall ordering of goods is possible. And to be educated into the culture of a liberal social order is, therefore, characteristically to become the kind of person to whom it appears normal that a variety of goods should be pursued, each appropriate to its own sphere, with no overall good supplying any overall unity to life. To notice a passage from John Rawls once more: "Human good is heterogeneous because the aims of the self are heterogeneous. Although to subordinate all our aims to one end does not strictly speaking violate the principles of rational choice . . . it still strikes us as irrational or more likely as mad. The self is disfigured. . . ." So Rawls equates the human self with the liberal self in a way which is atypical of the liberal tradition only in its clarity of conception and statement.

The liberal self then is one that moves from sphere to sphere, compartmentalizing its attitudes. The claims of any one sphere to attention or to resources are once again to be determined by the summing of individual preferences and by bargaining. So it is important for all areas of human life and not only for explicitly political and economic transactions that there should be acceptable rules of bargaining. And what each individual and each group has to hope for from these rules is that they should be such as to enable that individual or that group to be as effective as possible in implementing his, her, or their preferences. This kind of effectiveness thus becomes a central value of liberal modernity.

Within this liberal scheme the rules of justice have a distinctive function. The rules of distributive justice are both to set constraints upon the bargaining process, so as to ensure access to it by those otherwise disadvantaged, and to protect individuals so that they may have freedom to express and, within limits, to implement their preferences. The stability of property, for Hume an overriding value, is valued by liberals only insofar as it contributes to that protection and does not exclude the disadvantaged from due consideration. Desert is, except in some of those subordinate associations in which groups pursue particular chosen goods, irrelevant to justice. So both the Aristotelian and the Humean accounts of justice are incompatible with liberal justice, and they are so in a way which parallels the like incompatibility of both Aristotelian and Humean accounts of the genesis of action with the way in which individuals understand both themselves and others as preference-expressing agents in liberal societies.

For in the liberal public realm individuals understand each other and themselves as each possessing his or her own ordered schedule of preferences. Their actions are understood as designed to implement those preferences, and indeed it is by the way in which individuals act that we are provided with the best evidence as to what their preferences are. Each individual, therefore, in contemplating prospective action has first to ask him or herself the question: What are my wants? And how are they ordered? The answers to this question provide the initial premise for the practical reasoning of such individuals, a premise expressed by an utterance of the form: 'I want it to be the case that such and such' or of some closely cognate form.

At once this characteristically modern form of practical reasoning exhibits another difference from both Aristotle and Hume. 'I want it to be the case that such and such', as we noticed in chapter XVI above, cannot function as the expression of a good reason for action within Hume's scheme any more than within Aristotle's. The emergence of a type of practical reasoning in which this kind of expression can be the initiating premise of a practical argument marked a moment of post-Humean cultural change, one corresponding to that involved in coming to understand the arenas of public choice, not as places of debate, either in terms of one dominant conception of the human good or between rival and conflicting conceptions of that good, but as places where bargaining between individuals, each with their own preferences, is conducted. What had to happen for 'I want' to assume this new role?

Desires of course had always been recognized as motives for action, and someone could always explain his or her action by expressing the desire which had motivated by means of some such expression as 'I want'. Nor was there anything new about it being believed that it is good to satisfy certain desires or that the pleasure in so satisfying them is good. What was new was the transformation of first-person expressions of desire themselves, without further qualification, into statements of a reason for action, into premises for practical reasoning. And this transformation, I want to suggest, is brought about by a restructuring of thought and action in a way which accords with the procedures of the public realms of the market and of liberal individualist politics. In those realms the ultimate data are preferences. These are weighed against each other; how they were arrived at is irrelevant to the weight assigned to them. That people in general have such and such preferences is held to provide by itself a sufficient reason for acting so as to satisfy them. But if this is true in the polity at large, then surely each individual can equally find in his or her own preferences a sufficient reason for his or her acting similarly. And there will be an analogous procedure for weighing our individual desires against one another.

Wittgenstein drew our attention to the fact that certain types of first-person sentence—for example, 'I am in pain' or 'I am afraid'—may function primarily and originally as expressive, a replacement for something else, a groan perhaps or a scream, but then may come to function in another way: ". . . a cry, which cannot be called a description, which is more primitive than any description, for all that serves as a description of the inner life. A cry is not a description. But there are transitions" (*Philosophical Investigations,* Oxford, 1953, II, ix, 189e). The transitions are made by treating 'I am in pain' or 'I am afraid' as making a true or false statement in the same way as the third-person statements 'She is in pain' or 'He is afraid' do. We come to refer to ourselves with the same impersonality with which we refer to others. So it is also with 'I want', which instead of expressing a passion and so revealing a motive for action—as it still does, for example, in a Humean perspective—may come instead to function as a statement and so as a premise. Thereby it has come to possess the kind of impersonality required of a good reason for action.

My thesis is not that the procedures of the public realm of liberal individualism were cause and the psychology of the liberal individual effect nor vice versa. What I am claiming is that each required the other and that in coming together they defined a new social and cultural artefact, "the individual." In Aristotelian practical reasoning it is the individual *qua* citizen who reasons; in Thomistic practical reasoning it is the individual *qua* enquirer into his or her good and the good of his or her community; in Humean practical reasoning it is the individual *qua* propertied or unpropertied participant in a society of a particular kind of mutuality and reciprocity; but in the practical reasoning of liberal modernity it is the individual *qua* individual who reasons.

What is the structure of this kind of practical reasoning? Consider the procedure by which it has to be elaborated. From the initial premise of the form 'I want it to be the case that such and such' the reasoner must move to answer the question about how what he or she wants may be attained by action and which of the available alternative courses of action is preferable. But the conjunction of the initial premise 'I want it to be the case that such and such' and the secondary premise or premises obtained by answering this question will not of itself necessarily yield the conclusion as to what the reasoner should do. For it may well be that the course of action thus decided upon would in fact frustrate some other want of the reasoner. Hence an additional premise is required for any sound practical argument in which the initial premise is an expression of preference, and the following form of the set of required premises emerges: 'I want it to be the case that such and such; Doing so and so will enable me to achieve its being the case that such and such; There is no other way of so enabling me which I prefer; Doing so and so will not frustrate any equal or stronger preference'.

Contemporary analytic philosophers, who often take themselves to be representing the timeless form of practical reasoning as such, when they are in fact representing the form of practical reasoning specific to their own liberal individualist culture, confirm by their accounts that this is the general form of such practical reasoning, albeit and unsurprisingly differing among themselves over the details of how preferences are to be expressed (see G. H. von Wright *Explanation and Understanding,* Ithaca, 1971, chapter III; A. Goldman *A Theory of Human Action,* Englewood Cliffs, 1970, chapter IV; P. M. Churchland 'The Logical Character of Action Explanations' *Philosophical Review* 79, 2, 1970; R. Audi 'A Theory of Practical Reasoning' *American Philosophical Quarterly* 19, 1, 1982).

From this type of set of premises what type of conclusion follows? The connection between the preferences expressed in the premises of this kind of practical reasoning in modern liberal individualist society and any action which is to be generated by them is a good deal looser either than that between the premises of an Aristotelian practical syllogism and the action which is its conclusion or than that between a Humean passion and its expression in action. Neither the immediacy and necessity of the one nor the causal regularity of the other is involved in the way in which the relationships between the attitudes expressed in the premises and subsequent action are understood. It is true that, as G.E.M. Anscombe wrote, "The primitive sign of wanting is *trying to get* . . ." (*Intention,* Oxford, 1957, p. 67). But while it is true that someone who expresses a want is always thereby committed to trying to get what he or she wants in *some* circumstances or other, no more than this is necessarily involved.

Acting upon a particular want here and now, implementing a particular preference here and now, depends not only upon external circumstances permitting, but also upon no other want or preference presenting itself in such a way that the person does something else. And where as in modern liberal culture the range of desired goods is taken to be irreducibly heterogeneous and without any overall ordering, this is always liable to happen. So that even when someone has rehearsed all the premises of some piece of practical reasoning of this specific kind, the question of whether or not he or she is going to act accordingly still remains open. Hence between the rehearsal of the premises and the ensuing action there characteristically has to intervene a decision. Hence such premises logically terminate, not in some action as their conclusion, but in a practical judgment of the form "So I should do so and so." The decision whether to act in accordance with this judgment is not made simply by arriving at this conclusion.

Consider the resulting contrast between Aristotelian and such characteristically modern practical reasoning from the standpoint of our interpretation of the behavior of others. Someone who affirms the premises of an Aristotelian practical syllogism within the context of the kind of systematic activity from which those premises derive their peculiar force, knowing what he or she is doing, and who then fails to perform the action which should have been the conclusion of that syllogism, and not because it is not in that person's power to perform it, thereby lapses into the unintelligibility of blank inconsistency. But this is not at all the case with someone who similarly affirms the premise of a piece of modern practical reasoning and then does not act accordingly. So Robert Audi has argued compellingly that the reasoning of this kind which terminates in a practical judgment is thereby complete as a piece of practical reasoning; it does not require for its completion subsequent action by the reasoner in accordance with it or even a decision so to act. For not only may the reasoner suffer from weakness of will with respect to the performance of that particular possible action, but it can also be the case that "as he thinks about how he can do it, he changes his mind" (op. cit., p. 29). The range of possible intervening considerations which may interpose themselves between practical judgment and action and even between practical judgment and decision is at once too large and too indeterminate for there to be even an appearance of unintelligibility when practical reasoning produces no further outcome. Unsurprisingly in a culture dominated by this kind of practical reasoning, the making—and the unmaking—of decisions is a kind of activity which assumes a prominence unknown in other cultures.

In what, then, from the standpoint of those who engage in this kind of reasoning does practical rationality consist? First of all in the ordering of his or her preferences by each individual, so that those preferences may be ordinally ranked in their presentation in the public realm; second, in the soundness of the arguments whereby preferences are translated into decisions and actions; and third, in the ability to act so as to maximize the satisfaction of those preferences in accordance with their ordering. It is the first of these aspects of specifically modern rationality which makes the question of how preferences are to be summed, either by individuals or socially, so crucial, and Arrow's theorem and its heirs so relevant in modern social theory. It is the third which makes both the preoccupations of utilitarianism and its distinctive idiom so ineliminable from modern public discourse as well as from modern moral and political philosophy.

It is often the case, of course, that the preferences of different individuals and of groups of individuals conflict. And the need for some conception of justice is in this liberal culture no more and no less than the need for some set of regulating principles by which cooperation in the implementation of preferences may be so far as possible achieved and decisions made as to which kinds of preference have priority over others. Notice that according to the standards of this culture one can be fully rational without as yet being just. The priority of rationality is required so that the rules of justice may be justified by appeal to rationality. Compliance with the norms of justice may indeed on occasion be necessary for someone to satisfy his or her preferences effectively, and efficiency and rationality may therefore dictate such compliance. But no disposition to care for justice as such will be first required in order to be rational. What then is the function and notion of justice in such a cultural and social order?

The answer to this question requires attention to four different levels of activity and debate in the structure of a liberal and individualist order. The first is that at which different individuals and groups express their views and attitudes in their own terms, whatever these may be. Some of these individuals or groups may be members of synagogues or churches or mosques and express their views as injunctions to obey divine law. Some may be adherents of some nonreligious, say Aristotelian or quasi-Aristotelian, theory of the human good. Others again may espouse principles concerning, for example, universal human rights, which they simply treat as not requiring further grounding. What each standpoint supplies is a set of premises from which its proponents argue to conclusions about what ought or ought not to be done, conclusions which are often in conflict with those of other groups. The only *ra-*

tional way in which these disagreements could be resolved would be by means of a philosophical enquiry aimed at deciding which out of the conflicting sets of premises, if any, is true. But a liberal order, as we have already seen, is one in which each standpoint may make its claims but can do no more within the framework of the public order, since no overall theory of the human good is to be regarded as justified. Hence at this level debate is necessarily barren; rival appeals to accounts of the human good or of justice necessarily assume a rhetorical form such that it is as assertion and counterassertion, rather than as argument and counterargument, that rival standpoints confront one another. Nonrational persuasion displaces rational argument. Standpoints are construed as the expressions of attitude and feeling and often enough come to be no more than that. The philosophical theorists who had claimed that all evaluative and normative judgments *can* be no more than expressions of attitude and feeling, that all such judgments are emotive, turn out to have told us the truth not about evaluative and normative judgments as such, but about what such judgments become in this kind of increasingly emotivist culture (see chapters II and III of *After Virtue*).

When, therefore, the defense of rival moral and political standpoints is interpreted within the liberal order as the expression of preferences by those individuals who engage in such defenses, this interpretation is more than a matter of the status accorded to all expressions of opinion by liberal individualism. The culture of liberalism transforms expressions of opinion into what its political and moral theory had already said that they were. So debate at the first level has no outcome; but the participants in debate find that at a second level their points of view are included in that tallying and weighing of expressions of preference which the institutionalizations of liberalism always involve: counting votes, responding to consumer choice, surveying public opinion.

The first level, that of debate about the human good in general, is, as we have already seen, necessarily barren of substantive agreed conclusions in a liberal social order. The second level, that at which preferences are tallied and weighed, presupposes that the procedures and rules which govern such tallying and weighing are themselves the outcome of rational debate of quite another kind, that at which the principles of shared rationality have been identified by philosophical enquiry. It is therefore in some ways unsurprising, in the light of the argument so far, that liberalism requires for its social embodiment continuous philosophical and quasi-philosophical debate about the principles of justice, debate which, for reasons which have already been given, is perpetually inconclusive but nonetheless socially effective in suggesting that if the relevant set of principles has not yet been finally discovered, nonetheless their discovery remains a central goal of the social order.

This third level, once again a level of debate, thus provides a certain kind of sanction for the rules and procedures functioning at the second level. And even if the philosophical theorists of liberal individualism do not and cannot agree upon any precise formulation of the principles of justice, they are by and large agreed on what such principles should be designed to achieve. Just because the principles of justice are to govern the tallying and weighing of preferences, they must provide, so far as is possible, a justification to each individual *qua* individual for tallying and weighing his or her particular preferences in the way that they do. So any inequality in the treatment of individuals *qua* individuals requires justification. Justice is *prima facie* egalitarian. The goods about which it is egalitarian in this way are those which, it is presumed, everyone values: freedom to express and to implement preferences and a share in the means required to make that implementation effective. It is in these two respects that *prima facie* equality is required. But it is just here that argument between liberal theorists begins, argument in which the contributions of the greatest names in the foundation of liberalism, Kant, Jefferson, and Mill, have been continued by such distinguished contemporaries as Hart, Rawls, Gewirth, Nozick, Dworkin, and Ackerman. The continuing inconclusiveness of the debates to which they have contributed is of course also one more tribute to the necessary inconclusiveness of modern academic philosophy.

What has become clear, however, is that gradually less and less importance has been attached to arriving at substantive conclusions and more and more to continuing the debate for its own sake. For the nature of the debate itself and not of its outcome provides underpinning in a variety of ways for the fourth level at which appeals to justice may be heard in a liberal individualist order, that of the rules and procedures of the formal legal system. The function of that system is to enforce an order in which conflict resolution takes place without invoking any overall theory of human good. To achieve this end almost any position taken in the philosophical debates of liberal jurisprudence may on occasion be invoked. And the mark of a liberal order is to refer its conflicts for their resolution, not to those debates, but to the verdicts of its legal system. The lawyers, not the philosophers, are the clergy of liberalism.

Liberalism thus provides a distinctive conception of a just order which is closely integrated with the conception of practical reasoning required by public transactions conducted within the terms set by a liberal polity. The principles which inform such practical reasoning and the theory and practice of justice within such a polity are not neutral with respect to rival and conflicting theories of the human good. Where they are in force they impose a particular conception of the good life, of practical reasoning, and of justice upon those who willingly or unwillingly accept the liberal procedures and the liberal terms of debate. The overriding good of liberalism is no more and no less than the continued sustenance of the liberal social and political order.

Thus liberalism, while initially rejecting the claims of any overriding theory of the good, does in fact come to embody just such a theory. Moreover, liberalism can provide no compelling arguments in favor of its conception of the human good except by appeal to premises which collectively already presuppose that theory. The starting points of liberal theorizing are never neutral as between conceptions of the human good; they are always liberal starting points. And the inconclusiveness of the debates within liberalism as to the fundamental principles of liberal justice (see *After Virtue,* chapter 17) reinforces the view that liberal theory is best understood, not at all as an attempt to find a rationality independent of tradition, but as itself the articulation of an historically developed and developing set of social institutions and forms of activity, that is, as the voice of a tradition. Like other traditions, liberalism has internal to it its own standards of rational justification. Like other traditions, liberalism has its set of authoritative texts and its disputes over their interpretation. Like other traditions, liberalism expresses itself socially through a particular kind of hierarchy.

For in a society in which preferences, whether in the market or in politics or in private life, are assigned the place which they have in a liberal order, power lies with those who are able to determine what the alternatives are to be between which choices will be available. The consumer, the voter, and the individual in general are accorded the right of expressing their preferences for one or more out of the alternatives which they are offered, but the range of possible alternatives is controlled by an elite, and how they are presented is also so controlled. The ruling elites within liberalism are thus bound to value highly competence in the persuasive presentation of alternatives, that is, in the cosmetic arts. So a certain kind of power is assigned a certain kind of authority.

Liberals have, for reasons which are obvious in the light of the history of their doctrines, been reluctant to recognize that their appeal is not to some tradition-independent rationality as such. Yet increasingly there have been liberal thinkers who, for one reason or another, have acknowledged that their theory and practice are after all that of one more contingently grounded and founded tradition, in conflict with other rival traditions as such and like certain other traditions in claiming a right to universal allegiance, but unable to escape from the condition of a tradition. Even this, however, can be recognized without any inconsistency and has gradually been recognized by liberal writers such as Rawls, Rorty, and Stout.

From the fact that liberalism does not provide a neutral tradition-independent ground from which a verdict may be passed upon the rival claims of conflicting traditions in respect of practical rationality and of justice, but turns out itself to be just one more such tradition with its own highly contestable conceptions of practical rationality and of justice, it does not of course follow that there is no such neutral ground. And it is clear that there can be no sound *a priori* argument to demonstrate that such is impossible. What is equally clear, however, is that liberalism is by far the strongest claimant to provide such a ground which has so far appeared in human history or which is likely to appear in the foreseeable future. That liberalism fails in this respect, therefore, provides the strongest reason that we can actually have for asserting that there is no such neutral ground, that there is no place for appeals to a practical-rationality-as-such or a justice-as-such to which all rational persons would by their very rationality be compelled to give their allegiance. There is instead only the practical-rationality-of-this-or-that-tradition and the justice-of-this-or-that-tradition.

Liberalism, like all other moral, intellectual, and social traditions of any complexity, has its own problematic internal to it, its own set of questions which by its own standards it is committed to resolving. Since in its own internal debates as well as in the debate between liberalism and other rival traditions the success or failure of liberalism in formulating and solving its own problems is of great importance, just as the success or failure of the other traditions which we have considered in each carrying forward their own particular problematic is similarly important, it is worth taking note of two peculiarly central problems for liberalism, that of the liberal self and that of the common good in a liberal social order.

The classical statement of both these problems was by Diderot in *Le Neveu de Rameau,* but they both have also received powerful contemporary statements. The problem of the self in liberal society arises from the fact that each individual is required to formulate and to express, both to him or herself and to others, an ordered schedule of preferences. Each individual is to present him or herself as a single, well-ordered will. But what if such a form of presentation always requires that schism and conflict within the self be disguised and repressed and that a false and psychologically disabling unity of presentation is therefore required by a liberal order?

Those who have most cogently identified the relevant kind of schism and conflict within the self, such as Freud and Jacques Lacan, have often not appeared to be threatening the liberal view of the self by their views, because along with diagnosis they have offered their own therapeutic remedies. And within liberalism's social and culture order there has therefore not surprisingly been a preoccupation with the therapeutic, with means of curing the divided self (see P. Rieff *The Triumph of the Therapeutic,* London, 1966). Moreover, Lacan himself always emphasized his quarrel with Aristotle (*Encore,* Paris, 1973) and his debt to such liberals as Kant and de Sade ('Kant avec Sade' *Écrits,* Paris, 1966), in a way which should remind us that this issue of the unity and division of the self, how it is to be characterized and how, if at all, it is to be dealt with in practical life, arises for all the traditions which have been discussed and not only for liberalism. Nonetheless, it *is* a problem for liberalism.

Similarly, the problem of the common good which arises for liberalism has its analogue in at least some other traditions. Its most cogent recent statement has been by Robert A. Dahl in *Dilemmas of Pluralist Democracy* (New Haven, 1982). In what Dahl calls pluralist democracies, which are very much what I have called liberal political orders, individuals pursue a variety of goods, associating in groups to achieve particular ends and to promote particular forms of activity. None of the goods thus pursued can be treated as overriding the claims of any other. Yet if the good of liberalism itself, the good of the pluralist democratic polity rather than the goods of its constituent parts, is to be achieved, it will have to be able to claim an overriding and even a coerced allegiance. Or, to put the problem in another way, what good reasons could an individual find for placing him or herself at the service of the public good rather than of other goods? Dahl offers an acute and detailed account of "the extreme vulnerability of individualist civic virtue" and discusses possible remedies (op. cit., chapters 6 and 7), but, as he himself stresses, the problems are generated by the very forms of this kind of political order, and the task of institutionalizing any proposed remedies would confront the same set of questions which engendered the problems.

In emphasizing the fact that the problems which confront liberalism also confront other rival traditions I must take care to point out that success in dealing with these shared problems does not provide such traditions with a neutral standard in terms of which their respective achievements can be measured. Some problems are indeed shared. But what importance each particular problem has varies from tradition to tradition, and so do the effects of failing to arrive at a solution. Moreover, what counts as a satisfactory solution and the standards by reference to which different solutions are to be evaluated also differ radically from tradition to tradition. Thus once again any hope of discovering tradition-independent standards of judgment turns out to be illusory.

From this it may well appear to follow that no tradition can claim rational superiority to any other. For each tradition has internal to itself its own view of what rational superiority consists in in respect of such topics as practical rationality and justice, and the adherents of each will judge accordingly. And if this is the case, two further conclusions may seem to follow. The first is that at any fundamental level no rational debate between, rather than within, traditions can occur. The adherents of conflicting tendencies within a tradition may still share enough in the way of fundamental belief to conduct such debate, but the protagonists of rival traditions will be precluded at any fundamental level, not only from justifying their views to the members of any rival tradition, but even from learning from them how to modify their own tradition in any radical way.

Yet if this is so, a second conclusion seems to be in order. Given that each tradition will frame its own standpoint in terms of its own idiosyncratic concepts, and given that no fundamental correction of its conceptual scheme from some external standpoint is possible, it may appear that each tradition must develop its own scheme in a way which is liable to preclude even translation from one tradition to another. So it may appear that communication between traditions will at certain crucial points be too inadequate for each even to understand the other fully. A social universe composed exclusively of rival traditions, so it may seem, will be one in which there are a number of contending, incompatible, but only partially and inadequately communicating, overall views of that universe, each tradition within which is unable to justify its claims over against those of its rivals except to those who already accept them. Is this indeed what follows? It is to the problems posed by these two apparent and threatening conclusions that we must now turn.

XVIII

The Rationality of Traditions

This book has presented an outline narrative history of three traditions of enquiry into what practical rationality is and what justice is, and in addition an acknowledgment of a need for the writing of a narrative history of a fourth tradition, that of liberalism. All four of these traditions are and were more than, and could not but be more than, traditions of intellectual enquiry. In each of them intellectual enquiry was or is part of the elaboration of a mode of social and moral life of which the intellectual enquiry itself was an integral part, and in each of them the forms of that life were embodied with greater or lesser degrees of imperfection in social and political institutions which also draw their life from other sources. So the Aristotelian tradition emerges from the rhetorical and reflective life of the *polis* and the dialectical teaching of the Academy and the Lyceum; so the Augustinian tradition flourished in the houses of religious orders and in the secular communities which provided the environment for such houses both in its earlier, and in its Thomistic, version in universities; so the Scottish blend of Calvinist Augustinianism and renaissance Aristotelianism informed the lives of congregations and kirk sessions, of law courts and universities; and so liberalism, beginning as a repudiation of tradition in the name of abstract, universal principles of reason, turned itself into a politically embodied power, whose inability to bring its debates on the nature and context of those universal principles to a conclusion has had the unintended effect of transforming liberalism into a tradition.

These traditions of course differ from each other over much more than their contending accounts of practical rationality and justice: they differ in their catalogs of the virtues, in their conceptions of selfhood, and in their metaphysical cosmologies. They also differ on the way in which within each their accounts of practical rationality and of justice were arrived at: in the Aristotelian tradition through the successive dialectical enterprises of Socrates, Plato, Aristotle, and Aquinas; in the Augustinian through obedience to divine authority as disclosed in scripture, mediated by Neoplatonic thought; within the Scottish tradition it is by way of refutation of his predecessors, arguing from premises which they had come to accept, that Hume propounds his account; and within liberalism a succession of ringing accounts of justice continue in a debate rendered inconclusive in part by the accompanying view of practical rationality.

Moreover, these traditions have very different histories in respect of their relationships with each other. Adherents of the Aristotelian tradition have quarrelled among themselves as to whether it is or is not necessarily antagonistic to the Augustinian. And Augustinians have on the same issue also disagreed with one another. Both Aristotelians and Augustinians have found themselves necessarily at odds with Hume and also, on somewhat different grounds, with liberalism. And liberalism has had to deny certain of the claims of all the other major traditions. So the narrative history of each of these traditions involves both a narrative of enquiry and debate within that tradition and also one of debate and disagreement between it and its rivals, debates and disagreements which come to define the detail of these varying types of antagonistic relationship. Yet it is just here that further pursuit of the argument raises crucial questions.

The conclusion to which the argument so far has led is not only that it is out of the debates, conflicts, and enquiry of socially embodied, historically contingent traditions that contentions regarding practical rationality and justice are advanced, modified, abandoned, or replaced, but that there is no other way to engage in the formulation, elaboration, rational justification, and criticism of accounts of practical rationality and justice except from within some one particular tradition in conversation, cooperation, and conflict with those who inhabit the same tradition. There is no standing ground, no place for enquiry, no way to engage in the practices of advancing, evaluating, accepting, and rejecting reasoned argument apart from that which is provided by some particular tradition or other.

It does not follow that what is said from within one tradition cannot be heard or overheard by those in another. Traditions which differ in the most radical way over certain subject matters may in respect of others share beliefs, images, and texts. Considerations urged from within one tradition may be ignored by those conducting enquiry or debate within another only at the cost, by their own standards, of excluding relevant good reasons for believing or disbelieving this or that or for acting in one way rather than another. Yet in other areas what is asserted or enquired into within the former tradition may have no counterpart whatsoever in the latter. And in those areas where there are subject matters or issues in common to more than one tradition, one such tradition may frame its theses by means of concepts such that the falsity of theses upheld within one or more other traditions is entailed, yet at the same time no or insufficient common standards are available by which to judge between the rival standpoints. Logical incompatibility *and* incommensurability may both be present.

Logical incompatibility does of course require that at some level of characterization each tradition identifies that about which it is maintaining its thesis in such a way that both its adherents and those of its rival can recognize that it is one and the same subject matter about which they are making claims. But even so, each of course may have its own peculiar standards by which to judge what is to be accounted one and the same in the relevant respect. So two traditions may differ over the criteria to be applied in determining the range of cases in which the concept of justice has application, yet each in terms of its own standards recognizes that in certain of these cases at least the adherents of the other traditions are applying a concept of *justice* which, if it has application, excludes the application of their own.

So Hume and Rawls agree in excluding application for any Aristotelian concept of desert in the framing of rules of justice, while they disagree with each other on whether a certain type of equality is required by justice. So Aristotle's understanding of the class of actions for which someone can be held responsible excludes any application for Augustine's conception of the will. Each tradition can at each stage of its development provide rational justification for its central theses in its own terms, employing the concepts and standards by which it defines itself, but there is no set of independent standards of rational justification by appeal to which the issues between contending traditions can be decided.

It is not then that competing traditions do not share some standards. All the traditions with which we have been concerned agree in according a certain authority to logic both in their theory and in their practice. Were it not so, their adherents would be unable to disagree in the way in which they do. But that upon which they agree is insufficient to resolve those disagreements. It may therefore seem to be the case that we are confronted with the rival and competing claims of a number of traditions to our allegiance in respect of our understanding of practical rationality and justice, among which we can have no good reason to decide in favor of any one rather than of the others. Each has its own standards of reasoning; each provides its own background beliefs. To offer one kind of reason, to appeal to one set of background beliefs, will already be to have assumed the standpoint of one particular tradition. But if we make no such assumption, then we can have no good reason to give more weight to the contentions advanced by one particular tradition than to those advanced by its rivals.

Argument along these lines has been adduced in support of a conclusion that if the only available standards of rationality are those made available by and within traditions, then no issue between contending traditions is rationally decidable. To assert or to conclude this rather than that can be rational relative to the standards of some particular tradition, but not rational as such. There can be no rationality as such. Every set of standards, every tradition incorporating a set of standards, has as much and as little claim to our allegiance as any other. Let us call this the relativist challenge, as contrasted with a second type of challenge, that which we may call perspectivist.

The relativist challenge rests upon a denial that rational debate between and rational choice among rival traditions is possible; the perspectivist challenge puts in question the possibility of making truth-claims from within any one tradition. For if there is a multiplicity of rival traditions, each with its own characteristic modes of rational justification internal to it, then that very fact entails that no one tradition can offer those outside it good reasons for excluding the theses of its rivals. Yet if this is so, no one tradition is entitled to arrogate to itself an exclusive title; no one tradition can deny legitimacy to its rivals. What seemed to require rival traditions so to exclude and so to deny was belief in the logical incompatibility of the theses asserted and denied within rival traditions, a belief which embodied a recognition that if the theses of one such tradition were true, then some at least of the theses asserted by its rivals were false.

The solution, so the perspectivist argues, is to withdraw the ascription of truth and falsity, at least in the sense in which 'true' and 'false' have been understood so far within the practice of such traditions, both from individual theses and from the bodies of systematic belief of which such theses are constitutive parts. Instead of interpreting rival traditions as mutually exclusive and incompatible ways of understanding one and the same world, one and the same subject matter, let us understand them instead as providing very different, complementary perspectives for envisaging the realities about which they speak to us.

The relativist challenge and the perspectivist challenge share some premises and are often presented jointly as parts of a single argument. Each of them exists in more than one version, and neither of them was originally elaborated in terms of a critique of the claims to truth and rationality of *traditions*. But considered as such, they lose none of their force. Nonetheless I am going to argue that they are fundamentally misconceived and misdirected. Their apparent power derives, so I shall want to suggest, from their inversion of certain central Enlightenment positions concerning truth and rationality. While the thinkers of the Enlightenment insisted upon a particular type of view of truth and rationality, one in which truth is guaranteed by rational method and rational method appeals to principles undeniable by any fully reflective rational person, the protagonists of post-Enlightenment relativism and perspectivism claim that if the Enlightenment conceptions of truth and rationality cannot be sustained, theirs is the only possible alternative.

Post-Enlightenment relativism and perspectivism are thus the negative counterpart of the Enlightenment, its inverted mirror image. Where the Enlightenment invoked the arguments of Kant or Bentham, such post-Enlightenment theorists invoke Nietzsche's attacks upon Kant and Bentham. It is therefore not surprising that what was invisible to the thinkers of the Enlightenment should be equally invisible to those post-modernist relativists and perspectivists who take themselves to be the enemies of the Enlightenment, while in fact being to a large and unacknowledged degree its heirs. What neither was or is able to recognize is the kind of rationality possessed by traditions. In part this was and is because of the enmity to tradition as inherently obscurantist which is and was to be found equally among Kantians and Benthamites, neo-Kantians and later utilitarians, on the one hand, and among Nietzscheans and post-Nietzscheans on the other. But in part the invisibility of the rationality of tradition was due to the lack of expositions, let alone defenses, of that rationality.

Burke was on this matter, as on so many others, an agent of positive harm. For Burke ascribed to traditions in good order, the order as he supposed of following nature, "wisdom without reflection" (*Reflections on the Revolution in France,* ed. C. C. O'Brien, Harmondsworth, 1982, p. 129). So that no place is left for reflection, rational theorizing as a work of and within tradition. And a far more important theorist of tradition has generally been ignored by both Enlightenment and post-Enlightenment theorists, because the particular tradition within which he worked, and from whose point of view he presented his theorizing, was theological. I mean, of course, John Henry Newman, whose account of tradition was itself successively developed in *The Arians of the Fourth Century* (revised edition, London, 1871) and *An Essay on the Development of Christian Doctrine* (revised edition, London, 1878). But if one is to extend Newman's account from the particular tradition of Catholic Christianity to rational traditions in general, and to do so in a philosophical context very different from any envisaged by Newman, so much qualification and addition is needed that it seems better to proceed independently, having first acknowledged a massive debt.

What I have to do, then, is to provide an account of the rationality presupposed by and implicit in the practice of those enquiry-bearing traditions with whose history I have been concerned which will be adequate to meet the challenges posed by relativism and perspectivism. In the absence of such an account the question of how the rival claims made by different traditions regarding practical rationality and justice are to be evaluated would go unanswered, and in default of an answer from the standpoint of those traditions themselves, relativism and/or prospectivism might well appear to prevail. Notice that the grounds for an answer to relativism and perspectivism are to be found, not in any theory of rationality as yet explicitly articulated and advanced within one or more of the traditions with which we have been concerned, but rather with a theory embodied in and presupposed by their practices of enquiry, yet never fully spelled out, although adumbrations of it, or of parts of it, are certainly to be found in various writers, and more especially in Newman.

The rationality of a tradition-constituted and tradition-constitutive enquiry is in key and essential part a matter of the kind of progress which it makes through a number of well-defined types of stage. Every such form of enquiry begins in and from some condition of pure historical contingency, from the beliefs, institutions, and practices of some particular community which constitute a given. Within such a community authority will have been conferred upon certain texts and certain voices. Bards, priests, prophets, kings, and, on occasion, fools and jesters will all be heard. All such communities are always, to greater or lesser degree, in a state of change. When those educated in the cultures of the societies of imperialist modernity reported that they had discovered certain so-called primitive societies or cultures without change, within which repetition rules rather than transformation, they were deceived in part by their understanding of the claims sometimes made by members of such societies that they are obedient to the dictates of immemorial custom and in part by their own too simple and anachronistic conception of what social and cultural change is.

What takes a given community from a first stage in which the beliefs, utterances, texts, and persons taken to be authoritative are deferred to unquestioningly, or at least without systematic questioning, may be one or more of several types of occurrence. Authoritative texts or utterances may be shown to be susceptible to, by actually receiving, alternative and incompatible interpretations, enjoining perhaps alternative and incompatible courses of action. Incoherences in the established system of beliefs may become evident. Confrontation by new situations, engendering new questions, may reveal within established practices and beliefs a lack of resources for offering or for justifying answers to these new questions. The coming together of two previously separate communities, each with its own well-established institutions, practices, and beliefs, either by migration or by conquest, may open up new alternative possibilities and require more than the existing means of evaluation are able to provide.

What responses the inhabitants of a particular community make in the face of such stimuli toward the reformulation of their beliefs or the remaking of their practices or both will depend not only upon what stock of reasons and of questioning and reasoning abilities they already possess but also upon their inventiveness. And these in turn will determine the possible range of outcomes in the rejection, emendation, and reformulation of beliefs, the revaluation of authorities, the reinterpretation of texts, the emergence of new forms of authority, and the production of new texts. Since beliefs are expressed in and through rituals and ritual dramas, masks and modes of dress, the ways in which houses are structured and villages and towns laid out, and of course by actions in general, the reformulations of belief are not to be thought of only in intellectual terms; or rather the intellect is not to be thought of as either a Cartesian mind or a materialist brain, but as that through which thinking individuals relate themselves to each other and to natural and social objects as these present themselves to them.

We are now in a position to contrast three stages in the initial development of a tradition: a first in which the relevant beliefs, texts, and authorities have not yet been put in question; a second in which inadequacies of various types have been identified, but not yet remedied; and a third in which response to those inadequacies has resulted in a set of reformulations, reevaluations, and new formulations and evaluations, designed to remedy inadequacies and overcome limitations. Where a person or a text is assigned an authority which derives from what is taken to be their relationship to the divine, that sacred authority will be thereby in the course of this process exempt from repudiation, although its utterances may certainly be subject to reinterpretation. It is indeed one of the marks of what is taken to be sacred that it is so exempted.

The development of a tradition is to be distinguished from that gradual transformation of beliefs to which every set of beliefs is exposed, both by its systematic and by its deliberate character. The very earliest stages in the development of anything worth calling a tradition of enquiry are thus already marked by theorizing. And the development of a tradition of enquiry is also to be distinguished from those abrupt general changes in belief which occur when, for example, a community undergoes a mass conversion, although such a conversion might be the originating point for such a tradition. A rational tradition's modes of continuity differ from those of the former, its ruptures from those of the latter. Some core of shared belief, constitutive of allegiance to the tradition, has to survive every rupture.

When the third stage of development is reached, those members of a community who have accepted the beliefs of the tradition in their new form—and those beliefs may inform only a limited part of the whole community's life or be such as concern its overall structure and indeed its relationship to the universe—become able to contrast their new beliefs with the old. Between those older beliefs and the world as they now understand it there is a radical discrepancy to be perceived. It is this lack of correspondence, between what the mind then judged and believed and reality as now perceived, classified, and understood, which is ascribed when those earlier judgments and beliefs are called *false*. The original and most elementary version of the correspondence theory of truth is one in which it is applied retrospectively in the form of a correspondence theory of falsity.

The first question to be raised about it is: What is it precisely that corresponds or fails to correspond to what? Assertions in speech or writing, certainly, but these as secondary expressions of intelligent thought which is or is not adequate in its dealings with its objects, the realities of the social and rational world. This is a point at which it is important to remember that the presupposed conception of mind is not Cartesian. It is rather of mind as activity, of mind as engaging with the natural and social world in such activities as identification, reidentification, collecting, separating, classifying, and naming and all this by touching, grasping, pointing, breaking down, building up, calling to, answering to, and so on. The mind is adequate to its objects insofar as the expectations which it frames on the basis of these activities are not liable to disappointment and the remembering which it engages in enables it to return to and recover what it had encountered previously, whether the objects themselves are still present or not. The mind, being informed as a result of its engagement with objects, is informed by both images which are or are not adequate—for the mind's purposes—re-presentations of particular objects or sorts of objects and by concepts which are or are not adequate re-presentations of the forms in terms of which objects are grasped and classified. Representation is not as such picturing, but re-presentation. Pictures are only one mode of re-presenting, and their adequacy or inadequacy in functioning as such is always relative to some specific purpose of mind.

One of the great originating insights of tradition-constituted enquiries is that false beliefs and false judgments represent a failure of the mind, not of its objects. It is mind which stands in need of correction. Those realities which mind encounters reveal themselves as they are, the presented, the manifest, the unhidden. So the most primitive conception of truth is of the manifestness of the objects which present themselves to mind; and it is when mind fails to re-present that manifestness that falsity, the inadequacy of mind to its objects, appears.

This falsity is recognized retrospectively as a past inadequacy when the discrepancy between the beliefs of an earlier stage of a tradition of enquiry are contrasted with the world of things and persons as it has come to be understood at some later stage. So correspondence or the lack of it becomes a feature of a developing complex conception of truth. The relationship of correspondence or of lack of correspondence which holds between the mind and objects is given expression in judgments, but it is not judgments themselves which correspond to objects or indeed to anything else. We may indeed say of a false judgment that things are not as the judgment declares them to be, or of a true judgment that he or she who utters it says that what is is and what is not is not. But there are not two distinguishable items, a judgment on the one hand and that portrayed in the judgment on the other, between which a relationship of correspondence can hold or fail to hold.

The commonest candidate, in modern versions of what is all too often taken to be *the* correspondence theory of truth, for that which corresponds to a judgment in this way is a fact. But facts, like telescopes and wigs for gentlemen, were a seventeenth-century invention. In the sixteenth century and earlier 'fact' in English was usually a rendering of the Latin 'factum', a deed, an action, and sometimes in Scholastic Latin an event or an occasion. It was only in the seventeenth century that 'fact' was first used in the way in which later philosophers such as Russell, Wittgenstein, and Ramsey were to use it. It is of course and always was harmless, philosophically and otherwise, to use the word 'fact' of what a judgment states. What is and was not harmless, but highly misleading, was to conceive of a realm of facts independent of judgment or of any other form of linguistic expression, so that judgments or statements or sentences could be paired off with facts, truth or falsity being the alleged relationship between such paired items. This kind of correspondence theory of truth arrived on the philosophical scene only comparatively recently and has been as conclusively refuted as any theory can be (see, for example, P. F. Strawson 'Truth' in *Logico-Linguistic Papers,* London, 1971). It is a large error to read it into older formulations concerning truth, such as "*adaequatio mentis ad rem*," let alone into that correspondence which I am ascribing to the conception of truth deployed in the early history of the development of traditions.

Those who have reached a certain stage in that development are then able to look back and to identify their own previous intellectual inadequacy or the intellectual inadequacy of their predecessors by comparing what they now judge the world, or at least part of it, to be with what it was then judged to be. To claim truth for one's present mindset and the judgments which are its expression is to claim that this kind of inadequacy, this kind of discrepancy, will never appear in any possible future situation, no matter how searching the enquiry, no matter how much evidence is provided, no matter what developments in rational enquiry may occur. The test for truth in the present, therefore, is always to summon up as many questions and as many objections of the greatest strength possible; what can be justifiably claimed as true is what has sufficiently withstood such dialectical questioning and framing of objections. In what does such sufficiency consist? That too is a question to which answers have to be produced and to which rival and competing answers may well appear. And those answers will compete rationally, just insofar as they are tested dialectically, in order to discover which is the best answer to be proposed so far.

A tradition which reaches this point of development will have become to greater or lesser degree a form of enquiry and will have had to institutionalize and regulate to some extent at least its methods of enquiry. It will have had to recognize intellectual virtues, and questions lie in wait for it about the relationship of such virtues to virtues of character. On these as on other questions conflicts will develop, rival answers will be proposed and accepted or rejected. At some point it may be discovered within some developing tradition that some of the same problems and issues—recognized as the same in the light of the standards internal to this particular tradition—are being debated within some other tradition, and defined areas of agreement and disagreement with such an other tradition may develop. Moreover, conflicts between and within tradition-constituted enquiries will stand in some relationship to those other conflicts which are present in a community which is the bearer of traditions.

There characteristically comes a time in the history of tradition-constituted enquiries when those engaged in them may find occasion or need to frame a theory of their own activities of enquiry. What kind of theory is then developed will of course vary from one tradition to another. Confronted with the multiplicity of uses of "true," the adherents of one kind of tradition may respond by constructing an analogical account of those uses and of their unity, as Aquinas did, exhibiting in the way in which he went about his task the influence of Aristotle's treatment of the multiplicity of uses of "good." By contrast the same multiplicity may evoke an attempt to identify some single, perhaps complex, mark of truth. Descartes, who ought to be understood as a late follower of the Augustinian tradition as well as someone who attempted to refound philosophy *de novo,* did precisely this in appealing to clarity and distinctness as marks of truth. And Hume concluded that he could find no such reliable mark (*Treatise* I,4,7).

Other elements of the theories of rational enquiry so proposed will also vary from tradition to tradition. And it will be in part these differences which result in still further different and rival conclusions concerning the subject matter of substantive enquiries, including topics such as those of justice and of practical rationality. Nonetheless, to some degree, insofar as a tradition of rational enquiry is such, it will tend to recognize what it shares as such with other traditions, and in the development of such traditions common characteristic, if not universal, patterns will appear.

Standard forms of argument will be developed, and requirements for successful dialectical questioning established. The weakest form of argument, but nonetheless that which will prevail in the absence of any other, will be the appeal to the authority of established belief, merely as established. The identification of incoherence within established belief will always provide a reason for enquiring further, but not in itself a conclusive reason for rejecting established belief, until something more adequate because less incoherent has been discovered. At every stage beliefs and judgments will be justified by reference to the beliefs and judgments of the previous stage, and insofar as a tradition has constituted itself as a successful form of enquiry, the claims to truth made within that tradition will always be in some specifiable way less vulnerable to dialectical questioning and objection than were their predecessors.

The conception of rationality and truth as thus embodied in tradition-constituted enquiry is of course strikingly at odds with both standard Cartesian and standard Hegelian accounts of rationality. Because every such rational tradition begins from the contingency and positivity of some set of established beliefs, the rationality of tradition is inescapably anti-Cartesian. In systematizing and ordering the truths they take themselves to have discovered, the adherents of a tradition may well assign a primary place in the structures of their theorizing to certain truths and treat them as first metaphysical or practical principles. But such principles will have had to vindicate themselves in the historical process of dialectical justification. It is by reference to such first principles that subordinate truths will be justified within a particular body of theory, and it is by reference to such first principles that, as we have seen, in both Platonic and Aristotelian theories of practical reasoning both particular practical judgments and actions themselves will be justified. But such first principles themselves, and indeed the whole body of theory of which they are a part, themselves will be understood to require justification. The kind of rational justification which they receive is at once dialectical and historical. They are justified insofar as in the history of this tradition they have, by surviving the process of dialectical questioning, vindicated themselves as superior to their historical predecessors. Hence such first principles are not self-sufficient, self-justifying epistemological first principles. They may indeed be regarded as both necessary and evident, but their necessity and their evidentness will be characterizable as such only to and by those whose thought is framed by the kind of conceptual scheme from which they emerge as a key element, in the formulation and reformulation of the theories informed by that historically developing conceptual scheme. It is instructive to read Descartes himself as providing both in the *Regulae* and in the *Meditations* just such an account of a process of dialectical justification for *his* first principles and, in so doing, discarding tradition in a highly traditional way, and thus taking the Augustinian tradition to a point at which Descartes learns from it what he from then onward cannot acknowledge having learned from it. And in so doing Descartes became the first Cartesian.

Yet if in what it moves from, tradition-constituted enquiry is anti-Cartesian, in what it moves toward, tradition-constituted enquiry is anti-Hegelian. Implicit in the rationality of such enquiry there is indeed a conception of a final truth, that is to say, a relationship of the mind to its objects which would be wholly adequate in respect of the capacities of that mind. But any conception of that state as one in which the mind could by its own powers know itself as thus adequately informed is ruled out; the Absolute Knowledge of the Hegelian system is from this tradition-constituted standpoint a chimaera. No one at any stage can ever rule out the future possibility of their present beliefs and judgments being shown to be inadequate in a variety of ways.

It is perhaps this combination of anti-Cartesian and anti-Hegelian aspects which seems to afford plausibility to the relativist and the perspectivist challenges. Traditions fail the Cartesian test of beginning from unassailable evident truths; not only do they begin from contingent positivity, but each begins from a point different from that of the others. Traditions also fail the Hegelian test of showing that their goal is some final rational state which they share with all other movements of thought. Traditions are always and ineradically to some degree local, informed by particularities of language and social and natural environment, inhabited by Greeks or by citizens of Roman Africa or medieval Persia or by eighteenth-century Scots, who stubbornly refuse to be or become vehicles of the self-realization of *Geist*. Those educated or indoctrinated into accepting Cartesian or Hegelian standards will take the positivity of tradition to be a sign of arbitrariness. For each tradition will, so it may seem, pursue its own specific historical path, and all that we shall be confronted with in the end is a set of independent rival histories.

The answer to this suggestion, and indeed more generally to relativism and to perspectivism, has to begin from considering one particular kind of occurrence in the history of traditions, which is not among those so far cataloged. Yet it is in the way in which the adherents of a tradition respond to such occurrences, and in the success or failure which attends upon their response, that traditions attain or fail to attain intellectual maturity. The kind of occurrence is that to which elsewhere I have given the name "epistemological crisis" ('Epistemological Crises, Dramatic Narrative and the Philosophy of Science' *The Monist* 69, 4, 1977). Epistemological crises may occur in the history of individuals—thinkers as various as Augustine, Descartes, Hume, and Lukács have left us records of such crises—as well as in that of groups. But they can also be crises in and for a whole tradition.

We have already noticed that central to a tradition-constituted enquiry at each stage in its development will be its current problematic, that agenda of unsolved problems and unresolved issues by reference to which its success or lack of it in making rational progress toward some further stage of development will be evaluated. At any point it may happen to any tradition-constituted enquiry that by its own standards of progress it ceases to make progress. Its hitherto trusted methods of enquiry have become sterile. Conflicts over rival answers to key questions can no longer be settled rationally. Moreover, it may indeed happen that the use of the methods of enquiry and of the forms of argument, by means of which rational progress had been achieved so far, begins to have the effect of increasingly disclosing new inadequacies, hitherto unrecognized incoherences, and new problems for the solution of which there seem to be insufficient or no resources within the established fabric of belief.

This kind of dissolution of historically founded certitudes is the mark of an epistemological crisis. The solution to a genuine epistemological crisis requires the invention or discovery of new concepts and the framing of some new type or types of theory which meet three highly exacting requirements. First, this in some ways radically new and conceptually enriched scheme, if it is to put an end to epistemological crisis, must furnish a solution to the problems which had previously proved intractable in a systematic and coherent way. Second, it must also provide an explanation of just what it was which rendered the tradition, before it had acquired these new resources, sterile or incoherent or both. And third, these first two tasks must be carried out in a way which exhibits some fundamental continuity of the new conceptual and theoretical structures with the shared beliefs in terms of which the tradition of enquiry had been defined up to this point.

The theses central to the new theoretical and conceptual structures, just because they are significantly richer than and escape the limitations of those theses which were central to the tradition before and as it entered its period of epistemological crisis, will in no way be derivable from those earlier positions. Imaginative conceptual innovation will have had to occur. The justification of the new theses will lie precisely in their ability to achieve what could not have been achieved prior to that innovation. Examples of such successfully creative outcomes to more or less serious epistemological crises, affecting some greater or lesser area of the subject matter with which a particular tradition-constituted enquiry is concerned, are not hard to come by, either in the traditions with whose history I have been concerned here or elsewhere. Newman's own central example was of the way in which in the fourth century the definition of the Catholic doctrine of the Trinity resolved the controversies arising out of competing interpretations of scripture by a use of philosophical and theological concepts whose understanding had itself issued from debates rationally unresolved up to that point. Thus that doctrine provided for the later Augustinian tradition a paradigm of how the three requirements for the resolution of an epistemological crisis could be met. In a very different way Aquinas provided a new and richer conceptual and theoretical framework, without which anyone whose allegiance was given to both the Aristotelian and Augustinian traditions would necessarily have lapsed either into incoherence or, by rejecting one of them, into a sterile onesidedness. And in a different way again, perhaps less successfully, Reid and Stewart attempted to rescue the Scottish tradition from the incoherence with which it was threatened by a combination of Humean epistemological premises with anti-Humean moral and metaphysical conclusions.

In quite other areas of enquiry the same patterns of epistemological crisis are to be found: thus Boltzmann's 1890 derivation of paradoxes from accounts of thermal energy framed in terms of classical mechanics produced an epistemological crisis within physics which was only to be resolved by Bohr's theory of the internal structure of the atom. What this example shows is that an epistemological crisis may only be recognized for what it was in retrospect. It is far from the case that physicists in general understood their discipline to be in crisis between Boltzmann and Bohr. Yet it was, and the power of quantum mechanics lies not only in its freedom from the difficulties and incoherences which came to afflict classical mechanics but also in its ability to furnish an explanation of why the problematic of classical mechanics was bound in the end to engender just such insoluble problems as that discovered by Boltzmann.

To have passed through an epistemological crisis successfully enables the adherents of a tradition of enquiry to rewrite its history in a more insightful way. And such a history of a particular tradition provides not only a way of identifying the continuities in virtue of which that tradition of enquiry has survived and flourished as one and the same tradition, but also of identifying more accurately that structure of justification which underpins whatever claims to truth are made within it, claims which are more and other than claims to warranted assertibility. The concept of warranted assertibility always has application only at some particular time and place in respect of standards then prevailing at some particular stage in the development of a tradition of enquiry, and a claim that such and such is warrantedly assertible always, therefore, has to make implicit or explicit references to such times and places. The concept of truth, however, is timeless. To claim that some thesis is true is not only to claim for all possible times and places that it cannot be shown to fail to correspond to reality in the sense of "correspond" elucidated earlier but also that the mind which expresses its thought in that thesis is in fact adequate to its object. The implications of this claim made in this way from within a tradition are precisely what enable us to show how the relativist challenge is misconceived.

Every tradition, whether it recognizes the fact or not, confronts the possibility that at some future time it will fall into a state of epistemological crisis, recognizable as such by its own standards of rational justification, which have themselves been vindicated up to that time as the best to emerge from the history of that particular tradition. All attempts to deploy the imaginative and inventive resources which the adherents of the tradition can provide may founder, either merely by doing nothing to remedy the condition of sterility and incoherence into which the enquiry has fallen or by also revealing or creating new problems, and revealing new flaws and new limitations. Time may elapse, and no further resources or solutions emerge.

That particular tradition's claims to truth can at some point in this process no longer be sustained. And this by itself is enough to show that if part of the relativist's thesis is that each tradition, since it provides its own standards of rational justification, must always be vindicated in the light of those standards, then on this at least the relativist is mistaken. But whether the relativist has claimed this or not, a further even more important possibility now becomes clear. For the adherents of a tradition which is now in this state of fundamental and radical crisis may at this point encounter in a new way the claims of some particular rival tradition, perhaps one with which they have for some time coexisted, perhaps one which they are now encountering for the first time. They now come or had already come to understand the beliefs and way of life of this other alien tradition, and to do so they have or have had to learn, as we shall see when we go on to discuss the linguistic characteristics of tradition, the language of the alien tradition as a new and second first language.

When they have understood the beliefs of the alien tradition, they may find themselves compelled to recognize that within this other tradition it is possible to construct from the concepts and theories peculiar to it what they were unable to provide from their own conceptual and theoretical resources, a cogent and illuminating explanation — cogent and illuminating, that is, by their own standards — of why their own intellectual tradition had been unable to solve its problems or restore its coherence. The standards by which they judge this explanation to be cogent and illuminating will be the very same standards by which they have found their tradition wanting in the face of epistemological crisis. But while this new explanation satisfies two of the requirements for an adequate response to an epistemological crisis within a tradition—insofar as it *both* explains why, given the structures of enquiry within that tradition, the crisis had to happen as it did *and* does not itself suffer from the same defects of incoherence or resourcelessness, the recognition of which had been the initial stage of their crisis —it fails to satisfy the third. Derived as it is from a genuinely alien tradition, the new explanation does not stand in any sort of substantive continuity with the preceding history of the tradition in crisis.

In this kind of situation the rationality of tradition requires an acknowledgment by those who have hitherto inhabited and given their allegiance to the tradition in crisis that the alien tradition is superior in rationality and in respect of its claims to truth to their own. What the explanation afforded from within the alien tradition will have disclosed is a lack of correspondence between the dominant beliefs of their own tradition and the reality disclosed by the most successful explanation, and it may well be the only successful explanation which they have been able to discover. Hence the claim to truth for what have hitherto been their own beliefs has been defeated.

From the fact that rationality, so understood, requires this acknowledgment of defeat in respect of truth, it does not of course follow that there will be actual acknowledgment. When the late medieval physics of nature was defeated in just this way by Galileo and his successors, there were not lacking physicists who continued to deny both the facts of the epistemological crisis which had afflicted impetus theory and Galileo's, and later Newton's success in providing a theory which not only did not suffer from the defects of impetus theory, but which was able to furnish the materials for an explanation of why nature is such that impetus theory could not have avoided the discovery of its own resourcelessness and incoherence, at just the points at which these defects in fact appeared. The physics of Galileo and Newton identified the phenomena of nature in such a way as to reveal the lack of correspondence between what impetus theory asserted about the phenomena of motion and the character which those phenomena had now turned out to possess and, in so doing, deprived impetus theory of warrant for its claim to truth.

It is important to remember at this point that not all epistemological crises are resolved so successfully. Some indeed are not resolved, and their lack of resolution itself defeats the tradition which has issued in such crises, without at the same time vindicating the claims of any other. Thus a tradition can be rationally discredited by and in the light of appeal to its very own standards of rationality in more than one way.

These are the possibilities which the relativist challenge has failed to envisage. That challenge relied upon the argument that if each tradition carries within it its own standards of rational justification, then, insofar as traditions of enquiry are genuinely distinct and different from each other, there is no way in which each tradition can enter into rational debate with any other, and no such tradition can therefore vindicate its rational superiority over its rivals. But if this were so, then there could be no good reason to give one's allegiance to the standpoint of any one tradition rather to that of any other. This argument can now be seen to be unsound. It is first of all untrue, and the preceding argument shows it to be untrue, that traditions, understood as each possessing its own account of and practices of rational justification, therefore cannot defeat or be defeated by other traditions. It is in respect of their adequacy or inadequacy in their responses to epistemological crises that traditions are vindicated or fail to be vindicated. It does of course follow that something like the relativist charge would hold of any self-contained mode of thought which was not developed to the point at which epistemological crises could become a real possibility. But that is not true of the type of tradition of enquiry discussed in this book. So far as they are concerned therefore, the relativist challenge fails.

To this the relativist may reply that I have at least conceded that over long periods of time two or more rival traditions may develop and flourish without encountering more than minor epistemological crises, or at least such as they are well able to cope with out of their own resources. And where this is the case, during such extended periods of time no one of these traditions will be able to encounter its rivals in such a way as to defeat them, nor will it be the case that any one of them will discredit itself by its inability to resolve its own crises. This is clearly true. As a matter of historical fact for very long periods traditions of very different kinds do indeed seem to coexist without any ability to bring their conflicts and disagreements to rational resolution: theological, metaphysical, moral, political, and scientific examples are not hard to find. But if this is so, then it may seem that by restricting itself to such examples the relativist challenge can still be sustained, at least in moderated form.

There is, however, a prior question to be answered by the relativist: Who is in a position to issue such a challenge? For the person who is to do so must during such period of time *either* be him or herself an inhabitant of one of the two or more rival traditions, owning allegiance to its standards of enquiry and justification and employing them in his or her reasoning, *or* be someone outside all of the traditions, him or herself traditionless. The former alternative precludes the possibility of relativism. Such a person, in the absence of serious epistemological crisis within his or her tradition, could have no good reason for putting his or her allegiance to it in question and every reason for continuing in that allegiance. What then of the latter alternative? Can the relativist challenge be issued from some standpoint outside all tradition?

The conclusion of the preceding chapter was that it is an illusion to suppose that there is some neutral standing ground, some locus for rationality as such, which can afford rational resources sufficient for enquiry independent of all traditions. Those who have maintained otherwise either have covertly been adopting the standpoint of a tradition and deceiving themselves and perhaps others into supposing that theirs was just such a neutral standing ground or else have simply been in error. The person outside all traditions lacks sufficient rational resources for enquiry and *a fortiori* for enquiry into what tradition is to be rationally preferred. He or she has no adequate relevant means of rational evaluation and hence can come to no well-grounded conclusion, including the conclusion that no tradition can vindicate itself against any other. To be outside all traditions is to be a stranger to enquiry; it is to be in a state of intellectual and moral destitution, a condition from which it is impossible to issue the relativist challenge.

The perspectivist's failure is complementary to the relativist's. Like the relativist the perspectivist is committed to maintaining that no claim to truth made in the name of any one competing tradition could defeat the claims to truth made in the name of its rivals. And this we have already seen to be a mistake, a mistake which commonly arises because the perspectivist foists on to the defenders of traditions some conception of truth other than that which is theirs, perhaps a Cartesian or an Hegelian conception of truth or perhaps one which assimilates truth to warranted assertibility.

The perspectivist, moreover, fails to recognize how integral the conception of truth is to tradition-constituted forms of enquiry. It is this which leads perspectivists to suppose that one could temporarily adopt the standpoint of a tradition and then exchange it for another, as one might wear first one costume and then another, or as one might act one part in one play and then a quite different part in a quite different play. But genuinely to adopt the standpoint of a tradition thereby commits one to its view of what is true and false and, in so committing one, prohibits one from adopting any rival standpoint. Hence the perspectivist could indeed *pretend* to assume the standpoint of some one particular tradition of enquiry; he or she could not in fact do so. The multiplicity of traditions does not afford a multiplicity of perspectives among which we can move, but a multiplicity of antagonistic commitments, between which only conflict, rational or nonrational, is possible.

Perspectivism, in this once more like relativism, is a doctrine only possible for those who regard themselves as outsiders, as uncommitted or rather as committed only to acting a succession of temporary parts. From their point of view any conception of truth but the most minimal appears to have been discredited. And from the standpoint afforded by the rationality of tradition-constituted enquiry it is clear that such persons are by their stance excluded from the possession of any concept of truth adequate for systematic rational enquiry. Hence theirs is not so much a conclusion about truth as an exclusion from it and thereby from rational debate.

Nietzsche came to understand this very well. The perspectivist must not engage in dialectical argument with Socrates, for that way would lie what from our point of view would be involvement in a tradition of rational enquiry, and from Nietzsche's point of view subjection to the tyranny of reason. Socrates is not to be argued with; he is to be mocked for his ugliness and his bad manners. Such mockery in response to dialectic is enjoined in the aphoristic paragraphs of *Götzen-Dammerung*. And the use of aphorism is itself instructive. An aphorism is not an argument. Gilles Deleuze has called it "a play of forces" (and see more generally 'Pensée Nomade' in *Nietzsche aujourd'hui*, Paris, 1973), something by means of which energy is transmitted rather than conclusions reached.

Nietzsche is of course not the only intellectual ancestor of modern perspectivism and perhaps not at all of modern relativism. Durkheim, however, provided a clue to the ancestry of both when he described in the late nineteenth century how the breakdown of traditional forms of social relationship increased the incidence of *anomie,* of normlessness. *Anomie,* as Durkheim characterized it, was a form of deprivation, of a loss of membership in those social institutions and modes in which norms, including the norms of tradition-constituted rationality, are embodied. What Durkheim did not foresee was a time when the same condition of *anomie* would be assigned the status of an achievement by and a reward for a self, which had, by separating itself from the social relationships of traditions, succeeded, so it believed, in emancipating itself. This self-defined success becomes in different versions the freedom from bad faith of the Sartrian individual who rejects determinate social roles, the homelessness of Deleuze's nomadic thinker, and the presupposition of Derrida's choice between remaining "within," although a stranger to, the already constructed social and intellectual edifice, but only in order to deconstruct it from within, or brutally placing oneself outside in a condition of rupture and discontinuity. What Durkheim saw as social pathology is now presented wearing the masks of philosophical pretension.

The most obtrusive feature of this kind of philosophy is its temporariness; dwelling too long in any one place will always threaten to confer upon such philosophy the continuity of enquiry, so that it becomes embodied as one more rational tradition. It turns out to be forms of tradition which present a threat to perspectivism rather than vice versa.

So we are still confronted by the claims to our rational allegiance of the rival traditions whose histories I have narrated, and indeed, depending upon where and how we raise the questions about justice and practical rationality, by a number of other such traditions. We have learned that we cannot ask and answer those questions from a standpoint external to all tradition, that the resources of adequate rationality are made available to us only in and through traditions. How then are we to confront those questions? To what account of practical rationality and of justice do we owe our assent? How we do in fact answer these latter questions, we now have to notice, will depend in key part upon what the language is which we share with those together with whom we ask them questions and to what point the history of our own linguistic community has brought us.

XIX

Tradition and Translation

A precondition of the adherents of two different traditions understanding those traditions as rival and competing is of course that in some significant measure they understand each other. This understanding is sometimes to be achieved only by a set of related historical transformations; either or both of the traditions may have had to enrich itself significantly in order to be able to provide a representation of some of the characteristic positions of the other, and this enrichment will have involved both conceptual and linguistic innovation, and quite possibly social innovation too. Yet the achievement of the understanding of one tradition by the adherents of another may have as its sequel a number of different types of outcome: to understand may entail immediate rejection in respect of that upon which they are divided; or to understand may lead to the conclusion that the issues which divide the two traditions cannot be decided; and in certainly rare but crucial types of cases, as we have already noticed, to understand may lead to a judgment that by the standards of one's own tradition the standpoint of the other tradition offers superior resources for understanding the problems and issues which confront one's own tradition.

Some philosophers have argued that insofar as the protagonists of two rival points of view are successful in understanding one another, it must be the case that they share standards of rational evaluation, such that the issues dividing them must in broad outline, if not in detail, be capable of being brought to resolution. Translatability in their view entails commensurability. It has also been argued that such commensurability has to be assumed not only in order to carry through such a work of translation but even in the elementary task of identifying the speakers of some alien language who inhabit some alien culture as *having a language,* indeed as having a mind. Thus Donald Davidson has written that "finding the common ground is not subsequent to understanding, but a condition of it. . . . A creature that cannot in principle be understood in terms of our own beliefs, values, and modes of communication is not a creature that may have thoughts radically different from our own: it is a creature without what we mean by thoughts" (*Expressing Evaluations,* Lawrence, 1984, p. 20).

Davidson unfortunately does not tell us how different difference has to be in order to be radical difference, and since his claim is a claim about what is the case "in principle," it can be interpreted as saying no more than what would be conceded, I take it, by anyone: that there will always be something in common between any two languages or any two sets of thoughts. But he has sometimes at least been understood to be asserting claims incompatible with the account which I have given of the types of relationship which can obtain between different traditions.

It is therefore important that I should expand this account in order to identify and to characterize the types of relationship of translatability and untranslatability, the linguistic relationships which can hold between traditions. For without such an expansion certain key elements in the very conception of a tradition, in the very idea of rival, historically developing conceptual schemes, will have been omitted. Notice, however, that this concern with the linguistic embodiment of traditions, however important, is not to be taken as a move to a more fundamental level of philosophical enquiry. Some recent philosophers have supposed that semantics is first philosophy, having displaced epistemology from that fundamental position, and have written as if it is at the level of semantic enquiry that philosophical disagreements have to be resolved first, the answers to epistemological, metaphysical, and ethical questions then being derived, at least in part, from the findings of semanticists. But there is no particular reason to believe this. *Prima facie* it is as reasonable to draw conclusions about what must be the case in the philosophy of language from what is the case, say, epistemologically as vice versa. Moreover, the semantics which has dominated recent philosophy of language has been highly abstract and uninformed for the most part by attention to empirical enquiry either about the differing uses of language in specific cultures or about the historical transformations of languages. Hence it is scarcely surprising that theses which emerge from an ahistorical semantics should sometimes be in conflict with theses which arise from philosophical and historical enquiry into the linguistic embodiment of actual traditions.

Every tradition is embodied in some particular set of utterances and actions and thereby in all the particularities of some specific language and culture. The invention, elaboration, and modification of the concepts through which both those who found and those who inherit a tradition understand it are inescapably concepts which have been framed in one language rather than another. When the adherents of such a tradition first entertain the project of extending it from one linguistic community to another, they have first to identify within the new language not only what types of utterance can be recognized as instances of saying the same as certain utterances in the language or languages through which the tradition has up till now expressed itself but also what it is which cannot as yet be said in the new language, which is so far and at that particular time untranslatable.

In similar fashion, when a tradition is expressing itself within a linguistic community whose language is not the originating language of that tradition, but one of its heirs and successors, it can only preserve its relationship to its past through a recognition of the presence of the originating language, and indeed of any intermediate languages, within the language in which it is now spoken and written. So Judaism, after it had become Greek-speaking, had to recognize the presence within the Septuagint of specifically Hebrew forms, concepts, and idioms, a recognition which involved at least an implicit acknowledgment that the Greek of the Septuagint was thereby a transformed Greek and that Greek prior to the Septuagint, Greek without the Septuagint, could not say, could not provide a translation for, what the Hebrew had said. So also when Greek philosophy came to be written in Latin, those who continued the Greek tradition of philosophical enquiry had to be able to recognize the originating Greek in the Latin in a way which also recognized the previous singularly unphilosophical character of Latin, thus acknowledging the extraordinary achievement of those who like Cicero both translated from Greek and neologized Latin, so that it acquired these new resources.

We thus have two distinct species of translation, translation by same-saying and translation by linguistic innovation, through which a tradition may be transmitted from its originating language, Hebrew or Greek or whatever, to later languages. Notice that these two relations of translation may hold between texts or other bodies of utterance not only in languages as different from each other as Hebrew, Greek, and Latin but also between what could be accounted two different stages or periods in the same language: the task of translating either by same-saying or by linguistic innovation, say, from the type of English which was the language of non-Gaelic Scotland in the age of Dunbar into the Anglicized eighteenth-century English of Hume and Adam Smith was and is in substance the same kind of task as that of translating from Greek into Latin or from Latin into either version of English.

The conception of language presupposed in saying this is that of a language as it is used in and by a particular community living at a particular time and place with particular shared beliefs, institutions, and practices. These beliefs, institutions, and practices will be furnished expression and embodiment in a variety of linguistic expressions and idioms; the language will provide standard uses for a necessary range of expressions and idioms, the use of which will presuppose commitment to those same beliefs, institutions, and practices. There was no way to discuss political matters in Cicero's Rome except within a framework supplied by the standard uses of '*respublica*', '*auctoritas*' (originally a technical term in the procedures of the senate), '*dignitas*', '*libertas*', '*imperium*', and the like. The predicates applied to individual heroic or unheroic deeds in the *Iliad* presuppose one particular catalog of the virtues, embodied in a stock of available adjectives; those applied to such deeds in Irish seventeenth-century verse tales of the Fianna presuppose a somewhat different catalog expressible in a different stock of adjectives. Limits to the possibilities of speaking otherwise than in accordance with the dominant beliefs of such communities are set by the language-in-use of those communities; breaking those limits would set on foot to greater or lesser extent the process by which one language-in-use is transformed into another.

It will be obvious that on this view of language there can be no such language as English-as-such or Hebrew-as-such or Latin-as-such. There are not even, it must seem, such languages as classical Latin or early modern Irish. There is only Latin-as-written-and-spoken-in-the-Rome-of-Cicero and Irish-as-written-and-spoken-in-sixteenth-century-Ulster. The boundaries of a language are the boundaries of some linguistic community which is also a social community. This conception of language does require supplementation in one way. There was indeed no such language as fourteenth-century-English-as-such but only such languages as the-fourteenth-century-English-of-Lancashire-and-surrounding-districts, in which *Gawain and the Green Knight* was written. But there is, for better or for worse, late twentieth-century English, an internationalized language, which like other late twentieth-century internationalized languages—such as the late twentieth-century versions of Spanish, German, and Japanese—has been developed so as apparently to become potentially available to anyone and everyone, whatever their membership in any or no community. Not all internationalized languages are of this twentieth-century kind; versions of both high medieval Latin and of medieval Arabic, for example, which still presupposed some large degree of shared tradition and belief, nonetheless became the languages of the inhabitants of a variety of different social and political orders, thus moving toward, although not falling into, the condition of late twentieth-century internationalized languages.

We can therefore compare and contrast languages in respect of the degree to which some particular language-in-use is tied by its vocabulary and its linguistic uses to a particular set of beliefs, the beliefs of some specific tradition, so that to reject or modify radically the beliefs will require some corresponding kind of linguistic transformation. Initially I want to focus attention upon those types of language in which the tie between language and communal belief is relatively close; how can and do the members of one such linguistic community come to understand the language of some other very different and alien such community? Anthropologists have for a long time insisted that no alien culture can be adequately characterized, let alone understood, without actually living in it for a certain length of time. And the evidence that anthropologists have as a result accumulated makes it difficult to disagree; at the very least, understanding requires knowing the culture, so far as is possible, as a native inhabitant knows it, and speaking, hearing, writing, and reading the language as a native inhabitant speaks, hears, writes, and reads it. Moreover, the learning of the language and the acquisition of cultural understanding are not two independent activities. Gestures, modes of ritual behavior, choices, and silences may all on occasion express utterances, and utterances themselves will be one class of deeds, classified just as deeds are classified.

What this kind of language learning by someone from another culture with another language involves is only in very small part in the earliest stages a matter of starting out from one's own first language by matching sentence with sentence. Instead one has, so to speak, to become a child all over again and to learn this language — and the corresponding parts of the culture — as a second first language. Just as a child does not learn its first language by matching sentences with sentences, since it initially possesses no set of sentences of its own, so an adult who has in this way become a child again does not either.

Obviously this process of language learning is best understood in the case of those who, like anthropologists in training, go to live in the society of the other culture and transform themselves, so far as is possible, into native inhabitants. But it seems clear that where we have sufficient textual and other materials from a culture which no longer exists, those with the requisite linguistic and historical skills can so immerse themselves that they can become almost, if not quite, surrogate participants in such societies as those of fifth-century Athens or twelfth-century Iceland. The acquisition of this kind of second first language is going to be testable in ways analogous to that in which the anthropologist's knowledge is testable. In the latter case we ask: How far can he or she pass as a native? In the former the corresponding question might be, for example: Can he or she, when acting in a play by Aristophanes, introduce a piece of comic improvisation in which the best scholarship could detect no relevant difference from the original? This is why in a genuine old-fashioned classical education the composition of Greek and Latin verse of widely diverse kinds played a key part, and the dropping of this requirement from the classical curriculum therefore signaled either a lack of interest in knowing whether someone really knows Greek or Latin or else a lack of knowledge of what knowing a language involves.

The characteristic mark of someone who has in either of these two ways acquired two first languages is to be able to recognize where and in what respects utterances in the one are untranslatable into the other. Such untranslatability may be of more than one kind. It may be the result, as we noticed earlier, of one of the two languages possessing resources of concept and idiom which the other lacks, or perhaps of each of the two possessing in different areas resources unavailable in the other. So it was not only the case that Greek lacked certain resources possessed by Hebrew before the Septuagint's translators partially transformed Greek but also that Hebrew till later still lacked philosophical resources which Greek itself had had to acquire through a radical set of linguistic innovations, themselves deeply alien to archaic Greek. You cannot express some of Plato's key thoughts in the Hebrew of Jeremiah or even of the Wisdom literature, but you also cannot express them in Homeric Greek (see Charles Kahn *The Verb 'Be' in Ancient Greek*, Part 6, *The Verb 'Be' and Its Synonyms,* ed. J.M.W. Verhaar, Dordrecht, 1973).

Such examples are however, although illuminating, already moving too far away from those societies in which linguistic use is tied most closely to the kind of shared belief which characteristically informs traditions at their points of origin and original growth. And only by attending to examples drawn from such societies shall we be able to understand barriers to translation which do not arise only from a lack of conceptual and linguistic resources in one of the two languages in question. Moreover, it is of the languages-in-use of just such societies that it is most important to remember what the anthropologists have to teach: they cannot be acquired as a second language by adding to one's first language skill in sentence-matching or even in paraphrase. They have to be learned as second first languages or not at all.

Two features of such primary languages-in-use are of peculiar importance: their practices of naming persons and places, and the particular ways in which by saying something a speaker or writer communicates more and other than he or she has actually said. Both these features continue to be important in later languages-in-use in which to some varying degree belief and language use are less closely tied together than they are in the type of example from which I shall begin, but which are also the heirs and successors of this earlier type of language-in-use. Yet for the moment let us concern ourselves with examples from the type of community which provides the starting points for those histories which constitute traditions.

In such cultures to name persons and places is to name them as members of some set. The kinds of names conferred will vary from set to set: the kind of name used of a person will differ from that used of a place or of a day of the week. This distinctive use of kinds has broken down to some degree in late twentieth-century English; it would once have been impossible to use "Tuesday" as a person's name, and to call someone "Man Friday" was to cast doubt on his status as a person. Consider how in what I shall call a primary linguistic community of the requisite kind the names of persons are used. I choose as an example the mode of personal naming recorded by Robin Fox on Tory Island off the north coast of Donegal in 1962 ('Structure of Personal Names on Tory Island' *Man,* 1963, reprinted in 'Personal Names' chapter 8 *Encounter with Anthropology,* New York, 1973), just because we have a good contemporary account of it. The systems of naming in ancient Rome and other tradition-engendering communities have many of the same characteristics.

On Tory Island there were—and are—three sets of such names, one used only in Irish on relatively formal occasions; one used in those local everyday relationships in which Irish is the normal language, but English is also used; and one used in English in relationship to such outside bodies as employers in Britain or Irish government agencies (the Irish-in-use of Tory Island is or was sufficiently different from the Irish-in-use of Dublin civil servants that it is or was often easier to conduct transactions with them in English). Names of both the first and second types furnish sufficient information to distinguish the person named from everyone else in the community. Thus in the second set of names a man has his first name added to his father's, or perhaps mother's, grandfather's, or grandmother's first names unless some special feature needs to be conveyed, as that his grandfather was an immigrant; so one man was called (in English) 'Owen-John-Dooley from Malin.' The string is as long as it needs to be to convey the information necessary to distinguish that person from everyone else in the community.

The relationship of such a name to its bearer is that he or she answers to it, when addressed by it, may be summoned by its use, introduced to someone else by it, identified by it as the person about whom something has been said, or spoken of by it directly. The notion of a name as standing in a unique, single relationship to its bearer is in such contexts not so much mistaken as misleading. The mode of life in which the name is related to its bearer in all these different ways provides a necessary background for understanding what makes *this name* the name of *that* particular person; 'reference' is no more than a name for the unity in the diversity of use, and if the diversity of use were abstracted, what would remain would not be some pure referential relationship. Instead nothing at all would remain.

Naming in this scheme is naming someone *as* a member of the local community; it also names *as* a member of his or her kinship group. In the use of the name beliefs about kinship are necessarily presupposed. The force of "necessarily" can be brought out in the following way. Kripke has argued that when we use the name 'Aristotle' we cannot mean, in part for example, 'the teacher of Alexander,' because it is always possible that we should discover that Aristotle did not in fact teach Alexander, and this discovery could not be expressed if 'teacher of Alexander' was part of the meaning of the name 'Aristotle' (Saul A. Kripke *Naming and Necessity,* Cambridge, Mass., 1980, pp. 61–62). What this argument shows is, not that the names of persons do not or cannot have informational content, but that *either* they lack such content *or* it is true of them that their use presupposes commitment to a belief, such that were this belief discovered to be false, the name could not continue to be used in the same way. This latter possibility is the one which Kripke did not entertain, and he was perhaps right not to entertain it in respect of the use of the name 'Aristotle' by those speaking some language of modernity in our society now. But it is the possibility which is realized in the system of personal names on Tory Island and in many other such systems of naming. In such systems names are used on the assumption that certain beliefs entrenched in the social order are true. If and insofar as the use of a name presupposes such beliefs, no translation into the language of a different community with different beliefs can be achieved by simply reproducing the name or some version of it (as 'Aristotle' is the English and '*Aristote*' the French version of the Greek '*Aristoteles*'). The use of the name will have to be accompanied by an explanation perhaps of that name only, perhaps of the whole system of naming, depending upon what body of utterances it is which has to be translated.

Thus in the case of a certain type of use of proper names translation requires gloss and explanation as an indispensable part of its work. Such explanation has to include reference not only to the classificatory and informative character of this type of name but also to the way in which status and authority are ascribed and communicated by the use of certain names. Personal names which express someone's place in a kinship system often thereby ascribe status, and to use a particular type of personal name may ascribe legitimate political authority: such and such a one is 'the O'Kane' or 'the O'Neill'. Notice also that there may be rival systems of naming, where there are rival communities and traditions, so that to use a name is at once to make a claim about political and social legitimacy and to deny a rival claim. Consider as an example the two rival place names 'Doire Columcille' in Irish and 'Londonderry' in English.

'Doire Columcille' embodies the intention of a particular and historically continuous Irish and Catholic community to name a place which has had a continuous identity ever since it became St. Columba's oak grave in 564—'Doire Columcille' is the description 'St. Columba's oak grave' turned into a name—while 'Londonderry' embodies the intention of a particular and historically continuous English-speaking and Protestant community to name a settlement made in the seventeenth century, information about whose commercial origin in London, England, is conveyed as effectively by its name as the corresponding religious information is conveyed by 'Doire Columcille'. To use either name is to deny the legitimacy of the other. Consequently there is no way to translate 'Doire Columcille' into English, except by using 'Doire Columcille' and appending an explanation. 'Londonderry' does not translate 'Doire Columcille'; nor does 'St. Columba's oak grave', for in English there is no such name.

What this brings out is that in such communities the naming of persons and places is not only naming as; it is also naming for. Names are used *as* identification *for* those who share the same beliefs, the same justifications of legitimate authority, and so on. The institutions of naming embody and express the shared standpoint of the community and characteristically its shared traditions of belief and enquiry. What then happens to the use of such names when they are used to identify those persons or places whose names they are by someone from outside the community, by, for example, a stranger who had noticed a place name, the name on a map but knows nothing of the background beliefs governing and presupposed by its intracommunal use? Such a stranger may use such a name in either of two ways. He or she may use the name desiring and intending to identify the place in question by using *its* name, or he or she may use it simply to identify *that* place by a name which will successfully achieve the task of identification. When the latter is the case, the name has been used simply as a referring expression for which an appropriate, definite description or in the right circumstances a gesture of pointing could be used instead. *Naming* has then become detached from *naming as* and *naming for,* and the relationship of the name to that which it names is reduced to that which holds between any identifying label successfully used and that of which it is used. What makes two uses of 'Londonderry' or 'Aristotle' uses of one and the same name, when employed in this way, is no more and no less than that they are uses of tokens of the same spoken or written type used of the same object. The absence of shared background beliefs makes any informational context attached to the names redundant to their function as names. So the conception of pure reference, of reference as such, emerges as the artefact of a particular type of social and cultural order, one in which a minimum of shared beliefs and allegiances can be presupposed. And it is indeed the case that the relationship of names to their bearers in this type of order can be mapped with little or no complexity on to the relationship of names to their bearers in an interpreted version of the first-order predicate calculus, thus creating the illusion of some semantic theorists that there is a single essential relation of reference.

We are now in a position to identify two other sets of problems about translatability. The first concerns those situations in which the task of translation is from the language of one community whose language-in-use is expressive of and presupposes a particular system of well-defined beliefs into the different language of another such community with beliefs which in some key areas are strongly incompatible with those of the first community. The second set of problems arises when the task is to translate from any one such language into one of the internationalized languages of modernity. In both types of case the task of translation will clearly require not only same-saying and paraphrase but also a possibly extensive use of interpretative glosses and explanations. The problems which will arise in evaluating such interpretative glosses and translations will, however, differ.

As an example of the problems which can be engendered by translation of the first kind—that is, from the language-in-use of one community whose use of its language is closely tied to its beliefs to that of another such community with incompatible beliefs—let us consider the case where the beliefs are not only incompatible but also incommensurable. We have already seen that from the fact that two communities with such rival belief-systems are able to agree in identifying one and the same subject matter as that identified, characterized, and evaluated in their two rival systems and are able to recognize that the applicability of certain of the concepts in the one scheme of belief precludes certain concepts in the other scheme from having application, it does not follow that the substantive criteria which govern the application of those concepts—the standards, that is, by which truth or falsity and rational justification or the lack of it are judged—cannot differ radically. The incommensurability of two schemes of belief in no way precludes their logical incompatibility.

Examples of such incommensurability can be drawn from the beliefs expressed in rival schemes of naming. The translator from language-in-use A to language-in-use B of such a scheme will have to explain the scheme of naming in A to those whose language is B in terms of the beliefs of the members of this latter community. The scheme of naming in A, that is, will have to be explained in terms of its differences from naming in B, but so to explain will be to exhibit A's scheme of naming as lacking in justification, as in some ways defective. To understand the translation-plus-explanation into B will entail for those whose language is B rejecting the beliefs so explained.

Consider as another type of example what it would have been to translate with the aid of such explanations the Latin of the opening line of the fifth ode in Horace's third book of Odes into the Hebrew of the contemporary first-century BCE Jewish community in Palestine: "Caelo tonantem credidimus Jovem regnare: praesens divus habebitur Augustus . . ." ("We have believed that Juppiter thundering reigns in the sky; Augustus will be held a present divinity . . ."). What Horace said could only have emerged in Hebrew as at once false and blasphemous; the Hebrew explanation of the Roman conception of a god could only have been in terms of an idolatrous regard for evil spirits. It is in the course of just this type of explanation that '*daimōn*' is transformed into 'demon'.

In consequence, in this type of case one standard test of translation and of translatability cannot be applied. When someone, a text from whose first first language has been translated into his or her second first language, agrees that were he or she to translate the resultant text back into his or her first language what would then in turn result would be substantially the same as the original text, we have what is perhaps the strongest single test by which to judge a translation. But in the type of case which we are considering, because adequacy of explanation is relative to the beliefs of those to whom something is being explained, and because each scheme of belief involves the rejection of the other, what counts as a good translation by paraphrase or same-saying plus in the one language-in-use will differ from what so counts in the other.

The features of such languages in use which generate this kind of contested translatability extend far beyond their practices in using proper names. Problems precisely analogous to those of supplying the relevant explanation in the case of proper names will arise when the two languages-in-use embody different and incompatible catalogs and understandings of the virtues, including justice, or a different and incompatible stock of psychological descriptions of how thinking may generate action. And in all three cases—proper names, the language of the virtues, the language of the genesis of action—the problem of translatability is aggravated by two other features of such languages-in-use.

The first derives from the way in which shared background schemes of belief permit a speaker by saying one thing to give his or her hearers to understand certain other things. By offering one particular explanation of an action a speaker rules out a certain range of alternative explanations. By ascribing a particular virtue to someone a speaker precludes that person's having a certain range of vices. Understanding what is being denied when something is asserted, or vice versa, in this type of case requires far more than a comprehension of the negation sign.

A second feature of such languages-in-use intensifies this type of difficulty as well as adding some complexities of its own. It is a feature which in part derives from characteristics of languages as such and in part from the specific characteristics of those languages-in-use which embody a tradition or traditions. The relevant characteristic of languages as such can best be explained by considering the difference between the utterances of someone who has mastered a particular language, whether as first first language or as second first language, and the utterances of someone who is using a phrase-book to speak in a language which he or she has not mastered.

The latter speaks in units in which each sentence or short set of sentences has a discrete function, so that when sentences or short sets of sentences (types, not tokens) are matched to sentences or similar short sets in the speaker's language, and both are matched to certain types of well-defined and easily recognized context, the speaker can reasonably expect to produce some desired effect by the use of corresponding tokens. The measure of success in the matching is therefore pragmatic. Does the use of this set of sentences result in the purchase of a clay pot? Does the use of that set ensure that I am at the bus station on time? The better the phrase book is the more effective it will be in realizing the expectations of the alien culture which the foreign visitor brings to it; it is these which inform the choice of phrases. So a current Irish phrase book enables those foreign visitors who desire to pretend to speak Irish to say "Biadh deoch agat" ("Have a drink"), while users of *Easy Vietnamese* in the late sixties and early seventies learned to say *Đừng bắn!* ("Don't shoot").

What cannot be learned from the matching of sentence with sentence and of sentence with context, no matter how sophisticated the phrase book writer, is not only how the kinds of system of naming and classificatory schemes which we have already discussed are used but also and even more fundamentally how a grasp of a language-in-use enables a competent language user to move from one kind of use of expression in the context of one sentence to another notably different kind of use of the same expression in the context of another and perhaps then go on to innovate by inventing a third kind of use for that very same expression in yet another sentential context. It is this knowing how to go on and go further which is the badge of elementary linguistic competence. Someone who knows that it is appropriate to assent to "Snow is white" if and when snow is white does not as yet thereby evidence a grasp of "white" in English. Such a grasp would be evidenced by being able to say, for example, "Snow is white and so are the members of the Ku Klux Klan, and white with fear is what they were in snow-covered Arkansas last Friday." That is the kind of thing you cannot learn how to say from phrase books or indeed from any recursively enumerable set of individual English sentences.

Knowing how to go on and to go further in the use of the expressions of a language is that part of the ability of every language-user which is poetic. The poet by profession merely has this ability in a pre-eminent degree. It is in hearing and learning and later in reading spoken and written poetic texts that the young in the type of society with which we are concerned learn the paradigmatic uses of key expressions at the same time and inseparably from their learning the model exemplifications of the virtues, the legitimating genealogies of their community, and its key prescription. Learning its language and being initiated into their community's tradition or traditions is one and the same initiation. When asked in such a society "What is x?" or "What does 'x' mean?" one standard way of answering is to quote a line or two from a poem. So the meanings of key expressions are fixed in part by reference to standard authoritative texts, which also provide the paradigmatic examples used in instructing the same young as to how to extend concepts, to find new uses for established expressions, and to move through and on from that multiplicity of uses, acquaintance with which provides the background for introducing such distinctions as those between the literal and the metaphorical, the joking, the ironic, and the straightforward, and later, when the going becomes theoretical, the analogical, the univocal, and the equivocal. All tradition-informed language-use tends thereby in some measure toward the condition of multiple meanings finally achieved in *Finnegan's Wake,* that last of all paradigmatic texts which is itself a wake for all other texts — or at least the pretext of a wake.

Knowing how to go on and to go further is part, so I have suggested, of linguistic capacity as such; making this knowledge in key part dependent upon the reading of texts whose writing required this capacity to an exemplary degree provides just the kind of linguistic foundation which a tradition constituted in part by philosophically sophisticated enquiry requires. For such a tradition, if it is to flourish at all, as we have already learned, has to be embodied in a set of texts which function as the authoritative point of departure for tradition-constituted enquiry and which remain as essential points of reference for enquiry and activity, for argument, debate, and conflict within that tradition. Those texts to which this canonical status is assigned are treated both as having a fixed meaning embodied in them and also as always open to rereading, so that every tradition becomes to some degree a tradition of critical reinterpretation in which one and the same body of texts, with of course some addition and subtraction, is put to the question, and to successively different sets of questions, as a tradition unfolds.

Thus at any particular stage in the development of a tradition the beliefs which characterize that stage of that particular tradition carry with them a history in which the successive rational justification of their predecessors and themselves are embodied, and the language in which they are expressed is itself inseparable from a history of linguistic and conceptual transformations and translations: *velle* (first in everyday speech and then as a legal term), *voluntas, voluntary; auctoritas* (first as a legal-political term and then more generally), *authority, author; polis, politikē koinōnia; civitas, civil society; dikaiosunē, ius, iustitia, justice* — these are strings which can be read as aphoristic versions of such histories, of just the kind which are embodied in the narrative accounts of Greek, medieval, and early modern Scottish traditions in this book. And the names which genealogically punctuate those histories are for those inhabiting such traditions like the names on Tory Island: 'Aristotle' is inseparable in meaning and use from 'the pupil of Plato, the pupil of Socrates,' and 'Justinian' from 'the imperial author of the *Institutions.*'

When we are considering, as we have been so far, the tasks of translation from the texts of one tradition-informed community, whose language-in-use is closely tied to the expression of the shared beliefs of that tradition, into the different language-in-use of just such another community, with its own very different tradition and beliefs, this historical dimension peculiar to each tradition-bearing community merely adds to the kind of difficulty which arises from such practices as those of naming and of classification. But the historical dimension creates another kind of difficulty of its own when the task of translation to be performed is *from* just such a language-in-use but *into* one of the internationalized languages of modernity.

Just because it is characteristic of such languages that they are tied very loosely to any particular set of contestable beliefs but are rich in modes of characterization and explanation which enable texts embodying alien schemes of systematic belief to be reported on—not in the light of some other rival scheme of belief, by reference to which they would necessarily be exhibited as true or false, reasonable or unreasonable, but rather in detachment from all substantive criteria and standards of truth and rationality—the problems arising from a translation part of whose end product is an explanation of the meaning of a text unacceptable to those whose text it was or is, do not at first sight seem to arise.

What do I mean by "in detachment from all substantive criteria and standards of truth and rationality"? Just because and insofar as the internationalized languages-in-use of late twentieth-century modernity have minimal presuppositions in respect of possibly rival belief systems, their shared criteria for the correct application of such concepts as "is true" and "is reasonable" must also be minimal. And in fact truth is assimilated, so far as is possible, to warranted assertibility, and reasonableness, so far as possible, is relativized to social context. Hence when texts from traditions with their own strong, substantive criteria of truth and rationality, as well as with a strong historical dimension, are translated into such languages, they are presented in a way that neutralizes the conceptions of truth and rationality and the historical context. How is this achieved?

The conceptions of truth and rationality become not part of a presupposed framework of beliefs to which the author appeals in addressing an audience who shares or shared that same framework but are relegated to an explanation to an audience characterized as not possessing any such framework. The particular history out of which the author wrote and which it is his or her purpose to carry one stage further also disappears from view as the presupposed context of the work and appears instead, if at all, as an explanatory appendage to it. In these two ways a kind of text which cannot be read as *the text it is* out of context is nevertheless rendered contextless. But in so rendering it, it is turned into a text which is no longer the author's, nor such as would be recognized by the audience to whom it was addressed. The task of translation into such a language has been achieved at the cost of producing something which would not be recognized or accepted by speakers and writers for whom the original language-in-use was their first first language, but who had learned the particular internationalized language as their second first language.

This distortion by translation out of context—from the standpoint of those who inhabit the traditions from which the distorted texts are taken—is of course apt to be invisible to those whose first first language is one of the internationalized languages of modernity. For them it must appear that there is nothing which is not translatable into their language. Untranslatability—if cautious, they may say untranslatability in principle—will perhaps appear to them as a philosophical fiction.

This belief in its ability to understand everything from human culture and history, no matter how apparently alien, is itself one of the defining beliefs of the culture of modernity. It is evident in the way in which the history of art is taught and written, so that the objects and the texts produced by other cultures are brought under our concept of art, allowing us to exhibit what were in fact very different and heterogenous kinds of objects under one and the same aesthetic rubric in new artificial neutral contexts in our museums, museums which in an important way have become *the* public buildings of this kind of educated modernity, just as the temple was for Periclean Athens or the cathedral for thirteenth-century France.

The type of translation characteristic of modernity generates in turn its own misunderstanding of tradition. The original locus of that misunderstanding is the kind of introductory Great Books or Humanities course, so often taught in liberal arts colleges, in which, in abstraction from historical context and with all sense of the complexities of linguistic particularity removed by translation, a student moves in rapid succession through Homer, one play of Sophocles, two dialogues of Plato, Virgil, Augustine, the *Inferno,* Machiavelli, *Hamlet,* and as much else as is possible if one is to reach Sartre by the end of the semester. If one fails to recognize that what this provides is not and cannot be a reintroduction to the culture of past traditions but is a tour through what is in effect a museum of texts, each rendered contextless and therefore other than its original by being placed on a cultural pedestal, then it is natural enough to suppose that, were we to achieve consensus as to a set of such texts, the reading of them would reintegrate modern students into what is thought of as *our* tradition, that unfortunate fictitious amalgam sometimes known as "the Judeo-Christian tradition" and sometimes as "Western values." The writings of self-proclaimed contemporary conservatives, such as William J. Bennett, turn out in fact to be one more stage in modernity's cultural deformation of our relationship to the past.

It is then perhaps unsurprising that recent postmodernist doctrines of the text, although at the level of theory they have marked a radical break from their immediate predecessors, nonetheless in their theory did no more than provide a rationale for practices which were of fairly long standing in peculiarly modern education. Every text, so the radical postmodernist proclaims, is susceptible of indefinitely many interpretative readings. The understanding of the text is not controlled by authorial intention or by any relationship to an audience with specific shared beliefs, for it is outside context except the context of interpretation. So Roland Barthes could assert that a work of literature is unlike an utterance with practical import in which pragmatic considerations drawn from the context of utterance disambiguate it: "That is not the case with a work (*oeuvre*): the work is without circumstance and it is indeed perhaps what defines it best: the work is not circumscribed, designated, protected, directed by any situation, no practical life is there to tell what meaning to give to it . . . in it ambiguity is wholly pure: however extended it may be, it possesses something of the brevity of the priestess of Apollo, sayings conforming to a first code (the priestess did not rave) and yet open to a number of meanings, for they were uttered outside every *situation*—except indeed the situation of ambiguity . . ." (*Critique et Verité,* Paris, 1966, p. 56). This is a splendid description of what traditional texts detached from the context of tradition must become, presented by Barthes as though it were an account of how necessarily texts always are.

The indefinite multiplicity of possible interpretations is matched by the indefinite multiplicity of translations, since every translation is an interpretation. Indeed, mistranslation becomes in these circumstances increasingly difficult to achieve, since the canons of accuracy are necessarily relaxed in the name of creativity of interpretation. And here again modern conservatives are interestingly at one with postmodernist radicals: Ezra Pound's renderings of Propertius and Heidegger's treatment of the pre-Socratics anticipated in those translators' practice what Barthes and others would somewhat later proclaim as theory.

The thought which modernity, whether conservative or radical, rejects is that there may be traditional modes of social, cultural, and intellectual life which are as such inaccesible to it and to its translators. The argument that only insofar as we can come to understand what it is that is allegedly inaccessible to us could we have grounds for believing in such inaccessibility, and that the acquisition of such understanding is of itself sufficient to show that what was alleged to be inaccessible is in fact not so, carries conviction only when it is supposed that the acquisition of the understanding of the inaccessible is a matter of translating it into our own language-in-use. But if it is in the case, as I have argued here, that a condition of discovering the inaccessible is in fact a matter of two stages, in the first of which we acquire a second language-in-use as a second first language and only in the second of which can we learn that we are unable to translate what we are now able to say in our second first language into our first first language, then this argument loses all its force.

From the standpoint of any particular tradition it is a question of entirely contingent fact whether or not the language-in-use of some other different tradition will or will not be comprehensible to those who inhabit it or vice versa. Rival traditions may of course be very different from each other in some ways while sharing a great deal in others: texts, modes of evaluation, whole practices, such as games, crafts, and sciences. Insofar as this is so, translation will generally be able to proceed almost entirely by same-saying. But the less that is shared, the more difficult and cumbrous the work of translation will be, and the more possibilities of untranslatability will seem to threaten. But 'threaten' is not in fact the right word.

The possibility to which every tradition is always open, as I argued earlier, is that the time and place may come, when and where those who live their lives in and through the language-in-use which gives expression to it may encounter another alien tradition with its own very different language-in-use and may discover that while in some area of greater or lesser importance they cannot comprehend it within the terms of reference set by their own beliefs, their own history, and their own language-in-use, it provides a standpoint from which once they have acquired its language-in-use as a second first language, the limitations, incoherences, and poverty of resources of their own beliefs can be identified, characterized, and explained in a way not possible from within their own tradition.

It follows that the only rational way for the adherents of any tradition to approach intellectually, culturally, and linguistically alien rivals is one that allows for the possibility that in one or more areas the other may be rationally superior to it in respect precisely of that in the alien tradition which it cannot as yet comprehend. The claim made within each tradition that the presently established beliefs shared by the adherents of that tradition are true entails a denial that this is in fact going to happen in respect of those beliefs, but it is the possibility of this nonetheless happening which, as we also noticed earlier, gives point to the assertion of truth and provides assertions of truth and falsity with a content which makes them other than even idealized versions of assertions of warranted assertibility. The existence of large possibilities of untranslatability and therefore of potential threats to the cultural, linguistic, social, and rational hegemony of one's own tradition, either in some particular area or overall, is therefore more and other than a threat. Only those whose tradition allows for the possibility of its hegemony being put in question can have rational warrant for asserting such a hegemony. And only those traditions whose adherents recognize the possibility of untranslatability into their own language-in-use are able to reckon adequately with that possibility.

The argument to this conclusion requires one footnote: the condition which I have described as that characteristic of the late twentieth-century language of internationalized modernity is perhaps best understood as an ideal type, a condition to which the actual languages of the metropolitan centers of modernity approximate in varying and increasing degrees, especially among the more affluent. And the social and cultural condition of those who speak that kind of language, a certain type of rootless cosmopolitanism, the condition of those who aspiring to be at home anywhere—except that is, of course, in what they regard as the backward, outmoded, undeveloped cultures of traditions—are therefore in an important way citizens of nowhere is also ideal-typical. It is the fate toward which modernity moves precisely insofar as it successfully modernizes itself and others by emancipating itself from social, cultural, and linguistic particularity and so from tradition. (For a different account of the relevance of the problems of reference and translation to the issue of rival moral standpoints see David B. Wong *Moral Relativity,* Berkeley, 1984.)

XX

Contested Justices, Contested Rationalities

This is a point in the argument at which it is important to remind ourselves that the discussion of the nature of tradition-constituted and tradition-constitutive enquiry has been undertaken not for its own sake but in order to arrive, so far as is possible, at a true account of justice and of practical rationality. The enquiry into justice and practical rationality was from the outset informed by a conviction that each particular conception of justice requires as its counterpart some particular conception of practical rationality and vice versa. Not only has that conviction been reinforced by the outcome of the enquiry so far, but it has become evident that conceptions of justice and of practical rationality generally and characteristically confront us as closely related aspects of some larger, more or less well-articulated, overall view of human life and of its place in nature. Such overall views, insofar as they make claims upon our rational allegiance, give expression to traditions of rational enquiry which are at one and the same time traditions embodied in particular types of social relationship.

So Aristotle's conception of justice and practical rationality articulated the claims of one particular type of practice-based community, partially exemplified in the *polis,* while Aquinas', like Ibn Roschd's or Maimonides', expressed the claims of a more complex form of community in which religious and secular elements coexist within an integrated whole. So Hume's conception of justice and of the relationship of reasoning to action was both at home in and expressed the claims of a particular form of English or Anglicizing society ordered in terms of mutualities and reciprocities of passion and interest. That Aristotle, Aquinas, and Hume, and indeed those other philosophers with whom we have been concerned, were historically situated in the way that they were, themselves members of just such forms of community, who were inescapably involved in the conflicts central to the historically developing life of those communities at those times and places, is not then a merely accidental or peripheral fact about the philosophy of each. Not only do we have to understand each philosophy as a whole, so that the distinctive conceptions of justice and practical rationality elaborated by each thinker are understood as parts of that whole, but we have to understand each philosophy in terms of the historical context of tradition, social order, and conflict out of which it emerged.

In so doing we have to avoid two opposed types of error, one characteristic of many past histories of philosophy, the other of some work at least in the sociology of knowledge. Historians of philosophy have often enough presented the historical context of each philosopher's life as mere background. They have been compelled by the way in which later philosophers comment upon earlier to recognize some types of historical sequence, but sometimes little more than this. So the development of philosophical thought has been presented as though relatively autonomous, as a socially disembodied enterprise concerned with relatively timeless problems. By contrast some sociologists of knowledge have given accounts of philosophical thought and enquiry which make these dependent upon, or even nothing but, masks worn by antecedently definable social, political, or economic interests of particular groups. What on this view produces change cannot be progress in rationality; such progress could at best be the accidental outcome of what are taken to be more fundamental types of change.

By contrast, on the view which has emerged here from the discussion of tradition-constituted and tradition-constitutive enquiry such thought and enquiry have a history neither distinct from, nor intelligible apart from, the history of certain forms of social and practical life, nor are mere dependent variables. Philosophical theories give organized expression to concepts and theories already embodied in forms of practice and types of community. As such they make available for rational criticism and for further rational development those socially embodied theories and concepts of which they provide an understanding. Forms of social institution, organization, and practice are always to great or lesser degree socially embodied theories and, as such, more or less rational according to the standards of that type of rationality which is presupposed by tradition-constituted enquiry. The reductionism which appears recurrently in the sociology of knowledge rests upon the mistake of supposing that preconceptual interests, needs, and the like can operate in sustained forms of social life in independence of theory-informed presuppositions about the place of such interests and needs in human life. The apparently antithetical illusion of the autonomy of philosophical thought unintentionally reinforces such reductivism by treating the realm of theories and concepts as one distinct from that of interests, needs, and forms of social organization.

So theories of justice and practical rationality confront us as aspects of traditions, allegiance to which requires the living out of some more or less systematically embodied form of human life, each with its own specific modes of social relationship, each with its own canons of interpretation and explanation in respect of the behavior of others, each with its own evaluative practices. This does not mean that one cannot be an Aristotelian without membership in an actual *polis,* or that one cannot be a Humean outside the specific hierarchically ordered relationships of eighteenth-century England. Were this so, the study of either Aristotelian or Humean theory could be only of antiquarian interest. What it does mean is that it is only insofar as those features of the *polis* which provide an essential context for the exercise of Aristotelian justice and for the action-guiding and interpretative uses of the Aristotelian schema of practical reasoning can be reembodied in one's own life and that of one's time and place that one can be an Aristotelian. And it is likewise only insofar as those features of the social order in terms of which Hume framed his accounts of justice and of action can be reproduced that one can actually *be* a Humean. So also and correspondingly with other traditions of enquiry.

It is indeed a feature of all those traditions with whose histories we have been specifically concerned that in one way or another all of them have survived so as to become not only possible, but actual, forms of practical life within the domain of modernity. Even when marginalized by the dominant modern social, cultural, and political order, such traditions have retained the allegiance of the members of a variety of types of community and enterprise, not all of whom are aware of whence their conceptions of justice and practical rationality derive. The past of such traditions is encapsulated in the present and not always only in fragmented or disguised form.

So there are Humean modes of social existence, for which property relationships and their stability are all important, in which there are well-established reciprocities of pride and esteem, and in which the recognition of a common interest in sustaining the order within which these flourish can be appealed to against the partialities of self, group, and family interest. So there are also Aristotelian practice-based enterprises and communities in which a justice of desert is the social virtue of those who recognize the ordered goods which they pursue as specifying what for them in their circumstances is required for and of those whose *telos* is the good as such. And so, of course, there are religious and educational communities of Thomistic Christians as well as of other kinds of Augustinian Christian, both Catholic and Reformed. Moreover, it is once again important not to forget that there are traditions other than those discussed in this book, most notably more than one Jewish tradition and those of quite other cultures than our own which also have their contemporary social embodiments.

Each of those advances its claims, explicitly or implicitly, within an institutionalized framework largely informed by the assumptions of liberalism, so that the influence of liberalism extends beyond the effects of its explicit advocacy. And just as the older traditions are able to survive within liberal modernity, just because they afford expression to features of human life and modes of human relationship which can appear in a variety of very different social and cultural forms, so modern liberalism too has had its anticipations in earlier cultures, most notably, so far as the history which has been recounted here is concerned, in some aspects of Greek political thought and practice rejected by Socrates, Plato, and Aristotle but defended by, among others, certain sophists (see Eric A. Havelock *The Liberal Temper in Greek Politics,* New Haven, 1957). The historical particularities of traditions, the fact that each is only to be appropriated by a relationship to a particular contingent history, does not of itself mean that those histories cannot extend to and even flourish in environments not only different from but even hostile to those in which a tradition was originally at home.

Liberalism, as I have understood it in this book, does of course appear in contemporary debates in a number of guises and in so doing is often successful in preempting the debate by reformulating quarrels and conflicts with liberalism, so that they appear to have become debates within liberalism, putting in question this or that particular set of attitudes or policies, but not the fundamental tenets of liberalism with respect to individuals and the expression of their preferences. So so-called conservatism and so-called radicalism in these contemporary guises are in general mere stalking-horses for liberalism: the contemporary debates within modern political systems are almost exclusively between conservative liberals, liberal liberals, and radical liberals. There is little place in such political systems for the criticism of the system itself, that is, for putting liberalism in question.

It is then unsurprising that in contemporary debates about justice and practical rationality one initial problem for those antagonistic to liberalism is that of either discovering or constructing some institutional forum or arena within which the terms of the debate have not already predetermined its outcome. To consider the dimensions of this problem we must first return to the situation of the person to whom, after all, this book is primarily addressed, someone who, not as yet having given their allegiance to some coherent tradition of enquiry, is besieged by disputes over what is just and about how it is reasonable to act, both at the level of particular immediate issues—"Does justice require that I participate in or oppose this war?" "Is positive discrimination in favor of members of hitherto oppressed and deprived groups in appointing to this job now an injustice?"—and at the level at which rival systematic tradition-informed conceptions contend.

Such a person is confronted by the claims of each of the traditions which we have considered as well as by those of other traditions. How is it rational to respond to them? The initial answer is: that will depend upon who you are and how you understand yourself. This is not the kind of answer which we have been educated to expect in philosophy, but that is because our education in and about philosophy has by and large presupposed what is in fact not true, that there are standards of rationality, adequate for the evaluation of rival answers to such questions, equally available, at least in principle, to all persons, whatever tradition they may happen to find themselves in and whether or not they inhabit any tradition. When this false belief is rejected, it becomes clear that the problems of justice and practical rationality and of how to confront the rival systematic claims of traditions contending with each other in the *agōn* of ideological encounter are not one and the same set of problems for all persons. What those problems are, how they are to be formulated and addressed, and how, if at all, they may be resolved will vary not only with the historical, social, and cultural situation of the persons whose problems these are but also with the history of belief and attitude of each particular person up to the point at which he or she finds these problems inescapable.

What each person is confronted with is at once a set of rival intellectual positions, a set of rival traditions embodied more or less imperfectly in contemporary forms of social relationship and a set of rival communities of discourse, each with its own specific modes of speech, argument, and debate, each making a claim upon the individual's allegiance. It is by the relationship between what is specific to each such standpoint, embodied at these three levels of doctrine, history, and discourse, and what is specific to the beliefs and history of each individual who confronts these problems, that what the problems are for that person is determined. So that genuine intellectual encounter does not and cannot take place in some generalized, abstract way. The wider the audience to whom we aspire to speak, the less we shall speak to anyone in particular. How then ought we to characterize the different specific types of contemporary situation in which the problems of justice and practical rationality may arise, be pursued, and perhaps resolved by those not yet inheriting any one particular substantive tradition?

There is first of all that of the type of person for whom what an encounter with some particular tradition of thought and action in respect of these matters may provide is an occasion for self-recognition and self-knowledge. Such a person will characteristically have learned to speak and write some particular language-in-use, the presuppositions of whose use tie that language to a set of beliefs which that person may never have explicitly formulated for him or herself except in partial and occasional ways. He or she will characteristically have found themselves responsive to certain texts, less so or not at all to others, open to certain kinds of argumentative consideration, unpersuaded by others. Upon encountering a coherent presentation of one particular tradition of rational enquiry, either in its seminal texts or in some later, perhaps contemporary, restatement of its positions, such a person will often experience a shock of recognition: *this* is not only, so such a person may say, what I now take to be true but in some measure what I have always taken to be true. What such a person has been presented with is a scheme of overall belief within which many, if not all, of his or her particular established beliefs fall into place, a set of modes of action and of interpretative canons for action which exhibit his or her mode of reasoning about action as intelligible and justifiable in a way or to a degree which has not previously been the case, and the history of a tradition of which the narrated and enacted history of his or her life so far forms an intelligible part.

What rationality then requires of such a person is that he or she confirm or disconfirm over time this initial view of his or her relationship to this particular tradition of enquiry by engaging, to whatever degree is appropriate, both in the ongoing arguments within that tradition and in the argumentative debates and conflicts of that tradition of enquiry with one or more of its rivals. These two tasks are not at all the same. The latter requires, so far as is possible, the acquisition of the language-in-use of whatever particular rival tradition is in question, as what I have called a second first language, and that in turn requires a work of the imagination whereby the individual is able to place him or herself imaginatively within the scheme of belief inhabited by those whose allegiance is to the rival tradition, so as to perceive and conceive the natural and social worlds as they perceive and conceive them.

To possess the concepts of an alien culture in this secondary mode, informed by conceptual imagination, differs in important ways from possessing the concepts which are genuinely one's own. For insofar as one disagrees upon whether or not a particular concept has application — Hume's concept of justice, say, or Augustine's concept of the will — because one's own conceptual scheme precludes its having application, one will only be able to deploy it in the way in which an actor speaking his part may say things which he or she does not in his or her own person believe. We possess such concepts without being able to employ them in the first person, except as dramatic impersonators, speaking in a voice which is not our own. But this does not mean that we cannot understand what it is to be and to believe within another tradition by acts of empathetic conceptual imagination in some types of case; the limits of possibility here are those set by the kinds of untranslatability which were cataloged earlier.

So such a person comes both to inhabit one particular tradition-informed community of discourse in a way which enables him or her to enter into argumentative dialogue with the members of other such communities. This capacity for recognition of the self as being already to some degree at home in some tradition sharply differentiates this kind of person and this kind of encounter with a tradition of enquiry from the person who finds him or herself an alien to every tradition of enquiry which he or she encounters and who does so because he or she brings to the encounter with such tradition standards of rational justification which the beliefs of no tradition could satisfy.

This is the kind of post-Enlightenment person who responds to the failure of the Enlightenment to provide neutral, impersonal tradition-independent standards of rational judgment by concluding that no set of beliefs proposed for acceptance is therefore justifiable. The everyday world is to be treated as one of pragmatic necessities. Every scheme of overall belief which extends beyond the realm of pragmatic necessity is equally unjustified. There is no such scheme of belief within which such an individual is able to find him or herself at home, and the imaginative assumption of beliefs not actually held is not and cannot be for the purpose of investigating the rationality of that scheme, for it has already been concluded that all such schemes fail. Such an individual therefore views the social and cultural order, the order of traditions, as a series of falsifying masquerades. He or she can belong to no community of discourse, for the ties of the language which he or she speaks to any presupposed scheme of belief are as loose as it is possible to make them. So the natural languages of persons thus alienated are the internationalized languages of modernity, the languages of everywhere and of nowhere.

Such persons who take themselves to have escaped the deception and self-deception of such masquerades cannot understand the action of entering into any scheme of belief except as an act of arbitrary will, arbitrary, that is, in that it must lack sufficient supporting reasons. And to those who seem to them to have been deceived or to have deceived themselves into becoming accomplices in the masquerades they will characteristically ascribe just such unacknowledged acts of will. So beliefs, allegiances to conceptions of justice, and the use of particular modes of reasoning about action will appear to them as disguises assumed by arbitrary will to further its projects, to empower itself. How, if at all, could such a person as a result of an encounter with some particular tradition of enquiry come instead to inhabit that tradition as a rational agent? What kind of transformation would be required?

Such a transformation, understood from the standpoint of any rational tradition of enquiry, would require that those who adopt this stance become able not only to recognize themselves as imprisoned by a set of beliefs which lack justification in precisely the same way and to the same extent as do the positions which they reject but also to understand themselves as hitherto deprived of what tradition affords, as persons in part constituted as what they are up to this point by an absence, by what is from the standpoint of traditions an impoverishment. From a Humean point of view they have warped their sentiments in such a way as to render themselves incapable of reciprocity; from an Aristotelian they have refused to learn or have been unable to learn that one cannot think for oneself if one thinks entirely by oneself, that it is only by participation in rational practice-based community that one becomes rational; from an Augustinian point of view they have ignored even that standard internal to mind in whose light we are able to know our own deficiencies and consequently our inability to remedy them. In each case they are understood by the adherents of that particular tradition of enquiry to need for their correction, even for that minimal correction which would enable them to enter into dialogue with that tradition, what they have by their own attitude debarred themselves from being able to possess or to achieve. How then could such a transformation be possible?

Only, it seems, by a change amounting to a conversion, since a condition of this alienated type of self even finding a language-in-use, which would enable it to enter into dialogue with some tradition of enquiry, is that it becomes something other than it now is, a self able to acknowledge by the way it expresses itself in language standards of rational enquiry as something other than expressions of will and preference. In contrast with the type of self which in encounter with some tradition of enquiry achieves self-recognition and self-knowledge, because already informed by the dispositions, sentiments, language-in-use, and mind-set characteristic of that particular tradition, this latter type of self is equally estranged from and uninformed by any such set of dispositions, sentiments, thoughts, or language-in-use.

It may well be the case that such persons are portrayed in modern literary and philosophical texts more frequently than they are to be met with in everyday life. In both texts and actuality they represent a point of linguistic and moral extremity in relation to any tradition-constituted form of thought and life. Most of our contemporaries do not live at or even near that point of extremity, but neither are they for the most part able to recognize in themselves in their encounters with traditions that they have already implicitly to some significant degree given their allegiance to some one particular tradition. Instead they tend to live betwixt and between, accepting usually unquestioningly the assumptions of the dominant liberal individualist forms of public life, but drawing in different areas of their lives upon a variety of tradition-generated resources of thought and action, transmitted from a variety of familial, religious, educational, and other social and cultural sources. This type of self which has too many half-convictions and too few settled coherent convictions, too many partly formulated alternatives and too few opportunities to evaluate them systematically, brings to its encounters with the claims of rival traditions a fundamental incoherence which is too disturbing to be admitted to self-conscious awareness except on the rarest of occasions.

This fragmentation appears in divided moral attitudes expressed in inconsistent moral and political principles, in a tolerance of different rationalities in different milieus, in protective compartmentalization of the self, and in uses of language which move from fragments of one language-in-use through the idioms of internationalized modernity to fragments of another. (The simplest test of the truth of this is as follows: take almost any debatable principle which the majority of members of any given group profess to accept; then it will characteristically be the case that some incompatible principle, in some form of wording, often one employing an idiom very different from that used in formulating the first principle, will also receive the assent of a substantial fraction of that same group.) How can such persons be addressed by and become engaged in argumentative dialogue with any one tradition of enquiry, let alone with more than one?

What such an individual has to learn is how to test dialectically the theses proposed to him or her by each competing tradition, while also drawing upon these same theses in order to test dialectically those convictions and responses which he or she has brought to the encounter. Such a person has to become involved in the conversation between traditions, learning to use the idiom of each in order to describe and evaluate the other or others by means of it. So each such individual will be able to turn his or her own initial incoherences to argumentative advantage by requiring of each tradition that it supply an account of how these incoherences are best to be characterized, explained, and transcended. One of the marks of any mature tradition of rational enquiry is that it possesses the resources to furnish accounts of a range of conditions in which incoherence would become inescapable and to explain how these conditions would come about. So such individuals will invite a tradition of enquiry to furnish them with a kind of self-knowledge which they have not as yet possessed by first providing them with an awareness of the specific character of their own incoherence and then accounting for the particular character of this incoherence by its metaphysical, moral, and political scheme of classification and explanation. The catalogs of virtues and vices, the norms of conformity and deviance, the accounts of educational success and failure, the narratives of possible types of human life which each tradition has elaborated in its own terms, all these invite the individual educated into self-knowledge of his or her own incoherence to acknowledge in which of these rival modes of moral understanding he or she finds him or herself most adequately explained and accounted for.

What emerges from this account of the way in which different types of individual would have to engage with the claims of rival and competing traditions of enquiry is once again the specificity of the required kinds of dialogue. There is no way to engage with or to evaluate rationally the theses advanced in contemporary form by some particular tradition except in terms which are framed with an eye to the specific character and history of that tradition on the one hand and the specific character and history of the particular individual or individuals on the other. Abstract the particular theses to be debated and evaluated from their contexts within traditions of enquiry and then attempt to debate and evaluate them in terms of their rational justifiability to *any rational person,* to individuals conceived of as abstracted from their particularities of character, history, and circumstance, and you will thereby make the kind of rational dialogue which could move through argumentative evaluation to the rational acceptance or rejection of a tradition of enquiry effectively impossible. Yet it is just such abstraction in respect both of the theses to be debated and the persons engaged in the debate which is enforced in the public forums of enquiry and debate in modern liberal culture, thus for the most part effectively precluding the voices of tradition outside liberalism from being heard. Consider the ways in which this is so in the modern liberal university.

The foundation of the liberal university was the abolition of religious tests for university teachers. What the enforcement of religious tests ensured was a certain degree of uniformity of belief in the way in which the curriculum was organized, presented, and developed through enquiry. Each such preliberal university was therefore to some degree an institution embodying either one particular tradition of rational enquiry or a limited set of such traditions, a set whose agreements might well on occasion furnish a background for more or less intense conflict. So the Scottish universities of the seventeenth and eighteenth centuries articulated one kind of Protestant tradition of enquiry, as did the Dutch universities of the same period. So the University of Paris in the thirteenth century was the milieu for conflict both between contending Aristotelian and Augustinian thinkers and between the protagonists of alternative and competing resolutions of that conflict.

When universities without religious tests were founded or religious tests were abolished in universities formerly enforcing them, the consequence was not that such universities became places of ordered intellectual conflict within which the contending and alternative points of view of rival traditions of enquiry could be systematically elaborated and evaluated. Had this been the case, unity of belief would have been replaced by a multiplicity of contending beliefs, each permitted to provide its own framework for enquiry. Instead, what happened was that in the appointment of university teachers considerations of belief and allegiance were excluded from view altogether. A conception of scholarly competence, independent of standpoint, was enforced in the making of appointments. A corresponding conception of objectivity in the classroom required the appointed teachers to present what they taught *as if* there were indeed shared standards of rationality, accepted by all teachers and accessible to all students. And a curriculum was developed which, so far as possible, abstracted the subject matters to be taught from their relationship to conflicting overall points of view. Universities became institutions committed to upholding a fictitious objectivity.

Least harm was done thereby to the teaching of and research into the natural sciences. For they have been constituted in modern culture as a relatively autonomous tradition of enquiry, admission to which requires assent to whatever the basic shared tenets of that tradition are in a particular period. Radical dissent—the dissent of astrologers or phrenologists, for example—has always been extruded from the modern natural sciences. Most harm was done to the humanities, within which the loss of the contexts provided by traditions of enquiry increasingly has deprived those teaching the humanities of standards in the light of which some texts might be vindicated as more important than others and some types of theory as more cogent than others.

What the student is in consequence generally confronted with, and this has little to do with the particular intentions of his or her particular teachers, is an apparent inconclusiveness in all argument outside the natural sciences, an inconclusiveness which seems to abandon him or her to his or her prerational preferences. So the student characteristically emerges from a liberal education with a set of skills, a set of preferences, and little else, someone whose education has been as much a process of deprivation as of enrichment. Happily, of course, not *all* education in our culture is in this sense liberal, even in institutions whose dominant ethos is that of this kind of liberalism.

There is thus a deep incompatibility between the standpoint of any rational tradition of enquiry and the dominant modes of contemporary teaching, discussion, and debate, both academic and nonacademic. Where the standpoint of a tradition requires a recognition of the different types of language-in-use through which different types of argument will have to be carried on, the standpoint of the forums of modern liberal culture presupposes the possibility of a common language for all speakers or at the very least of the translatability of any one language into any other. Where the standpoint of a tradition involves an acknowledgment that fundamental debate is between competing and conflicting understandings of rationality, the standpoint of the forums of modern liberal culture presupposes the fiction of shared, even if unformulable, universal standards of rationality. Where the standpoint of a tradition cannot be presented except in a way which takes account of the history and the historical situatedness, both of traditions themselves and of those individuals who engage in dialogue with them, the standpoint of the forums of modern liberal culture presupposes the irrelevance of one's history to one's status as a participant in debate. We confront one another in such forums abstracted from and deprived of the particularities of our histories.

It follows that only by either the circumvention or the subversion of liberal modes of debate can the rationality specific to traditions of enquiry reestablish itself sufficiently to challenge the cultural and political hegemony of liberalism effectively. How could such circumvention and such subversion be carried through in a way which conformed to the requirements of justice and rationality? When this question is posed, we cannot but be reminded once more that what I have said about traditions of rational enquiry in general has been at best a sketch of a set of shared attitudes, beliefs, and presuppositions, developed in very different ways within each particular tradition and affording different and incompatible answers to such questions when developed as fully as the formulation of such answers requires. Hence the point in the overall argument has been reached—it may indeed have been reached somewhat earlier—at which it is no longer possible to speak except out of one particular tradition in a way which will involve conflict with rival traditions. There is a way of developing the argument of this book further which would be Aristotelian, but antagonistic to both Augustine and Hume; a way which would be Augustinian, necessitating a rejection of both Aristotle and Hume; a way which would be Thomist, synthesizing Aristotle and Augustine in a manner inimical to both Aristotelian anti-Augustinians and Augustinian anti-Aristotelians, let alone to Hume; and there would finally be a Humean way of developing it, one in which what were taken to be the limitations and superstitions of Aristotle, Augustine, and Aquinas would be exposed historically as well as philosophically.

There are, that is to say, at least four alternative ways of continuing the narratives of the earlier chapters, at least four alternative ways of moving this book toward further conclusions, but no one author could write more than one of them. For it is just here that contemporary substantive argument between, and for, and against particular traditions of enquiry, and indeed for and against antitradition in respect of both justice and rationality, has to begin. It is here that we have to begin speaking as protagonists of one contending party or fall silent. A book which ends by concluding that what we can learn from its argument is where and how to begin may not seem to have achieved very much. Yet, after all, Descartes may have been right about one thing: in philosophy to know how to begin is the most difficult task of all. We, whoever we are, can only begin enquiry from the vantage point afforded by our relationship to some specific social and intellectual past through which we have affiliated ourselves to some particular tradition of enquiry, extending the history of that enquiry into the present: as

Aristotelian, as Augustinian, as Thomist, as Humean, as post-Enlighten-ment liberal, or as something else.

For each of us, therefore, the question now is: To what issues does that particular history bring us in contemporary debate? What resources does our particular tradition afford in this situation? Can we by means of those resources understand the achievements and successes, and the failures and sterilities, of rival traditions more adequately than their own adherents can? More adequately by our standards? More adequately also by theirs? It is insofar as the histories narrated in this book lead on to answers to these questions that they also hold the promise of answering the questions: Whose justice? Which rationality?

Yet perhaps a little more may have been achieved quite incidentally in the course of reaching this point in this argument. At the close of the discussion of Aristotle's achievement I pointed out that it afforded a vantage point from which Socrates and Plato could be understood as having contributed to the constitution of a particular tradition of enquiry concerning justice and practical rationality, a tradition at that point most adequately articulated by Aristotle himself. Two further ex-tended episodes in the history of the further development of that same tradition have since been recounted.

In the first of these Aristotle's scheme of thought was developed by Aquinas in a way which enabled him to accommodate Augustinian claims and insights alongside Aristotelian theorizing in a single dialec-tically constructed enterprise. In the second the inability of the Scot-tish seventeenth-century Aristotelians both to provide a cogent reply to the new epistemological doubts about their first principles and to bring into an adequate relationship their Calvinist Augustinianism and their Aristotelianism led Hutcheson to his reformulations of older positions in terms of the way of ideas, and so rendered the whole Scot-tish tradition vulnerable to Hume's critique. By contrast the Aristote-lianism and the Augustinianism of the Thomistic dialectical snythesis were not thus vulnerable. That synthesis can provide a very different account of how the justification of first principles is to be carried through and of the relationship of philosophy to theology, one which invites no concessions to the premises from which Hume was to draw his sub-versive conclusions.

Hence the narratives of these two episodes combine to exhibit an Aristotelian tradition with resources for its own enlargement, correc-tion, and defense, resources which suggest that *prima facie* at least a case has been made for concluding first that those who have thought their way through the topics of justice and practical rationality, from the standpoint constructed by and in the direction pointed out first by Aristotle and then by Aquinas, have every reason at least so far to hold that the rationality of their tradition has been confirmed in its encounters with other traditions and, second, that the task of characterizing and accounting for the achievements and successes, as well as the frustrations and failures, of the Thomistic tradition in the terms afforded by rival traditions of enquiry, may, even from the point of view of the adherents of those traditions, be a more demanding task than has sometimes been supposed.

This conclusion will of course be unacceptable to all those who give their allegiance to rival traditions of enquiry, and there are no tradition-independent standards of argument by appeal to which they can be shown to be in error. It will be in key part by the way in which they turn out to be able to write their rival histories that they will, both from their own standpoint and from the Thomistic, further confirm or disconfirm this emerging Thomistic conclusion. The rival claims to truth of contending traditions of enquiry depend for their vindication upon the adequacy and the explanatory power of the histories which the resources of each of those traditions in conflict enable their adherents to write.

Index of Persons